HOW TO DRAW EVERYTHING

CAN'T DRAW, WANT TO DRAW? THIS BOOK SHOWS YOU HOW!

igloo

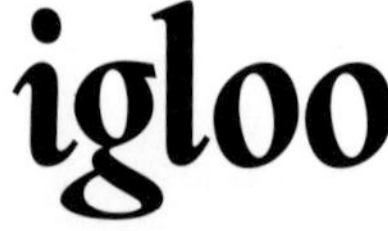

Published in 2007
by Igloo Books Ltd
Cottage Farm,
Sywell,
NN6 0BJ.
www.igloo-books.com

10 9 8 7 6 5 4 3

ISBN: 978 1 84561 197 2

Project management: Kandour Ltd

Editorial and design management: Emma Hayley and Jenny Ross
Coordinator: Adam Phillips
Author and illustrator: Richard Pashley
Cover and text design: Paul Barton
Layout: Kurt Young
With thanks to: Josephine Bacon, Victoria Chow and Beci Keys

Printed in China.

CONTENTS

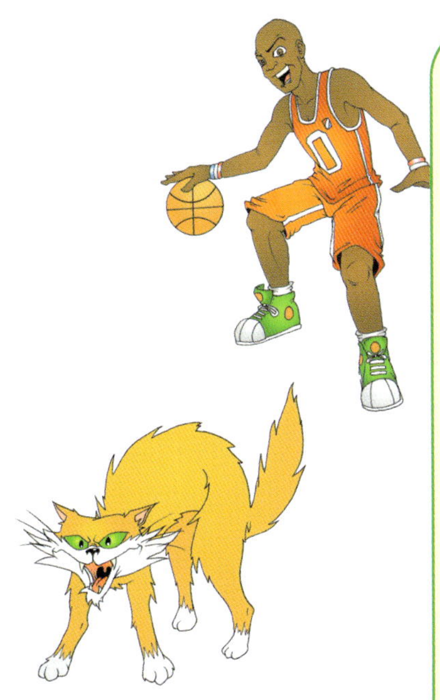

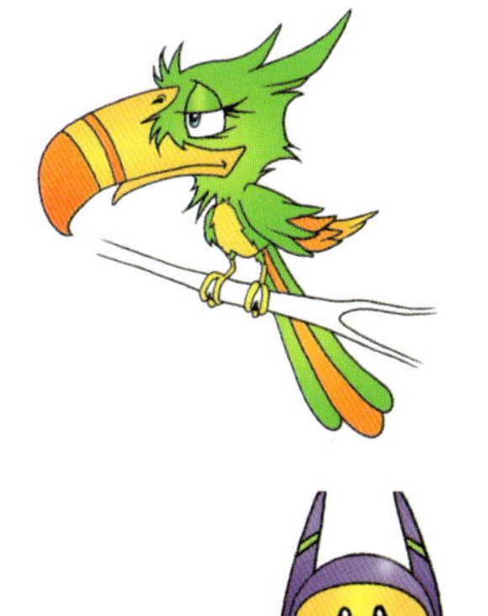

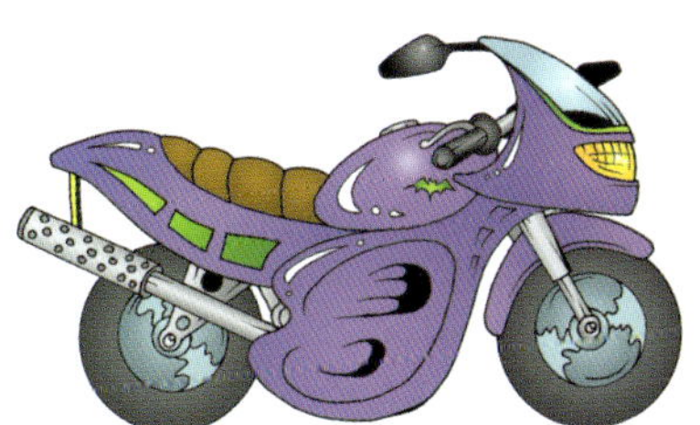

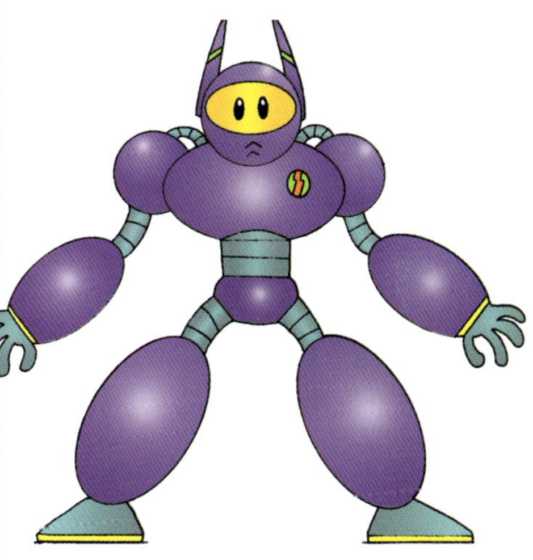

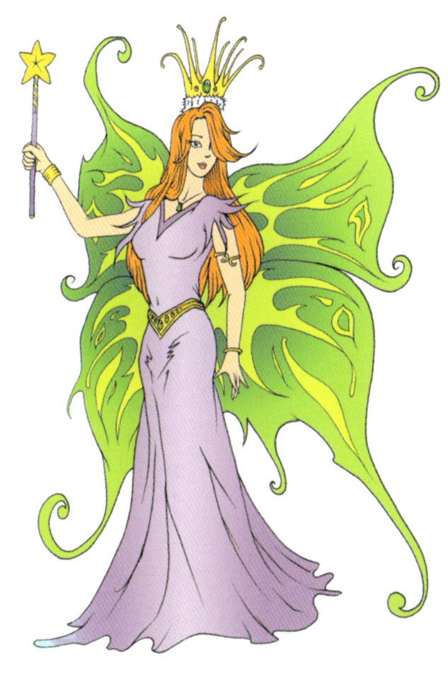

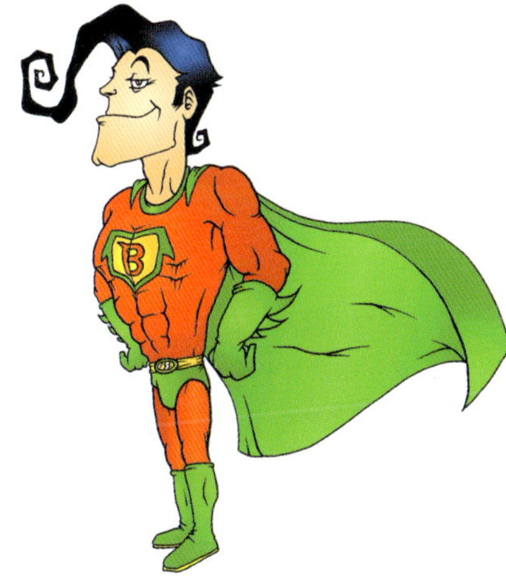

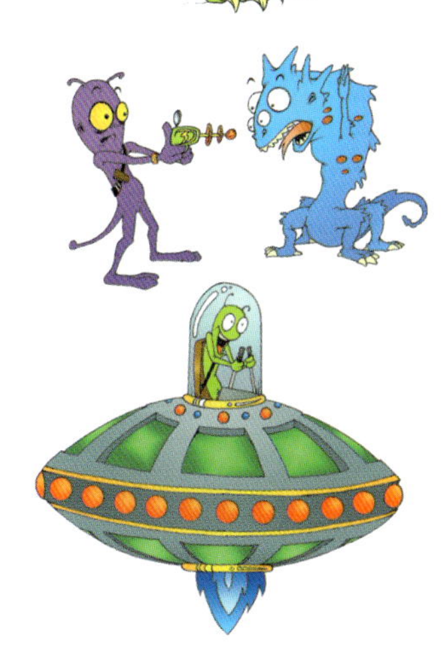

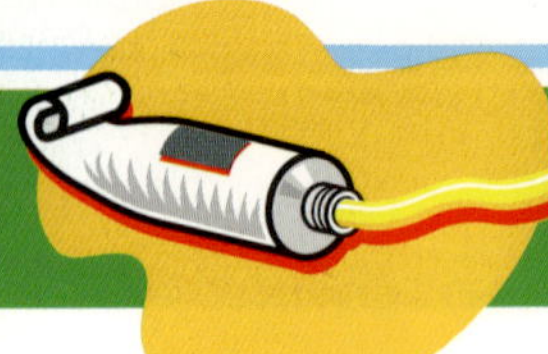

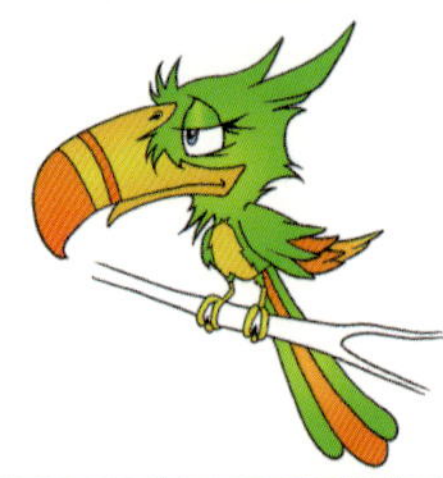

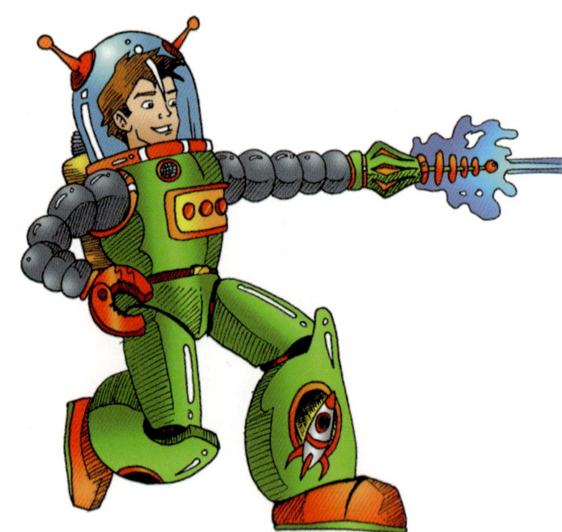

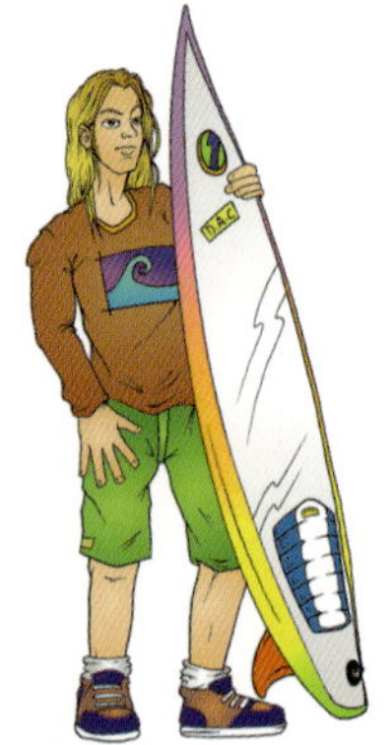

Welcome to **How To Draw Everything**. We all know that pictures can look really intimidating to attempt. They can seem complicated or difficult, and it is sometimes hard to even know where to start. The great thing about this book, though, is that it breaks down even the most detailed pictures into easily understandable steps, so you can start drawing almost right away.

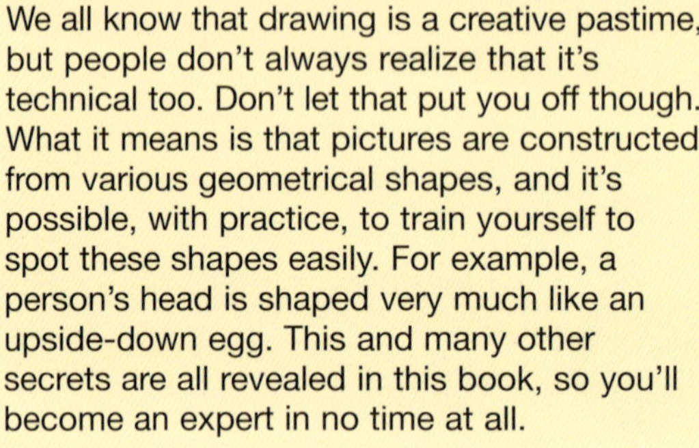

We all know that drawing is a creative pastime, but people don't always realize that it's technical too. Don't let that put you off though. What it means is that pictures are constructed from various geometrical shapes, and it's possible, with practice, to train yourself to spot these shapes easily. For example, a person's head is shaped very much like an upside-down egg. This and many other secrets are all revealed in this book, so you'll become an expert in no time at all.

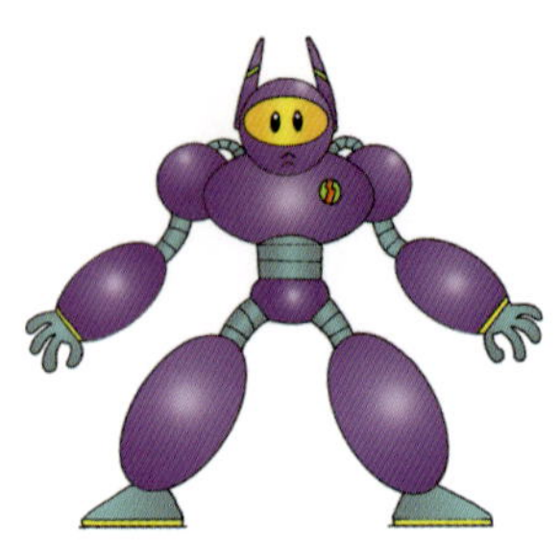

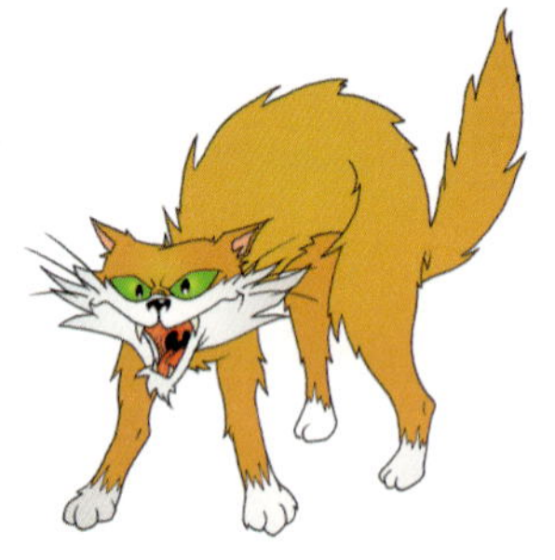

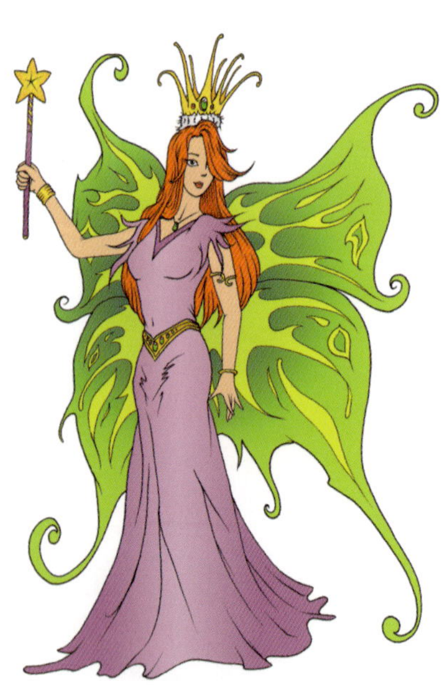

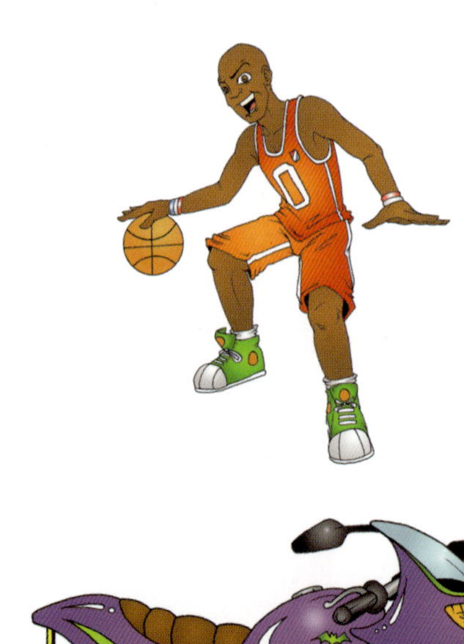

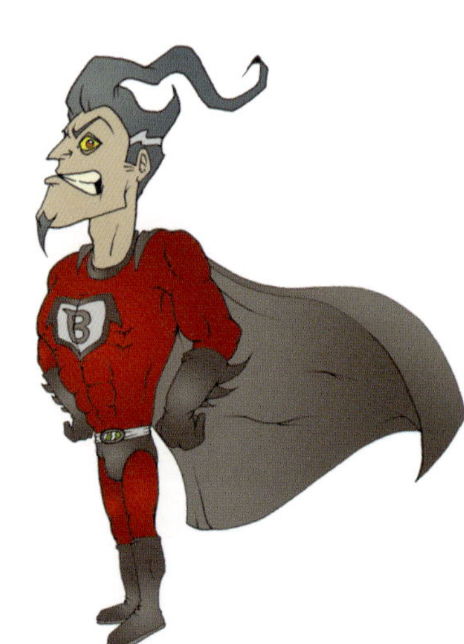

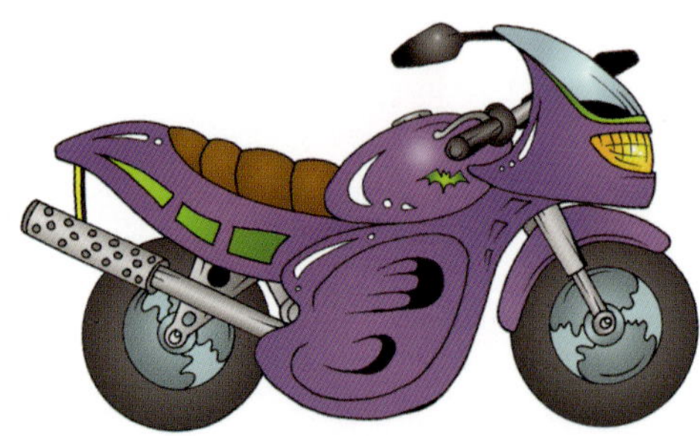

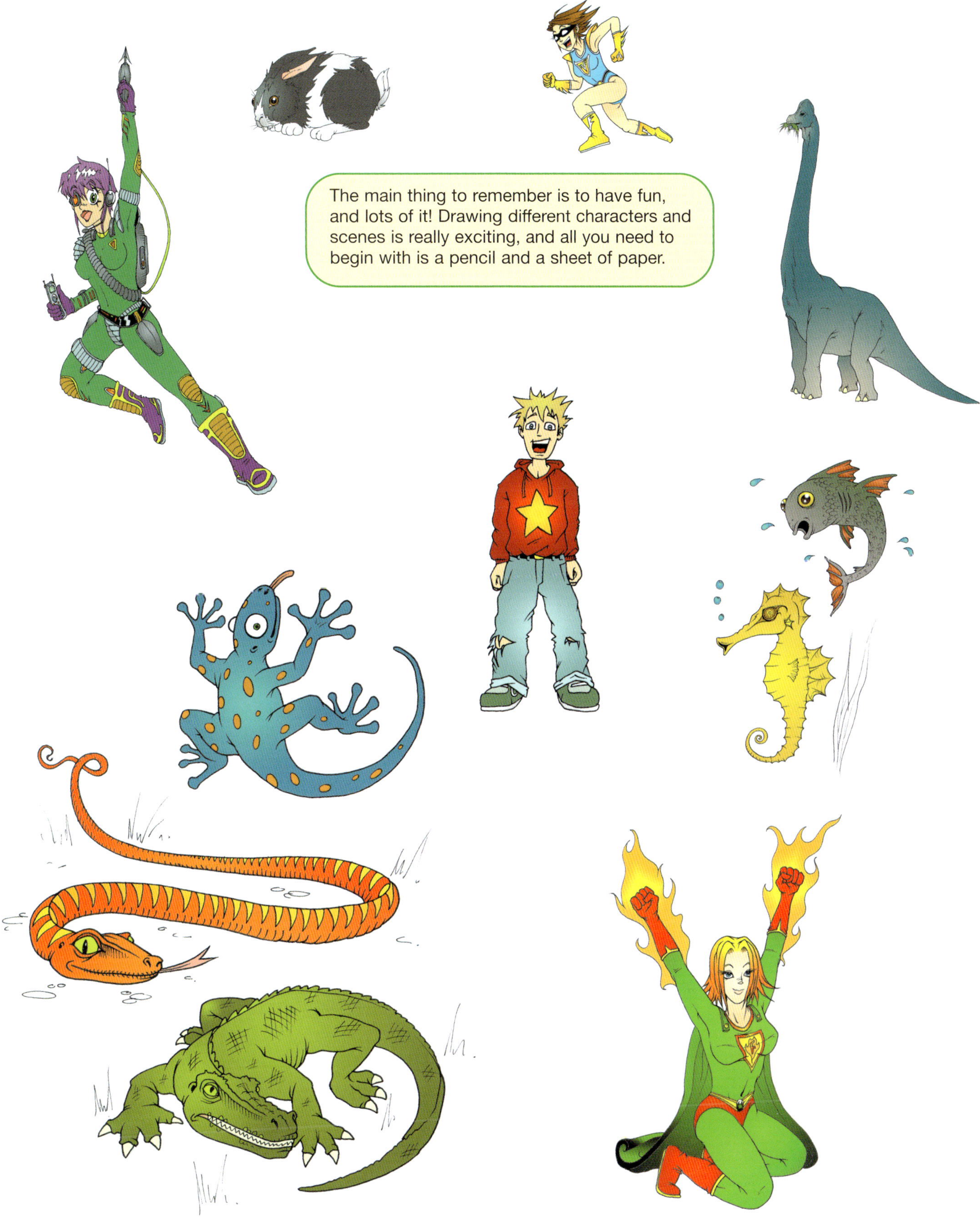

The main thing to remember is to have fun, and lots of it! Drawing different characters and scenes is really exciting, and all you need to begin with is a pencil and a sheet of paper.

MATERIALS

The most important materials you'll need for getting started are a pencil and some drawing paper. Pencils are graded from soft to hard. Hard pencils, such as a No. 3, produce a fine line that's good for technical drawings. Softer pencils, such as a No. 1, produce a much darker line that is ideal for artistic shading. A good general-purpose pencil to use is a standard No. 2. This will produce a solid line that is still easy to erase if you should happen to make a mistake.

Paper, like pencils, comes in many variations. There are so many different thicknesses, grades, and surface textures. For example, paper with a heavy grain is great for watercolor painting, but not so good for pen drawings. The best paper to use for reproducing the drawings in this book is plain photocopier paper. As well as being inexpensive to buy, it has a smooth surface, making it easier to erase pencil markings.

Obviously, you're going to need an eraser and a pencil sharpener too. Pencils need to be sharpened regularly so that they give an accurate and constant line. A ruler is also required for certain drawings, especially those that require making measurements, as is a black fine-line pen. Fine-line pens come in different thicknesses, and they help produce a strong outline to your work.

Other drawing tools you may want to consider are shape stencils. With some of the drawings in this book, it is easier, not to mention quicker, to use a circle and ellipse stencil. Stencils come in many other shapes, too. You can all these items from office supply outlets and hobby and craft stores.

Finally, you're going to need to use color for your pictures. Colored pencils are excellent, and you can be really accurate with them. You may prefer using watercolor paints, or you could even scan your work to copy it onto a computer so you can color it in with your mouse. It's up to you—it's all about whatever you feel most comfortable doing!

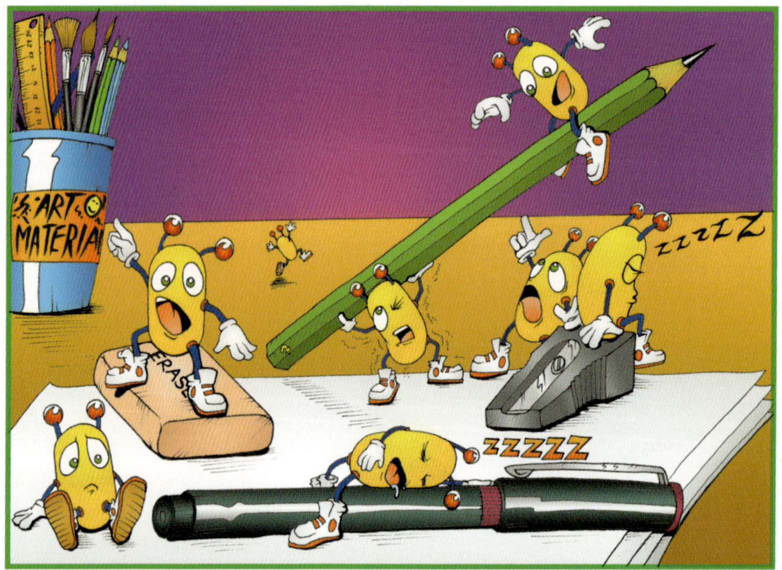

PEOPLE

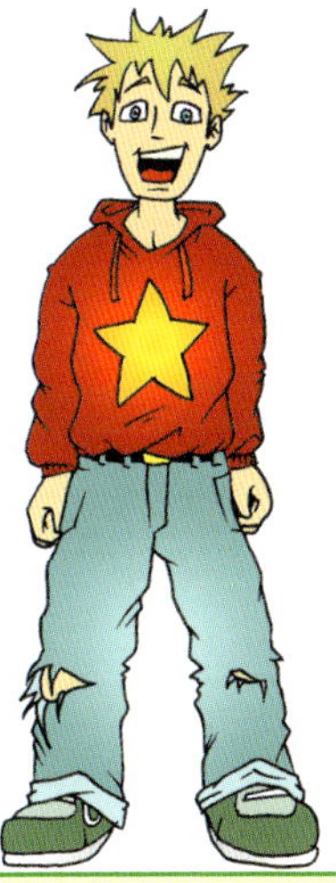

People come in all shapes and sizes, and our body shapes are constantly changing as we grow from a baby to an adult. In this chapter, we're going to look at how to draw people of different ages, and we'll also find out how to draw different facial expressions, hand shapes, and items of clothing.

In the first example, we'll be attempting to draw a young boy. The younger we are, the larger our head is in comparison with the rest of our body. This boy is roughly "five heads" tall. He has a huge grin on his face, and has clenched fists. He's wearing baggy jeans and a hooded sweatshirt.

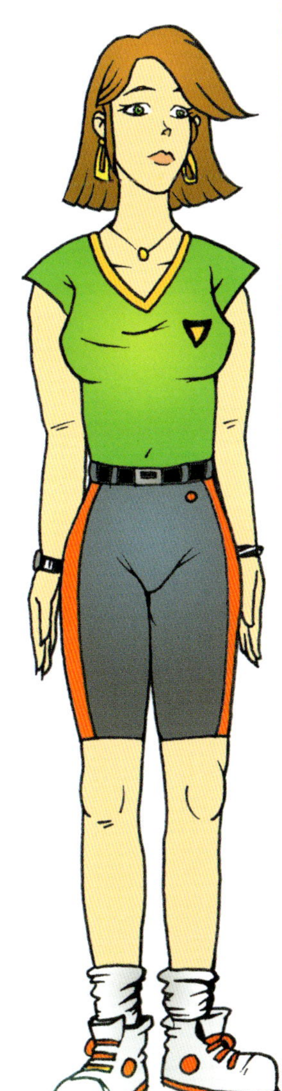

Next we have a teenage girl. At this age, she is about "seven heads" in height. She has an expression of boredom, and her hands are flat by her sides. The clothes she's wearing is tight-fitting sports gear.

In the final example, you'll be drawing a fully-grown man. He is "eight heads" tall and has an angry expression on his face. One of his hands is open, and the other hand is slightly clenched in frustration. His tee shirt is tight-fitting, while his combat pants are baggy.

This chapter will give you a very clear idea of how to draw figures and clothing, and this is important to making many of the following chapters easier to figure out!

STEP 1

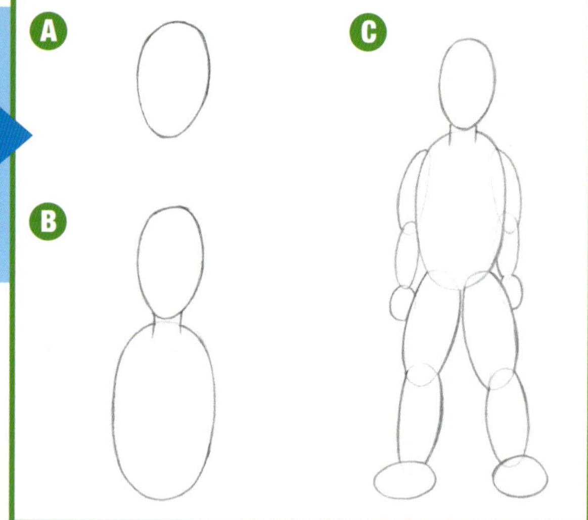

Head: Start by drawing the boy's head in the center of your page. As you can see, his head shape is oval, and is similar to an upturned egg, only a little more rounded.

Body: The boy's body is similar to the shape of his head. It's about 1.5 times the size of the head and is joined to it by a short neck.

It's time to create your boy's arms and legs:

Arms: The arms are made from two ovals, each of which is roughly half the length of his body. The boy's hands are going to be clenched fists, so start them off as simple circles.

Legs: The legs are also made using oval shapes, which are slightly fatter and 1.5 times the length of the arm sections. His feet are drawn head-on, which makes them oval-shaped.

Face: The young boy is looking straight at us, so, for his face, draw a feint line down the center. His features should be almost symmetrical—whatever you draw on one side of his face, repeat it on the other. The boy has a wide mouth, and his eyes sit roughly halfway up his face. Don't forget to pencil in his eyebrows—they are vital for adding expression.

2

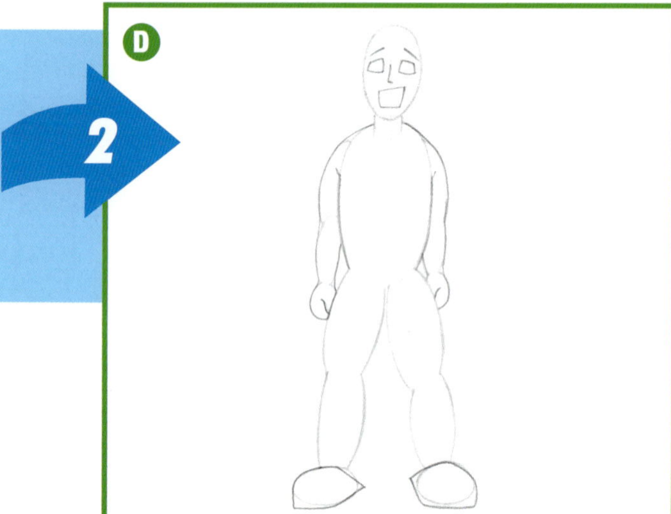

3

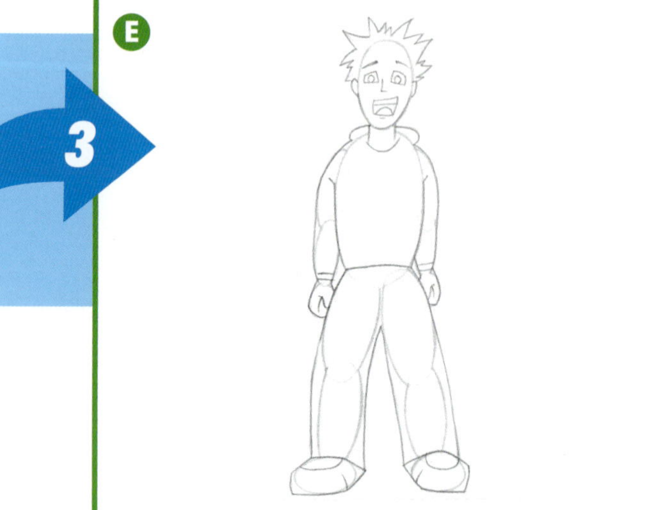

4

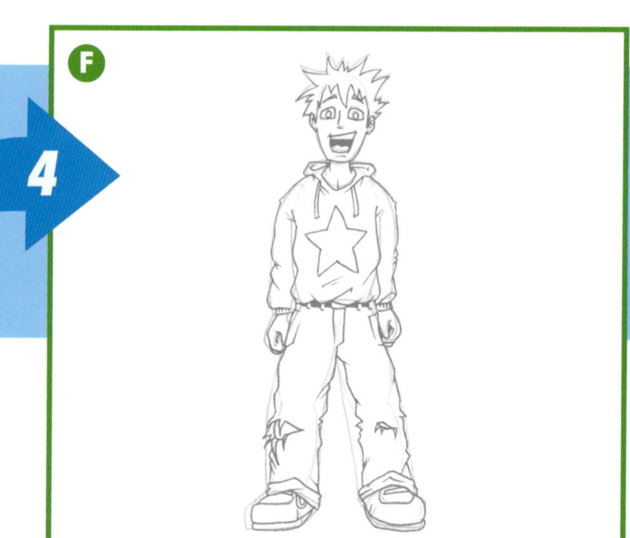

5

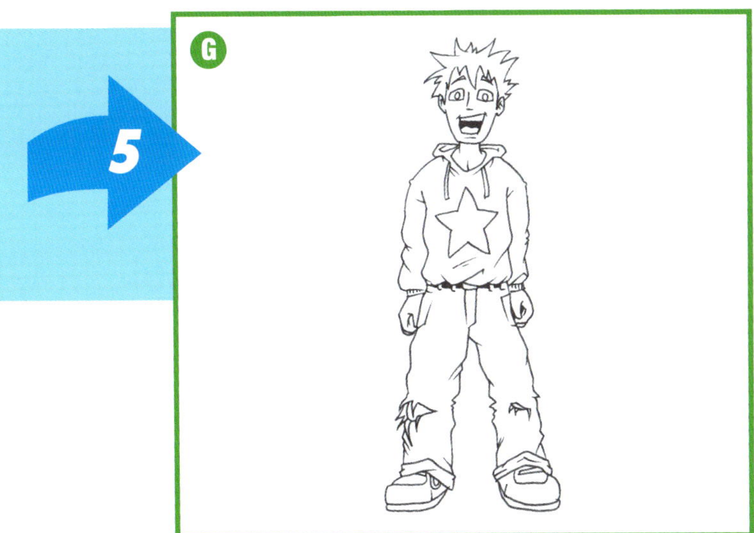

6

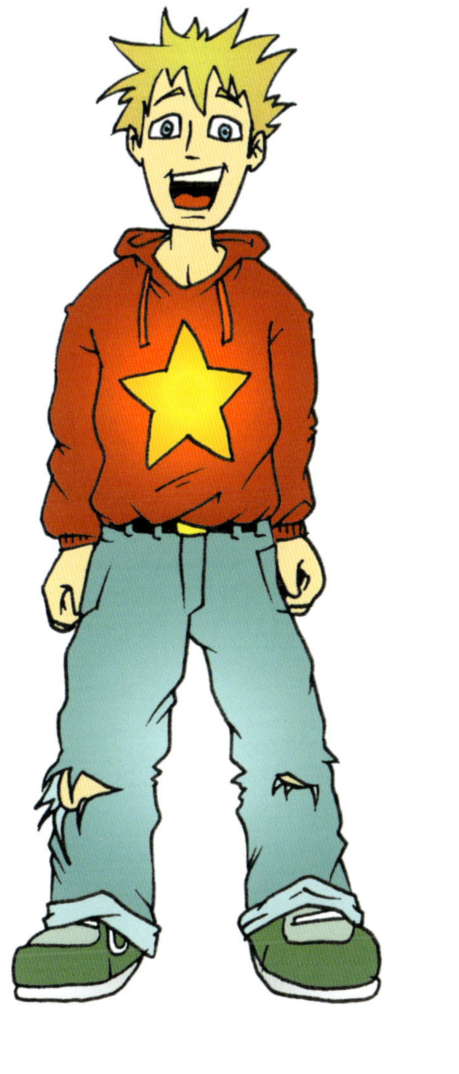

Arms: To get the overall shape of the boy's arms, join the two ovals with a flowing outline. Next, his hands are given definition by drawing a line where his thumb is tucked into his palm.

Feet: Give the feet a rounded toe each, with a flat base. You can also draw the line where his jeans meet his shoes.

E **Face:** Start putting some more detail on his face: the pupils in his eyes, the tongue and teeth, some spiked hair, and his ears.

Hands: Show where the skin at the base of the boy's thumb is creased slightly—this is important because he is clenching his fists.

Clothes: This boy is wearing a baggy, hooded sweatshirt and loose, ripped jeans. His hooded top billows out at the bottom because of its elastic waistband. The sleeves do the same. The jeans, however, hang off his waist and drape over his legs.

F **Clothes:** The boy's sweater has a large star emblem on it. He has creased and ripped pants with turn-ups. Give his shoes some detail, such as shoelaces and rubber soles.

Hands: Add depth to the boy's hands by showing where his other fingers are bent. Remember that they are obscured slightly because of the position of his hands.

G Draw over the picture of your boy using a thin black pen. Pen in the lines you want to keep, and then erase any leftover pencil lines. Now that he's ready to color, you can start thinking about what tones you want to use.

H This boy's jeans are blue. His top is bright red, because red is a vibrant, in-your-face color, and this boy has a confident look about him. Remember that color is a great way to enhance the character of your drawings, so try to choose colors that say something about the people you are drawing.

STEP 1

A

B

C

A **Head:** The head of the teenage girl is a similar egg-shape to the boy's, but is slightly sharper on the pointed side. This is because as we grow older, our features often become less rounded.

B **Body:** The girl's body is based on the shape of her head. It is twice the size of the head, but not as pointed.

C It's time to create your girl's arms and legs:

Arms: The arms consist of two ovals, each of which is just over half as long as the body. Her hands are shaped like upside-down teardrops.

Legs: Her legs consist of oval shapes. The upper leg is nearly as long as her body, while the lower leg is shorter and thinner. Her feet are drawn slightly turned outward, so use triangles.

D **Face:** The teenage girl's face is turned slightly away from us, so draw a curved feint line down her face, slightly offset to your right. This line represents the center of her face. Her features should be almost symmetrical—this means that whatever you draw on one side of her face, you should repeat on the other. Her eyes sit around halfway up her face.

2

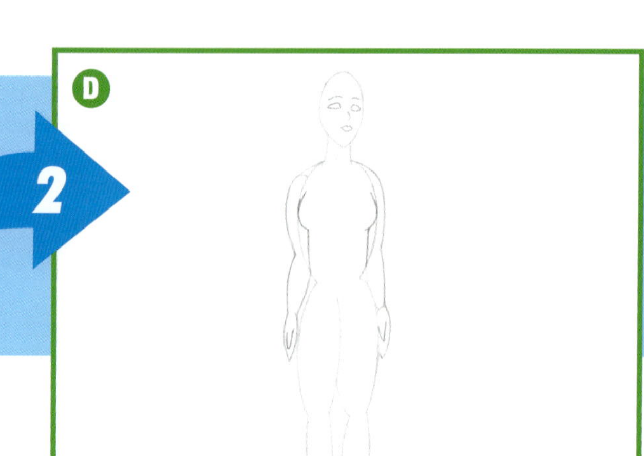

3

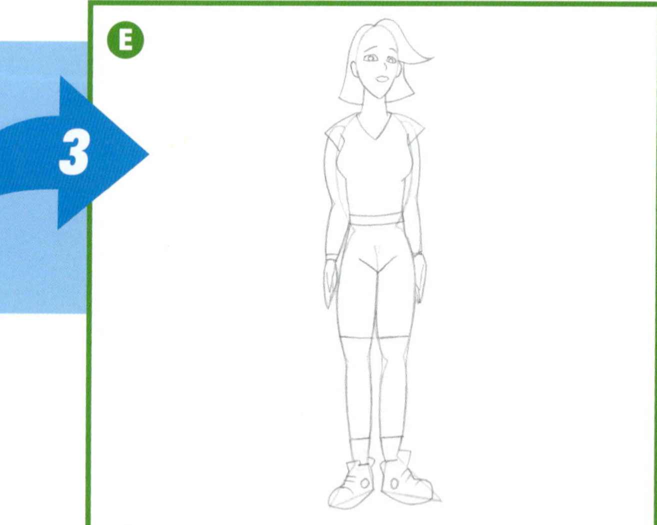

4

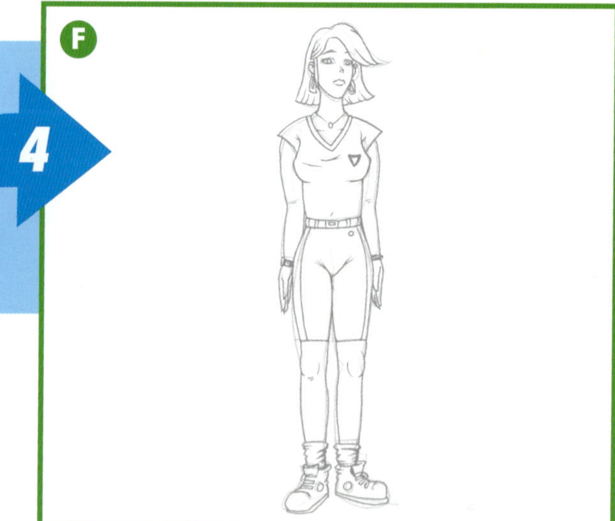

5

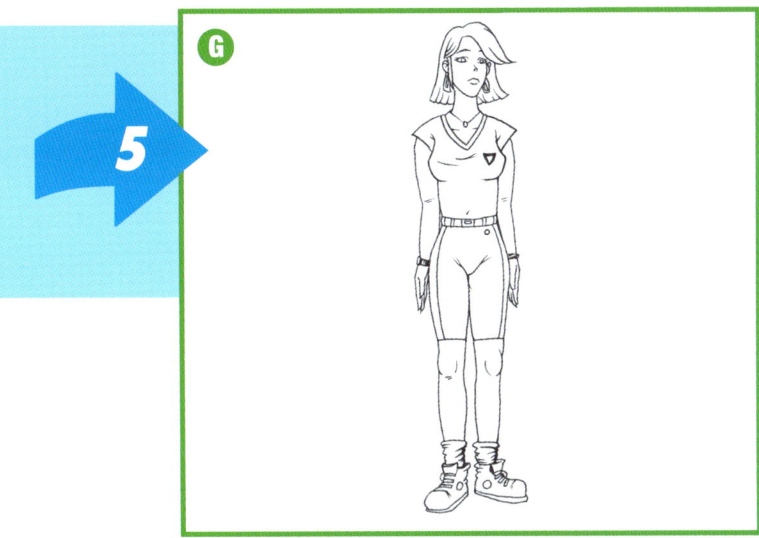

6

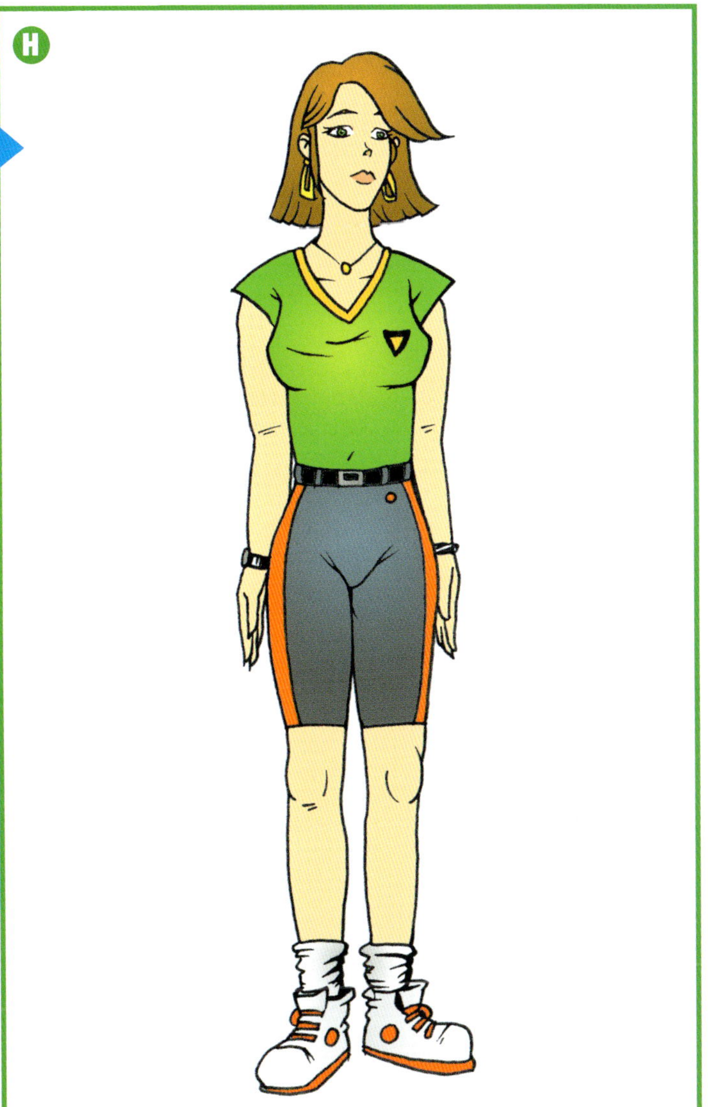

Arms: To get the full shape of her arms, join the two ovals with a flowing outline. Next, her hands have a thumb in the center of each "teardrop."

E

Body: Girls have a curvier figure than boys, particularly older girls and women. Start to define the shape of her chest and waist—she has an "hourglass" figure.

Feet: Give her feet rounded toes with a flat base. These are going to be her sneakers.

Face: Start putting some detail on her face—the pupils in her eyes, some mid-length straight hair, and her ears.

Hands: Give the girl's hands more definition by drawing separate fingers, tucked in by her side.

Clothes: The tight tee shirt that the girl is wearing follows the contours of her body. Her biking shorts are also smooth, and they come to just above her knees. Give her shoes detail like the laces and soles. Don't forget to give her some socks!

F

Clothes: Now put the finishing touches to her clothes. Her tee shirt has a triangular logo on it, and she is wearing big earrings and a necklace. Give your girl a watch and some stripes running down the sides of her shorts. Lastly, make her socks really wrinkled.

Hands: Add some final definition to the fingers, such as long fingernails.

Body: Draw marks where her knees show, and add creases where her elbows bend.

G

Draw over your teenage girl using a black pen and then erase the pencil lines. Now she's ready to color in!

H

Because this girl is so sporty, she is wearing brightly colored clothing. Her top is lime green, and her shorts have bright red stripes running down them. You may, of course, use whatever colors you want —so experiment as much as you like!

STEP 1

A

B

C

2

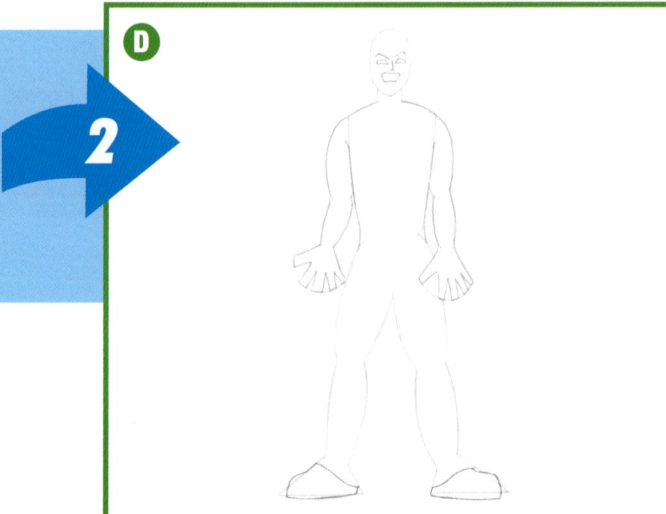

D

3

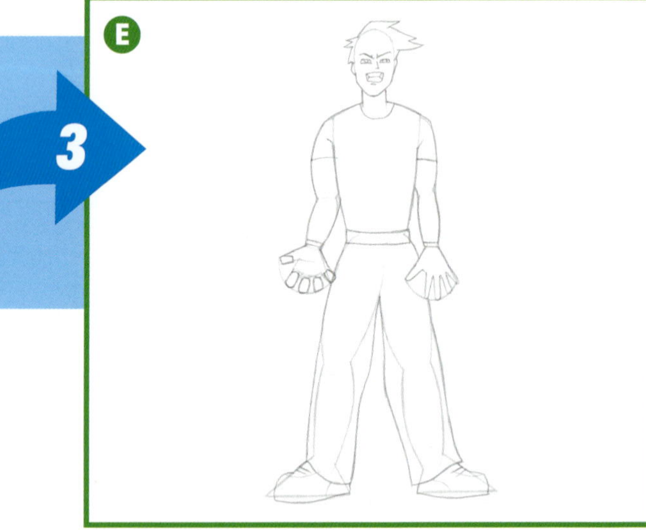

E

A **Head:** Start your picture by drawing the man's head. This, as with the other two characters, is oval. Bear in mind, though, that it has a more angular underside to it than the boy's or girl's—this is because it will eventually become his square jaw.

B **Body:** Your man's body is wider at the top (where his shoulders will be), and narrower toward the waist. It also has sides that curve out slightly.

C It's time to construct your man's arms and legs:

Arms: The arms consist of two ovals each, that are about half as long as his body. Because the left arm arm is bent, the lower oval is a touch shorter. His hands are fan-shaped.

Legs: His legs are also made of oval shapes. The upper leg is nearly as long as his body, while the lower leg is shorter and thinner. His feet are drawn sideways-on, so they are triangular in shape.

D **Face:** This man's face is looking straight at us, so draw a feint line down the center. His features should be almost symmetrical, so whatever you draw on one side of his face, repeat on the other. He has strong eyebrows, and his eyes sit halfway up his face.

Arms: To get the overall shape of his arms, join the two ovals with a flowing outline. Next, his hands are given five separate fingers by "cutting" triangular shapes out of the fan.

Feet: Give the feet rounded toes with a flat base. You can also draw the line where his combat pants meet his shoes.

E **Face:** Start drawing in the detail on his face: the pupils in his eyes, the teeth in his mouth, his choppy hair, and his two ears. This man also has a very square jaw.

Hands: This man's hands say a lot about his mood—give the right hand more pointed fingertips, and be sure to give the left hand bent fingers. Fingers are actually made up of three bones with bending joints.

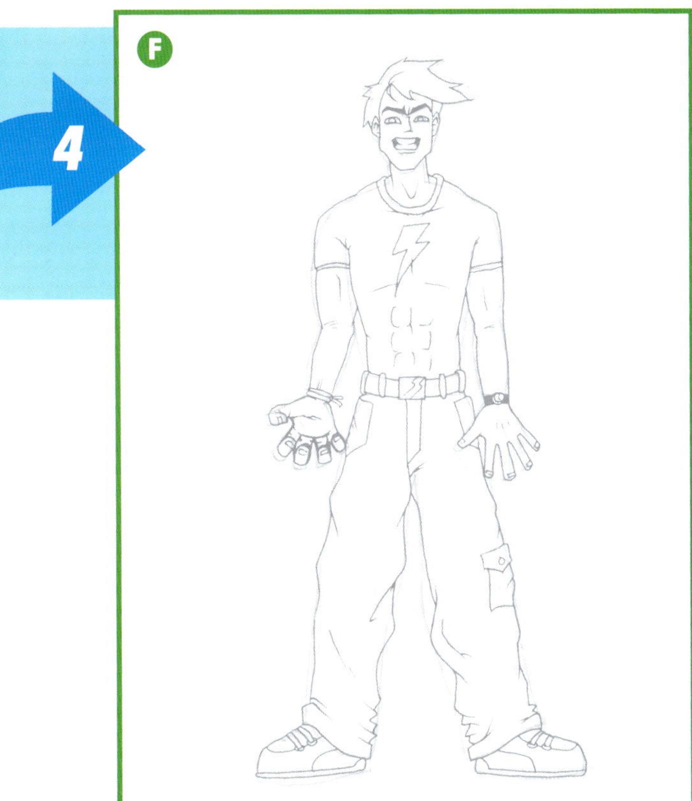

5

G

In this picture, we can only see the end bone on each finger as it is bent inward toward the palm of his hand.

Clothes: This man is wearing a tight tee shirt and baggy combat pants. The shirt simply follows the outline of his body and arms. The pants, however, are loose-fitting and hang off of his waist, draping down over his legs. Give him a watch on one wrist and a belt around his waist.

F **Clothes:** The tight tee shirt shows the man's "six-pack"(his stomach muscles), and also features a large lightning bolt emblem on it. He has creased pants that wrinkle and gather on his shoes. Now give the shoes soles and laces.

Hands: Add some creases to the skin of the man's hands where they bend, and give him some fingernails.

Body: Add creases where his elbows bend, before drawing in his arm muscles and his collar bone, which sticks out through his tee shirt slightly.

G Once you're happy with the look of your man, you can draw over him using a black pen. Remember only to draw over the lines you want to keep, and then erase all the pencil lines. Your man will then be ready to color in.

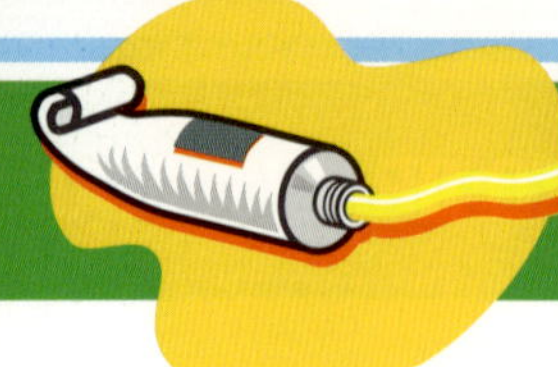

H

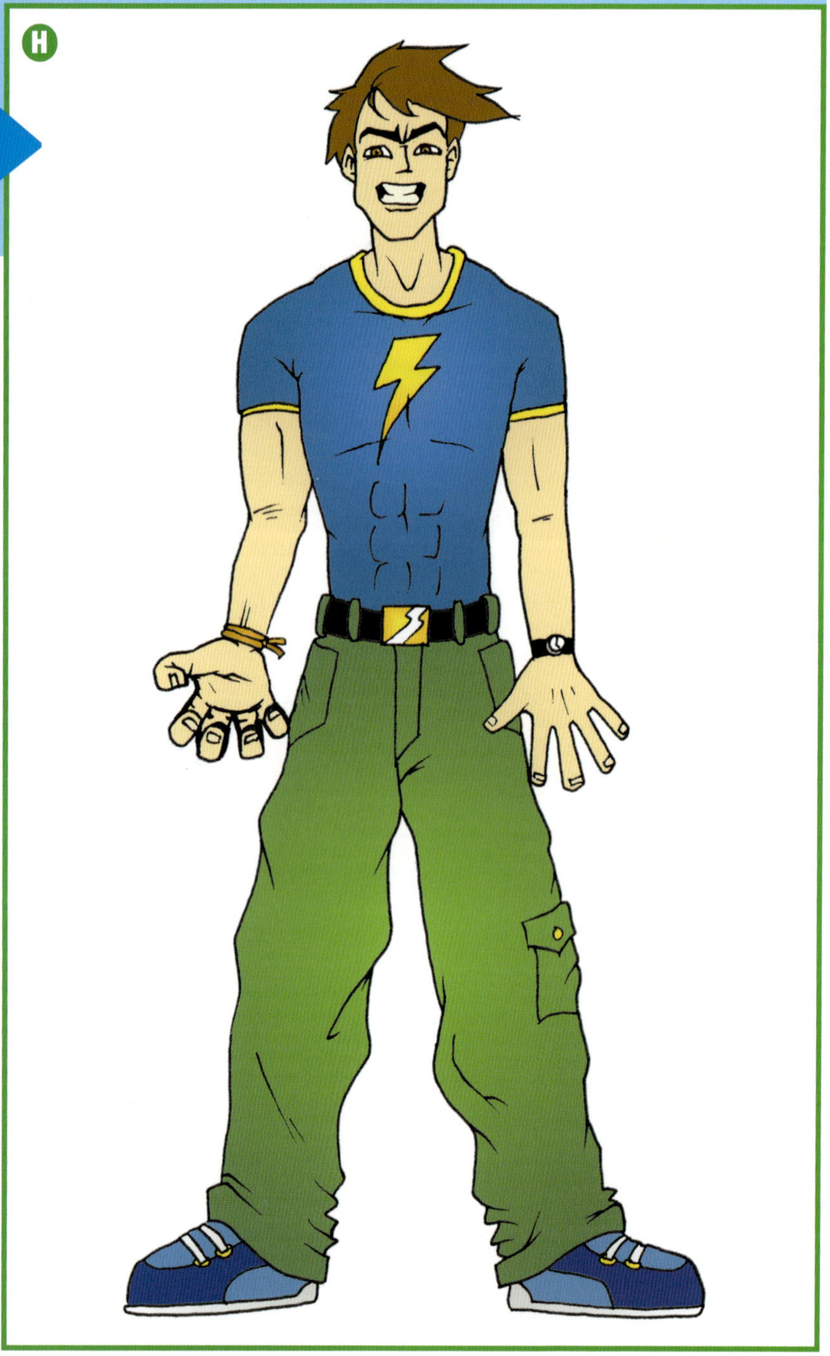

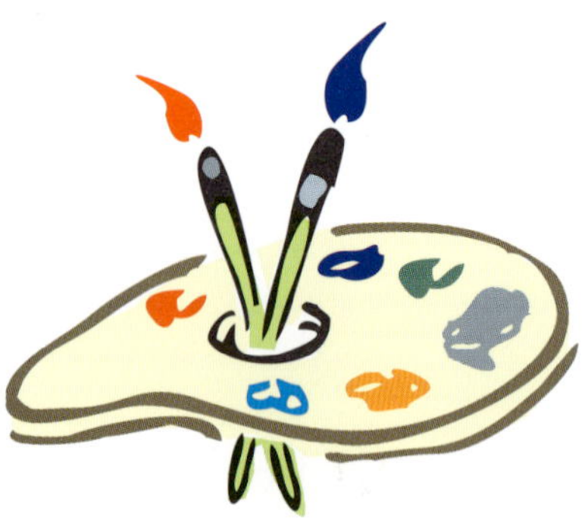

H Think about different color combinations before coloring your man in—look for shades that will go well together. In this picture, the man is wearing khaki combat pants and a dark blue tee shirt on which there is a yellow lightning bolt.

ANIMALS

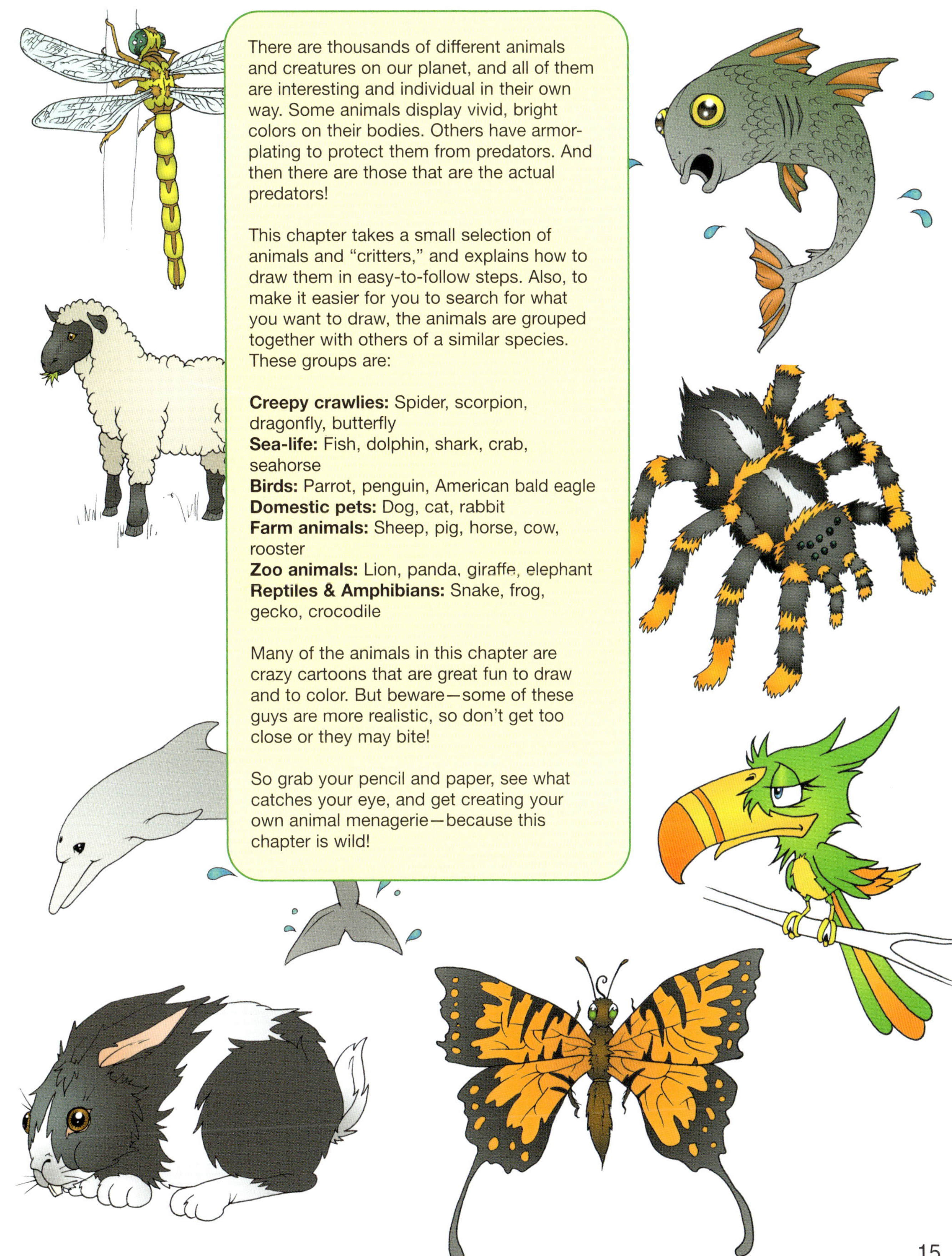

There are thousands of different animals and creatures on our planet, and all of them are interesting and individual in their own way. Some animals display vivid, bright colors on their bodies. Others have armor-plating to protect them from predators. And then there are those that are the actual predators!

This chapter takes a small selection of animals and "critters," and explains how to draw them in easy-to-follow steps. Also, to make it easier for you to search for what you want to draw, the animals are grouped together with others of a similar species. These groups are:

Creepy crawlies: Spider, scorpion, dragonfly, butterfly
Sea-life: Fish, dolphin, shark, crab, seahorse
Birds: Parrot, penguin, American bald eagle
Domestic pets: Dog, cat, rabbit
Farm animals: Sheep, pig, horse, cow, rooster
Zoo animals: Lion, panda, giraffe, elephant
Reptiles & Amphibians: Snake, frog, gecko, crocodile

Many of the animals in this chapter are crazy cartoons that are great fun to draw and to color. But beware—some of these guys are more realistic, so don't get too close or they may bite!

So grab your pencil and paper, see what catches your eye, and get creating your own animal menagerie—because this chapter is wild!

HOW TO DRAW A SPIDER

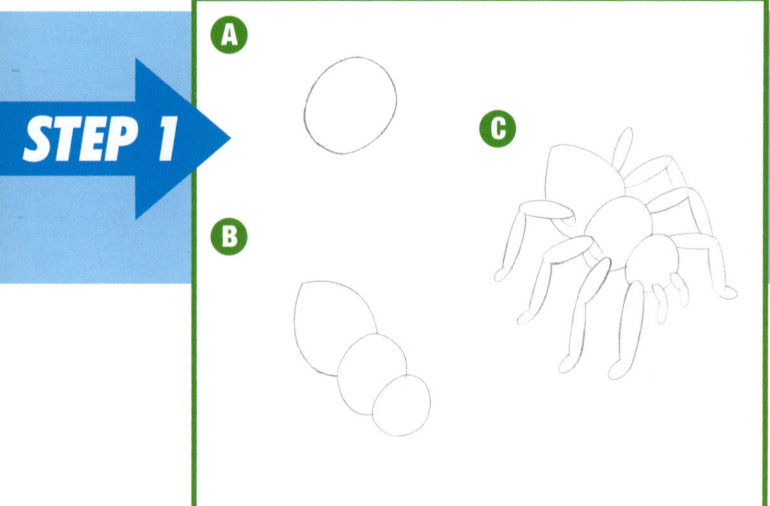

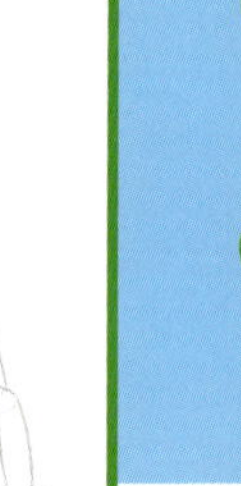

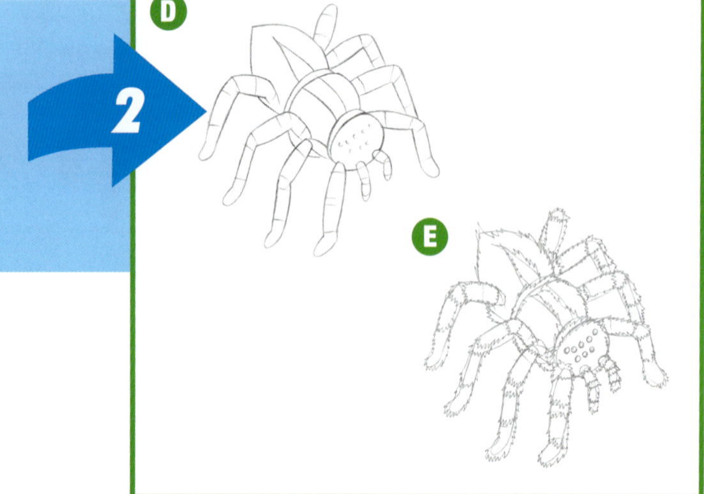

A The first stage of creating a gruesome tarantula is to sketch a large circle in the center of your page. This will be for the spider's thorax.

B Draw a smaller circle in front of this, which will form the head of your spider. Next, draw a fat teardrop shape behind the thorax, which is the tarantula's abdomen.

C Your spider's legs are constructed using long oval shapes. Its feet are tiny ovals that are the same width as the rest of the legs but set at an angle. The spider also has two small "feelers" on its head. These are constructed in the same way as its legs.

D Tarantulas have striped fur on their legs and body. The legs are candy-striped at the knees, feet, and where they join the body. There is also a large, pointed stripe running down the thorax onto the abdomen. Spiders have many eyes, so draw these on its head.

E In the final stage of pencil sketching, alter anything you aren't happy with before giving your spider an all-over "fuzzy" look. Do this with short, spiky pencil strokes.

F Draw over all of the pencil lines that you're happy with using a black pen before erasing the leftover pencil lines. Your spider is now ready to color.

G Your tarantula should be a deep gray or black color, with orange stripes on its legs and a large white stripe on its back. Give it deep green eyes, and you have one seriously creepy crawly!

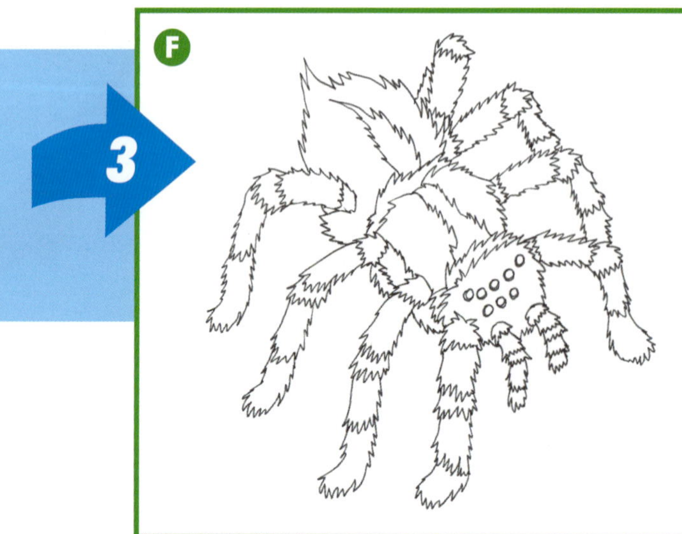

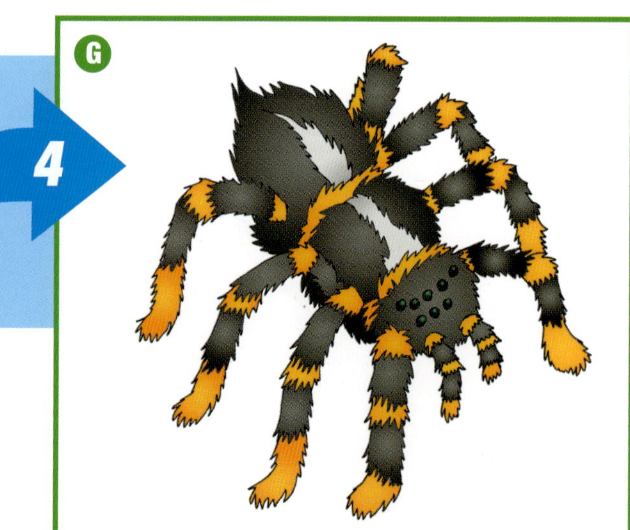

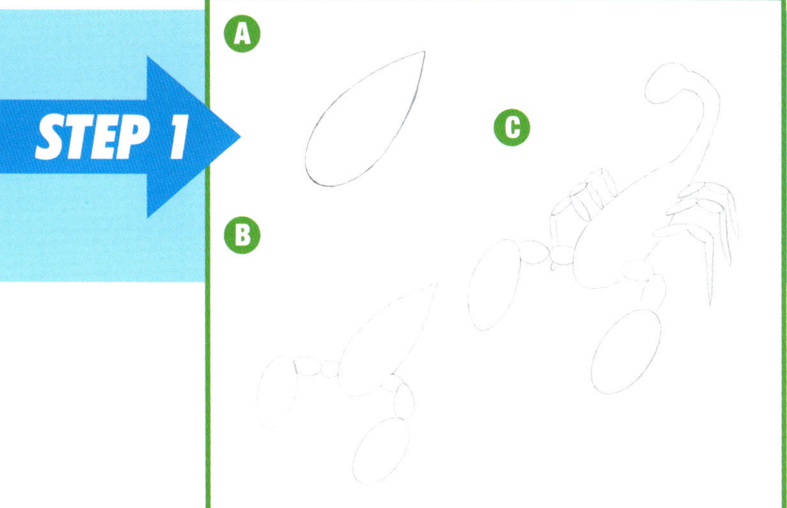

A The main body of your scorpion is teardrop-shaped, so begin by drawing this in the center of your paper.

B On either side of your teardrop, draw your scorpion's pincers. These are large oval shapes on the end of small arms.

C The rest of your scorpion's body is constructed using simple shapes. First of all, its tail extends from the back of the body and has a bulbous oval on top that will eventually be the sting. The legs of your scorpion are in three segments.

D You can now draw your scorpion's claw-like pincers and its body armor. The pincers are two joined teardrop shapes, one overlapping the other, and the body armor is made up of many sections. Finally, the sting has a sharp point on the end for piercing and paralyzing its victims!

E Start to add detail to the scorpion. Begin sketching in the eyes and some smaller pincers around the mouth area. Overlap each section of the armor on the scorpion's body.

F Draw over your lines in black pen and erase any pencil lines. You are now ready to color in your scorpion.

G Color your scorpion in your own choice of tones and hues. The one shown here features yellow that blends into black on each plate of armor. Once done, stand back from your page, and look at what you have drawn—it's very scary isn't it?

2

D

E

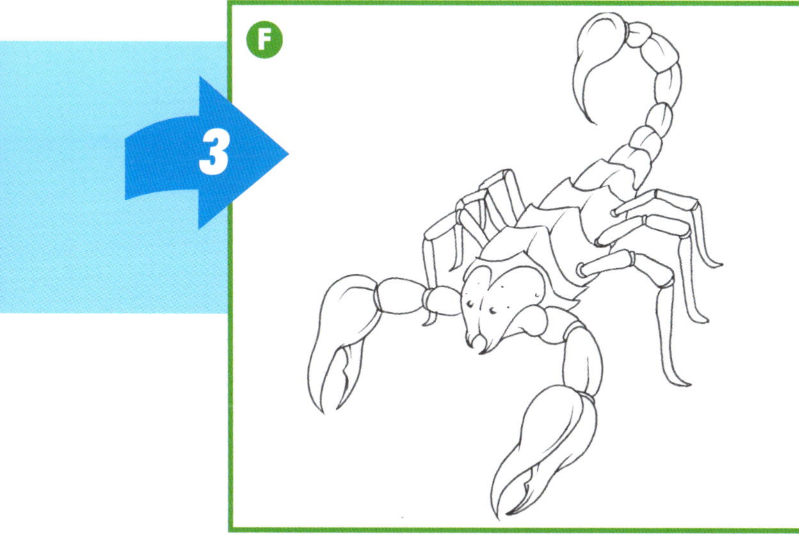

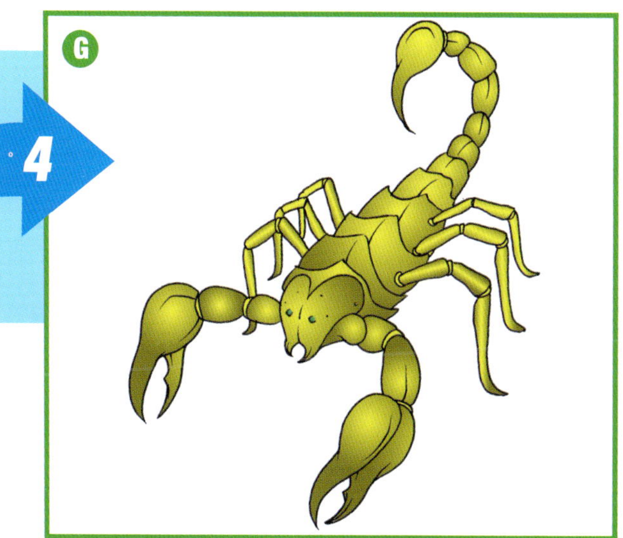

HOW TO DRAW A DRAGONFLY

STEP 1

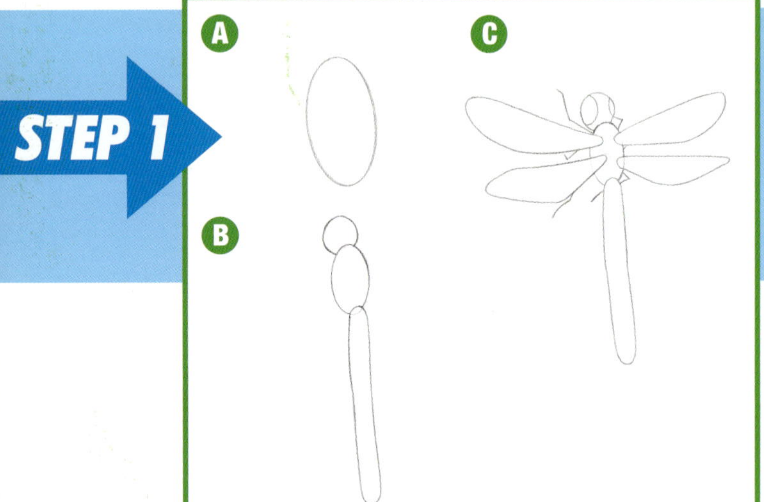

2

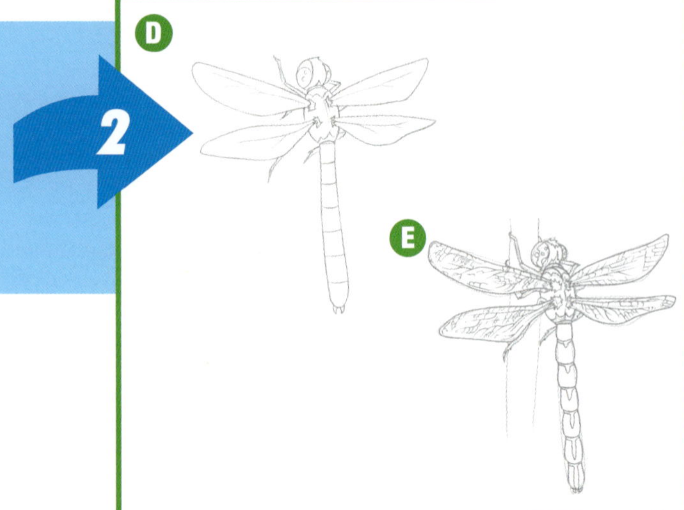

3

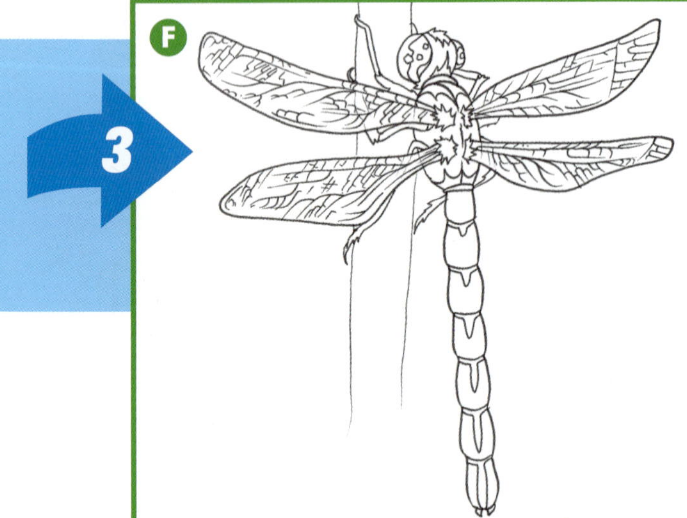

4

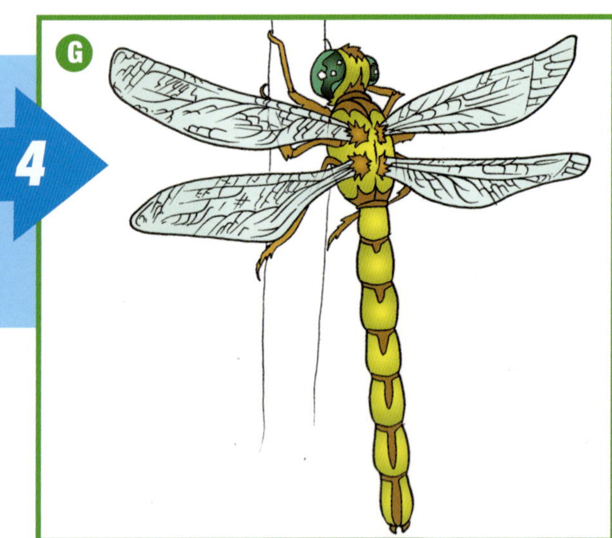

A Begin your dragonfly picture by drawing an oval shape in the center of your page. Remember to draw this at a slight angle. This oval is going to be the thorax of your dragonfly.

B Next, draw a long thin sausage shape directly below the thorax—this will be your dragonfly's abdomen. Now draw its head, a small circular shape sitting on top of the thorax.

C The dragonfly is going to need some legs and wings. The legs are simple sticks, and the wings are like large sails. It also has large, round, faceted eyes on either side of its head.

D Start adding the detail to your dragonfly. The wings have veins running down them, and the abdomen has stripes all the way along it. The dragonfly's eyes contain reflections from the sun. You can now fatten the legs a little.

E The dragonfly's wings are broken down into lots of patterned compartments, and you can place these quite randomly. The stripes on the abdomen are given extra detail down the center, and it has furry patches where the wings meet the thorax.

F When your dragonfly is looking the way you want it to, draw in the outline using a black pen, and erase the pencil marks.

G Insects look great painted in strong primary colors, so the dragonfly should be predominantly yellow, with green eyes and brown details. Blue or red would look just as good, though.

STEP 1

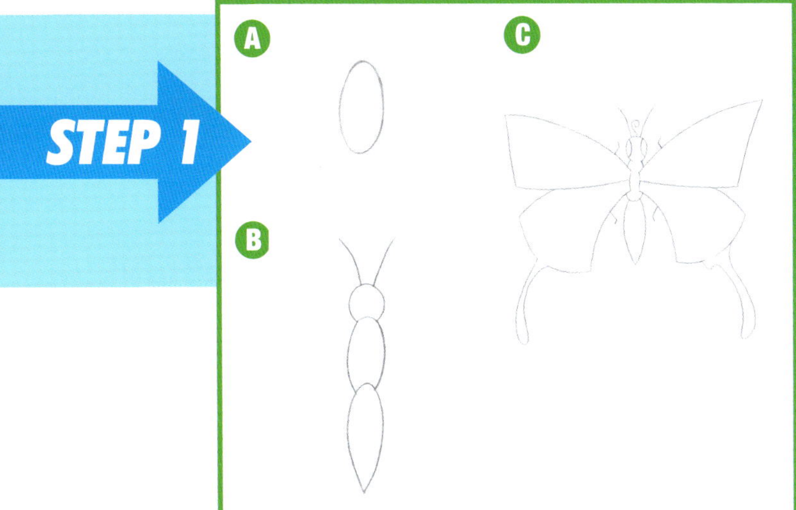

2

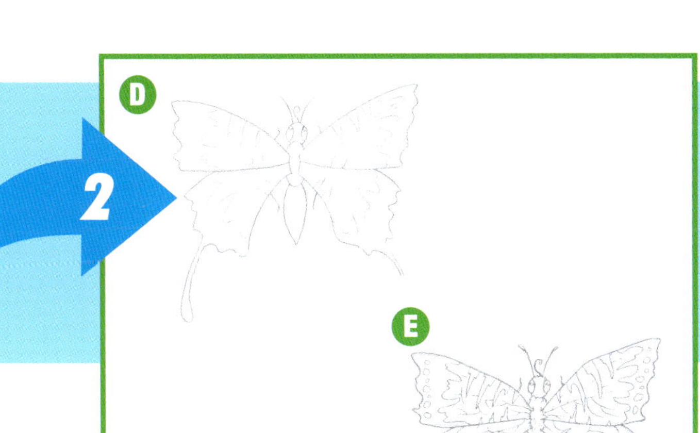

A Start your butterfly by drawing a small thin oval in the center of your paper. This is going to be the thorax for your butterfly.

B The other two parts of the butterfly's body are called the head and the abdomen. The head sits on top of the thorax, and is a small circle with two antennae on top. The abdomen is like an upside down teardrop, and is drawn under the thorax.

C To fly, your butterfly needs wings that are almost triangular in shape. The lower wings have "tails" hanging down from them that look like a trail of liquid paint. Next, draw eyes on either side of the head and a curled tongue on top.

D The details of butterfly are mainly on the wings, which can have fantastic patterns covering them. Remember the one important rule: keep it symmetrical—whatever you draw on one wing should be exactly mirrored on the other.

E Draw some final details on your butterfly's wings and make its body look "fuzzy" all over. You can now add some reflections in its eyes.

F Draw over your pencil sketch with a black pen in order to create your final outline. Then erase the pencil, and your butterfly is ready to color in.

G Any color goes with the butterfly but to make a real impact on the page, stick with "the brighter, the better" rule. The one shown here is actually a butterfly called a "Red Admiral," that is black and orange.

3

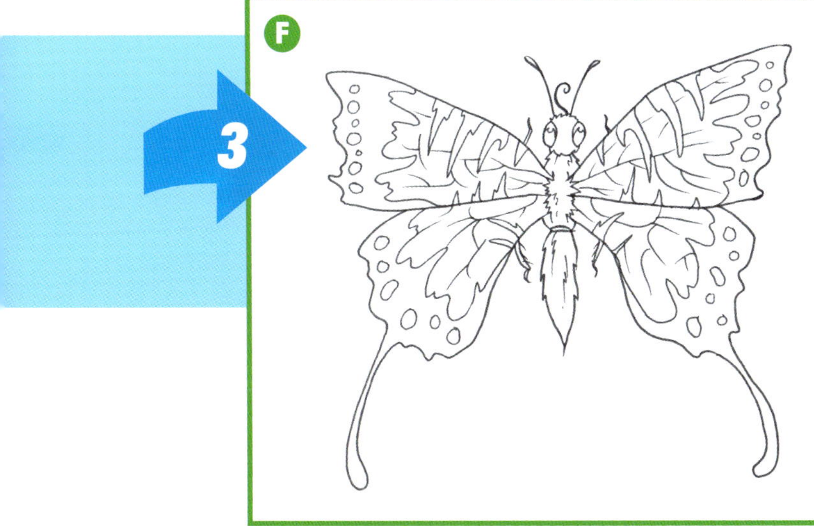

4

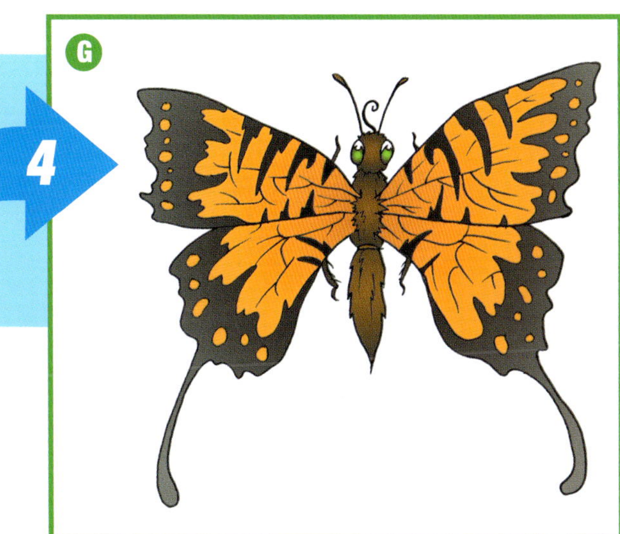

HOW TO DRAW A FISH

STEP 1

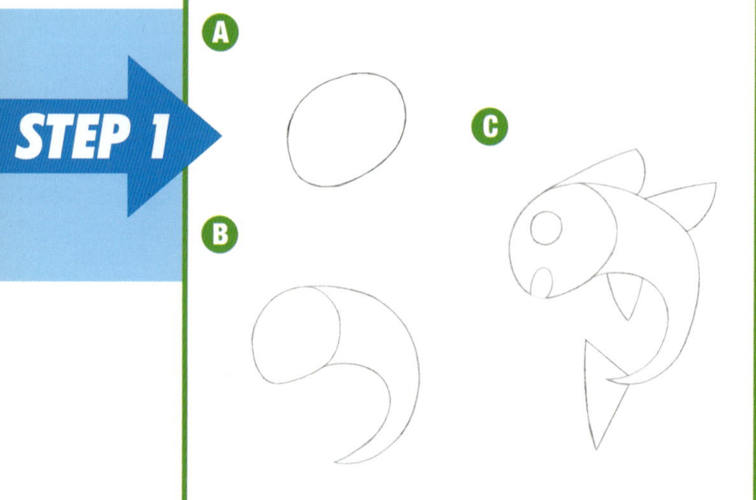

2

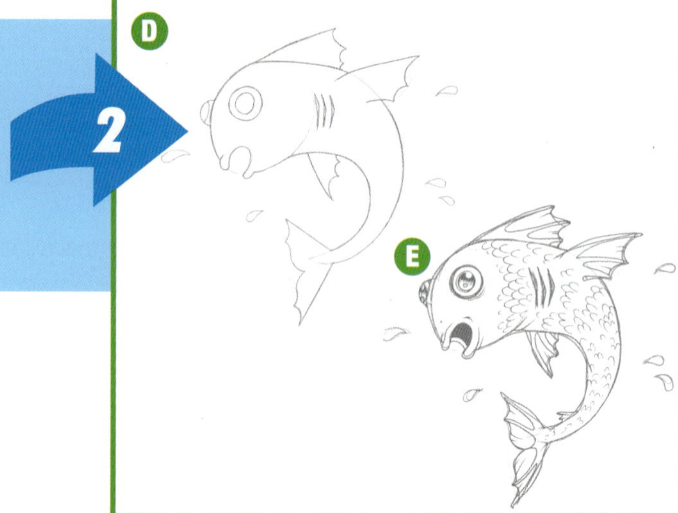

A A fish's head is shaped like a large egg. Start by drawing this shape in the center of your paper.

B The second stage is to draw the fish's tail, which is shaped like a large curved horn and is attached to the head.

C Your fish needs some fins to swim with! Make these from fan shapes. One is placed behind the head, two are placed on the sides, and a final fan shape makes up the tail. Draw a circular eye on the head, as well as an oval-shaped mouth cut into the outline of the head.

D Now you can start adding some simple detail to the fish's frame. Give it three thin gills behind its head, another eye bulging from the side of its head, and make sure the fan-shaped fins now have sharp edges. This fish also has curved spikes on the end of its tail, a rubbery mouth, and splashes of water around its body.

E You should create some texture on the fish's skin. Many fish have scales covering the skin, and you can create this effect by drawing small "C" shapes all along body. Next, add details to the glassy eyes. Finally, put some finishing touches to the fins.

F Once you're happy with how your fish looks, you can draw over the lines in black pen, before erasing the original pencil lines.

G Fish come in a wide variety of colors, but for a three-dimensional look, shade from one color to another like in the picture here.

3

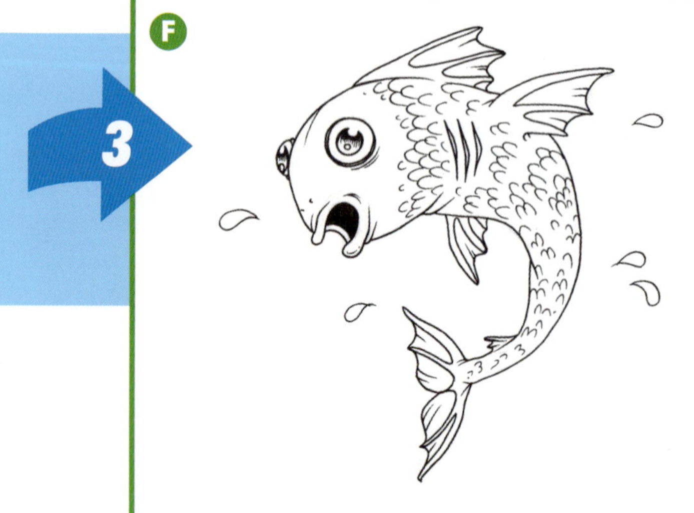

4

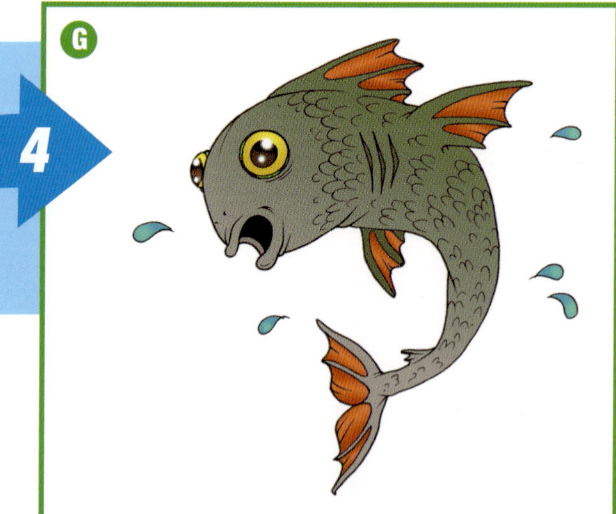

STEP 1

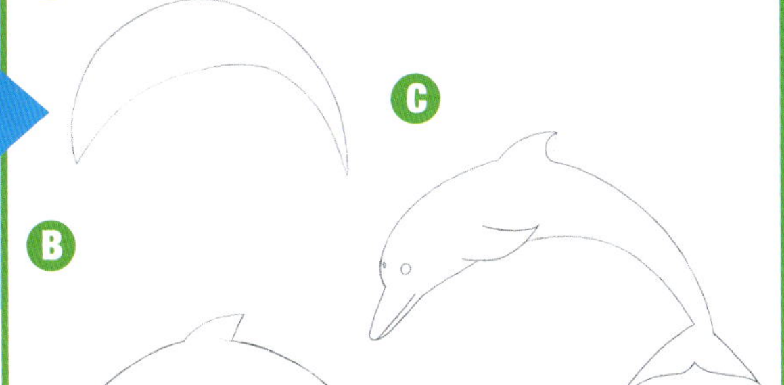

B

2

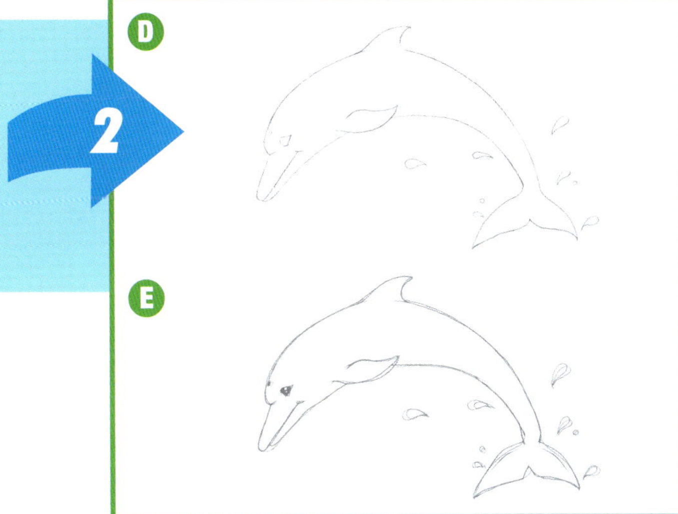

A Draw a large crescent moon shape on your page, with the pointed edges facing downward. This shape is the basic form of your dolphin.

B Your dolphin has fins shaped like a triangle with one curved edge, like a quarter of a circle. The tail is a larger triangle with a curved bottom edge.

C The shape of your dolphin's face is created by cutting into your crescent shape and giving it a curved snout and rounded forehead. Its face consists of a small eye, a smiling mouth, and a single "nostril" on the forehead. You should also give the top fin and tail a curvier look, using your pencil.

D After the dolphin's framework is finished, start adding some simple detail. The eye will look a lot friendlier if you give it a more fan-shaped eyelid. Draw splashes of water to make it look like the dolphin is leaping out of the ocean.

E Sketch detail onto your dolphin, such as wrinkles where the flippers meet the body, and a glint of light in the eye.

F Before adding any color to your dolphin, trace over your pencil version in black pen and erase the pencil lines. This will prevent any smudging of the outline when you add color.

G You can now color in your dolphin using gray tones. To achieve the best effect, shade gradually from a darker gray on top to a light gray on the underside.

3

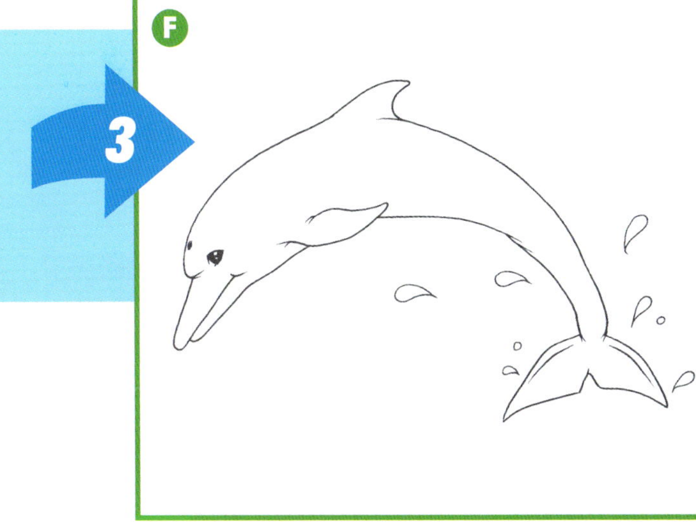

4

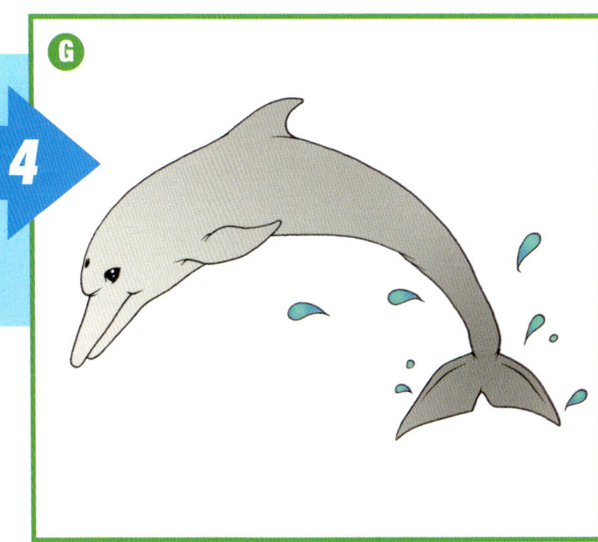

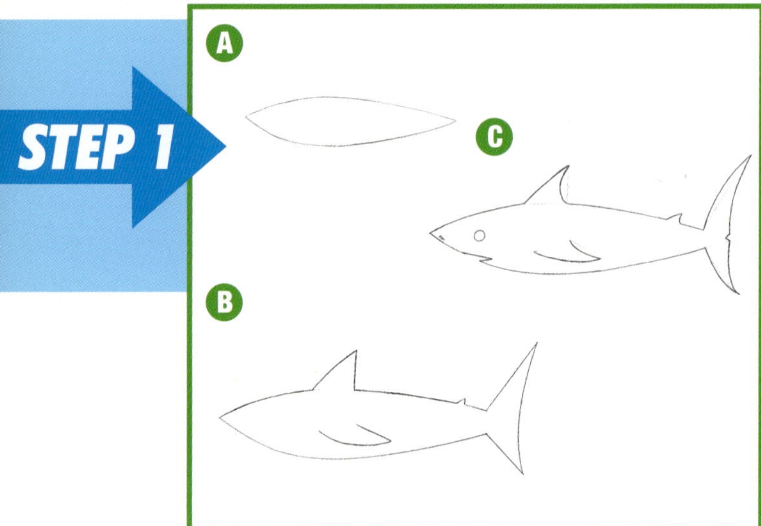

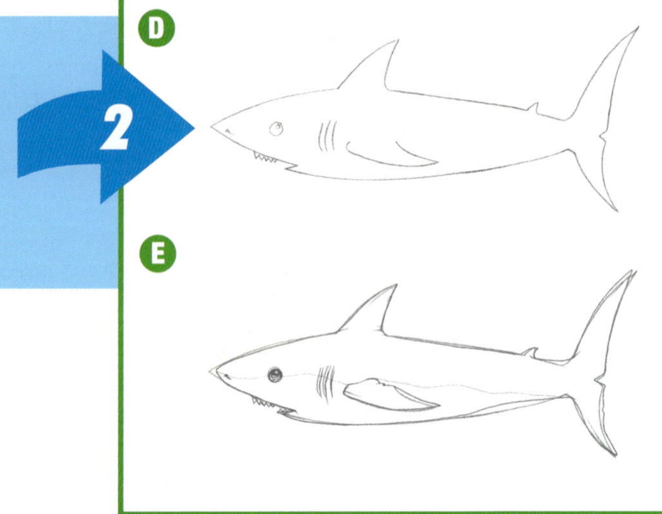

A Sketch a long almond shape in the center of the page—this is going to be your shark's body. The front edge of this is a little fatter than the back.

B Draw a curved triangular shape on top of the body to represent its main fin. The other fins are similar in shapes, and the tail is a large triangle with a curved section at the rear. Make the tail longer at the top than at the bottom.

C Your shark's face is constructed using simple shapes. Its mouth is a triangular shape cut into the main body, and the eye is a circle. Start to give the fins a more curved appearance, and scoop a small triangle from the tail.

D The shark's gills are drawn using three simple curved lines. Draw a row of sharp triangular teeth in its mouth and put a small circular reflection in the eye. Also start rounding off the edges where the fins and tail meet the body.

E Now alter anything you aren't happy with before sketching a feint wobbly line about halfway down the body from nose to tail. Great White sharks in particular have undersides that are much paler than the rest of their bodies, so this line will help separate that lighter underbelly from the dark upper body.

F Draw over the pencil lines that you want to use with a black drawing pen and erase any leftover pencil lines.

G Your man-eater is now ready to color! The shark here features a turquoise-gray combination.

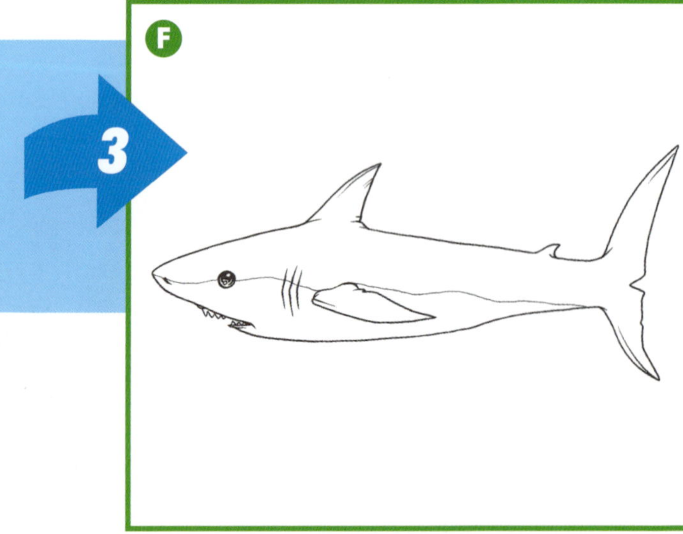

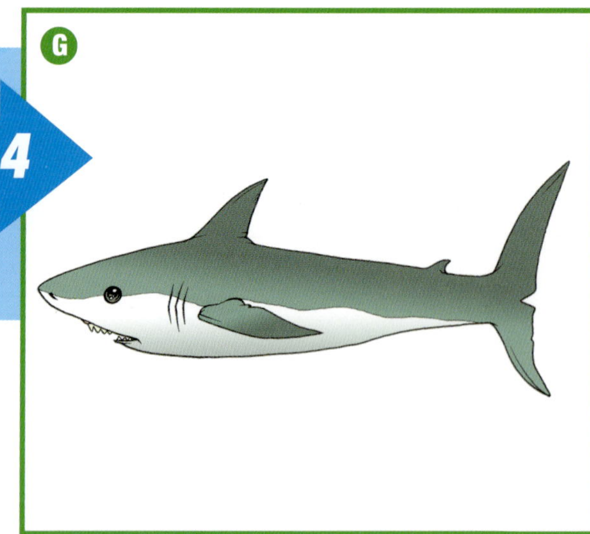

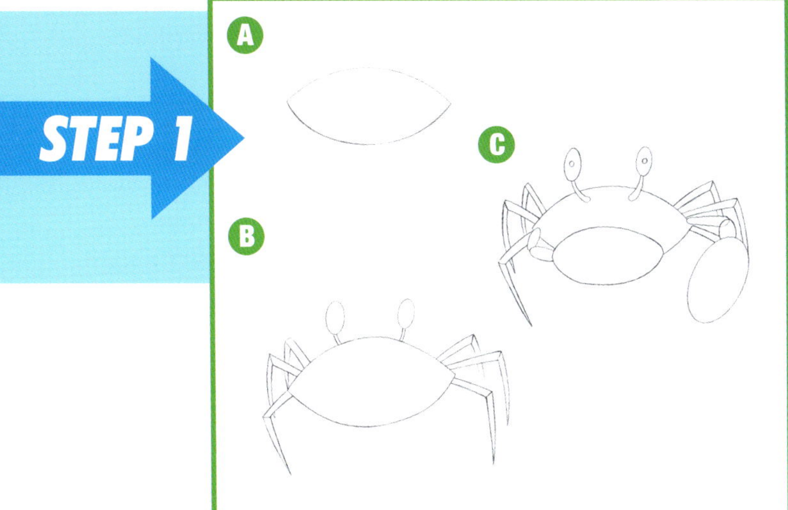

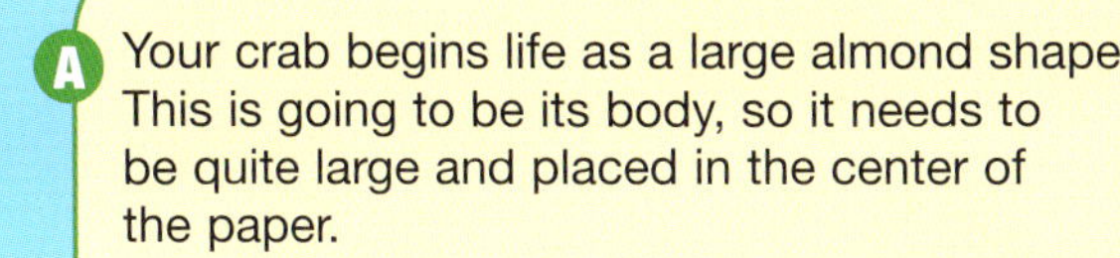

A Your crab begins life as a large almond shape. This is going to be its body, so it needs to be quite large and placed in the center of the paper.

B The legs of your crab consist of two sections, the lower one tapering to a point. Two fairly small ovals are joined to the body with stalks—these are your crab's eyes.

C Now your crab needs some arms. These are created using one oval as the upper arm, and another for the forearm. These are connected to the body at either side. Finally, it needs huge pincers on the end of each arm to fight enemies and catch food!

D Your crab is almost done, except for the final shape of the pincers. These claws are the sharp, curved shapes at the end of the arms. To draw these, split each oval into sharp, "teardrop" shapes. Next, give the eyelids and pupils some detail.

E Now add details to the crab's tough shell, such as stripes running along the top, and lines along the joints of the legs to give them a bony look.

F Once your crab is looking suitably "armored," you can draw over the pencil lines with a black pen, and erase any pencil lines that aren't needed.

G To complete your picture of the crab, it's time to color it in using colored pencils, felt-tip pens, pastels, or paints.

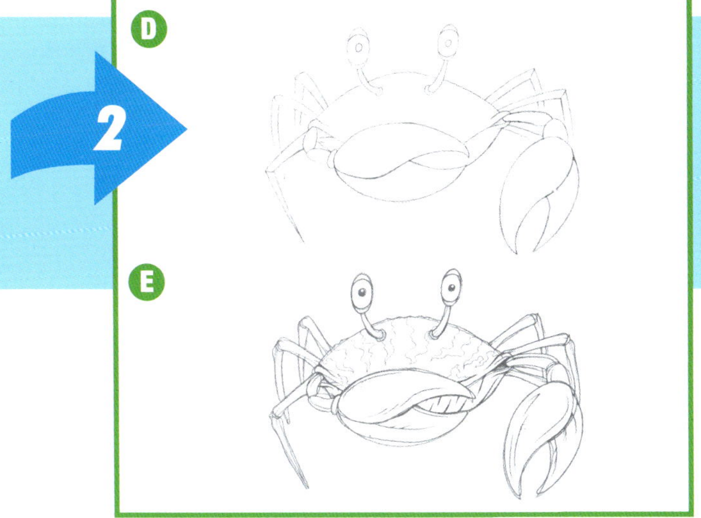

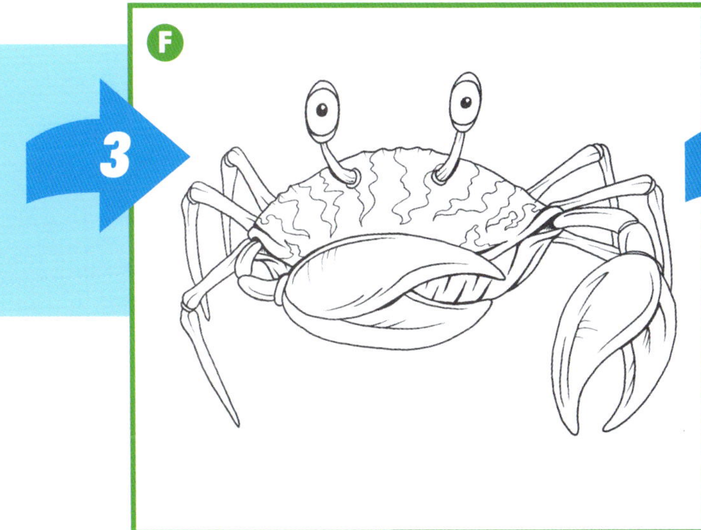

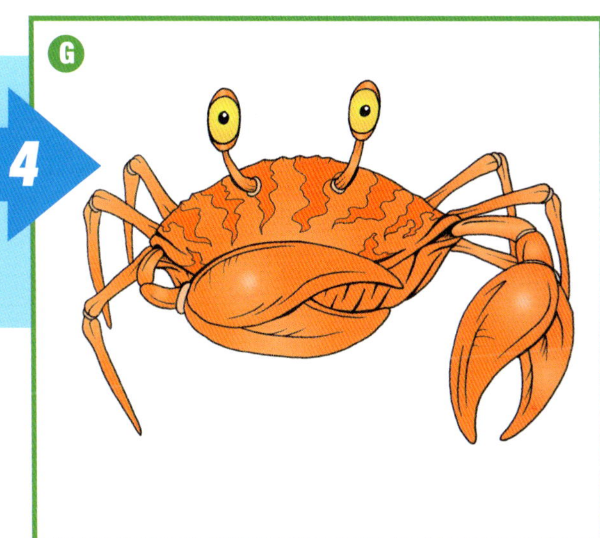

HOW TO DRAW A SEAHORSE

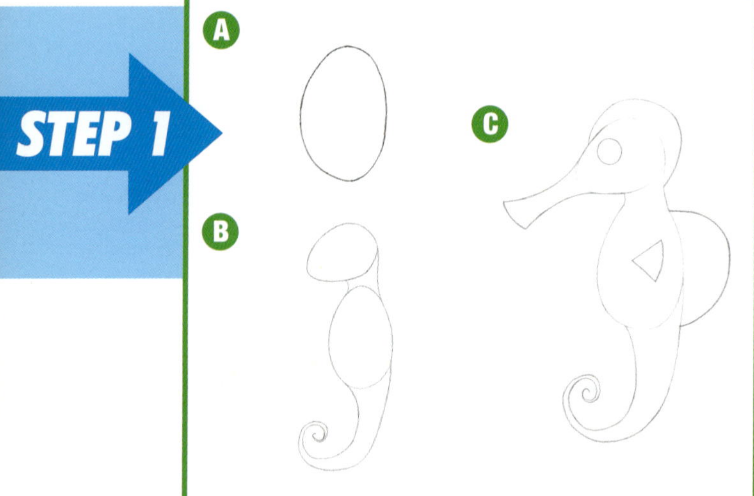

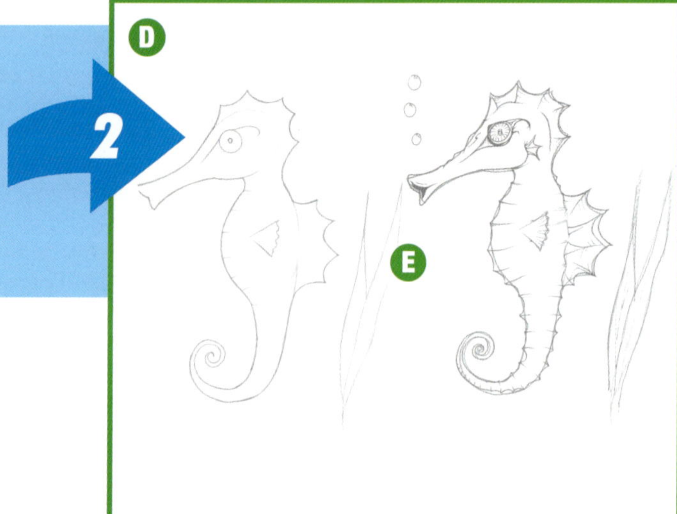

A The first stage of your seahorse drawing will look like a giant oval or "egg" shape—this is the seahorse's body.

B Draw another egg shape on top of the first, joined by a short neck. Next, add your seahorse's tail, a long, coiled horn shape.

C Give your seahorse a thin, trumpet-shaped snout, a circular eye, and a semi-circular crest on the head. The fin starts off as a triangular "fan" shape, and it has a large semi-circular "sail" on its back.

D Start adding simple detail to your seahorse, such as spiked edges on the crest and "sail," a frilled edge to the fin, and a tiny pupil in his eye. You can also begin sketching in some seaweed floating in the water beside it.

E Next, add the final touches to the face by adding lines in the eyes that branch out from the pupil. Give it a tiny fin, similar to the spiked crest, behind the head. Make the entire body outline look spiny by drawing lines down it, and joining these with the scooped lines. Finally, draw round bubbles coming out of its snout.

F Use a black pen to draw over your design before erasing the pencil lines.

G Seahorses are quite often sand-colored, so they can blend in with their surroundings and avoid predators. Use a few similar tones of color, and blend from one to the other to help your seahorse hide from hungry enemies!

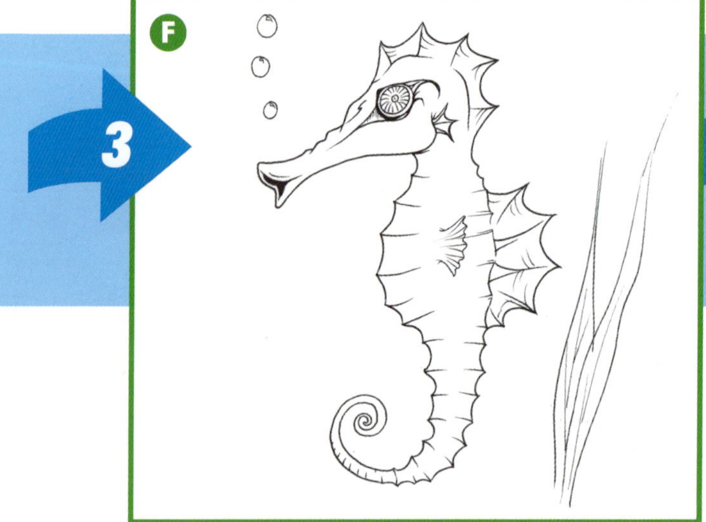

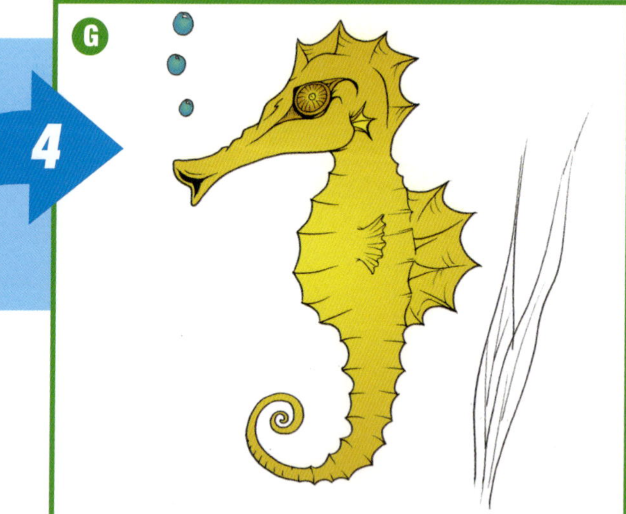

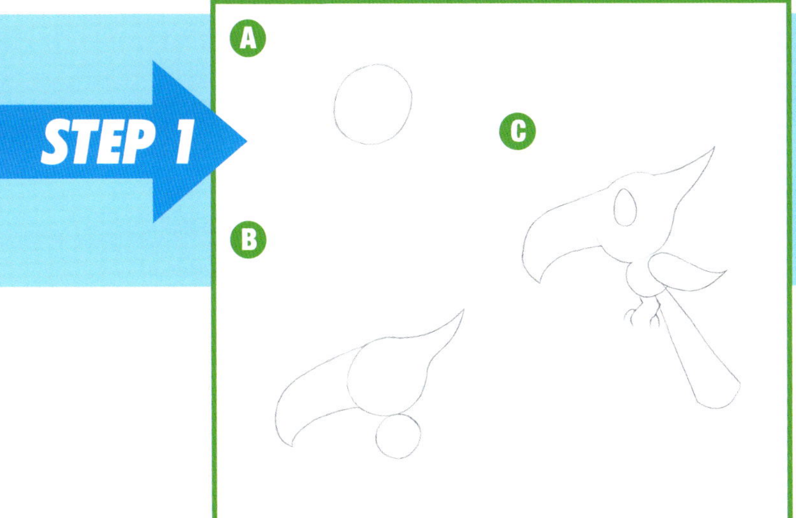

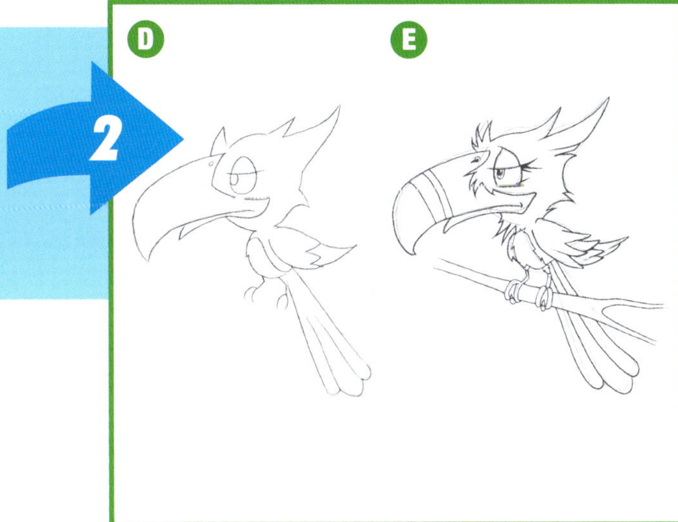

A The first shape you should draw on your page to create a parrot is a large circle. You don't have to be exact with this, as it is just the basic starting shape for your parrot's head.

B Draw a large beak on the left of the circle and a bent triangular shape on the right, to form your parrot's head. Next, draw a circle about half the size and below the first one to represent the parrot's body. Being a cartoon parrot means that it can get away with having a huge head, yet still fly!

C The parrot has tiny stick-like feet and a tear-drop-shaped wing. Its tail is a long fan shape, and the eyes start off by being egg-shaped.

D Now, sketch a few details onto your bird. It has a dumb-looking face, with half-open eyes and a head of ruffled feathers. The nostrils sit at the top of the beak, near the eyes. Separate the tail into three large feathers, and the wing into sections.

E To add to the realism of your character, layer the feathers over each other and draw some smaller, fluffy feathers around the beak. Draw lashes on the eyes if you want your parrot to look female, but if you want a boy parrot, leave these off. Finally, fatten the stick-like legs a little and draw the perch it's sitting on.

F Draw over the character with a thin black pen, before you erase the pencil lines.

G You can use pencils or paints to complete your character.

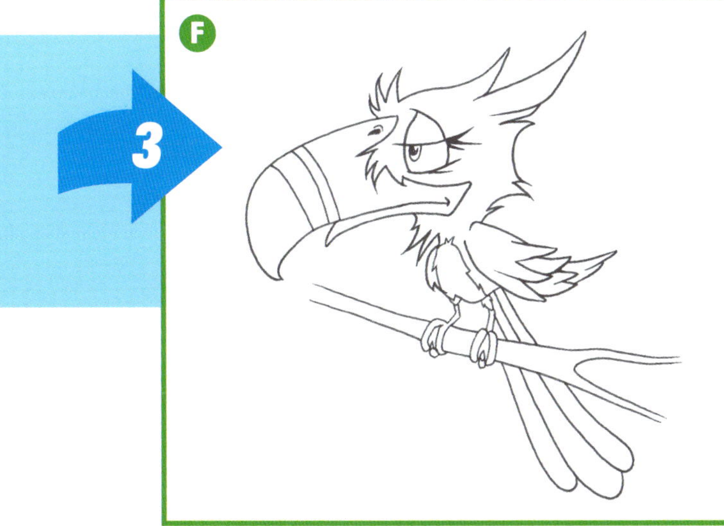

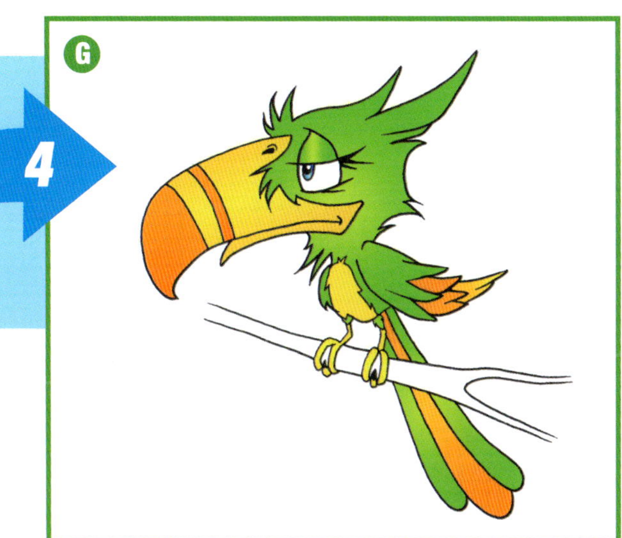

HOW TO DRAW A PENGUIN

STEP 1

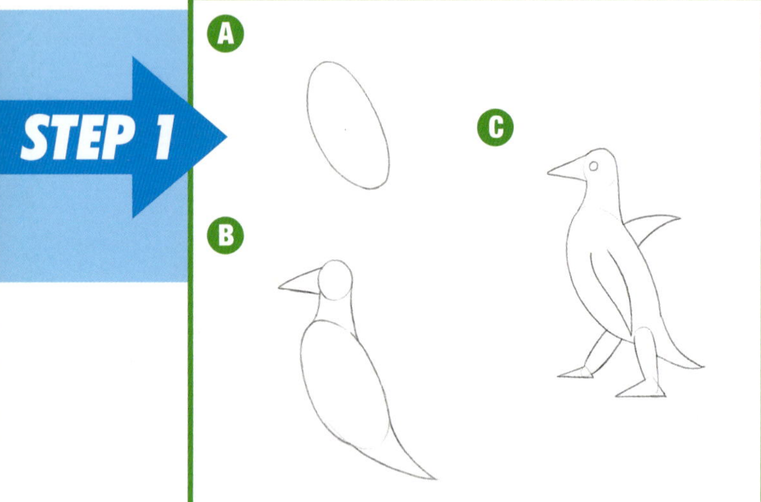

2

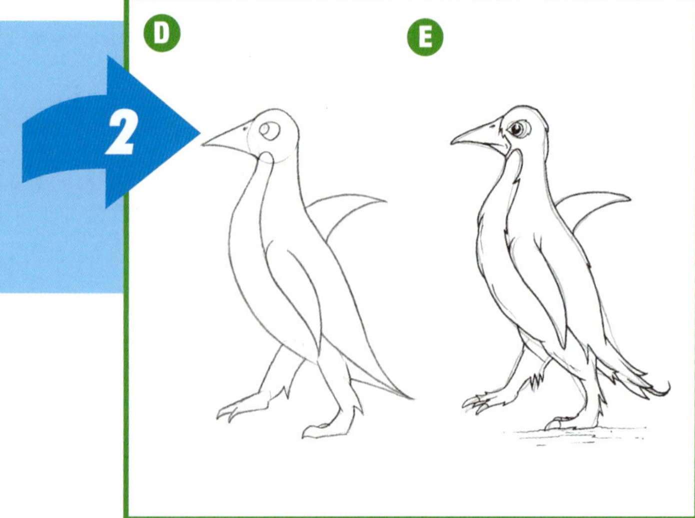

A For the penguin, draw a large oval in the center of your page, roughly twice as long as it is high, but don't worry about being exact. Draw this shape at an angle, as if it were falling over.

B Using the first shape as a guide, draw a small circle, joined by two lines, to the top of the large oval, and add a long triangular beak. The tail is a triangle that curves slightly upward.

C Draw two wings on your penguin—these resemble flippers, so they should be sleek and smooth. Next, draw your penguin's legs. These are thin oval shapes with triangles for feet. The left leg is slightly hidden behind the body.

D To complete the basic frame for your penguin, join all of your shapes together with a smooth outline. Draw its tiny, beady eye with a white ring behind it, and sketch a line down the body to separate the black top feathers from the white underside. Finally, give the legs some fluffy feathers and his feet curved toenails.

E Time to add those finishing touches—the most important thing is to make the penguin look like it has feathers, but not fluffy ones. Penguins have smooth, oily feathers to help them survive in Antarctic conditions.

F Draw over your penguin with a drawing pen. Wait a few minutes for the ink to dry, then erase any remaining pencil lines.

G Color your penguin using either felt-tip pen or colored pencils.

3

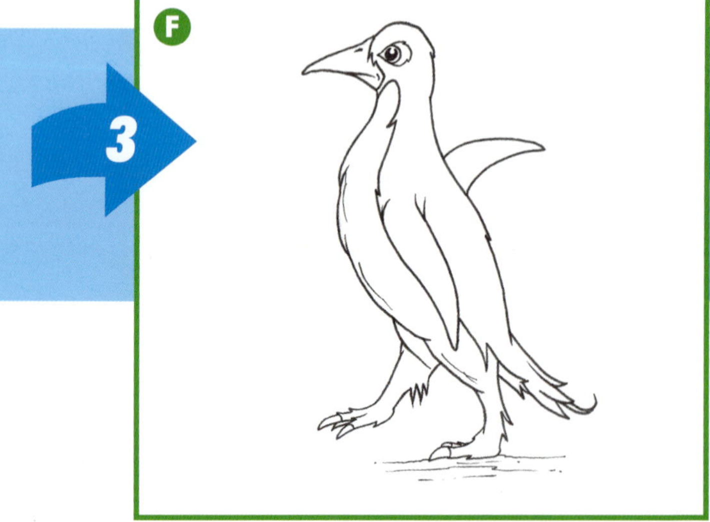

4

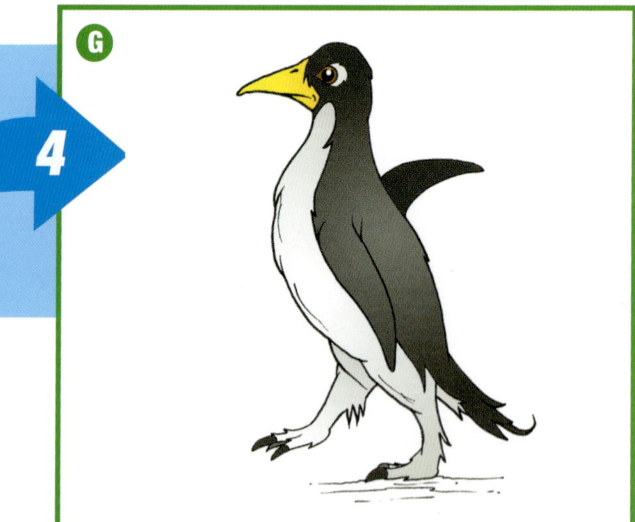

STEP 1

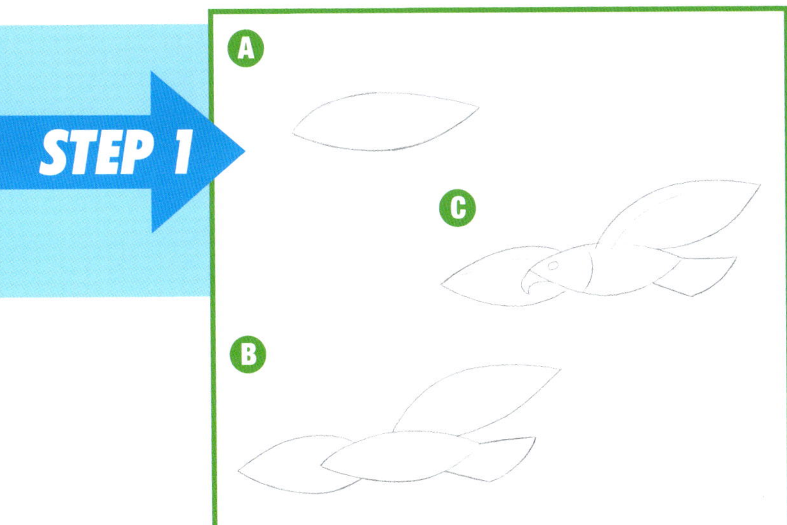

A Start your eagle by sketching a feint leaf shape on your paper. This is its body.

B The eagle's wings are a similar shape, but one wing overlaps the head slightly, so be careful with your pencil and don't press too hard. The tail is a simple fan shape.

C Your eagle's legs are tucked away while it flies, so you won't have to draw them. Draw a large hooked beak on the front of the head, an oval-shaped eye, and a collar where the white head feathers will begin on the neck.

D Start to add simple detail to your eagle. The sharp piercing eyes have small pupils that help it spot its prey, and the beak has a tiny nostril on the top. Start to draw the feathers by using jagged pencil lines around the "collar" and down the edge of the wings. Finally, the fan-shaped tail is split into five separate feathers.

E Final details can now be applied to your eagle such as sharp wispy feathers along the inside of the wings and a frowning face. Draw lots of curvy, jagged lines around the face to make it look like as if the ruffled feathers are being blown by the wind as the bird flies along.

F It's time to trace over the lines you've drawn with a black pen, and don't forget to erase any leftover pencil lines.

G Give the body feathers a deep, warm brown tone, leaving the face feathers white. The eyes are yellow, as is the powerful, curved beak.

2

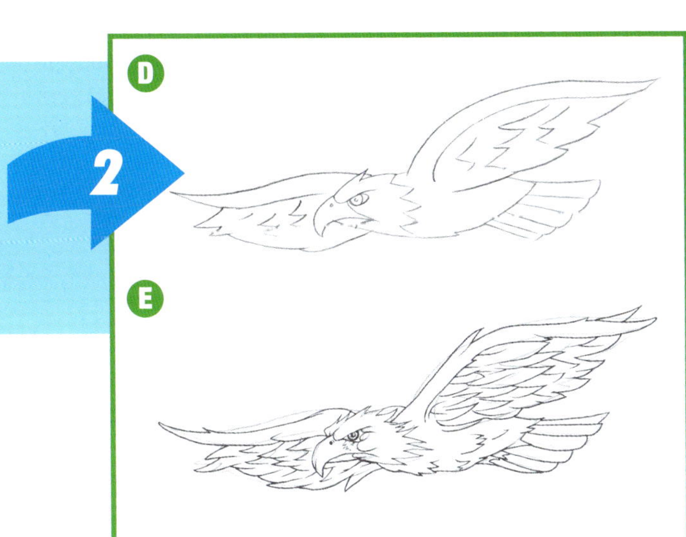

3

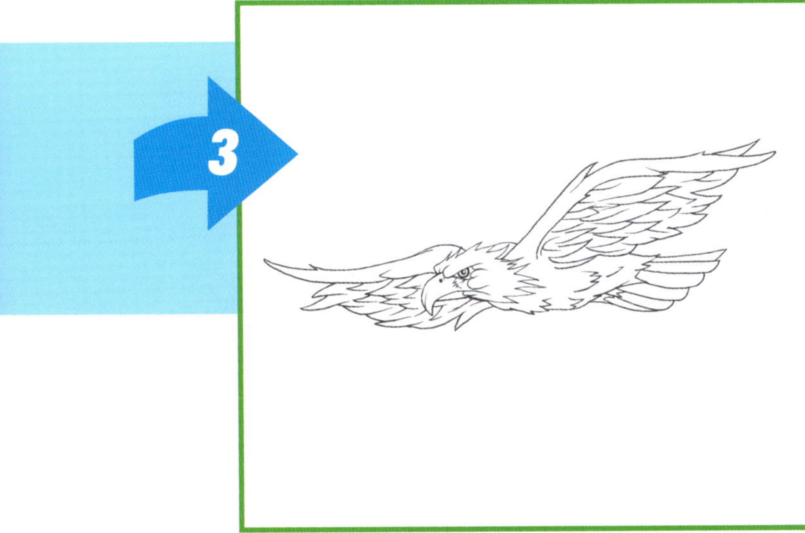

4

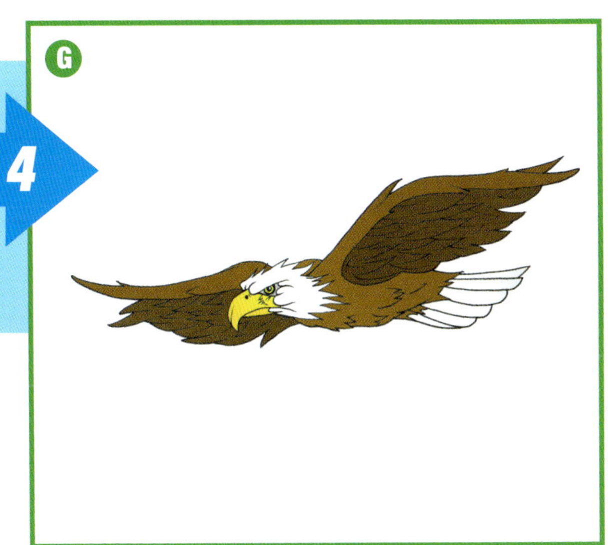

HOW TO DRAW A DOG

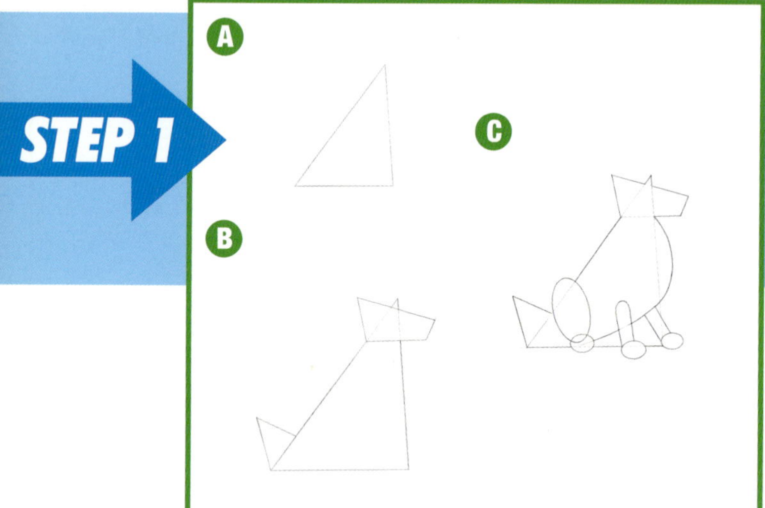

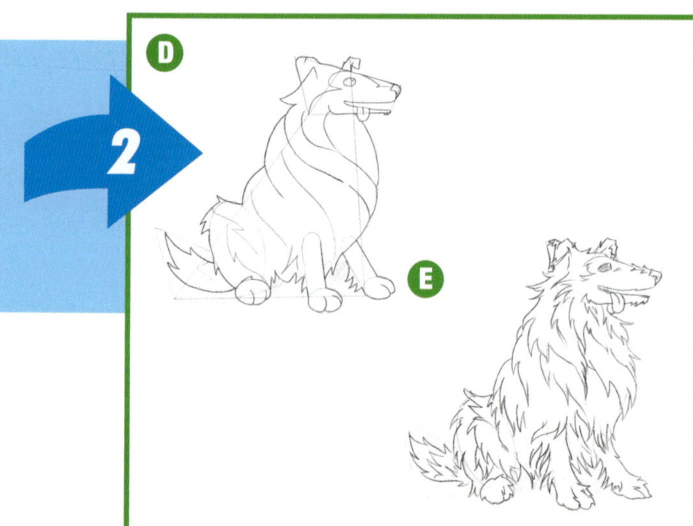

A Start your picture by drawing a tall, right-angled triangle in the center of your paper. This is going to be the main body of your dog.

B Now draw the head, which is also triangular, but with one of the corners cut off. Make this shape overlap the first triangle. Then draw a much smaller triangle near the base of the original triangle. This will be your dog's tail.

C Give your dog a rounded chest. Next, add the cylindrical front legs and the oval feet. Because the back legs are tucked in underneath this dog, you can only see one of them, and it needs to be oval-shaped.

D It's time for those details! Add simple facial features and start rounding off the sharp edges. Draw three separate toes on each of the dog's paws, and give it a wet nose and a lolling tongue. Finally, start to draw the fur. Begin by drawing lines that wrap around the body.

E Draw some final detail on your dog. The fur is separated into large sections, each of these sections can be a different color. Give the fur a shaggy appearance by using short, sharp strokes with your pencil.

F Draw over your sketch with a black pen. Then erase the pencil, and the dog is ready to color.

G This dog is a rough-coated Collie, so it should be colored in sandy browns, grays, and white. Color the tongue a fleshy pink and make the eye dark brown.

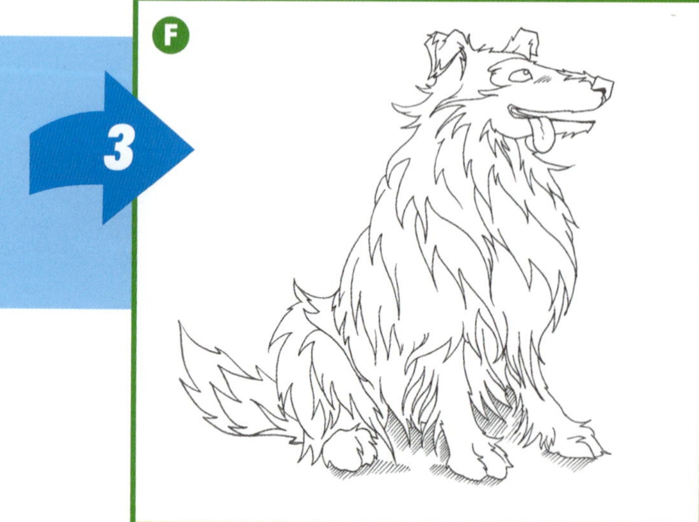

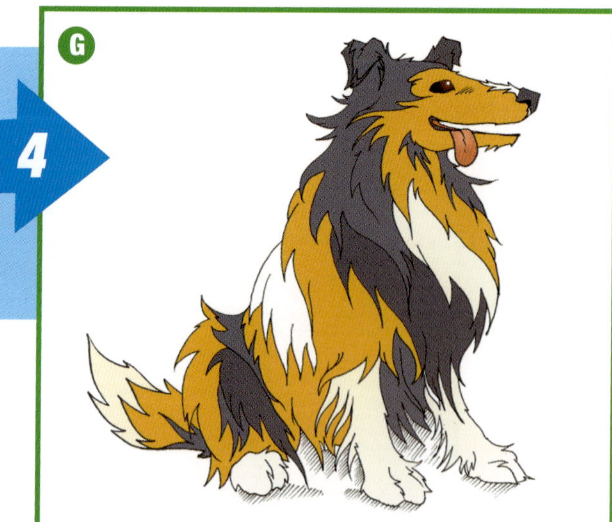

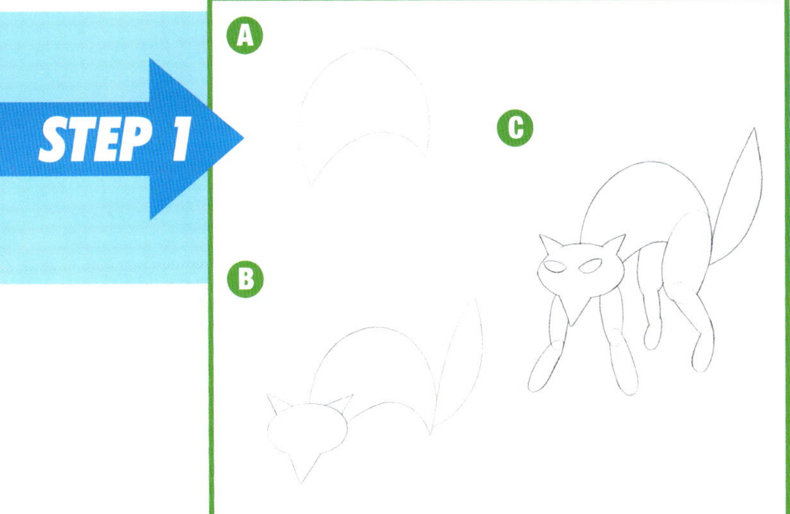

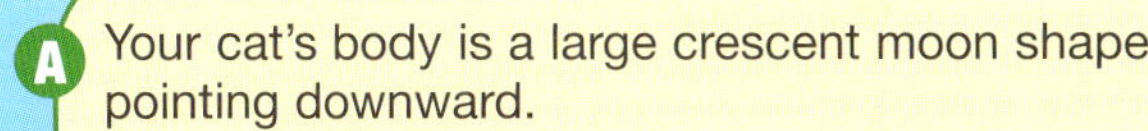

A Your cat's body is a large crescent moon shape, pointing downward.

B The head of your cat is an oval with two triangular ears and a triangle that will form its open mouth. It has an almond-shaped tail that it is waving in the air.

C The cat's legs are constructed using oval shapes. The front legs consist of two ovals, and the hind legs consist of three. Notice how the legs bend backward on a cat, unlike the human leg that bends forward from the knee. Once you've drawn the legs, give your cat two narrow, slanting eyes.

D Using the frame as a guide, start to add detail to your cat. Begin sketching the fur, which is jagged and standing on end. This cat isn't too happy! Next, give it three toes on each foot and start to sketch in an angry mouth.

E Your cat will need some sharp teeth and whiskers. It is hissing at a dog, so the mouth is wide open and the tongue is showing. Finally, give your cat white "socks" on the feet.

F Draw over your picture with a black drawing pen or narrow felt-tip pen. Once you have gone over all of the lines, erase the leftover pencil lines.

G Cats are usually black, white, ginger, or calico, so it's best to stick with these colors. This cat has bright green eyes to make it look mad, but maybe your cat could be a little more laid back? Experiment with different colors!

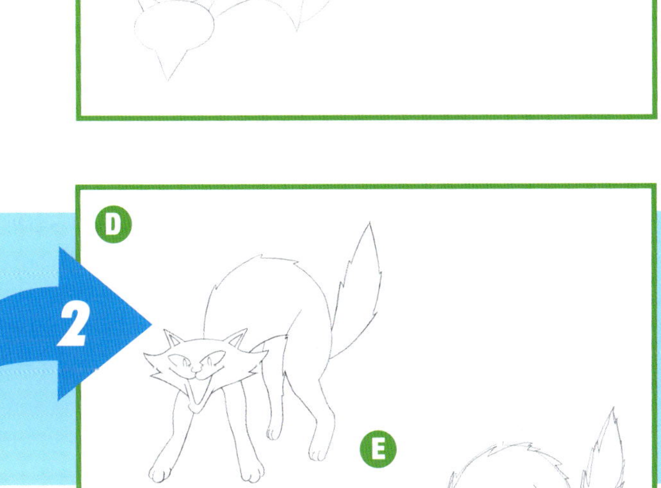

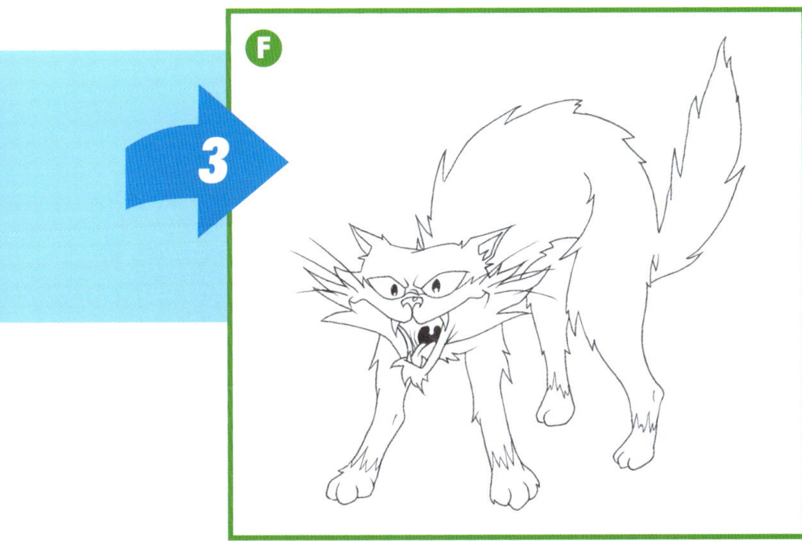

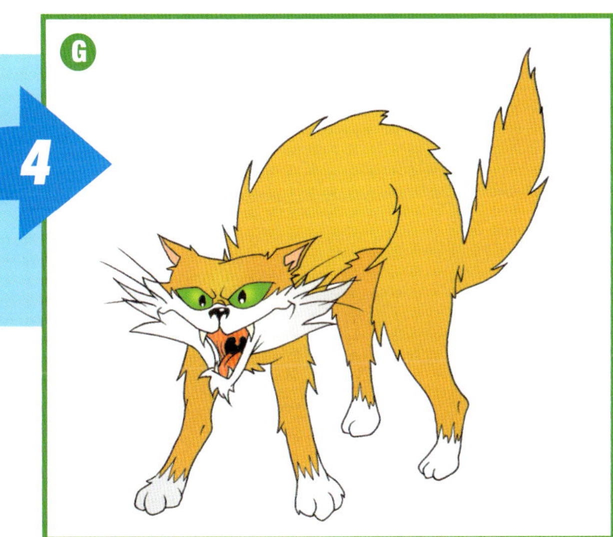

HOW TO DRAW A RABBIT

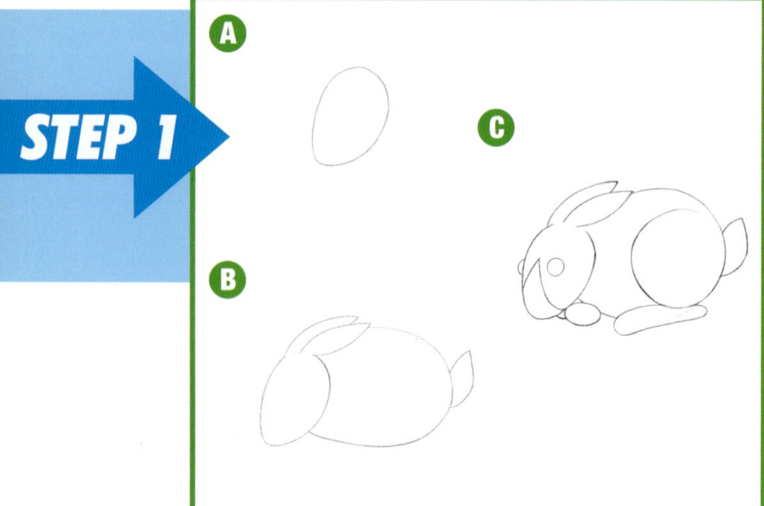

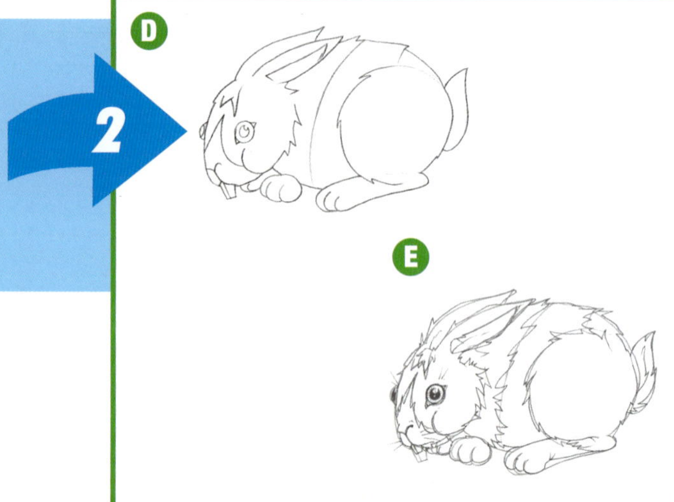

A To begin your picture, draw an oval shape for the rabbit's head.

B Draw two large ears on top of your oval. Then, slightly overlapping the head shape, draw a much larger oval for the rabbit's body. Finally, give your rabbit a little cotton-bud tail.

C To complete your rabbit's basic frame, it will need legs. The hind leg is quite large, and consists of a circle with a rounded cylindrical shape underneath. The front feet are oval shapes, tucked under the head. Next, give it two round eyes and a triangular stripe on the nose.

D Start adding simple details to your rabbit, such as the teeth and nostrils. Add some detail to the eyes, such as the pupils and a reflection. Use jagged lines when drawing the outline of your rabbit, as this will make it look furry.

E Add some final detail to your rabbit. Keep sketching jagged lines all over its body to give it that fluffy appearance, and separate the feet, drawing three toes on each of them.

F Before coloring your rabbit, draw over the pencil lines with a black pen, remembering not to trace over any lines that you don't want.

G You can color your rabbit in various ways. This one was colored in on a computer because it makes the fur look extra-glossy. If you don't have access to a computer, you can get excellent results with paints or colored pencils.

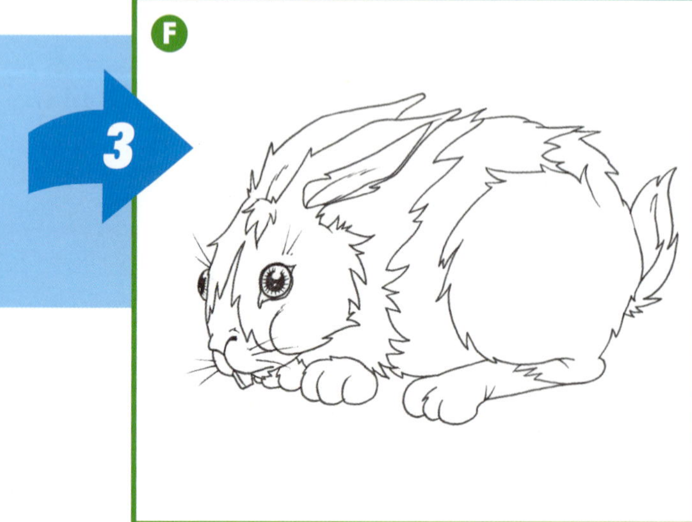

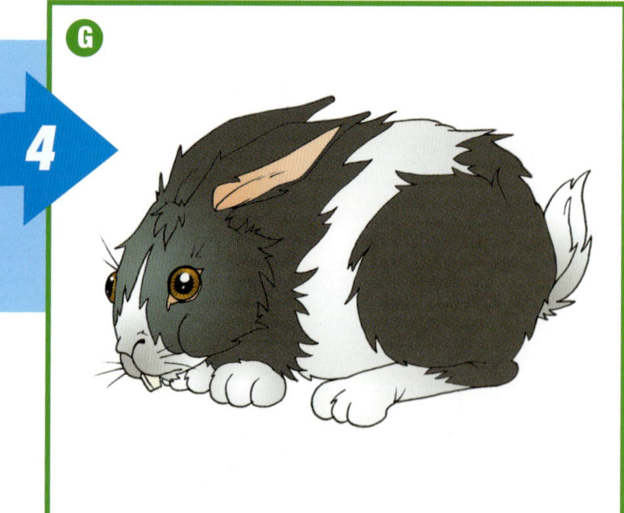

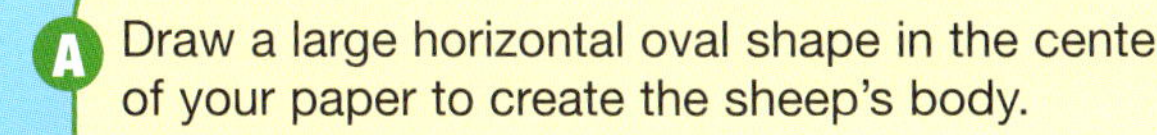

HOW TO DRAW A SHEEP

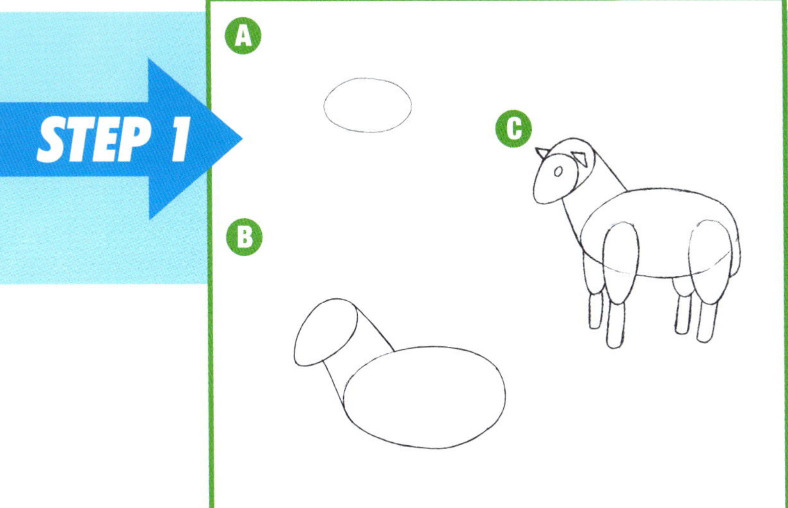

A Draw a large horizontal oval shape in the center of your paper to create the sheep's body.

B On the top of your oval shape, draw an egg shape connected to the oval by a wide collar. This should now look like a head and neck attached to the sheep's body.

C Give your sheep some legs to walk on. The tops of these are oval, with lower-leg "stick" shapes underneath. You should also add detail to your sheep's face, such as an oval eye and some pointed ears. Next, draw a short tail.

D Draw some hooves on your character and make the face a little shapelier. Finally, you can stick a clump of grass in its mouth. Sheep are grazing animals, so it's rare not to see one chewing!

E Your sheep is almost finished, but the fleece needs to be a lot fluffier: a little like cotton candy in fact. Add the "fluff" as if you are drawing a cloud, making lots of tiny curved lines. Give your sheep some pupils in the eye and some flared nostrils.

F Use a black pen to fill in the outline, and erase those pencil lines. You're now ready to start coloring in.

G Of course, it's best to use black and white for your sheep—after all, how often have you seen a purple sheep? Or an orange one? But, if you want to experiment with different colors, then don't let reality stop you—go for it! You may surprise yourself with the results.

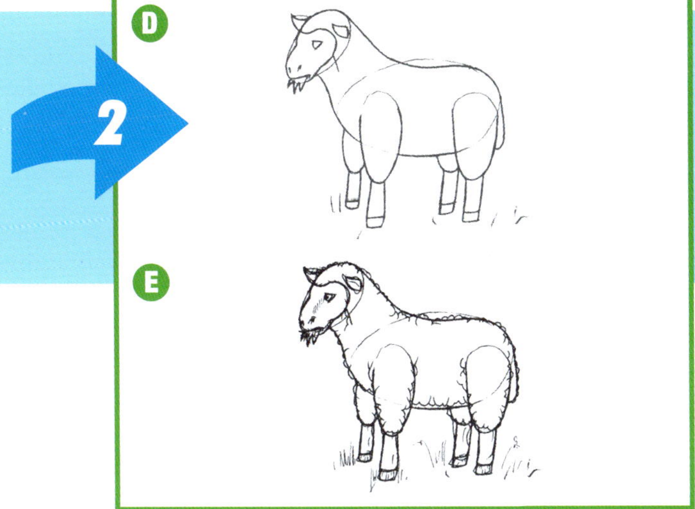

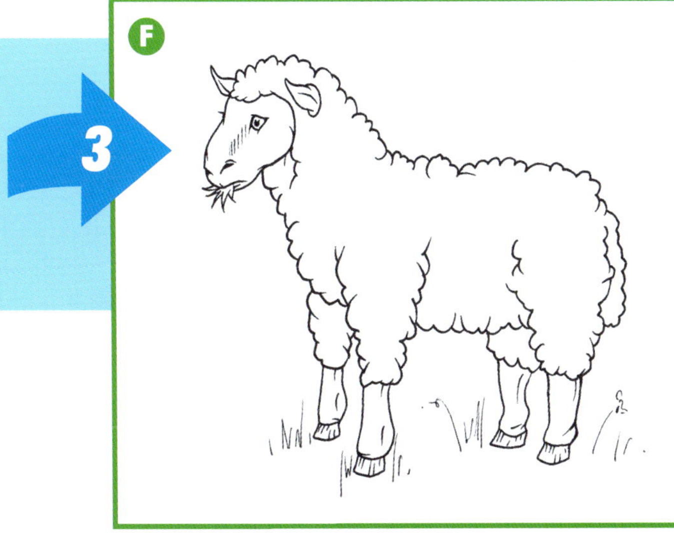

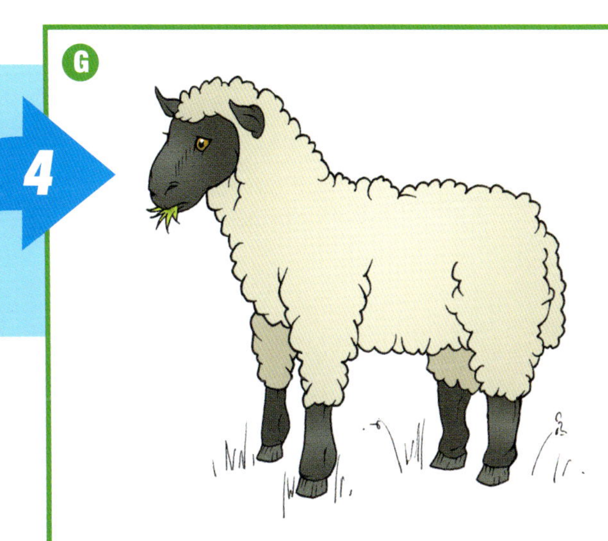

HOW TO DRAW A PIG

STEP 1

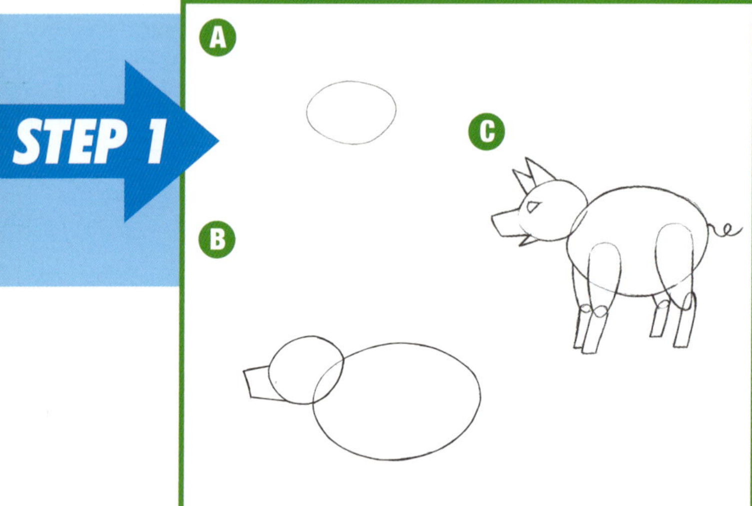

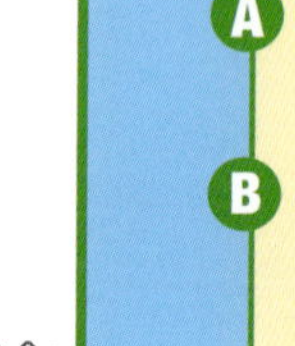

2

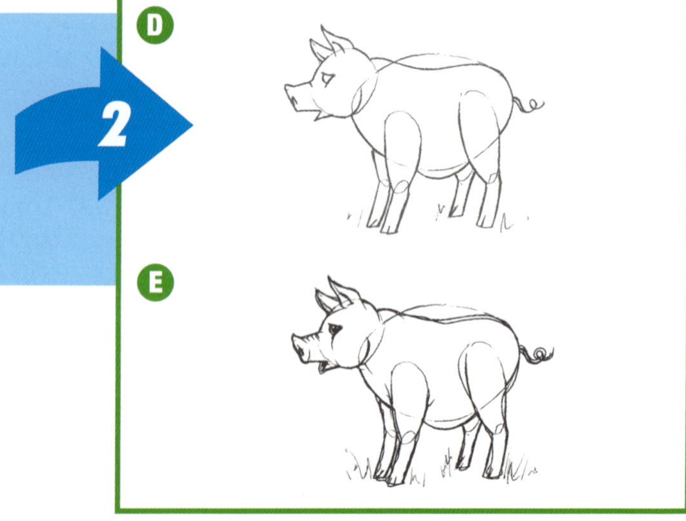

A Your pig's body is oval shaped and should be drawn fairly large in the center of your page.

B Like the body, this pig's head is oval but smaller of course. Set the head at the same angle as the body, and slightly overlapping, but make the shape a little fatter and rounder. Next, give the pig a short, boxy snout.

C Draw your pig's legs using simple shapes. The hind legs bend back at the knee, and are a touch bigger than the front legs. The feet are flat and quite narrow. It has a triangular bottom lip and large triangular ears. Don't forget the thin, curly tail!

D Start to pencil in your pig's facial features, such as the nostrils and half-open eye. Next, curve the ears a little and begin to give the feet some shape.

E The important final details on your pig are the face and skin. It has a very wrinkly snout and reflective eyes. The skin creases where the limbs meet the body, and the legs are quite thin and bony, in contrast to the fat, round body.

F Trace over your drawing using a black drawing pen. Then you can erase the pencil lines. Your porky pig or hog is now ready to color.

G You should ideally color your pig either pink or black, or a combination of the two. Or, if you're feeling daring, make it any color you want—experiment and see what happens!

3

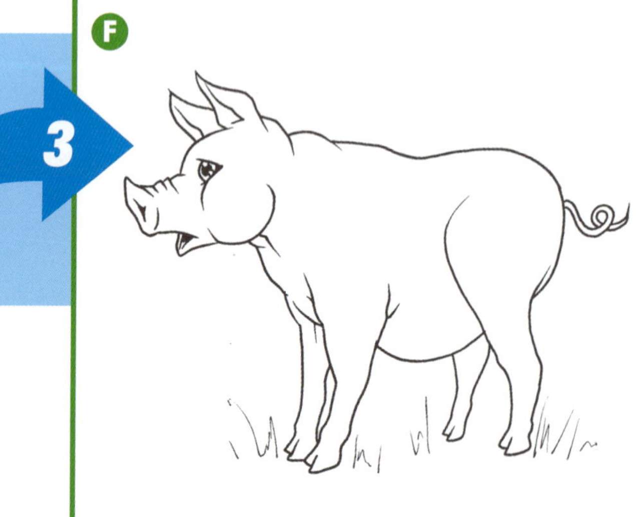

4

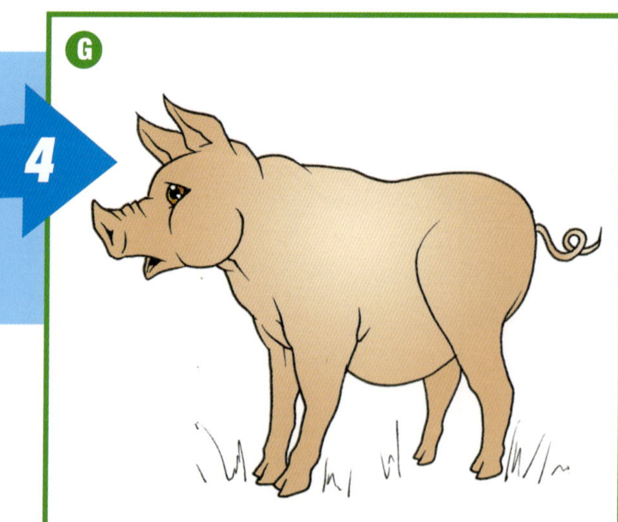

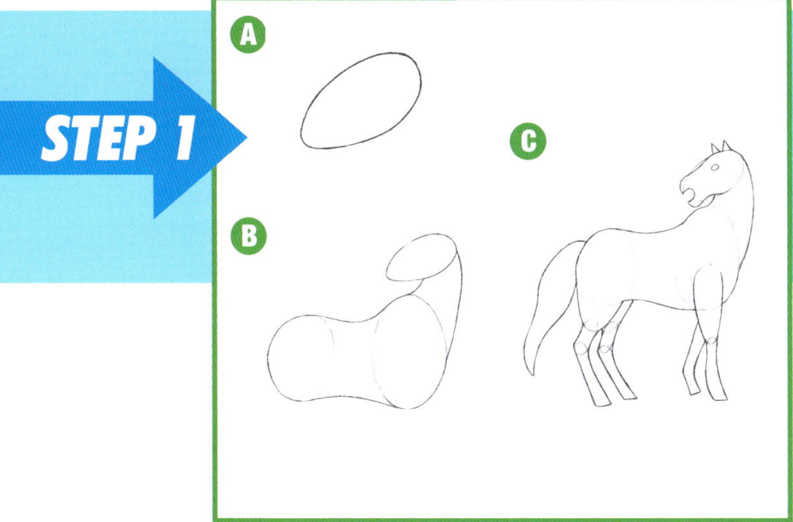

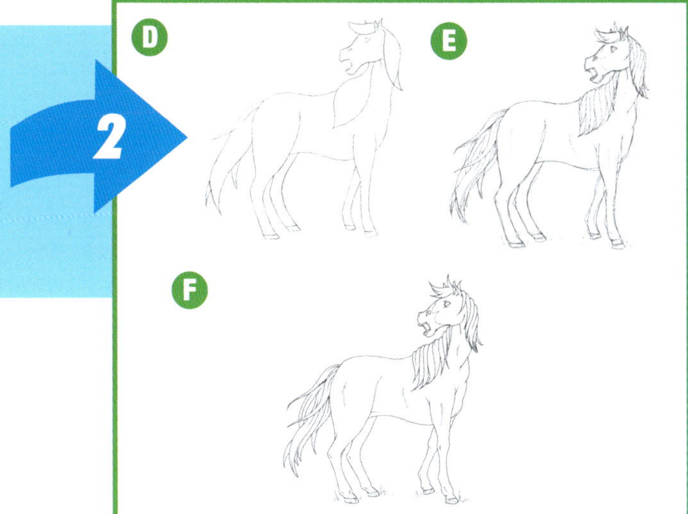

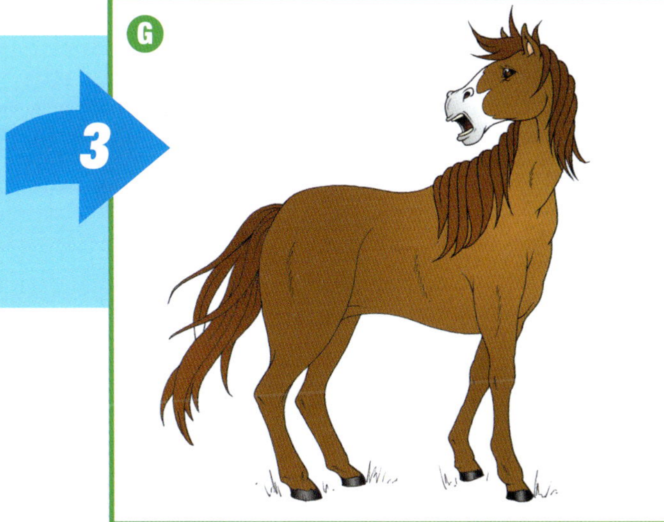

A The horse's head is shaped like an egg. Start by drawing this shape on the right-hand side of your paper, with the pointed part of the egg facing slightly downward.

B The horse's body consists of two large oval shapes, joined together by two dipping lines. The front oval is twice as long as the horse's head, while the back oval is about the same length, but a little fatter. Join this body shape to the head by drawing a thick neck.

C Draw your horse's back legs with three simple shapes—a large oval, a much smaller oval, and a stick shape. Its front legs consist of an oval and a stick shape. Give your horse a thick tail and then start to shape the face a little. The bridge of the nose should narrow slightly before widening again toward the mouth. It has triangular ears and an oval eye.

D Draw the outline of your horse by joining all the body shapes together with flowing lines. Now begin to add detail like the horse's mane and the white stripe on the end of its nose. Draw some extra spiky shapes on the tail so that it appears to be blowing in the wind.

E Use heavier pencil lines to give the eye long, pointed eyelashes and a reflection. The nostrils should flare, to look as if it is whinnying. Final touches to the legs, such as the hooves and bony knees, give the horse a more realistic look. The mane and tail are segmented into clumps of hair so that they give the impression of real movement.

F It's time to draw over the lines in black pen, before erasing the original pencil lines.

G This horse has a brown coat with a white flash on its nose, but horses can be white, black, or mottled. You can use colored pencils, pastels, or even a computer if you have access to one, to color your picture. Perhaps, though, you have your own horse? If so, you could use these tips to draw your own horse, color it in, and then pin the picture up in your horse's stable. Now there's an idea!

HOW TO DRAW A COW

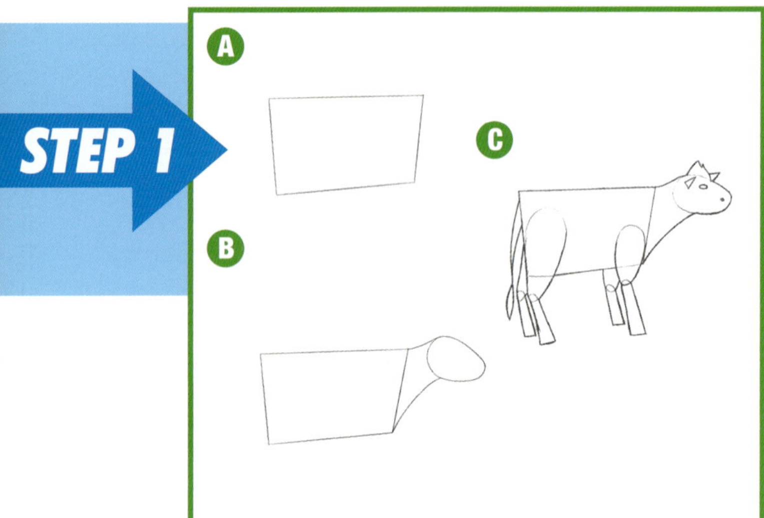

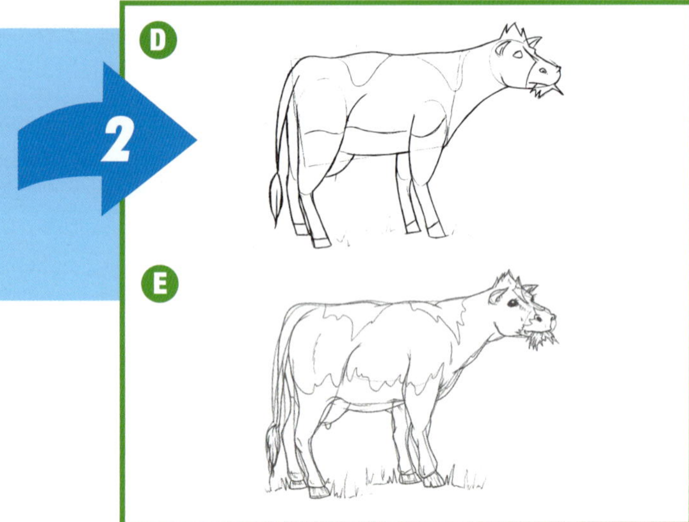

A Like all cows, the one featured here is quite a box-shaped character, so the first shape you should draw on your page is a large, irregular oblong.

B Draw an egg shape to form your cow's head. This is joined to the boxy body by making two curved lines to form a neck.

C All of the cow's legs are drawn with two shapes: an oval (which is larger on the hind legs) and a thin stick-like shape beneath them. Now, start to work on the face: she will have pointed ears and a fluffy patch of hair. She doesn't have any horns, though.

D Start to round off any sharp corners on your cow's body. Cows may be box-shaped, but there aren't any sharp corners on a real cow! The egg-shaped head should be narrower along the nose and she should have large, calm eyes. Sketch some grass in her mouth, and don't forget her udders: a simple cup shape.

E The pattern on the cow's fur helps to determine what breed of cow she is. Being a Friesian cow, this one has patches of white on her back, plus a white underside. She has sturdy, yet bony legs.

F Draw over the character with a thin black pen, before you erase the remaining pencil lines.

G You can use pencils, paints, or even a computer to color in your cow. Don't forget to give her a name!

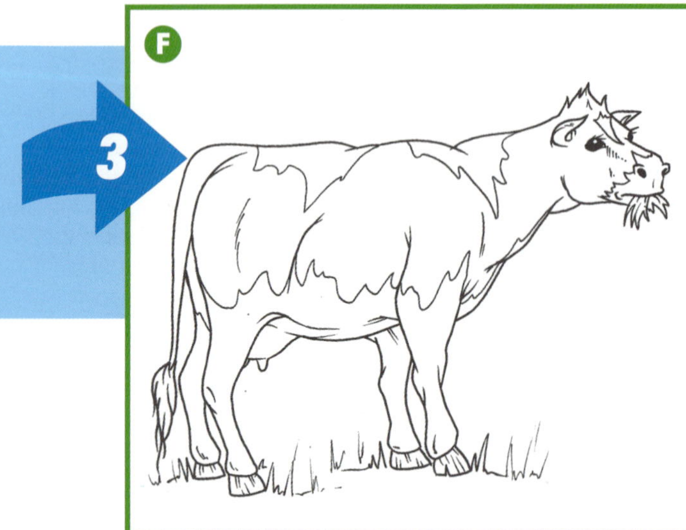

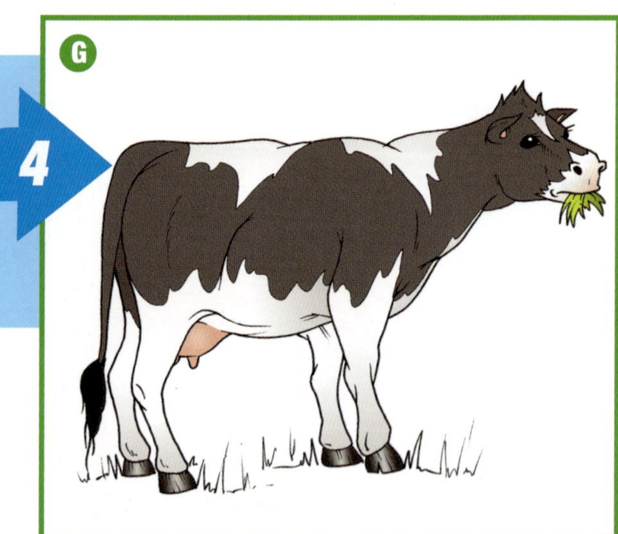

STEP 1

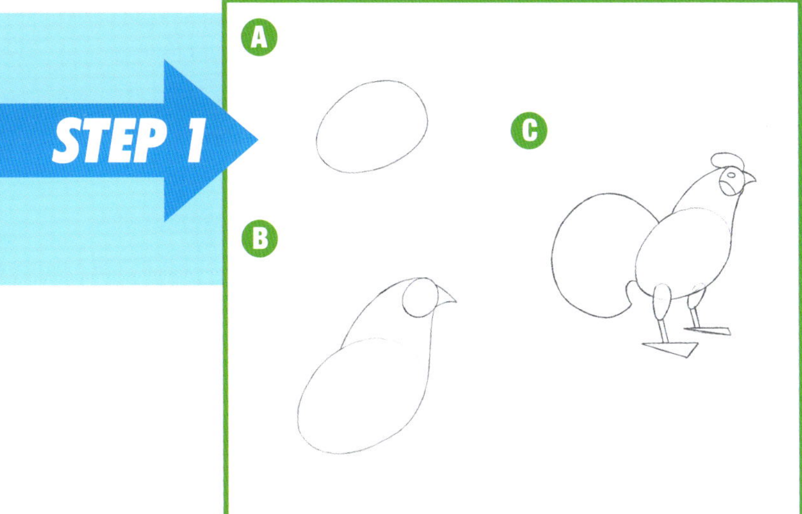

2

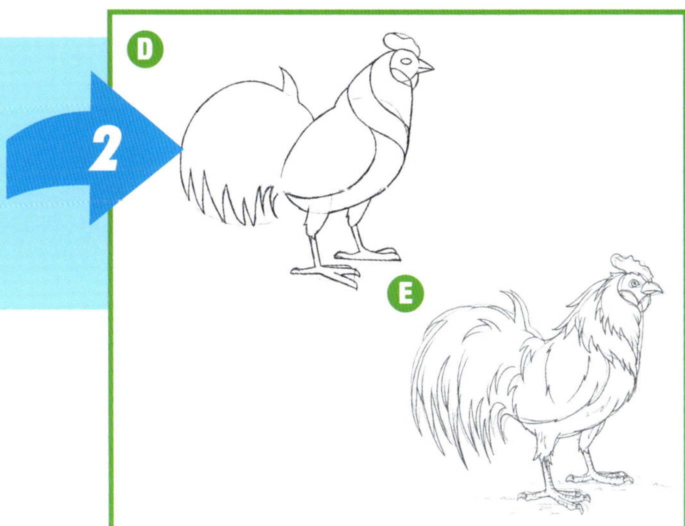

A The main body of the rooster is an oval, which you should draw at an angle in the center of your page.

B Draw a small circle that has two sweeping curved lines that join at the bottom of the circle and add a short, stumpy, triangular beak.

C Draw a large curved tail on your rooster. Next, draw his legs. These are thin oval shapes with stick-shaped lower legs and triangles for feet. The rooster has an oval eye and a simple crest shaped a little like a baked bean.

D To complete the basic frame of your rooster, start to sketch some fluffy feathers along the base of his tail and give his feet three toes, each with curved claws. The feathers on the rooster's chest start as curved lines that follow the contour of his body. You should also sketch the shape of the wing down the side of the body.

E When detailing, it is important to make your rooster look like he has lots of ruffled feathers! These are drawn using sweeping strokes for the large feathers and shorter jagged strokes for the small ones. Finally, his feet have tiny wrinkles all the way down them, and he has beady eyes.

F Draw over your rooster with a pen, and wait a few minutes for the ink to dry before erasing any remaining pencil lines.

G The final stage of your bird is adding color. Consider using watercolors because they are a great way to blend the colors on his tail and wing.

3

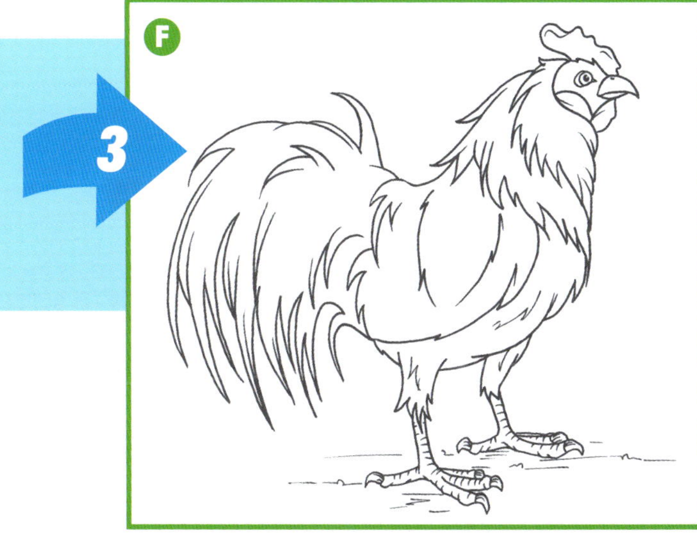

4

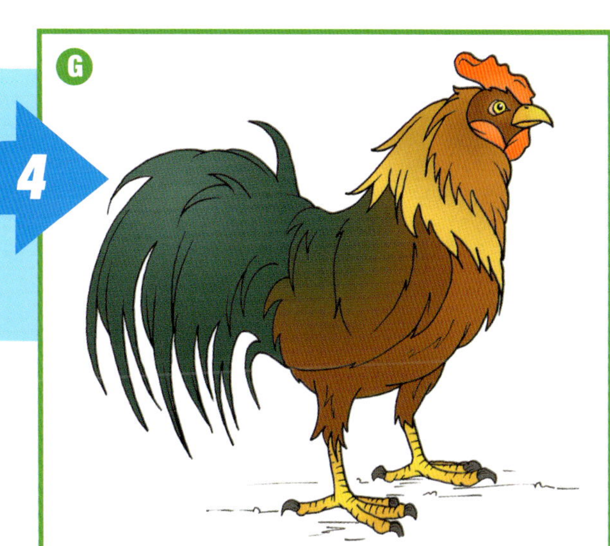

HOW TO DRAW A LION

STEP 1

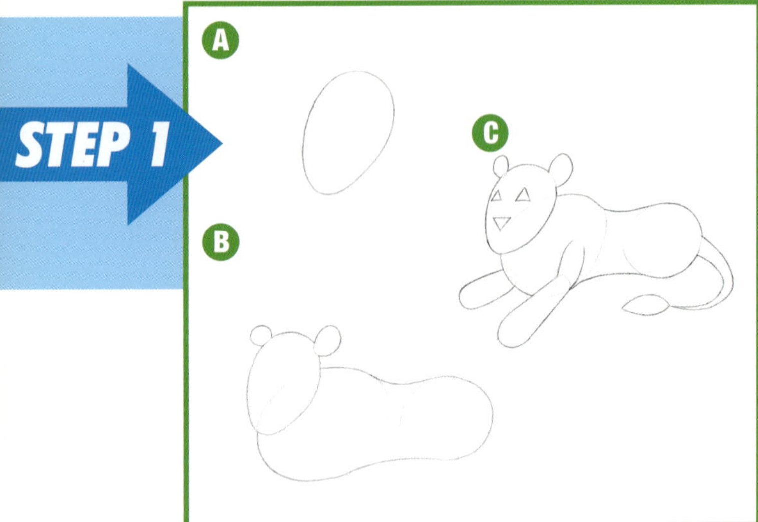

A First, draw an upturned egg shape for your lion's head. This should be fairly large, but remember that you'll need to fit his body on one side of it, so draw it on the left of the page.

B Draw a larger, longer egg under the first and overlap it slightly. This shape is going to be the front part of your lion's body. Then draw an egg about the same size as the head, joined to the front of his body by two dipped lines. The overall body shape should look like a footprint. Next, give your lion two small oval ears.

C Draw in his front legs and tail. The legs are created using simple shapes—the right leg is made out of two shapes, while the left leg is a single oval, hidden behind the lion's chest. His tail is long and thin with a tasselled tip, and his eyes and nose are triangles.

2

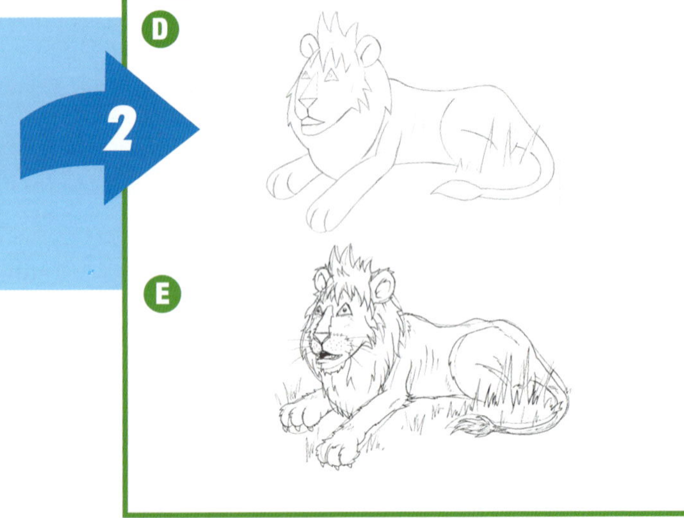

D Now add his face and his large shaggy mane. Draw three toes on each foot, and the crease of the back leg that is bent under him in the grass.

E Draw in his long whiskers, spiky fringe, and the stripe down his nose. The paws have claws protruding from them, and the ribs show slightly through the body fur.

F Before coloring your lion, draw over your pencil lines with a black pen.

G Lions are a yellow color with a darker mane. The eyes would normally be yellow too, but as this is a cartoon, he has more human-looking white eyes to add character.

3

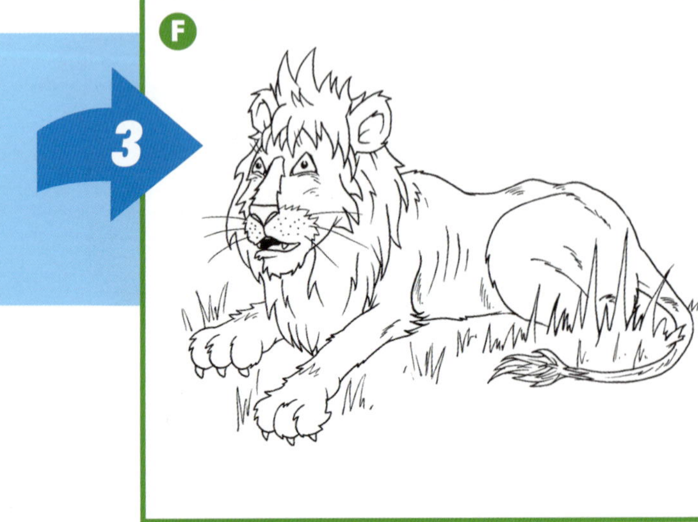

4

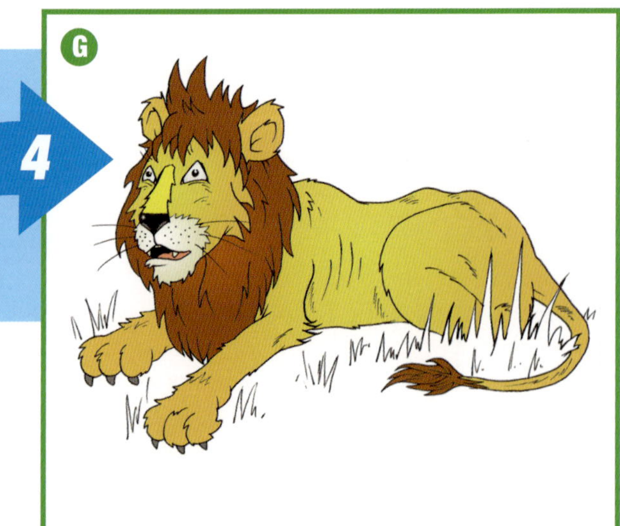

HOW TO DRAW A PANDA

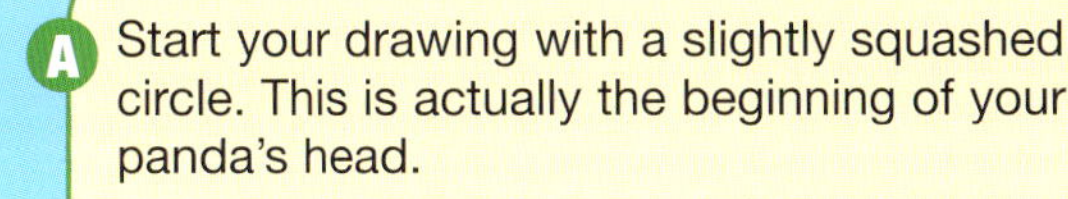

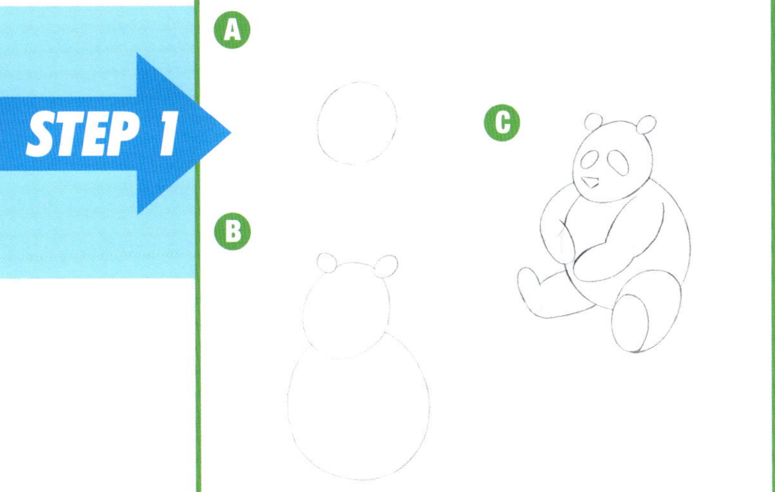

A Start your drawing with a slightly squashed circle. This is actually the beginning of your panda's head.

B Now draw a larger, overlapping circular shape beneath the head, before giving the head two small round ears.

C Complete the panda's body by giving it arms and legs. The right leg is in front, with the bottom of the foot showing. The other leg is stretched out further back, so it is drawn smaller and thinner to create perspective. The arms are each made of two oval shapes, bent at the elbow because the panda will be holding some leaves.

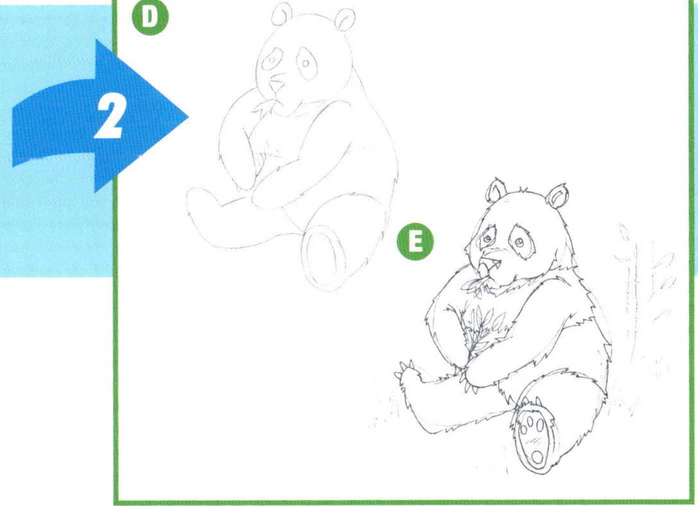

D Now start to give the panda a jagged, furry outline. Begin adding the facial features, such as the sad-looking eyes and the downturned mouth with a leaf in it.

E Add some final touches such as the pads on the bottom of the panda's front foot, and the small claws that help it grip its food. Draw a furry stripe around the body, and the arms and legs.

F Draw over your pencil sketch with a black pen in order to create a final outline. Then erase the pencil.

G Of course, you don't need much coloring for a panda—it's mainly black and white, but little touches, such as brown eyes and the green leaves it's holding and eating, will really stand out and bring the picture to life.

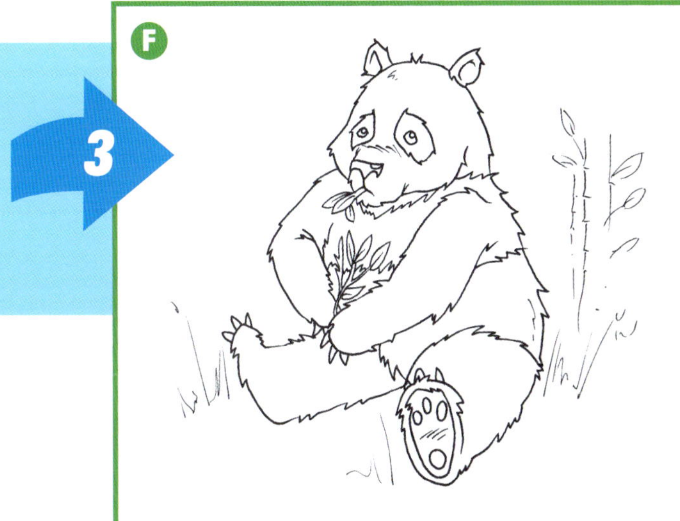

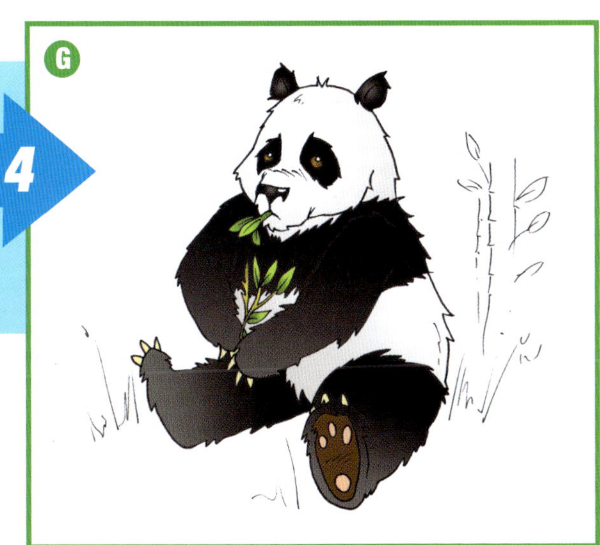

HOW TO DRAW A GIRAFFE

STEP 1

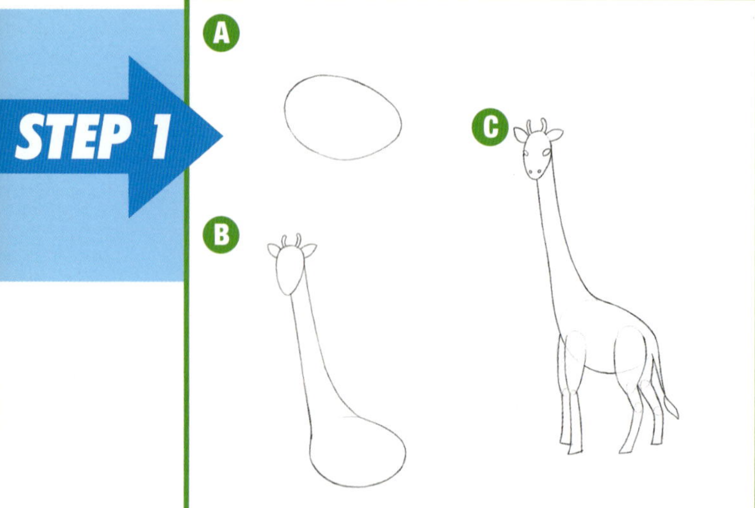

A Use an egg shape to create the giraffe's body. It needs to be quite large and low down on the paper so you have space for the long neck.

B The giraffe's head is also an oval shape, but it's less than half the size of its body. The head is joined to the body by an incredibly long neck that is thinner near the head, but widens slightly toward the body. Finish the head with two leaf-shaped ears and two little "horns."

C The giraffe's legs are created using oval shapes, with long pole shapes for the lower legs. Remember that the back legs are in three sections and bend backward. It has a thin tail with a tassel on the end.

2

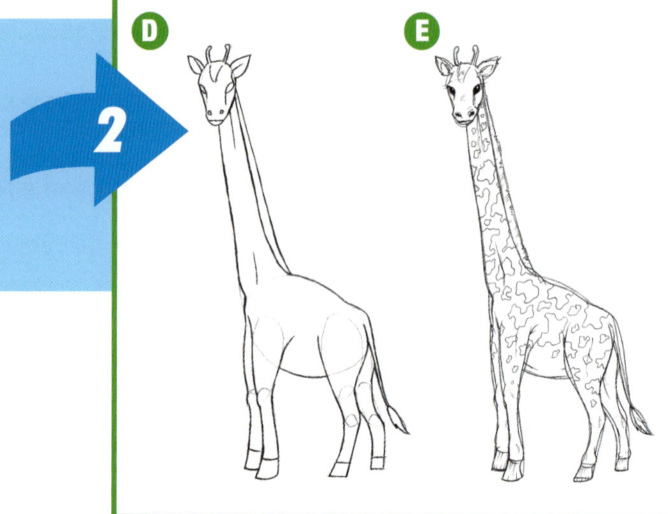

D Draw your giraffe's outline using the shapes as a guide. Connect the shapes, remembering which are supposed to overlap and which are not. Start sketching in the giraffe's face and give it a thin mane all the way down the neck. Next, give the legs some hooves.

E Now draw creases where the legs join the body. Giraffes have a kind of "jigsaw" pattern of patches on the body. Achieve this by drawing different sized uneven shapes. Be bold and try to vary the size of the pattern.

F You can now draw over the pencil lines with a black pen, and then erase any pencil lines.

G It's time to color in your drawing. Use yellow for the fur and brown for the "jigsaw" patches on the body.

3

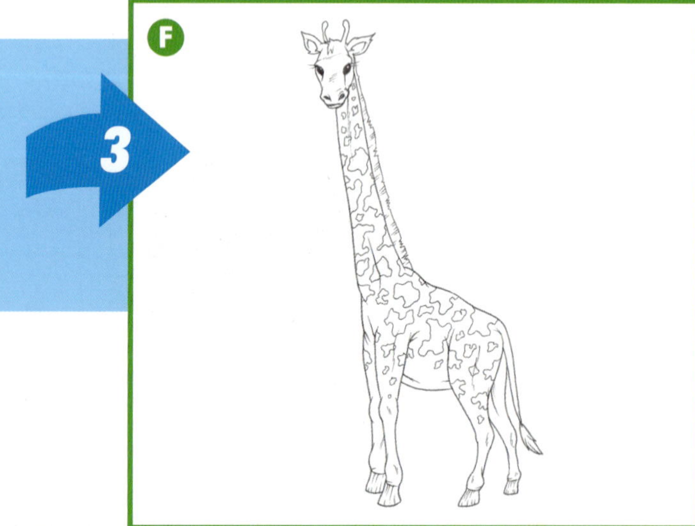

4

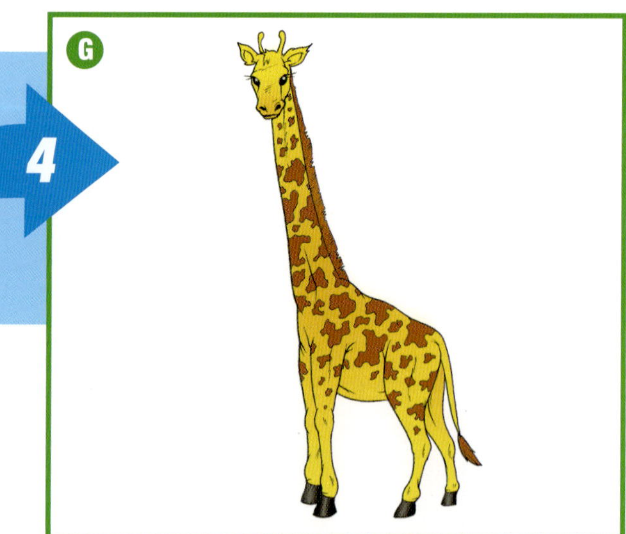

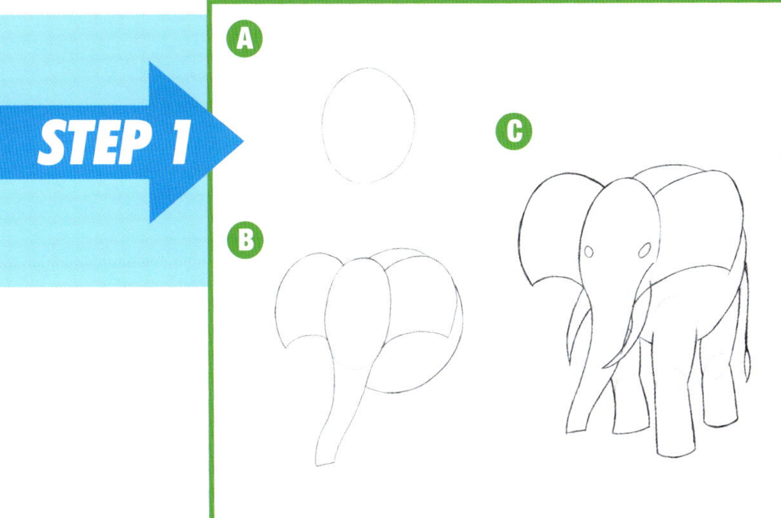

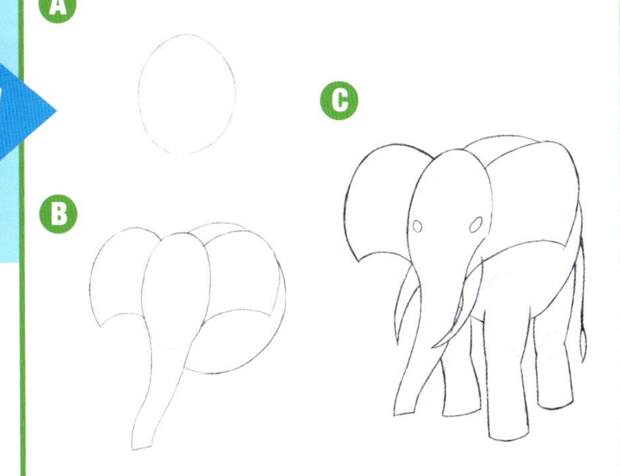

A Draw a large, round shape on the page to create the elephant's body.

B The head of the elephant is about half the size of its body. This oval shape overlaps the elephant's body. On either side of this shape, draw your elephant's ears, which are shaped like big sails. The elephant now needs a trunk. This is simply a long snake-like shape.

C Complete the elephant's frame by giving it some legs, tusks, and a tail. The legs are like tree trunks, but one of the back legs is hidden from view behind the front legs.

D Using the shapes as a guide, connect them using simple, bold lines. The ears are ragged along the bottom edge, and the feet have large, semi-circular toenails.

E Now finalize the elephant's facial features—it has a bald head and small, dark, almond-shaped eyes. Elephants are also quite wrinkly, and have very tough skin. Make the knees look wrinkled by drawing a swirl on each one.

F Now you're ready to trace over the lines with a black pen. Erase any pencil lines that are left over, and you are ready to color.

G Elephants are gray with cream-colored tusks. The one you see here has been colored using a computer, but don't worry if you don't have access to one—colored pencils, in particular, are just as good because they give a grainy appearance.

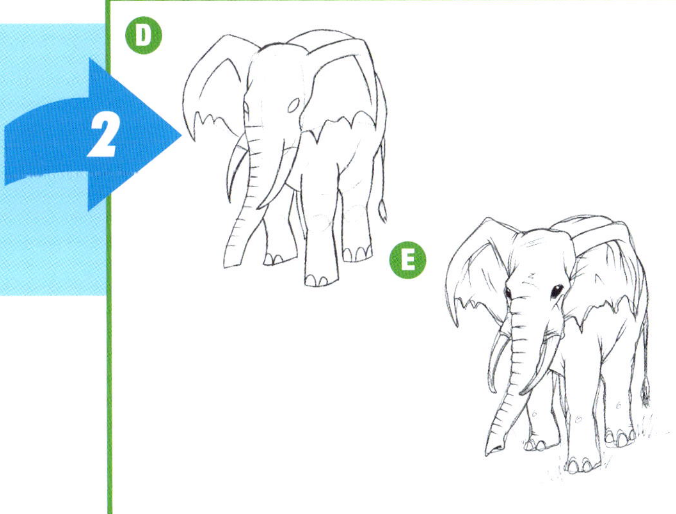

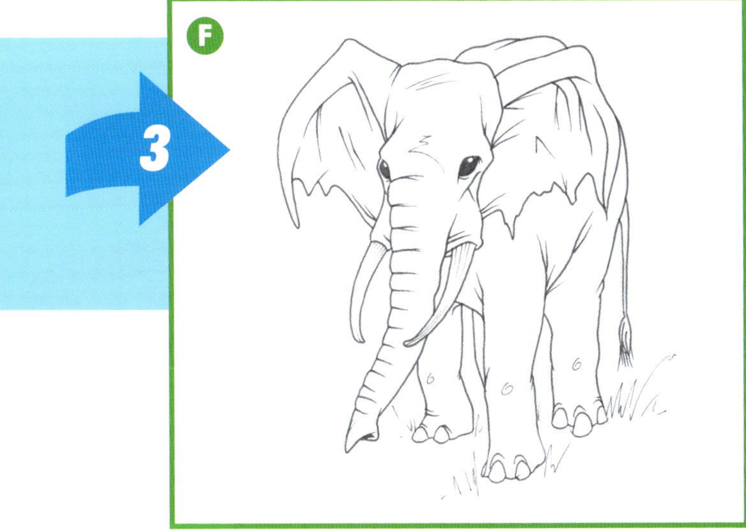

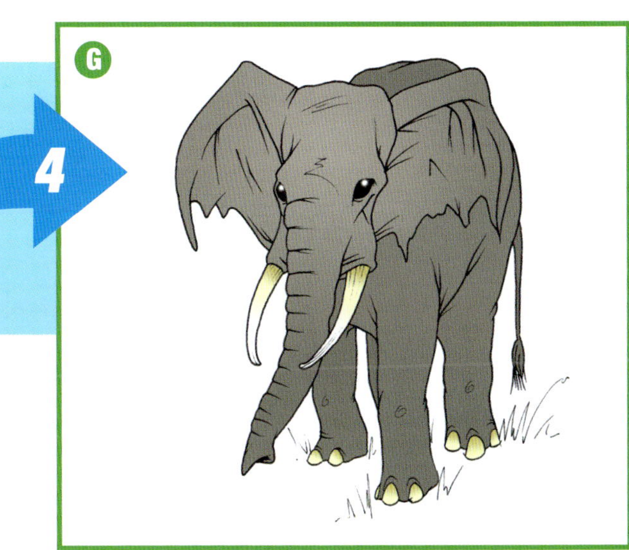

HOW TO DRAW A SNAKE

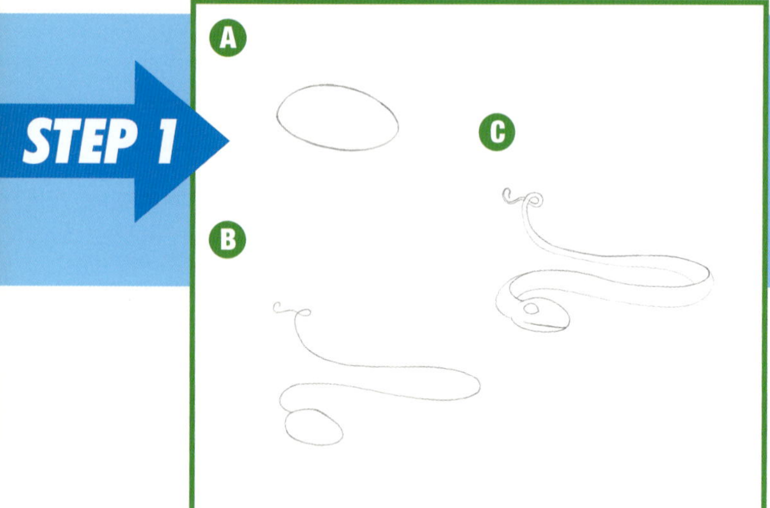

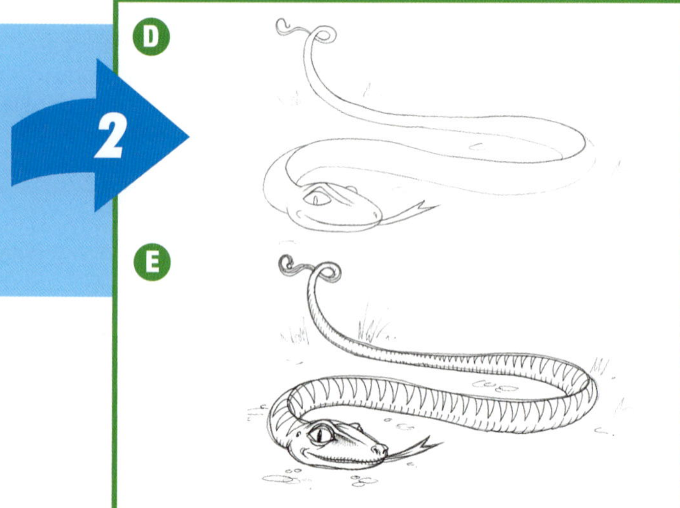

A Begin by drawing the snake's head in the shape of a large egg on your paper. The head should be closer to the bottom of the page, because the snake's body will be curling above its head.

B Draw a long, squiggly line up from the head to create the snake's body.

C The snake's body now needs to be fattened out. The line you drew in the previous step is actually the snake's "spine," so it should rest on the top of his body. Next, draw an almond-shaped eye and a mouth.

D Add some simple detail to your snake's face, such as a long, thin forked tongue and a slit-shaped pupil.

E To enhance the look of the snake's skin, draw triangular stripes down the length of the body. The snake featured here has fairly smooth skin, except for a few wrinkles, but you may want yours to have more scales and maybe a rattle at the tip of the tail.

F Now trace over your pencil lines with a thin black marker or drawing pen. Then you can erase the pencil lines, and your slithery snake is ready to color.

G You can color your snake any way you want to but it's a good idea to use bright colors. Some snakes are bright green, but the one featured is an attractive and eye-grabbing red and yellow. Don't be afraid to experiment and see what you can come up with!

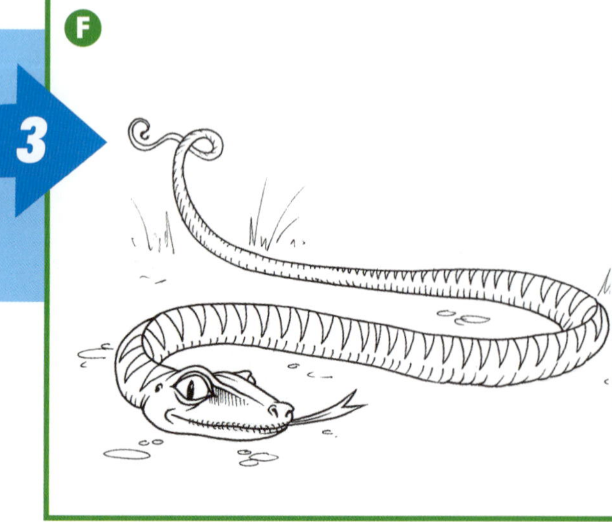

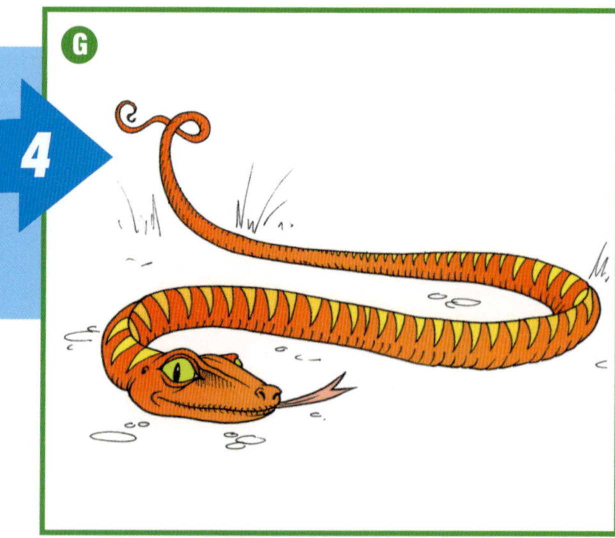

HOW TO DRAW A FROG

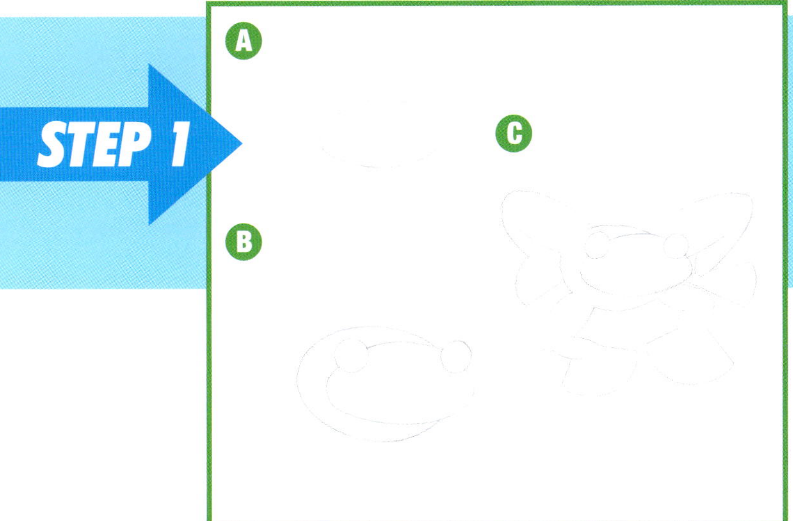

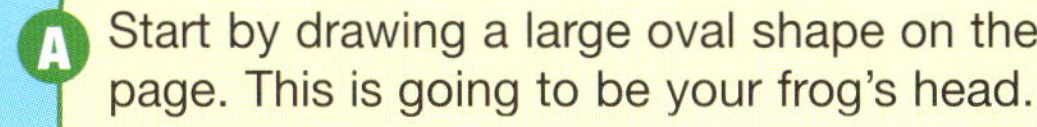

A Start by drawing a large oval shape on the page. This is going to be your frog's head.

B Draw a larger oval behind the head and slightly to the left. Next, draw two circles on top of the head, which are going to be the frog's distinctive, bug-eyes.

C Your frog's legs are made using two oval shapes, and two large fan shapes are used for its feet. The back legs are bent backward and tucked in behind the body.

D Begin adding detail to your frog's face and feet. Give the eyes pupils, and draw a long, thin mouth from one side of the head to the other. The front feet have four toes on each, while the back feet have three.

E Now that you have the basic shape of the frog, you can start to draw the skin. It has striped legs and webbed feet. Pencil in the nostrils and round off the toes. You could also draw a passing fly, that is unaware that it may be the frog's next meal!

F Trace over your picture with a pen, and then erase the original pencil lines. Color your frog using bright shades. Try watercolor pencils, pastels or even a computer if you have access to one. As for the colors, this frog has green skin, but your frog could be red, blue, yellow, or whatever color you want. Remember to experiment!

2 D

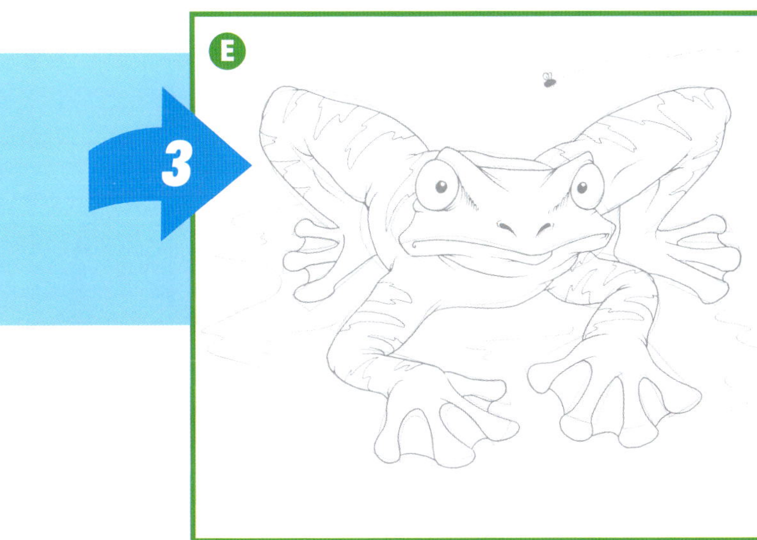

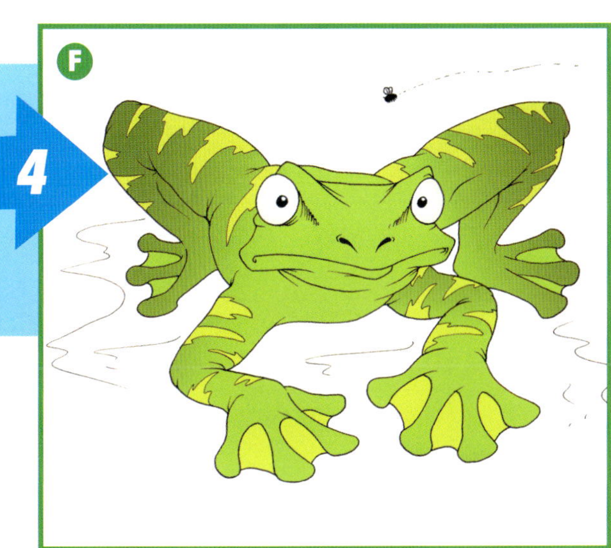

HOW TO DRAW A GECKO

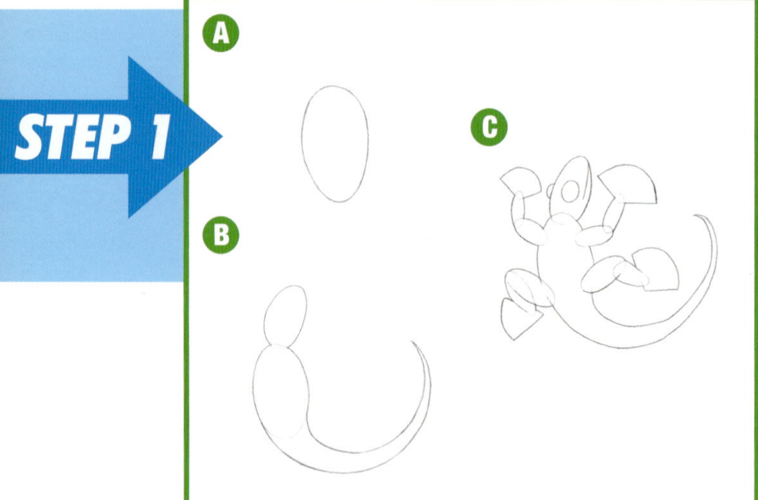

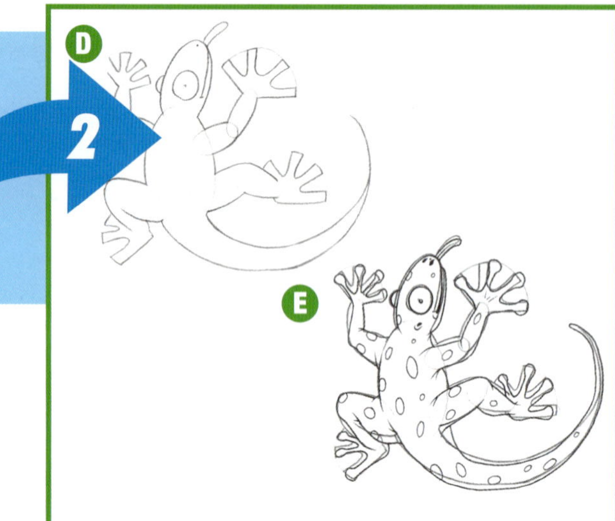

A Draw an oval shape—like an upside down egg in the center of your page.

B The gecko's body is an egg shape too, but is much larger. Make this oval overlap the head very slightly, and only lightly pencil in where it crosses the face because you'll need to erase this later. Next, draw a long, horn-shaped tail out of the bottom of the body.

C Your gecko now needs some legs. Draw two long ovals and a fan for each limb, making sure that the upper section is slightly fatter than the lower. Next, draw two large bug-eyes on the head.

D Join all the shapes together to create your gecko's basic outline. Its feet can also be drawn in now, each foot having four toes. Start to sketch its face and remember to give it a very long tongue.

E Begin sketching in some simple detail, such as the spotted skin. Round off the gecko's toes and sketch some wrinkles where the limbs meet its body.

F Now draw over the pencil lines you want to keep, using a fine black pen. Then erase the remaining pencil lines.

G Experiment with different color combinations on a separate piece of paper before coloring in your gecko—you can really go nuts with this one, as geckos are lots of crazy colors in real-life!

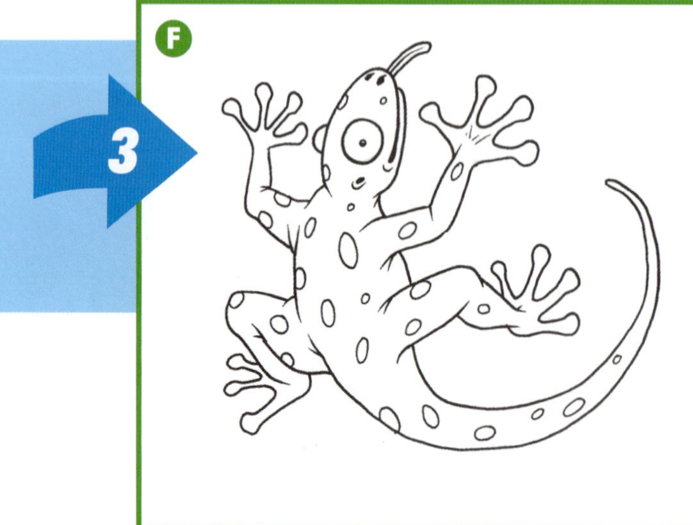

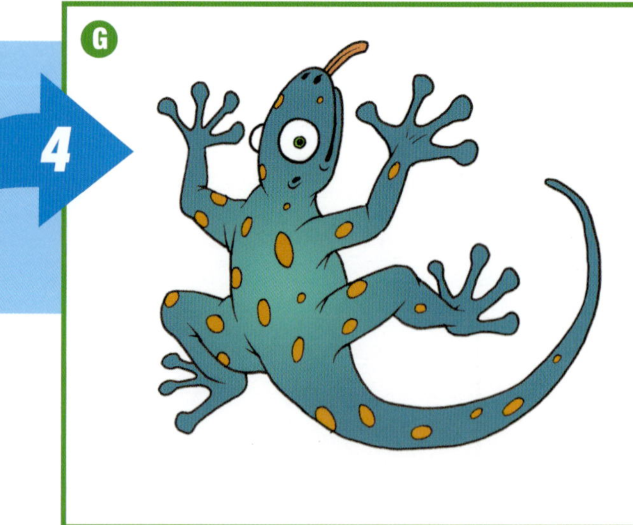

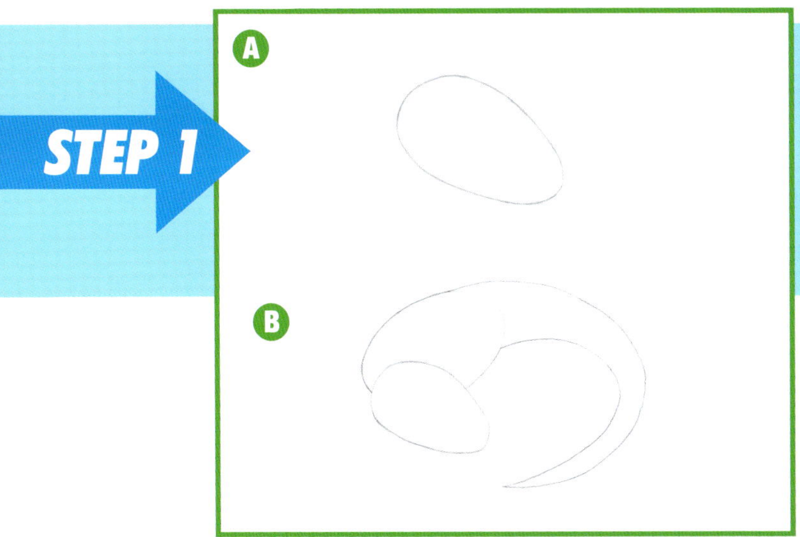

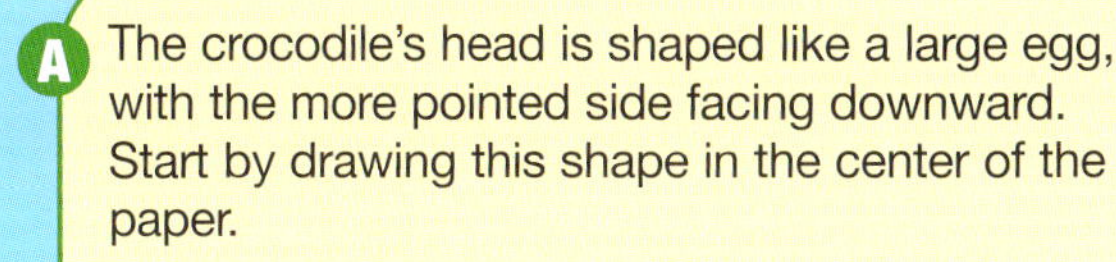

(A) The crocodile's head is shaped like a large egg, with the more pointed side facing downward. Start by drawing this shape in the center of the paper.

(B) Now draw the body and tail. The body is a very large egg shape, overlapping the head slightly. The part that overlaps will be hidden behind the head, so don't press too hard! The crocodile's tail is shaped like a large, curved horn.

(C) His legs are constructed using oval shapes for the upper and lower part of the legs, and a fan shape for each foot. Remember that two of his legs are hidden behind his body, so don't be too firm with your pencil because you will need to erase these lines later on.

(D) Now add simple detail to the crocodile's frame. Give him stubby toes on each foot, and draw in where his eye and mouth are going to be.

(E) Now add some texture on the crocodile's skin. These creatures have tough scaly skin, and you can create the effect of these scales by using a technique called "cross-hatching." This is when you use overlapping, sketchy diagonal lines. Next, put some folds of skin on his legs and add detail to the face, like some scales round the mouth, and a wrinkled nose.

→

2 (C)

3 (D)

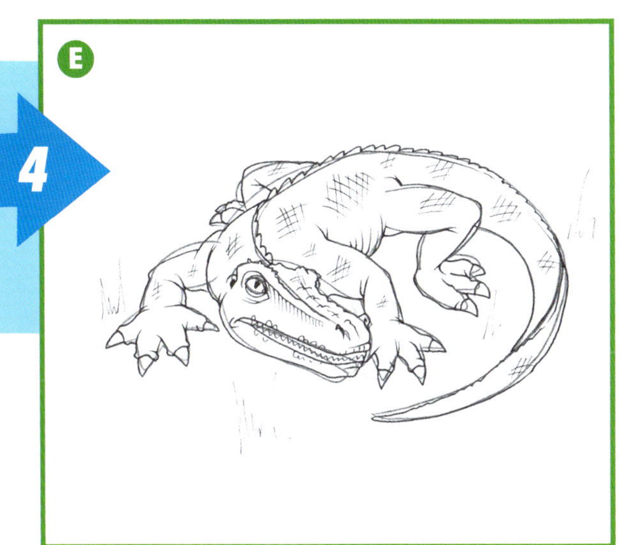

HOW TO DRAW A CROCODILE

5

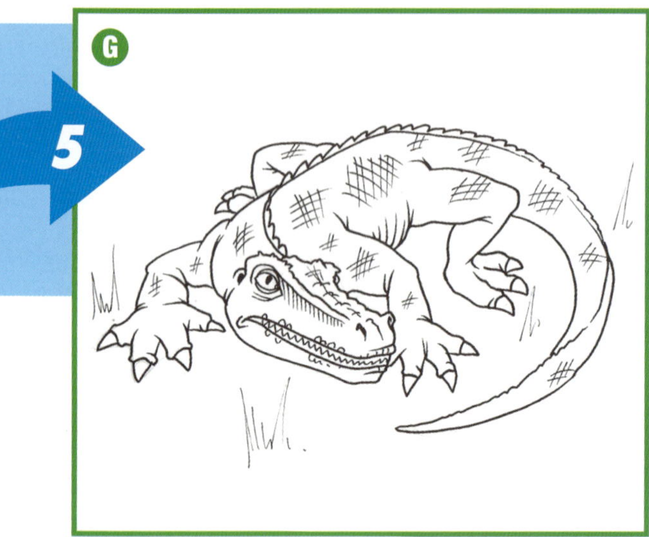

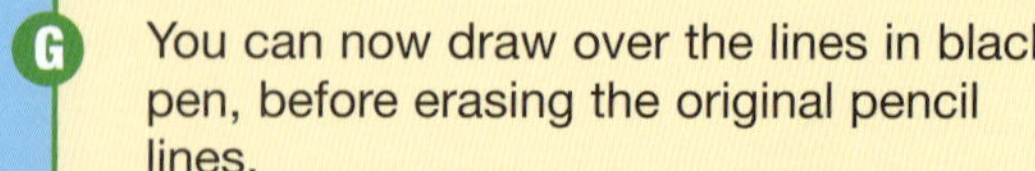

G You can now draw over the lines in black pen, before erasing the original pencil lines.

H This crocodile is colored green to give him a swamp-like look.

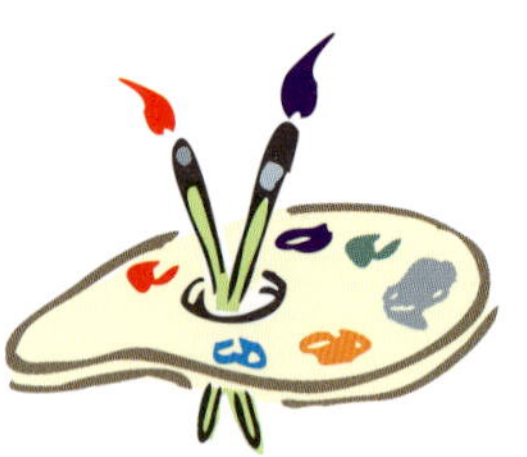

6

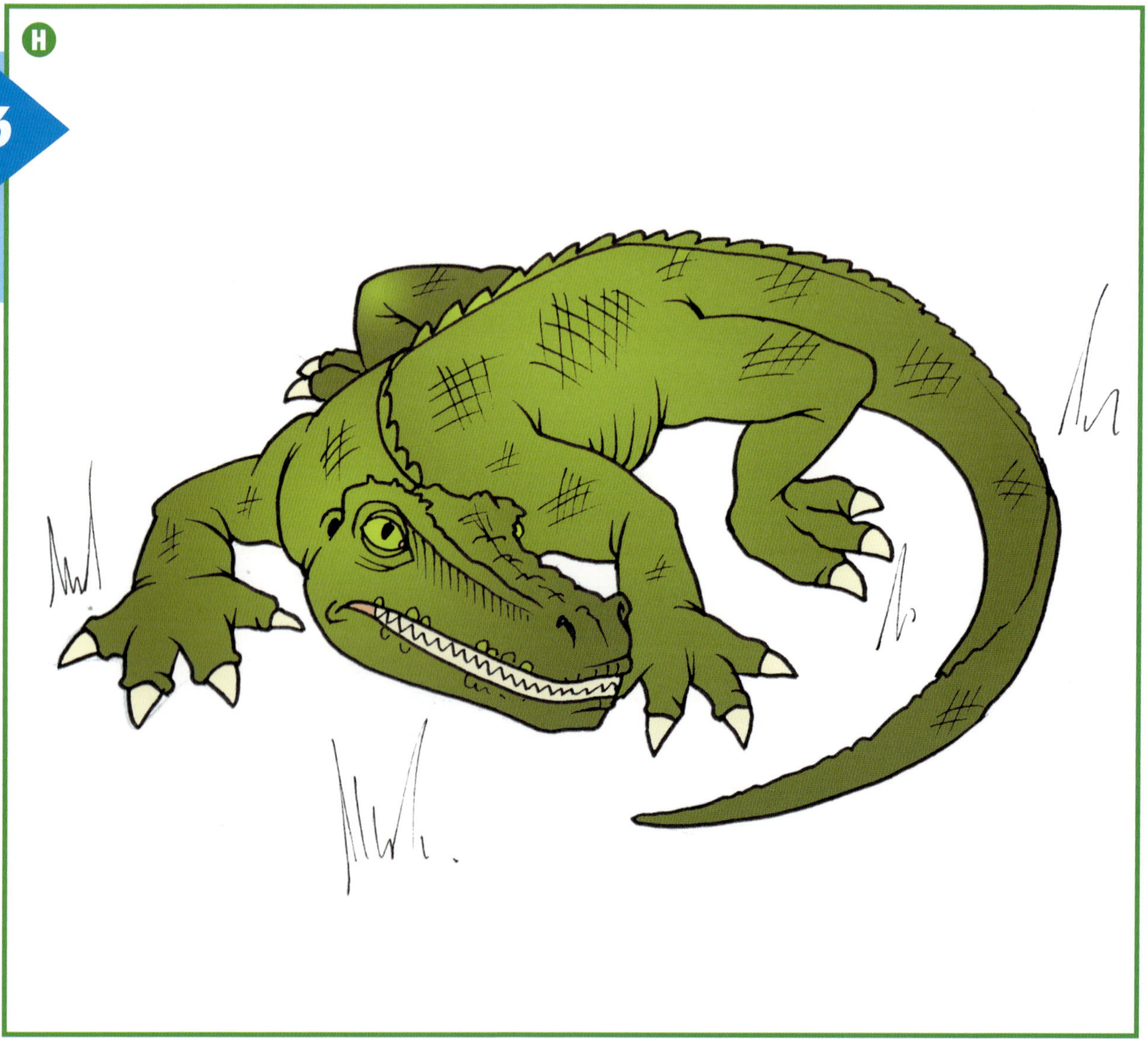

VEHICLES

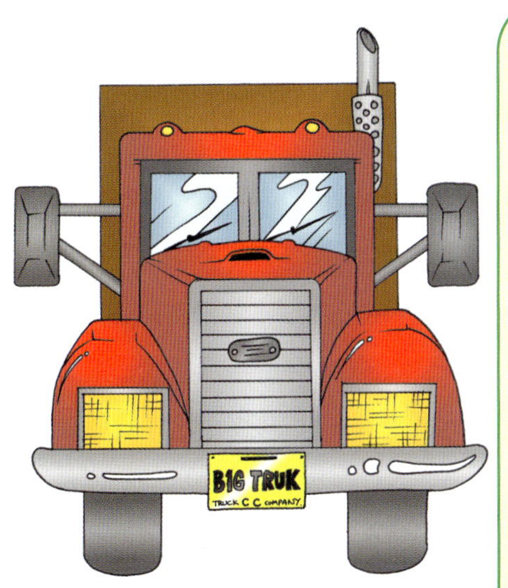

Imagine a world without automobiles or airplanes; a world where you had to walk everywhere! Well, if you take a look at your history books, that wasn't so long ago. Believe it or not, there was a time when the only form of transportation available to us was the humble horse.

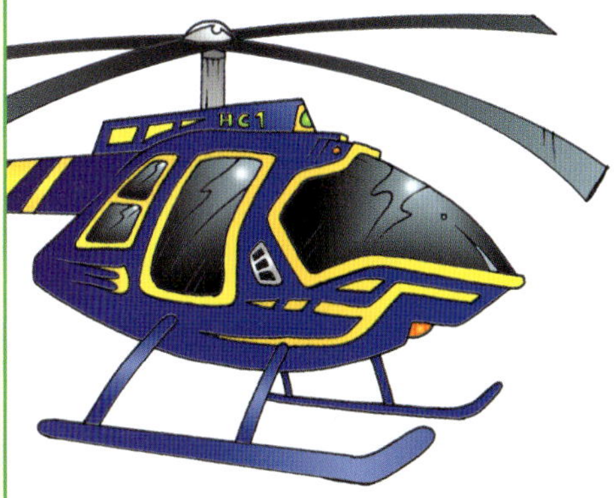

As time passed, new inventions were discovered to help us travel over long distances more quickly. But it's been a bumpy road getting there—inventions such as the bicycle were incredibly uncomfortable to ride at first because nobody had thought of shock absorbers. Without them, it meant riders felt every single lump and bump in the road. Ouch!

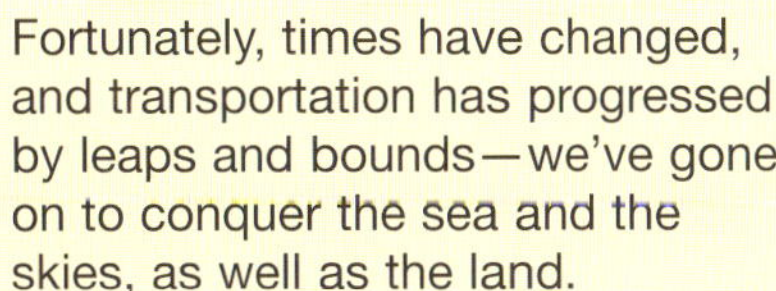

Fortunately, times have changed, and transportation has progressed by leaps and bounds—we've gone on to conquer the sea and the skies, as well as the land.

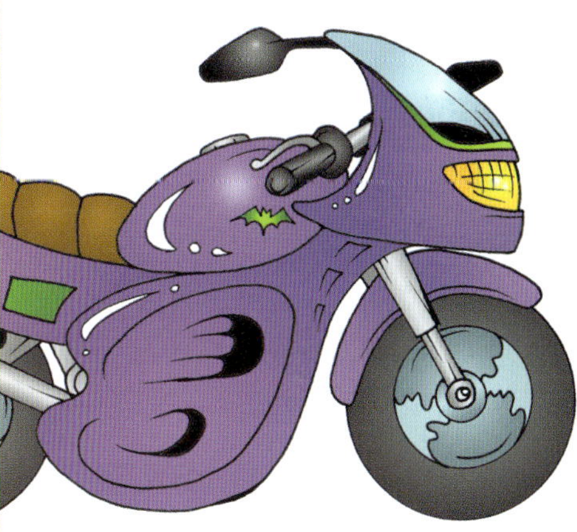

This chapter looks at how to draw six of the most common engine-powered vehicles of the modern age. These include the car, the motorbike, the truck, the speedboat, the plane, and the helicopter.

So, it's time to get your brain in top gear and your pencil in pole position. Strap in safely and enjoy the ride. You'll never forget this journey!

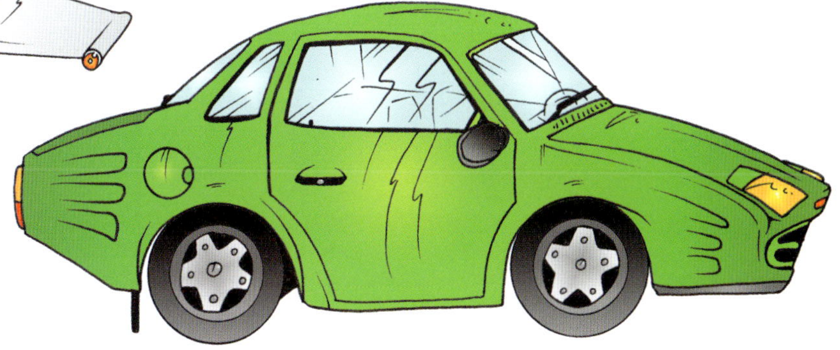

STEP 1

A

B

A Begin your car by drawing a very large semi-circle on your page, with the flat edge on the underside. This is going to be the auto body, so it needs to be quite large on the paper.

B The car will need some wheels—these are just simple circles, but make sure they actually overlap the car's body, otherwise it will look like your car's floating on its wheels! Next, focus on the front and rear elements of the car—the hood and trunk are simple boxy shapes at either end of your semi-circle.

C Now your car needs some windows. The front windshield is rectangular, while the rear window is triangular. Both side-windows are irregular four-sided shapes, slightly rectangular, but with angled sides.

D Draw some simple detail on your car, like the side-door (including a wing mirror), some hubcaps on the wheels, and the headlamps at the front. There is also a radiator grille on the front of the car, which is shaped like half an oval, and a circular cap to the gas tank above the rear wheel.

E Your car should be looking pretty good by now. All that's missing are some final touches—start adding reflections to the various surfaces of your car especially on the windows.

2

C

3

D

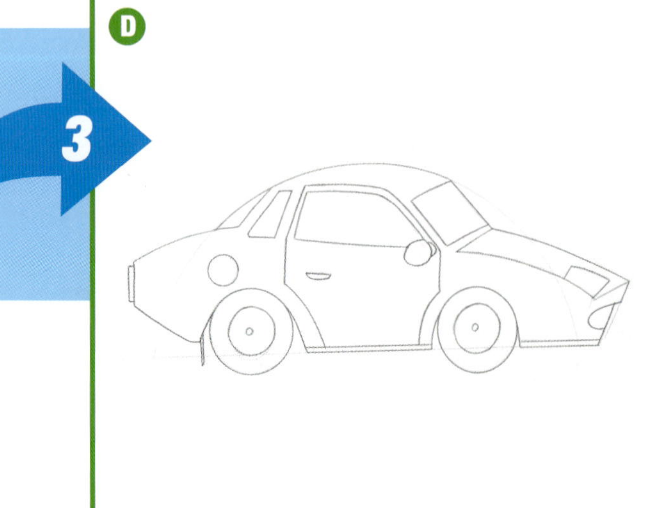

4

E

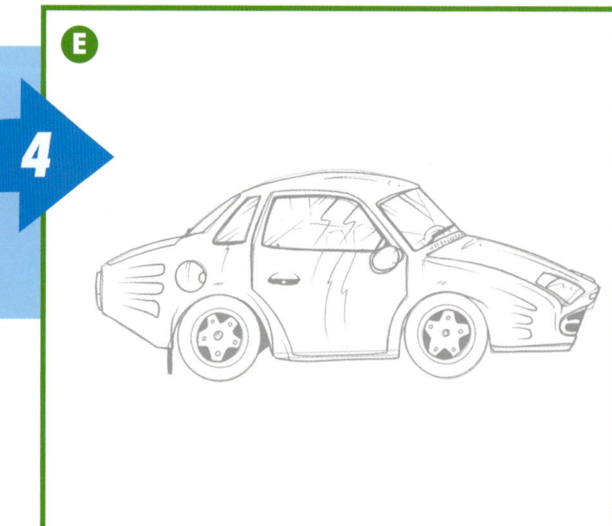

5

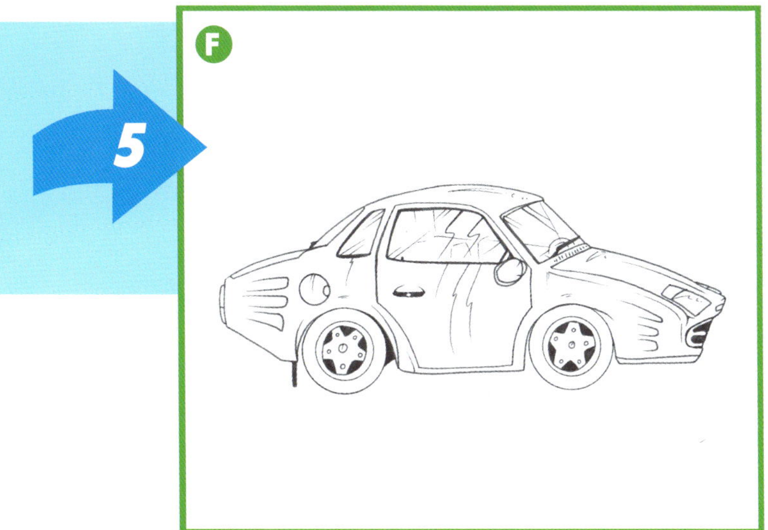

The hubcaps are star-shaped, and the radiator grille is shaped like a large letter "E," plus there are air intakes on the bodywork at the front and rear.

F Once your car is looking shiny and fast enough, you can draw over the pencil lines with a black pen, and then erase the rough frame.

G Color in your car using paints, colored pencils, felt-tip pens, or a computer. While the green used here is a traditional sports car color, try different colors—sports cars can be sprayed in bright colors that scream: "Look at me!" For instance, red is a great color to use, because it's vibrant and shouts: "Danger!"

6

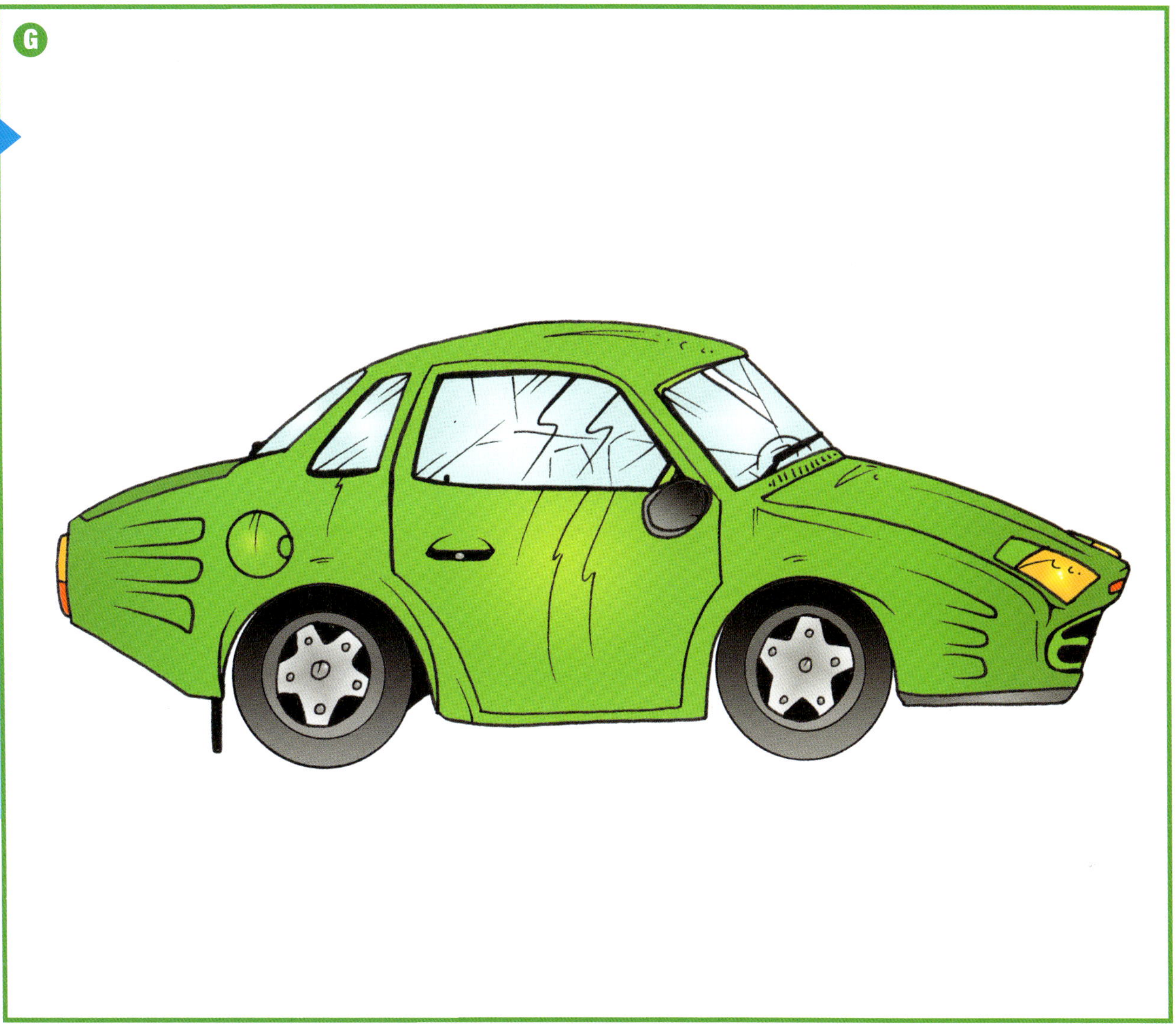

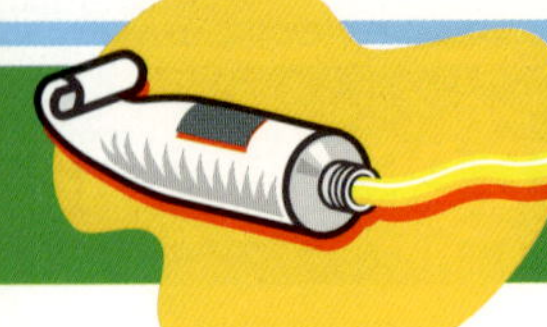

STEP 1

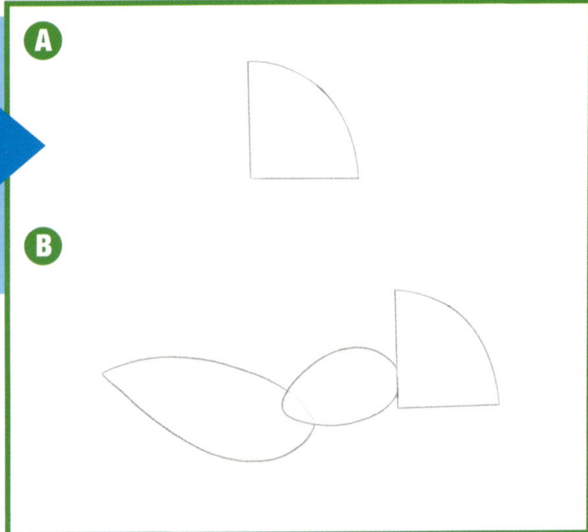

A When beginning your picture of a motorbike, the first shape you should draw is a quarter-circle. This shape is a little like a triangle with one of the edges semicircular. This is going to be the front of your bike.

B Draw a sideways egg-shape to the left of the first shape you drew. This shape is the gas tank of your motorbike, and should be angled slightly downward. Further back on your bike there is the seat—this is leaf-shaped and should overlap the gas tank slightly.

2

C

C Motorbikes have large wheels, fixed to the main body of the bike with "forks." The front fork on this bike is like a thin pole, while the rear fork is triangular. Both must line up with the center of each wheel. Next, the underside of the motorbike is a similar egg shape to the gas tank, only much larger and with the pointed side facing upward instead of down.

D Now it's time to sketch in some simple details to really bring your motorbike to life. The seat has a leather section for the rider to sit comfortably, and there is a long exhaust pipe in front of the rear wheel. Both wheels have thick tires and trims, and the front wheel has a mudguard above it. Finally, the "head" of the bike has a narrow headlamp, an angled handlebar, and two wing mirrors, one of which is slightly hidden from view because of the picture's angle.

3

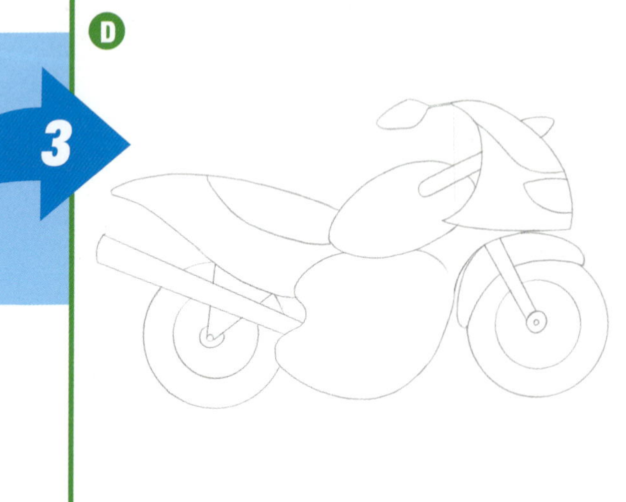

4

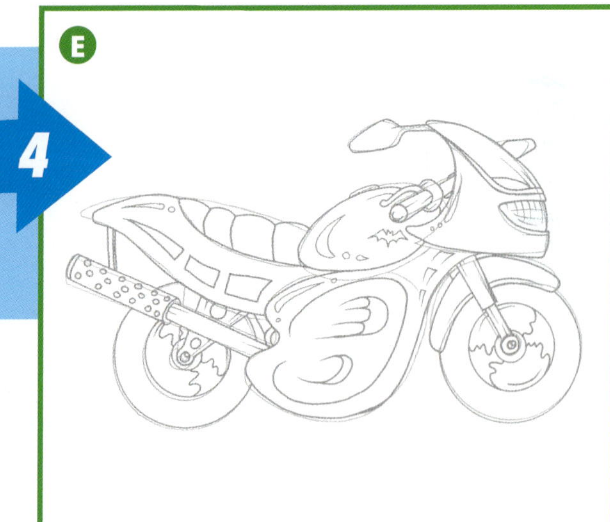

5

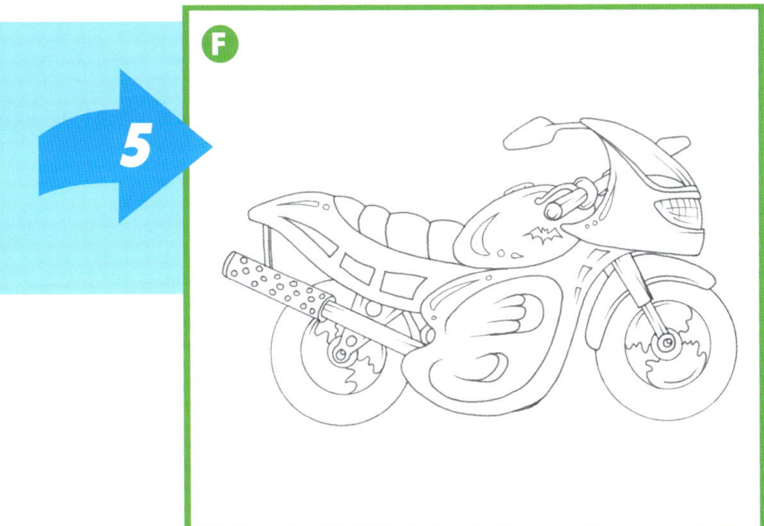

E Continue adding details to your motorbike. Give the exhaust pipe a few rows of holes—these help the pipe stay cool. Draw the padded leather surface of the seat, and add reflections to the bodywork to give the bike a three-dimensional look. Next, sketch some decals onto your bike.

F Draw over the motorbike drawing with a thin black pen, before erasing the remaining pencil lines.

G Motorbikes come in every color imaginable. You should try using metallic colors such as silver, which will give the bike a sleek and fast look.

6

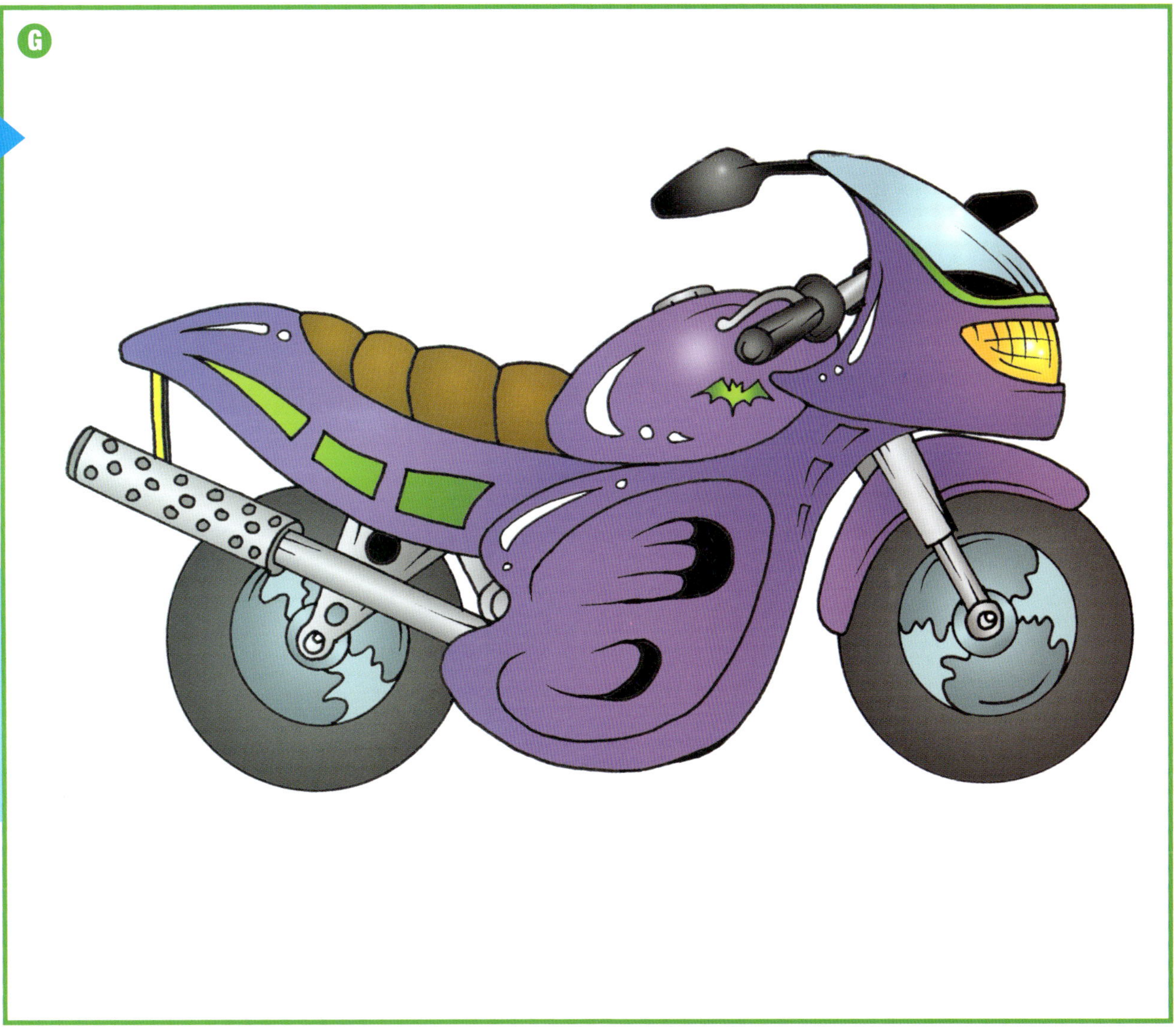

G

STEP 1

A

B

A The first thing you should remember is that the truck you are going to be drawing is from a head-on view, and is therefore symmetrical. So the rule from now on is to repeat on one side what you have drawn on the other! Bearing this mind, begin by drawing a large square shape for the truck's trailer.

B Draw a smaller square inside the first square you've drawn, with its lower edge lining up with the trailer's lower edge. This square will be the cab of the truck. The wing mirrors on either side are simply rectangles on the end of a triangular frame.

C Your truck's engine is housed in a boxy hood. The front radiator grille is rectangular, and the hood above this is slightly hump-backed in shape. The fenders on either side of the radiator are shaped like the top half of an egg. When you're happy with the hood and radiator, thicken the supports that are holding the wing mirrors onto the cab.

D To complete your truck's basic frame, it will need some wheels and a front fender. Then start adding simple details to your truck, such as the rectangular headlights on each wheel arch and the vent on top of the hood. Next, on the roof of your cab, draw a large pipe-shaped exhaust. Finish off by drawing two windshields on the front of the cab and a plaque on the radiator grille.

2

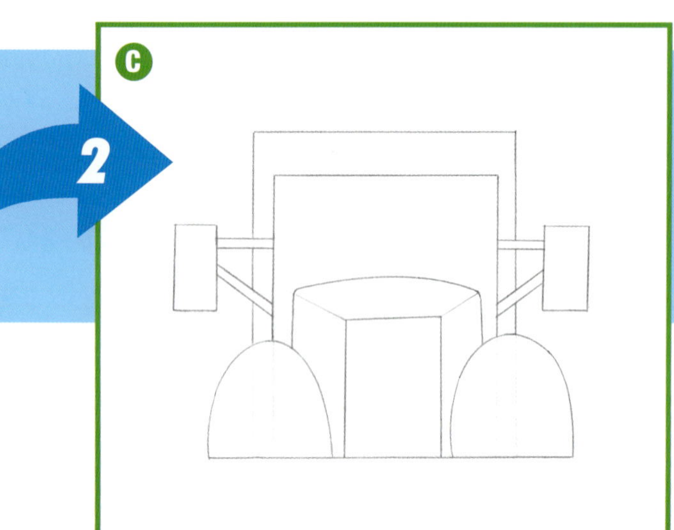

3

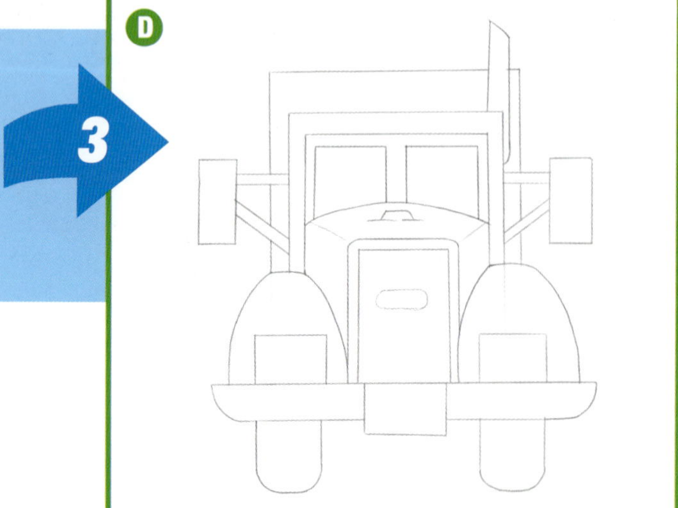

4

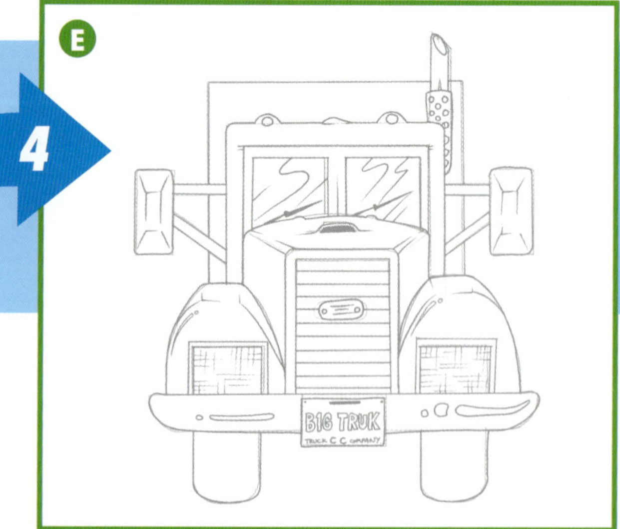

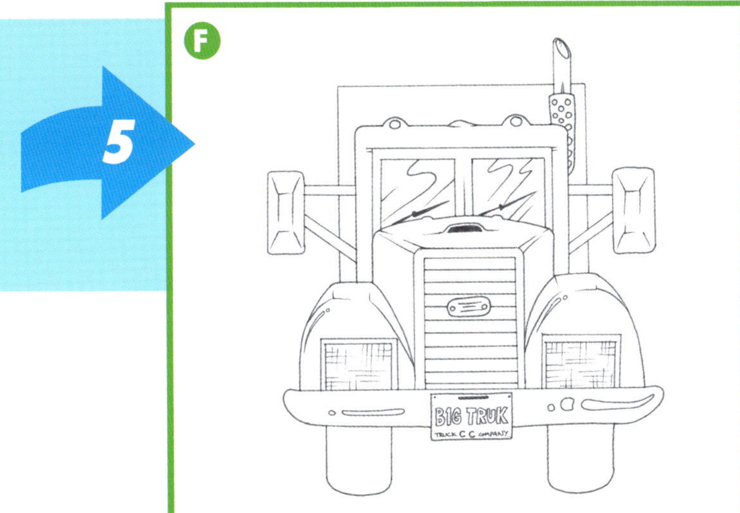

E It's time to add some final detail to your truck. Both the windows and the chrome bumper on the front are really shiny. Don't forget those windshield-wipers on the windshield either! Next, draw holes in the exhaust and place two tiny lights on the top of the cab. Finish the picture off with a personalized license plate—"B1G TRUK" seems fitting for this one!

F Before coloring your truck in, draw over your pencil lines with a black pen. Then erase the pencil lines, and you'll be ready to color in your truck.

G You can color your truck in many different ways, but using a computer gives a shiny, metallic look to the bodywork. If you don't have access to a computer, don't worry because you can get excellent results with colored pencils and marker pens.

6

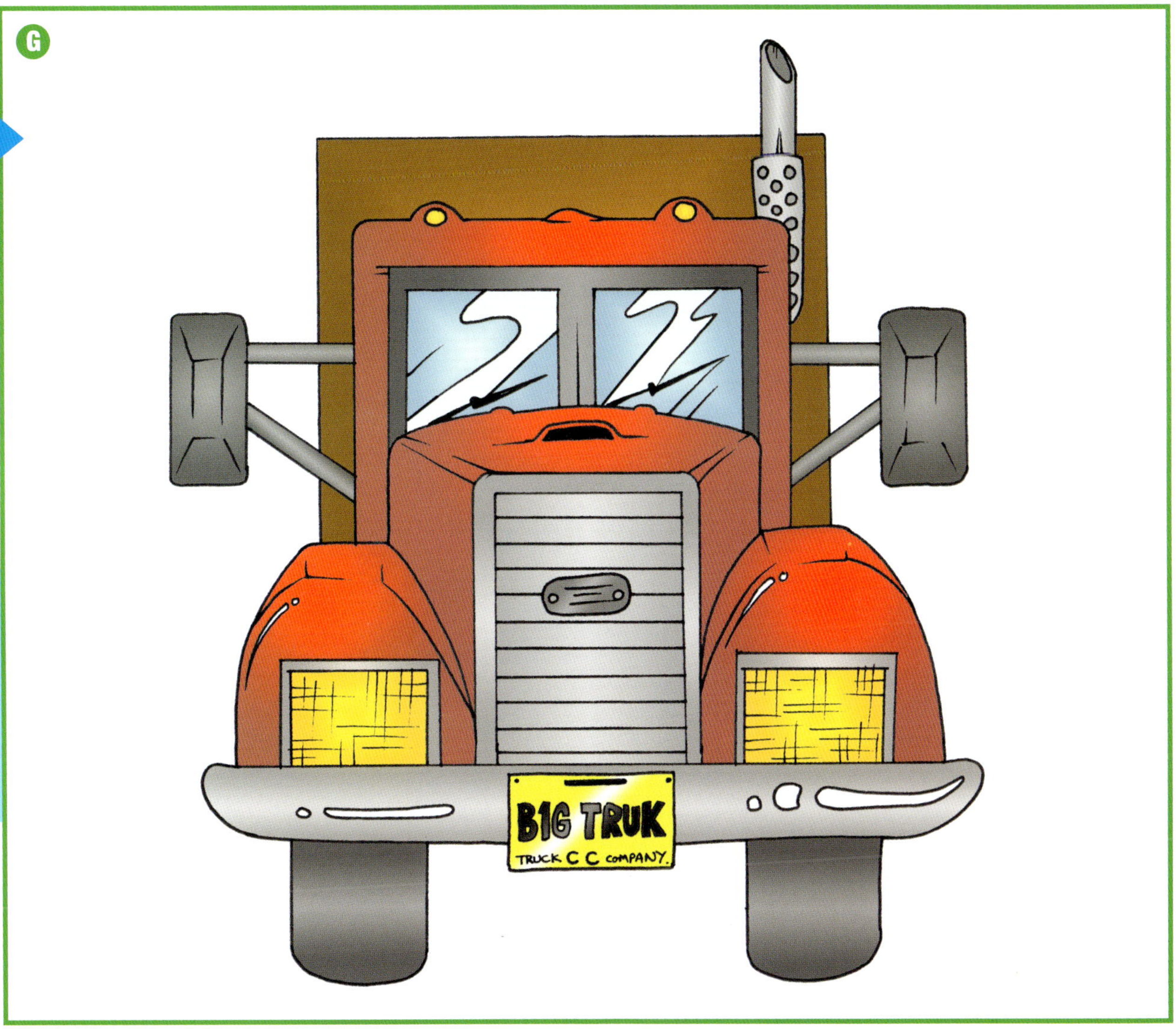

G

STEP 1

A

B

A In the middle of your page, draw a large angled almond shape with one of the ends chopped off. This is the basic shape of your speedboat.

B Next, your boat's body needs to be made three-dimensional. The side of the speedboat is quite shallow, and curves up gradually at the front of the boat, where it meets the front point of your first shape. The cockpit of the boat is a large square shape that sits slightly back from the center of the vessel.

C Begin sketching in some simple details, such as the thick painted stripe that runs down the center of your speedboat. Give the cockpit a windshield with a rectangular front and two triangular side-panes. Start to sketch the splashing water at the side and rear of the boat as it rockets along.

D The windshield you drew in the previous step has a thin frame that tapers back to a point on the side windows. Look at your picture—does the cockpit look a little empty? Yes? You're right—the speedboat needs a driver. He is made of simple shapes: an oval head with a larger egg-shaped chest and thin oval arms. His spiked hair is blowing back because the boat is going so fast.

E Now draw your driver in more detail. Add the final touches to his face, such as the pupils in

2

C

3

D

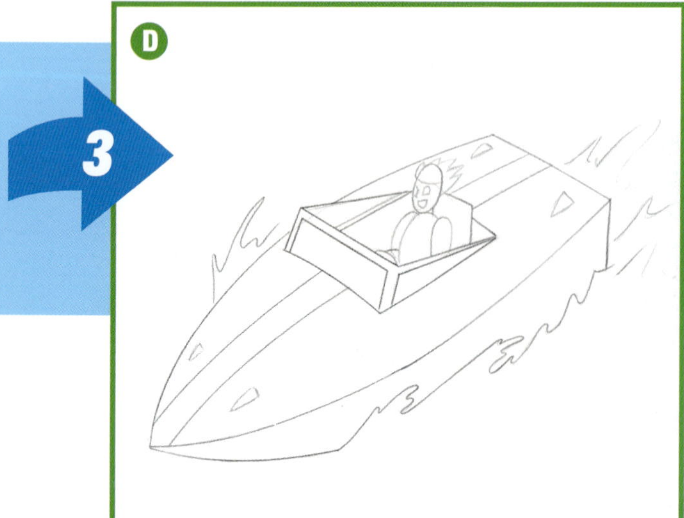

4

E

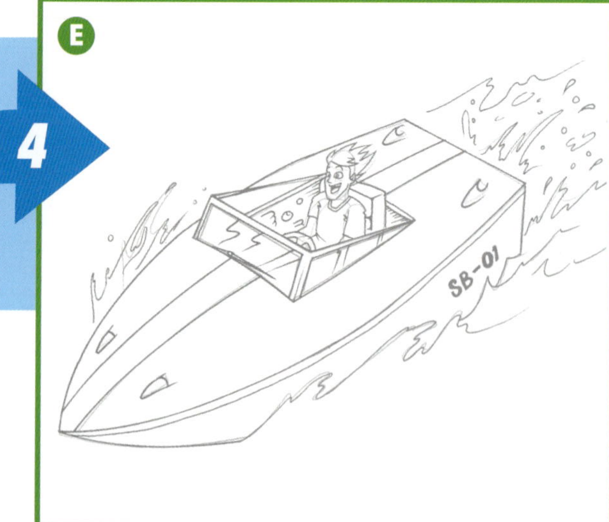

5

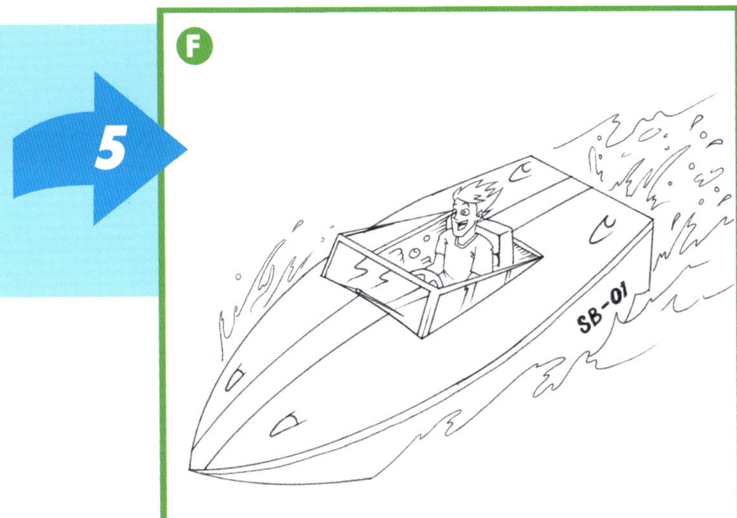

his eyes, and his tongue and teeth. Make sure he looks like he's having a good time out there on the water! Furnish the cockpit with a couple of lights and a padded seat. Then add some reflections in the windshield and give the boat a name.

F When you're happy with the overall look of your boat, you can draw over it using a fine black pen. Only draw over the lines you want to keep. Erase the pencil lines, and get ready to color.

G Boats are normally painted in pale colors. More often than not they're white, but you can be different and color your boat any way you want. Experiment and see what you can come up with.

6

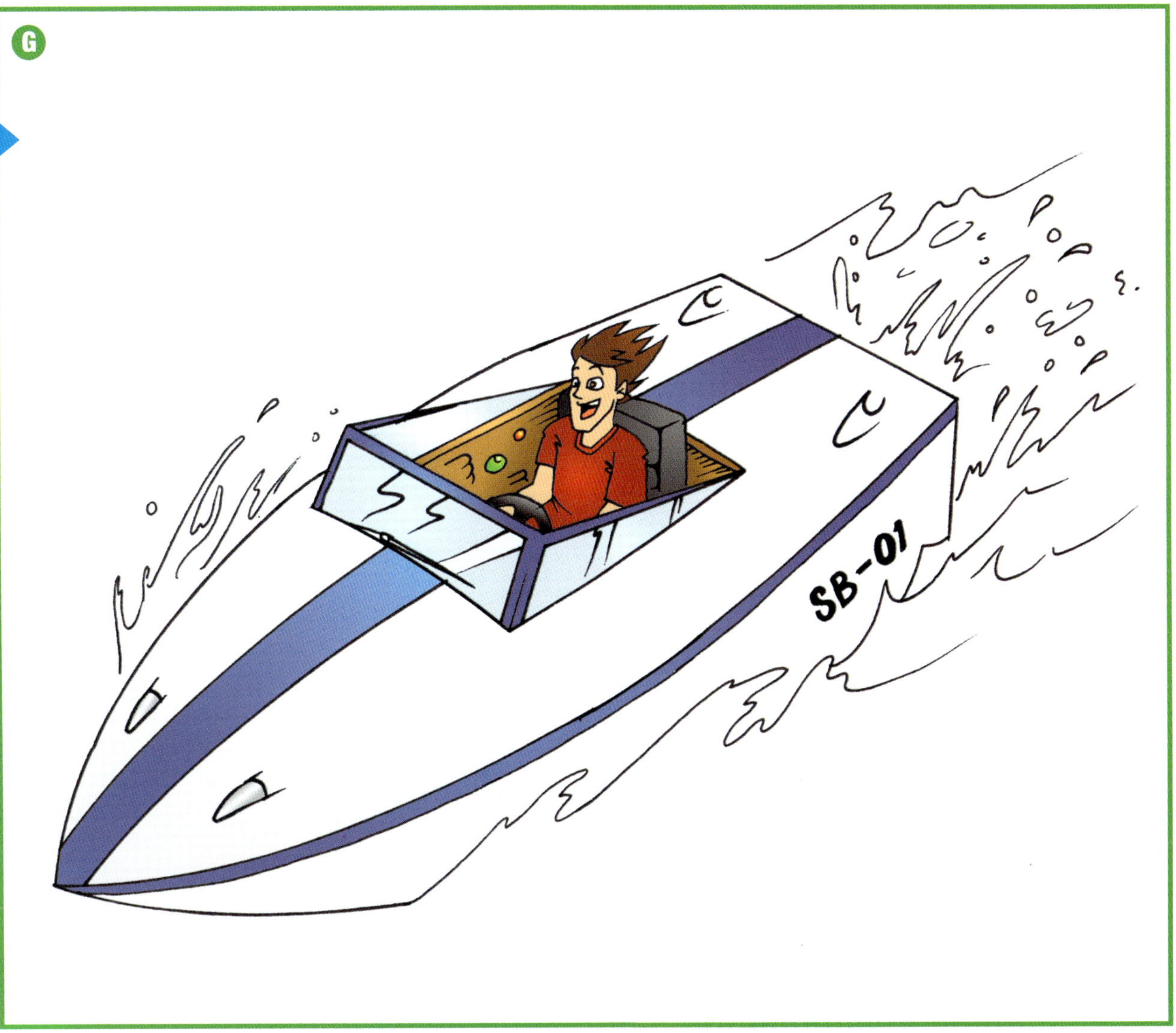

G

SB-01

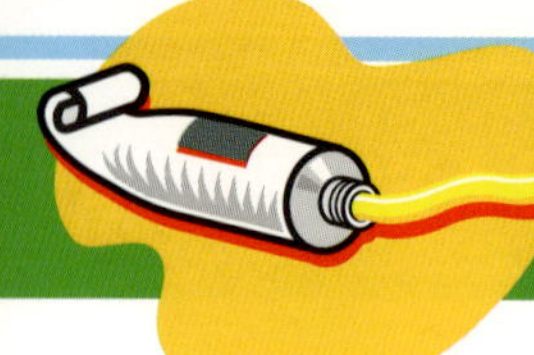

STEP 1

A

B

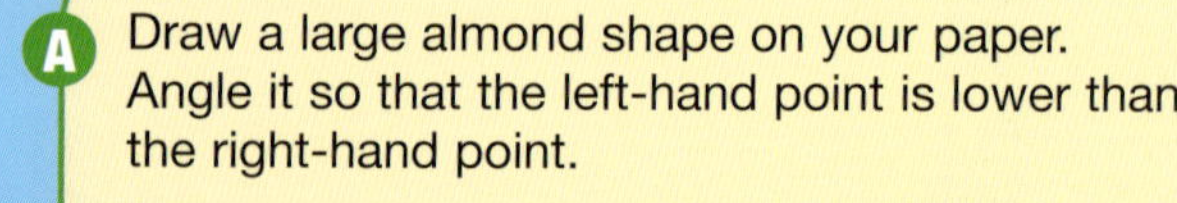

A Draw a large almond shape on your paper. Angle it so that the left-hand point is lower than the right-hand point.

B Through the middle of this original shape, you're going to draw the plane's wings, that are actually a triangle with its ends chopped off. Don't press down hard with your pencil, because the section of the triangle that overlaps the main body of the plane will need to be erased later.

C The engines that sit on your plane's wings are egg-shaped, with the most rounded parts facing forward. The left-hand engine will be partially obscured by the plane's body, so only mark your pencil lines lightly. Next, draw the rear wing on your plane—this consists of a large and a small triangle.

D There is a large windshield at the front of the plane, which is like a rectangle with curved sides. The front of the nose has a colored stripe, that is drawn with a single curved line separating it from the rest of the plane. Next, draw three windows down the side of the body and start to add extra detail to the engines and rear wing. Also include some lights at the very tip of the plane's wings.

E Draw some detail on the plane, such as the shiny metallic surface and the serial number on the side. Finally, you can make the boosters

2

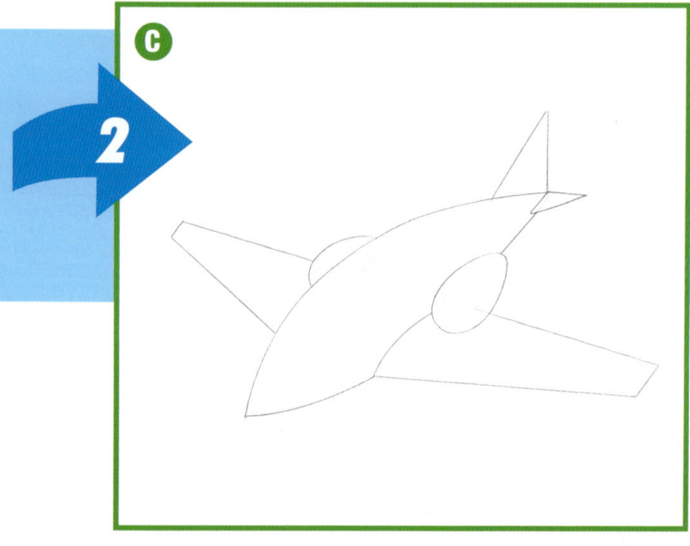

C

3

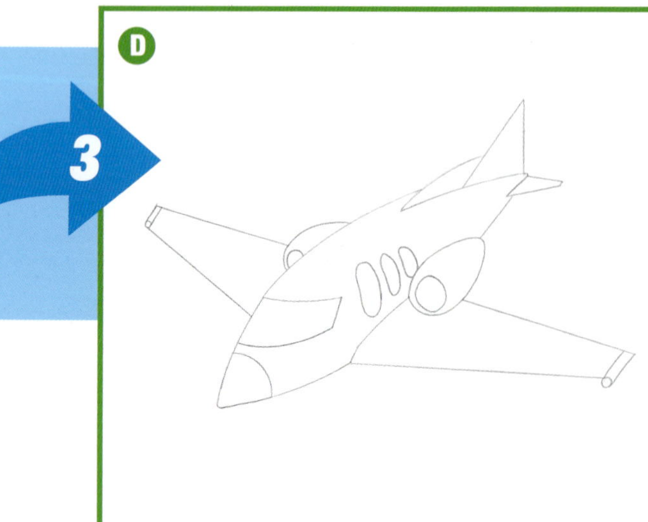

D

4

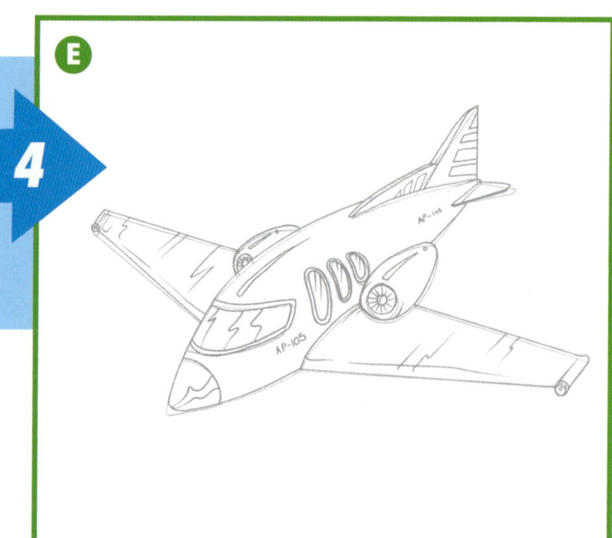

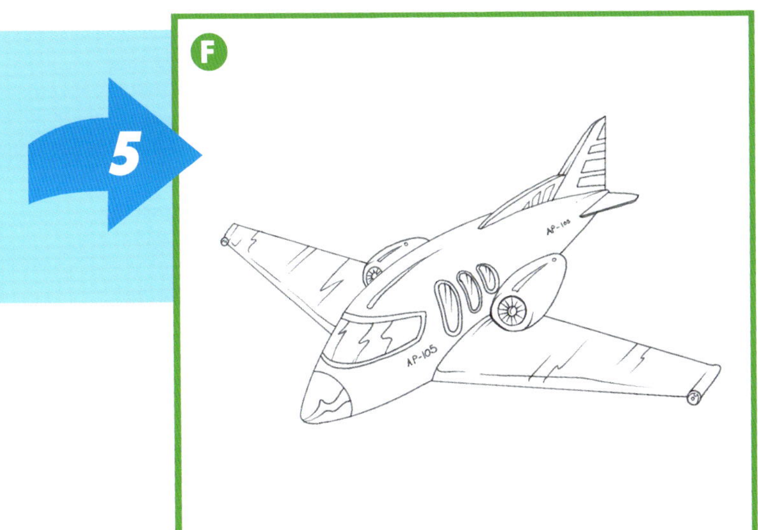

look more powerful by adding a fan in each one. These fans pull the air through, and you can draw them by creating a small circle in the center of each engine, with lines radiating outward from them.

F When you're happy with how your plane looks, trace over your drawing using a black pen and then erase the pencil marks.

G It's best to use metallic colors for an airplane, such as gray or silver. The details on the nose and side-windows are red, as this looks dynamic. Color really adds to your picture—after all, would a brown plane look as fast as a silver one? Color plays a major part in how we react to pictures, so choose wisely!

6

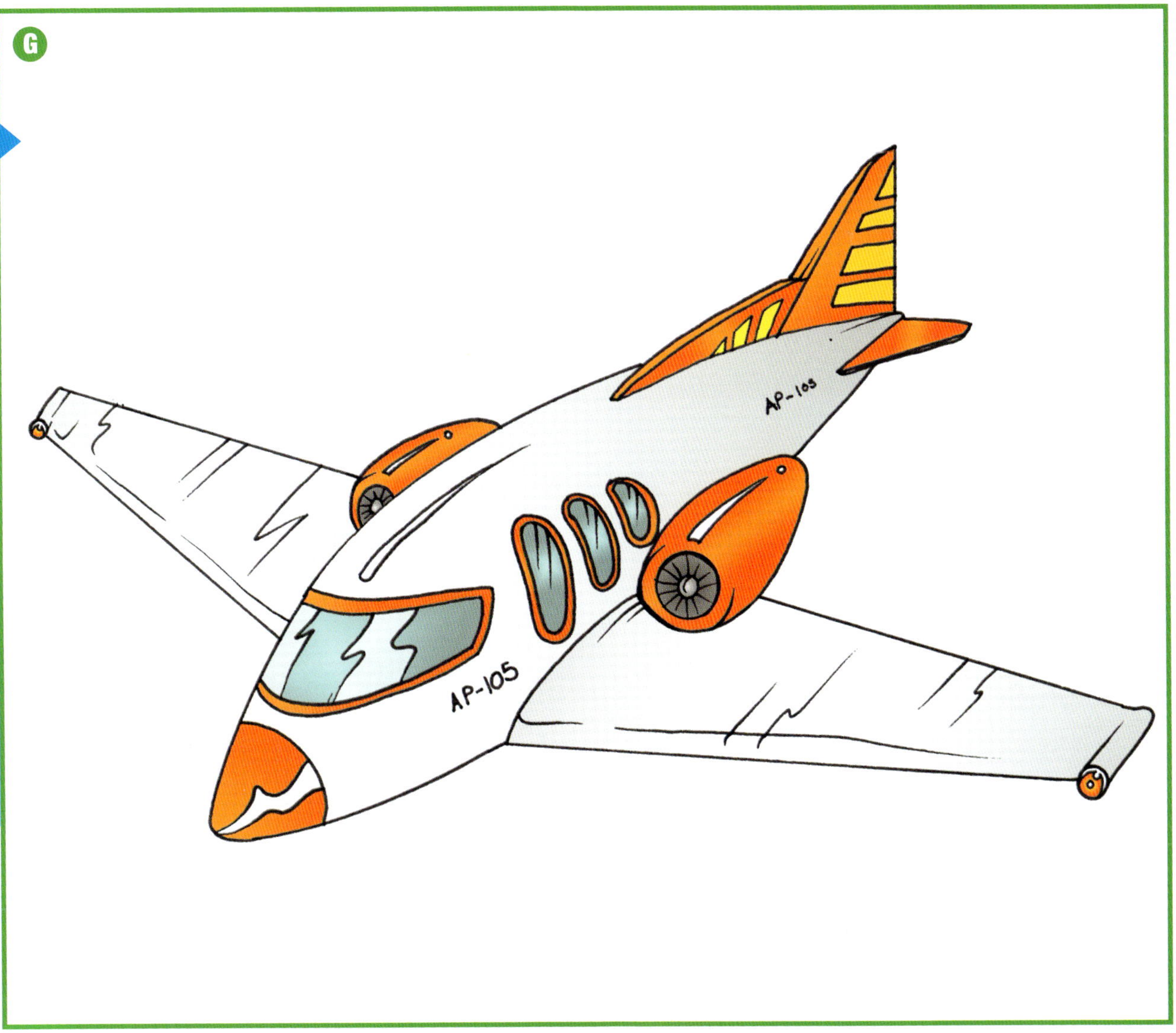

G

AP-105

HOW TO DRAW A HELICOPTER

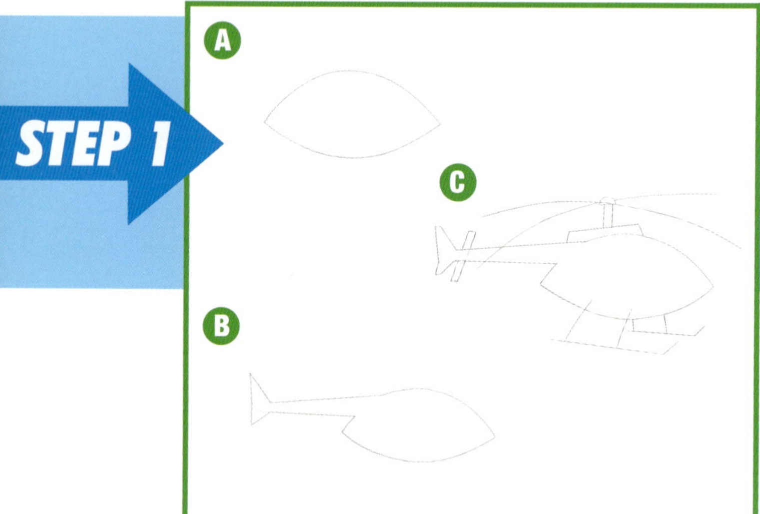

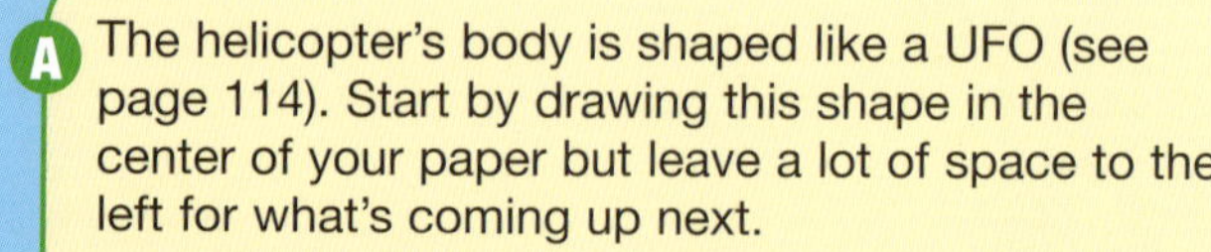

A The helicopter's body is shaped like a UFO (see page 114). Start by drawing this shape in the center of your paper but leave a lot of space to the left for what's coming up next.

B The tail consists of two shapes, a long, tapering cylinder shape and a triangular "wing" on the end of this. The cylinder attaches to the body of the helicopter, just above the point on the left-hand side of the first shape you drew.

C The helicopter's legs are shaped like skis, and are attached to the undercarriage by two struts. On the tail, just in front of the rear "wing," there is a rectangular propeller blade that helps the craft to steer. Now, draw the rotor blades—these are created by making a cross shape on a central pole.

D Start adding simple details to your picture, such as the front and side windows. Now thicken the blades on top of your craft—these narrow toward the central pole and become wider toward the tips. Don't forget to thicken the helicopter's legs.

E Begin to build up the detail, such as the reflective windows and the painted striped patterns below the front windshield. Give the craft a serial number on its tail and below the blades.

F You can now draw over the lines with a black pen, and then erase the pencil lines.

G This helicopter is dark blue with yellow markings. The windows are dark, tinted glass so no one can see who's piloting the helicopter—it's a spy helicopter, swift and deadly!

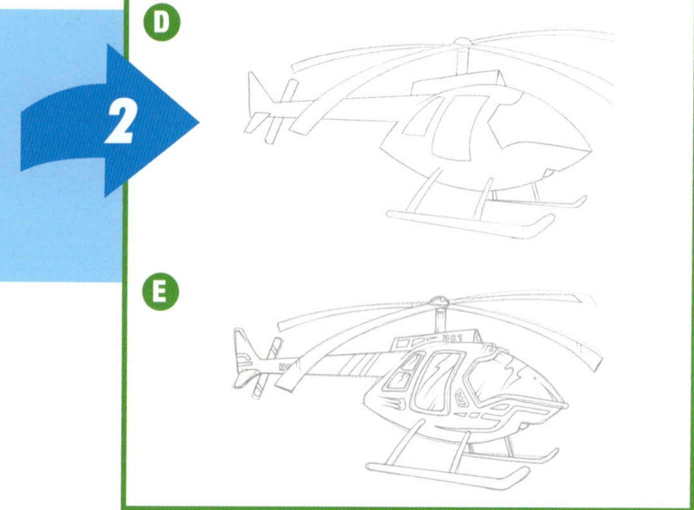

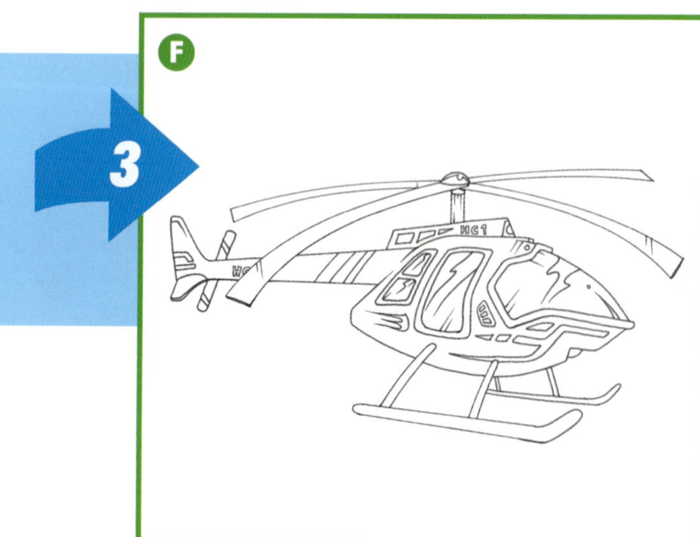

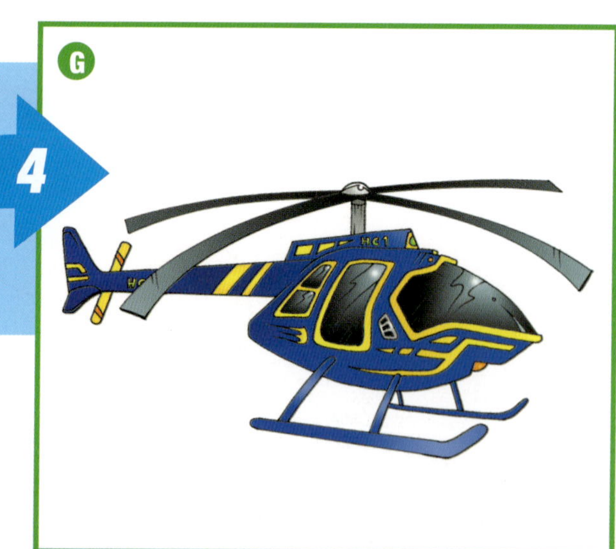

BUILDINGS AND PLANTS

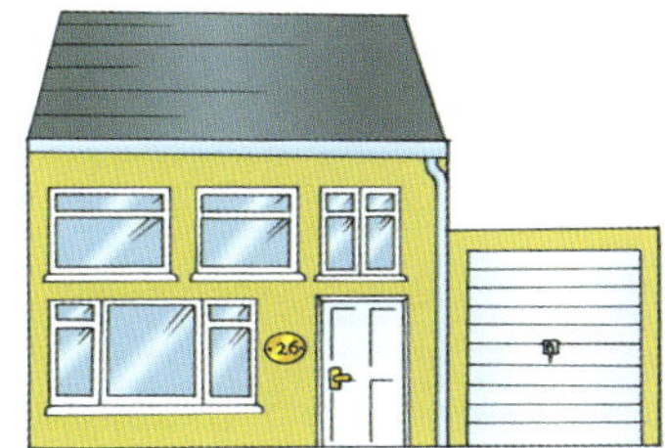

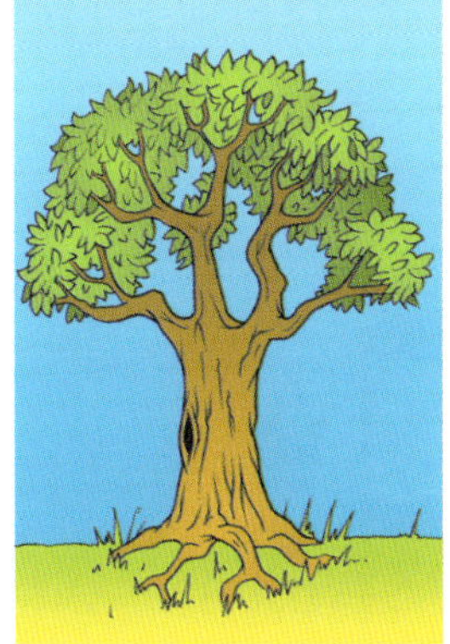

When drawing your characters, it's often helpful to know how to draw a backdrop behind them. This creates a scene and puts your characters in a specific situation or place.

Whether the background consists of downtown New York or deep in a secluded forest, the following section will give you some helpful hints on drawing plants and buildings.

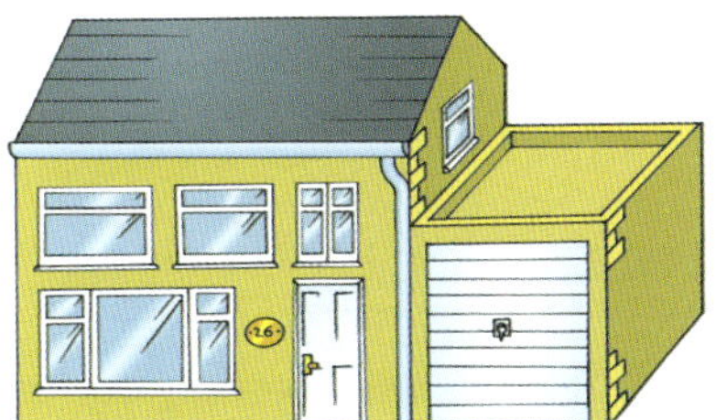

First, you're going to learn how to draw a suburban house. As well as finding out how to draw a house from a head-on view, you'll also discover how to convert this into a three-dimensional view.

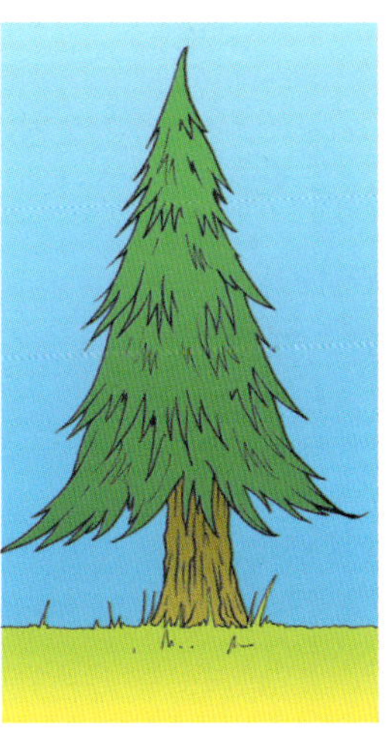

Trees are quite simple to draw, and they look really effective as a backdrop to any scene. You'll find out what different sizes and shapes trees grow into, and how to bring these to life in a few simple steps.

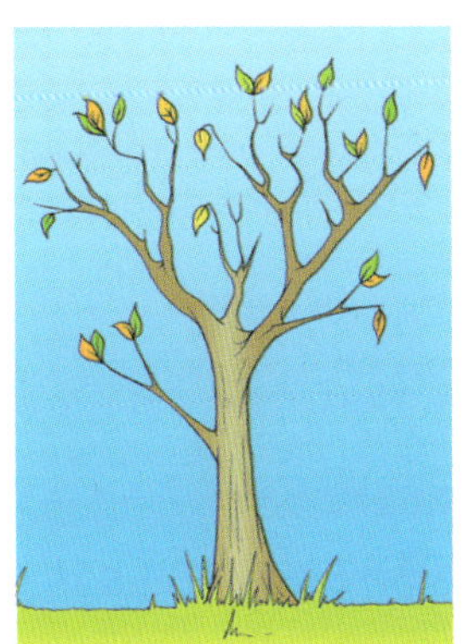

Finally, you'll be shown how to add flowers to your picture. These come in various shapes and sizes, and are easy to draw. Color is also an important consideration when drawing flowers—this chapter will help you though decide on the best use of your palette.

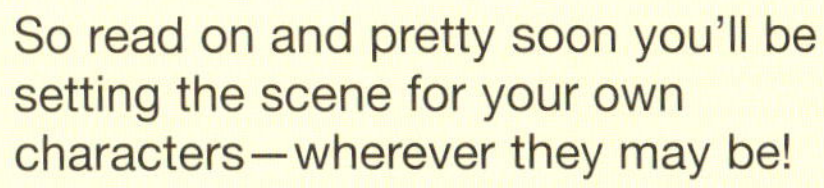

So read on and pretty soon you'll be setting the scene for your own characters—wherever they may be!

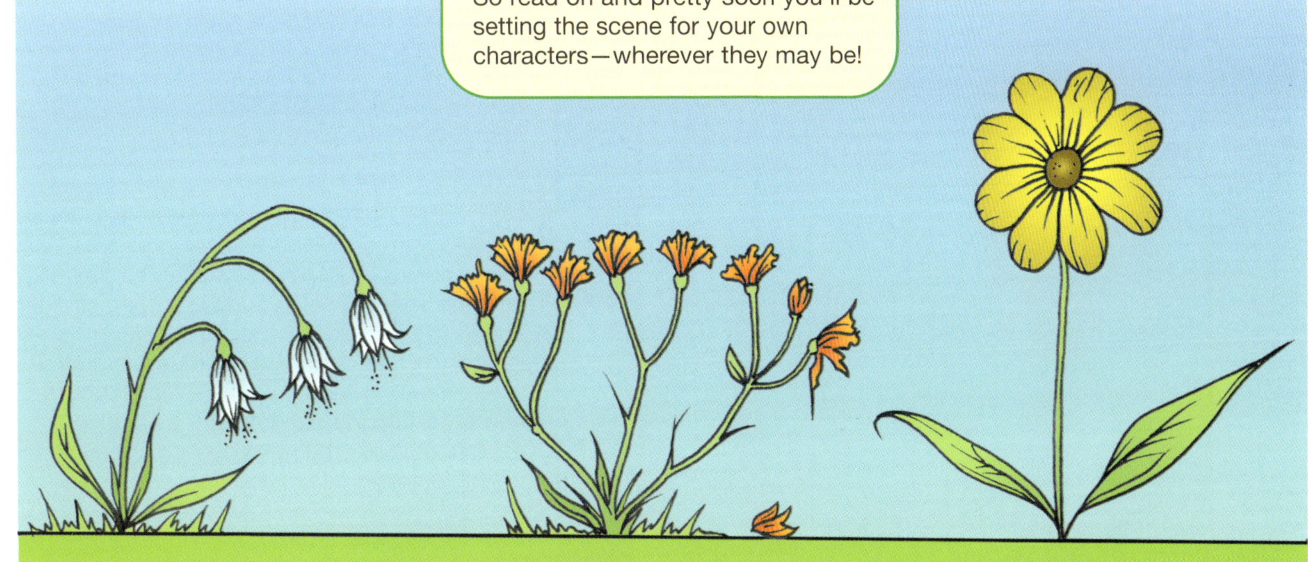

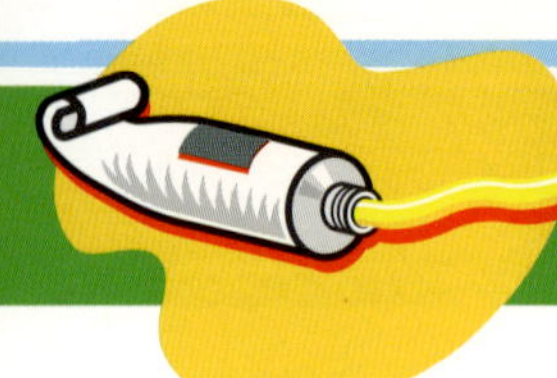

STEP 1

A

B

The first two steps to drawing a house are the same whether it is two- or three-dimensional.

A Start by drawing a square with sides measuring 4in on your page.

B Mark 1.2in down on either side of your square, and connect these marks with a straight, horizontal line. You should now have two rectangles. The larger of these will be the main house, and the smaller rectangle on top is going to be the roof. Next, draw a 2in square on the right-hand side of your house—this is your garage.

2

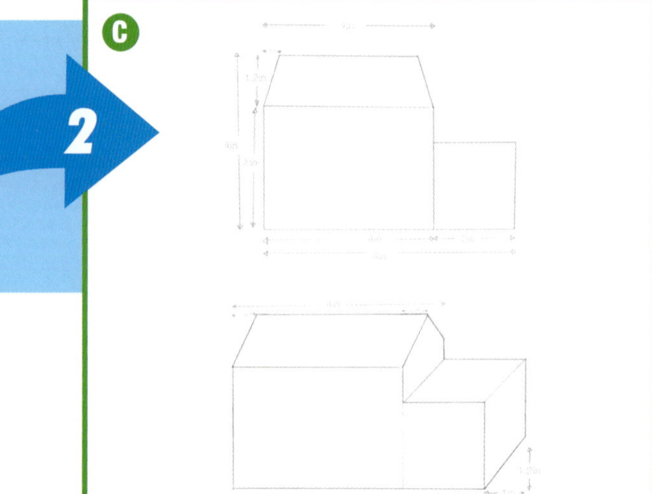

The following step is split into two for two- (2-D) and three-dimensional (3-D) houses.

C 2-D: The roof of your house needs to look as if it is slightly slanting backward. You can do this by measuring roughly half an inch in from both of your square's top corners, and marking these points. Then draw an angled line from these marks to the outer edges of the line below.

3-D: To give your house a three-dimensional look, it will need sidewalls. First though, measure 0.6in in from the top left corner of your square, and the same amount out from the top right corner. Join these points to the corners of the line below, and you will have a basic roof shape. Next, mark a dot that is 1in out and 1.2in up from the bottom right corner of your garage square.

Join this to the corner, and draw a vertical line that stretches 2in above this point. Join this next point to the top right corner of the original garage square and you will have a sidewall. The garage roof is constructed the same way—it is also 2in across. The sidewall of the house itself is made by drawing 0.6in up from the garage and connecting this to the top right corner of the house roof.

3

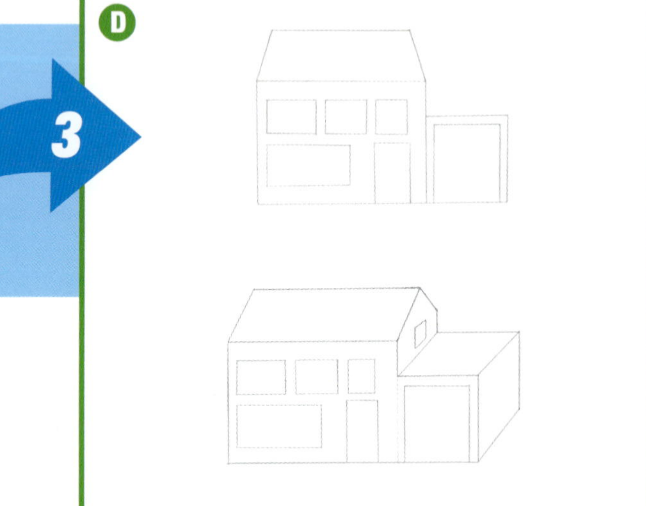

D When drawing windows on your house, it's a good idea to draw two parallel, horizontal lines through the house before starting to draw the shapes. This will help you to get them straight and in line with each other. The lower window is considerably larger than the upper three. If you're drawing the three-dimensional house, add an extra side-window at the same angle as your garage. You can get the right angle for this by drawing a feint line from one corner of

4

E

the wall to the other, and then another line parallel to the garage roof. The sides of this window should still be vertical, even though it's at an angle.

E This is the first detailing stage of your house picture. Each window is split into smaller glass panes. The top left two are split in two, while the top right is split into four panes. The lower window is split into one large pane, and four smaller side-panes of glass. The house door has four rectangular panels, while the garage door is split into many horizontal panels. You can make these by marking them down either side of the garage using equal spacing, and then joining the dots to create the perfect door.

F The second stage of detailing consists of adding reflections and window sills to each window. Be sure to also thicken the frames round each separate pane. Draw lines on your roof to represent tiles, put door handles on the house and garage, and finally give your house a number. If you're drawing the 3-D house then you could draw some clusters of bricks or draw lines to look like wood paneling on the sidewalls. It's up to you how realistic you want your house to look!

G Trace in your drawing with a black felt tip or fine-line pen, and then erase the leftover pencil lines. Now you're all set to start coloring your house in.

→

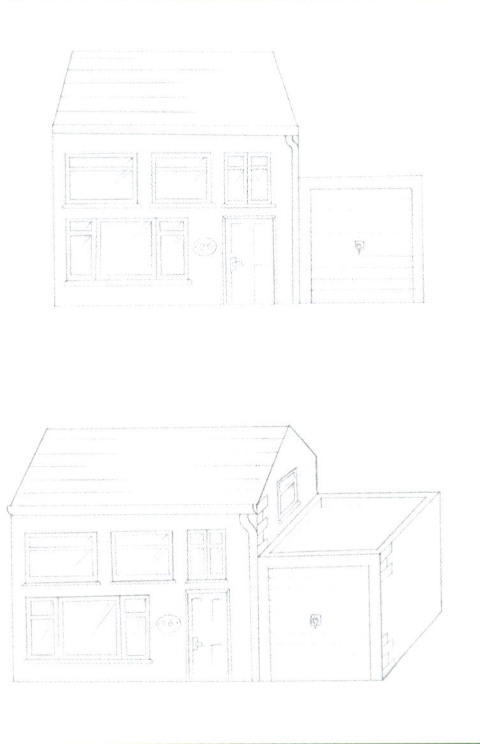

6

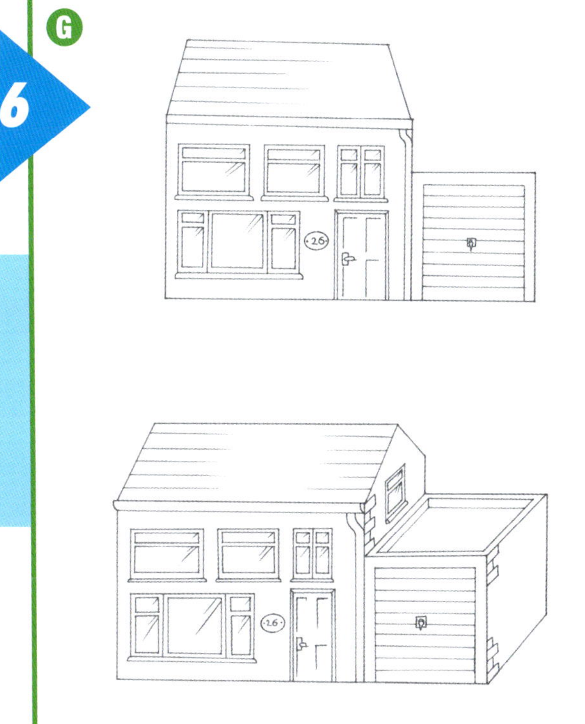

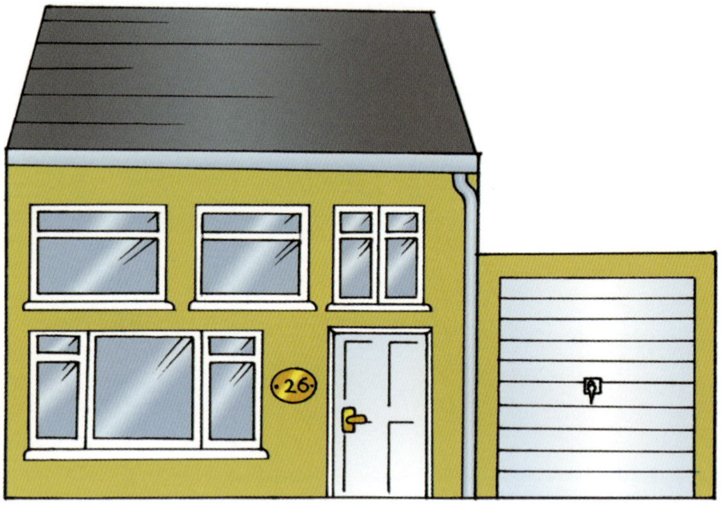

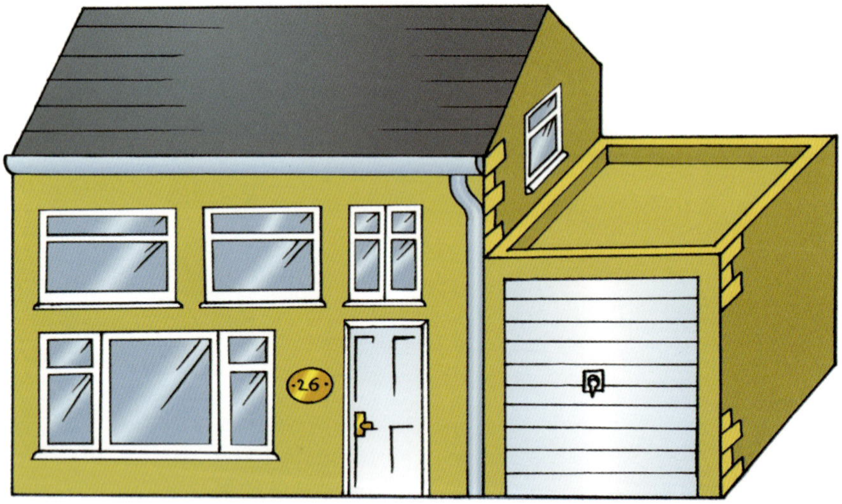

1 You can use whatever you like to color in your house, but colored pencils look great. You can get an excellent brick effect by putting a sheet of fine sandpaper underneath your paper and shading over this. If your house is made of bricks then reds, grays or yellows all look good. If your house is wooden, you can use browns. Take a look at the houses on your block if you can't make up your mind.

STEP 1

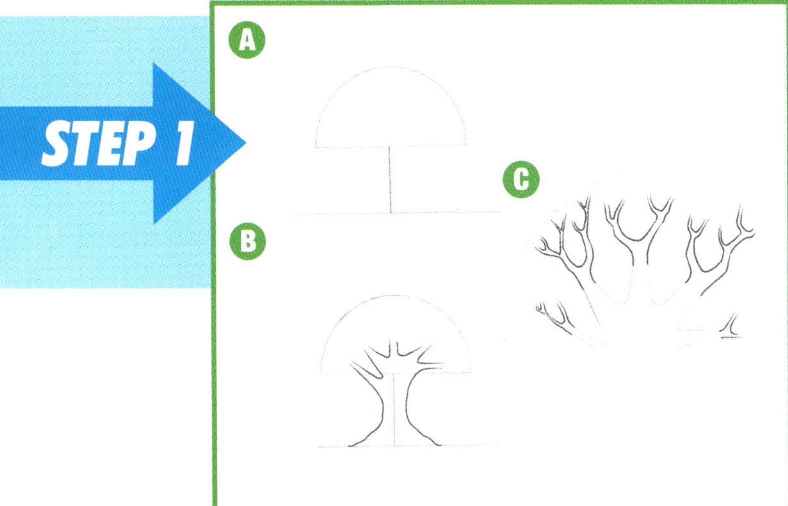

2

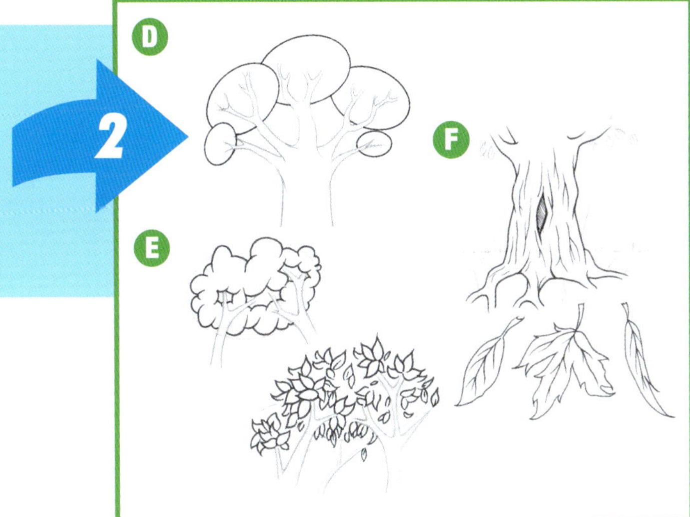

3

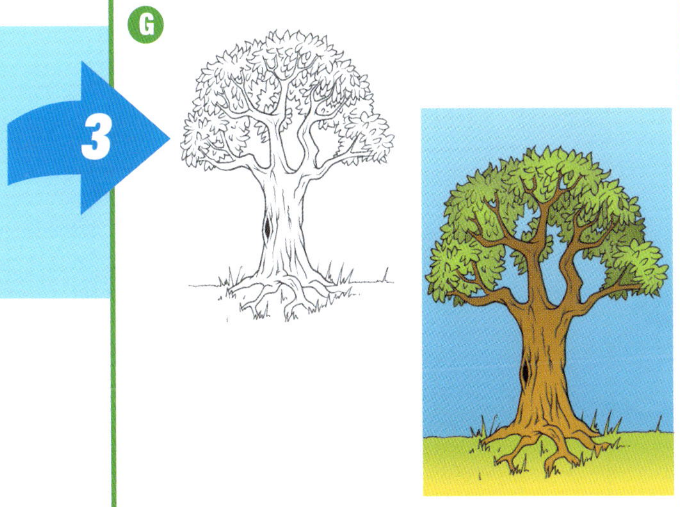

Oak tree

A When drawing a tree, the first basic shapes you sketch are very important in deciding what kind of tree it will become. A large tree, such as an oak, begins with a short trunk and a large, semi-circular shape ready for the branches.

B The second stage of drawing your tree consists of thickening the trunk. The trunk of this tree is very wide, with an even thicker base and five main branches sprouting out at the top.

C Each of the five branches at the top of your trunk splits off into two smaller branches, and each of these in turn splits off into two even smaller branches. Repeat this process until you reach the edges of your semi-circle.

D Foliage on trees often grows in clumps, so it's a good idea to use simple shapes, like the ovals featured here, and separate the foliage into different sized sections.

E Foliage can be as detailed, or as simple as you want it to be. Either draw fluffy cloud shapes, or if you're feeling really adventurous, sketch in lots of individual leaf shapes within your clump. Do bear in mind though that this takes much, much longer to accomplish.

F Bark details on your tree trunk can be achieved by using thin wavy lines that run vertically down the trunk. You can also draw holes in the trunk to show the tree's age, and sketch in roots at the base of the trunk—these are drawn in the same way as you drew the branches.

G Leaves, like trees, come in many different shapes and colors.

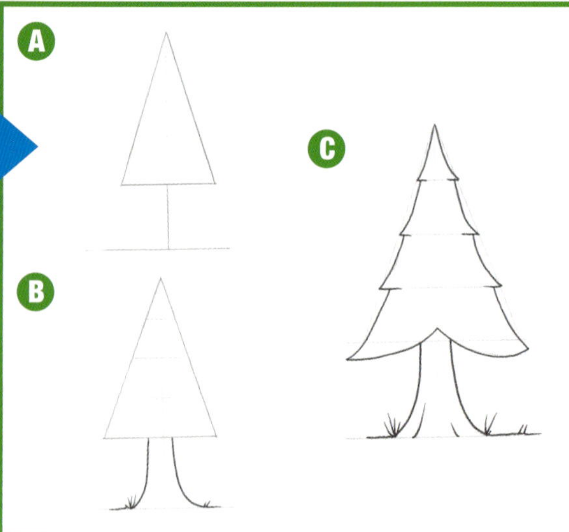

Fir tree

A A fir tree should begin with a small trunk like the oak tree, but have large triangle-shaped foliage on top.

B The next step is to make the trunk thicker. It should widen toward the ground. Next, draw lines across the triangle shape that you created in Step A.

C Using the pencil lines as a guide, draw curved "ledges" running down either side of your tree.

D E F Give the tree a shaggier look by drawing short, sharp triangular shapes all over it. Then draw over your lines with a pen, and then you are ready to color in your tree.

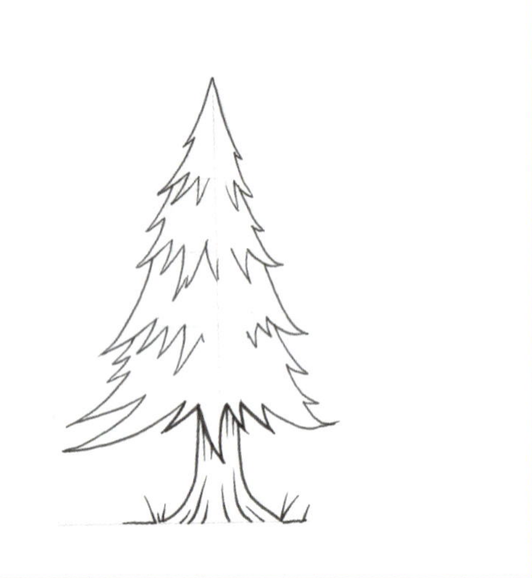

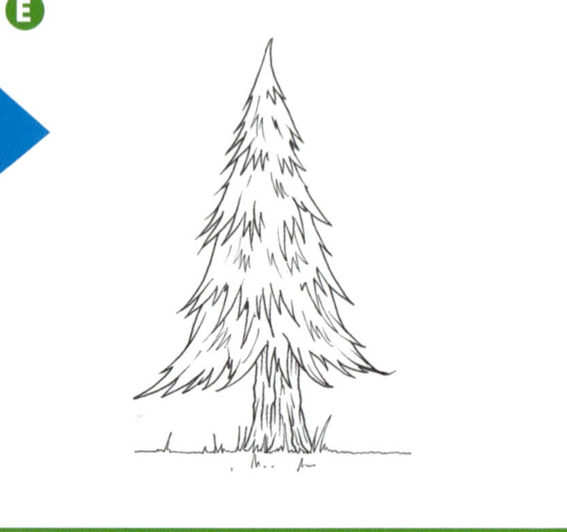

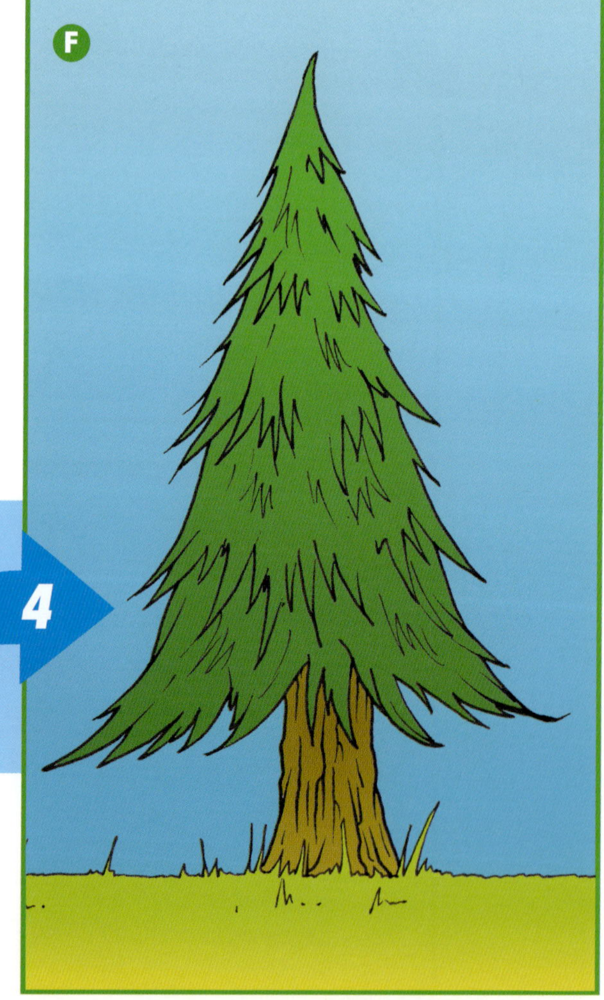

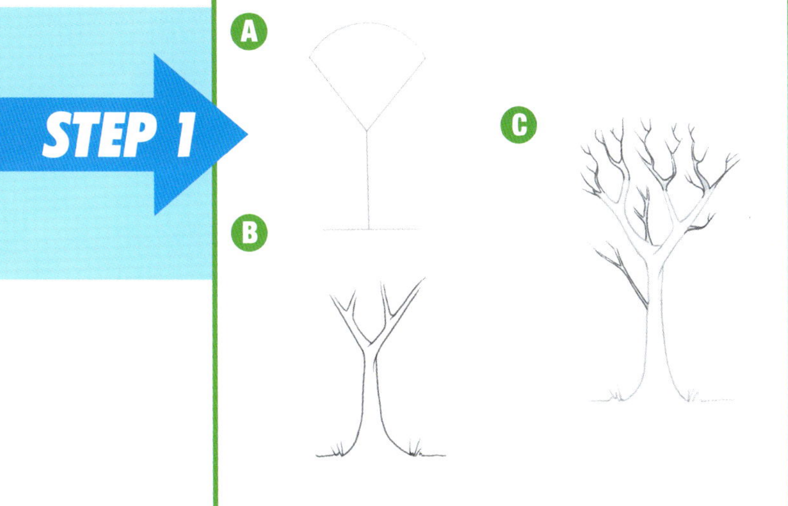

Winter tree

A Some trees are tall and thin with a smaller shape on top for the foliage and branches. This tree has a fan shape on top of the long thin stalk.

B The tree's trunk is a little thinner than those of the other trees featured in this chapter, and is split into two main branches at the top. It should look like a huge catapult. Next, split each of these branches into two more.

C Keep splitting the branches until you reach the outside of your original fan shape. Try not to split the branch too often, and also add one or two stray branches further down the trunk.

D E F The foliage on a tree in winter time is sparse at best, so all you need to do is draw a couple of leaves on each set of branches. Stagger the leaves as much as possible, so that your tree looks truly bare. Then draw over your lines with a pen and add your colors.

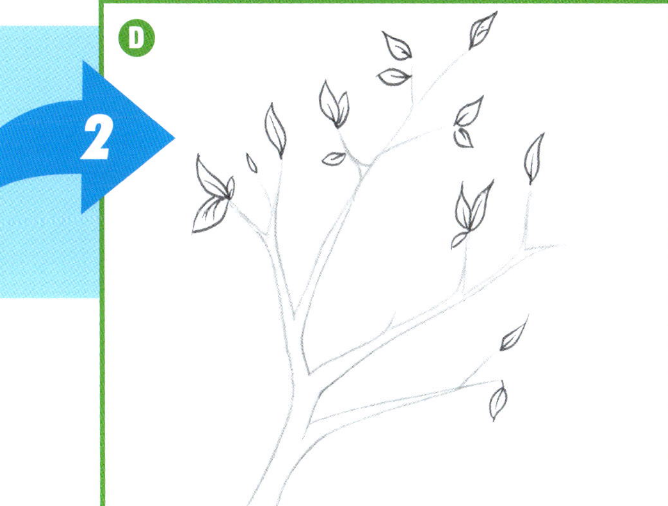

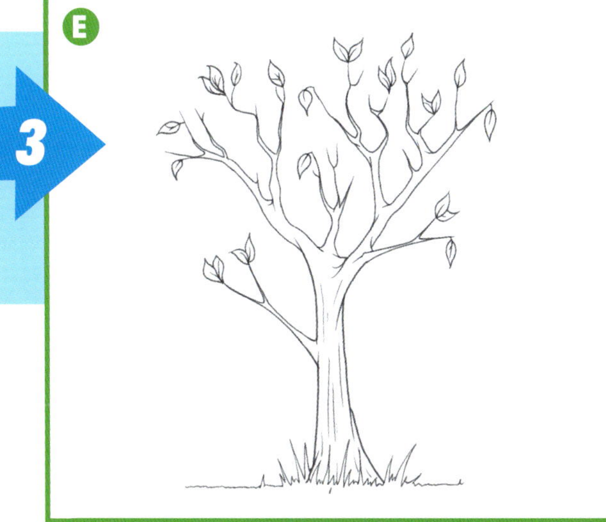

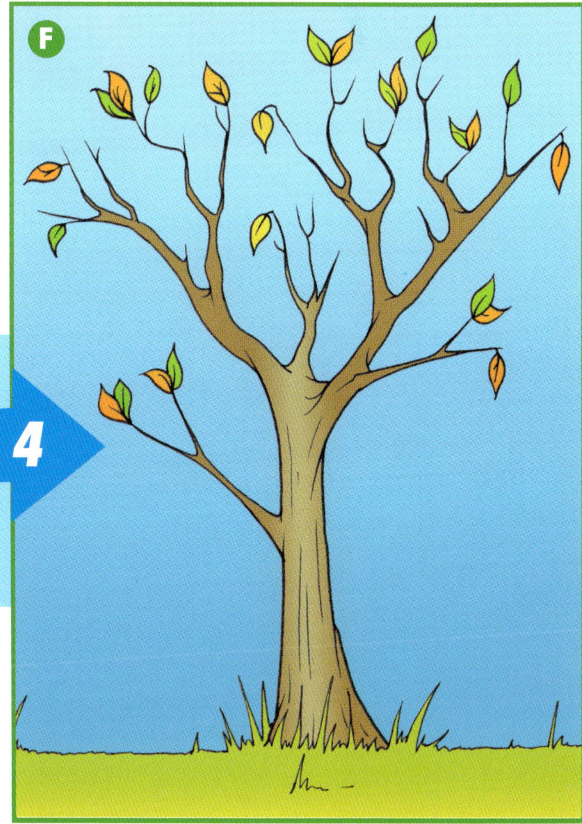

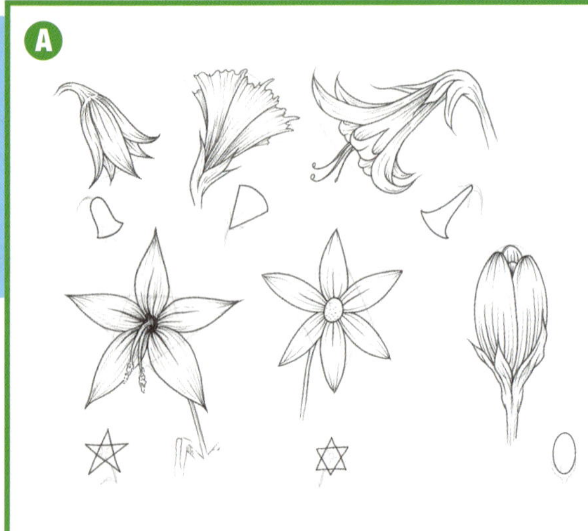

A Flowers come in various sizes: bells, fans, trumpets, stars, and more.

B Flower petals can be almost any color, and can vary in number from flower to flower.

Daisy

C A simple "daisy" style of flower starts as a circle on a stalk, a little like a lollipop. Draw two leaves at the base of the stem.

D Drawing a daisy requires you to split the circle into sections. This will help you draw its petals. First, draw a vertical line and a horizontal line that meet in the middle, and then split each of the resulting sections in two—this is going to be a flower with eight petals.

E Round each of the sections off at the outer edge of the circle, and draw a large F circular "face" in the center. Draw veins on your leaves and petals to complete the flower. Then pen in your lines and color the flower.

B

C

E

D

STEP 1

2

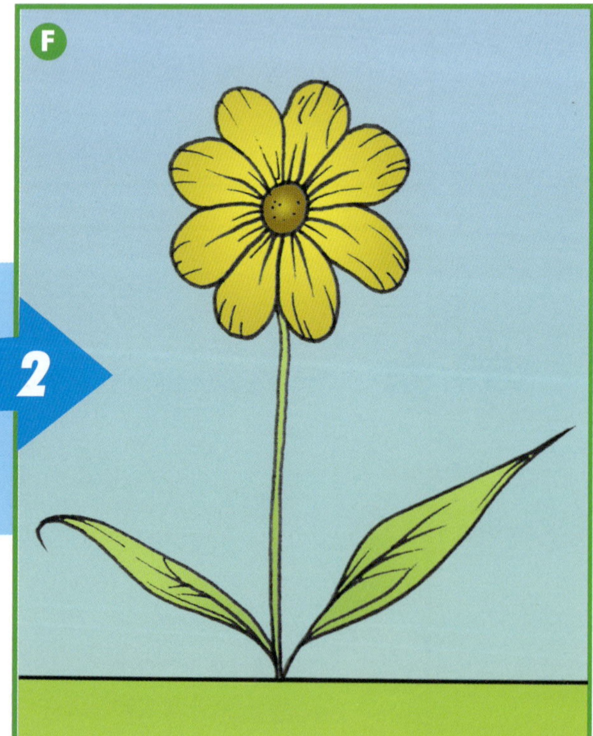

STEP 1

A

Teardrop

A The basic shape of a teardrop style of flower is a bell shape. This plant has three bell-shaped flowers hanging from a single stem, that splits into three halfway up.

B The next step is to separate the bell shapes into individual petals: three at the front of the flower, and two emerging from behind.

C D Finally, thicken the flower's stem and draw stamens coming from each flower head: these can be just a simple line with dots to represent the pollen. As with the daisy flower, draw veins on the leaves. Then pen in your lines and color the picture.

2

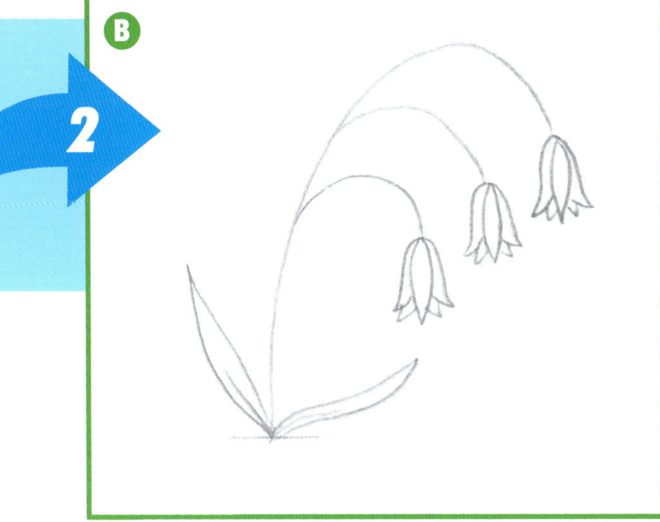

3

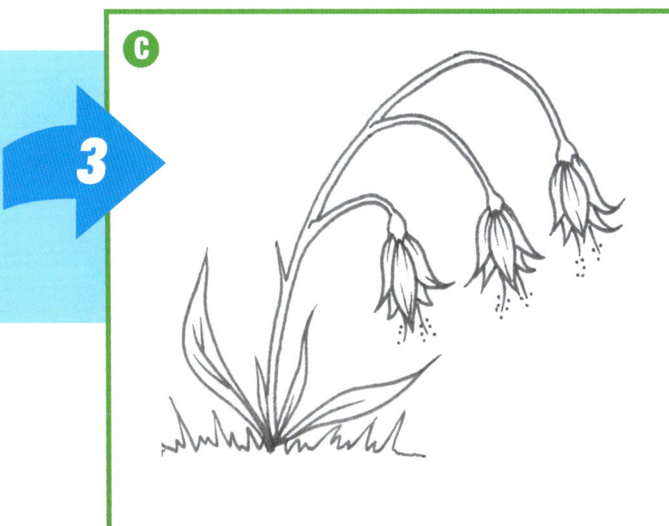

4

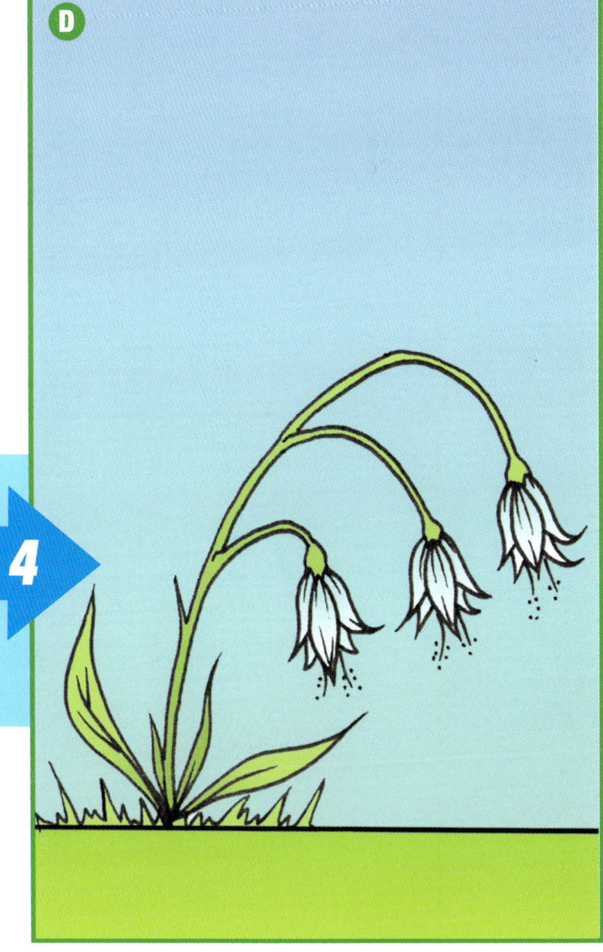

STEP 1

A

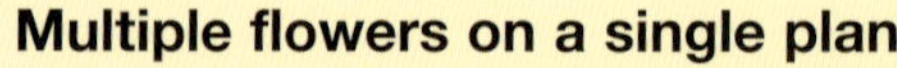

Multiple flowers on a single plant

A Some plants have many flowers on them, and these are drawn in a similar fashion to the trees featured in this chapter—keep splitting the main stem into two or even three new stems at certain points. This particular plant has fan-shaped flowers.

B Split each flower into three or four petals.

C **D** Thicken the stem and add the final detail to your flowers. These particular flowers have frilled edges, like a dress. You can also draw a couple of flower buds that haven't bloomed yet. Now you're ready to pen in your drawing and color the flowers.

2

B

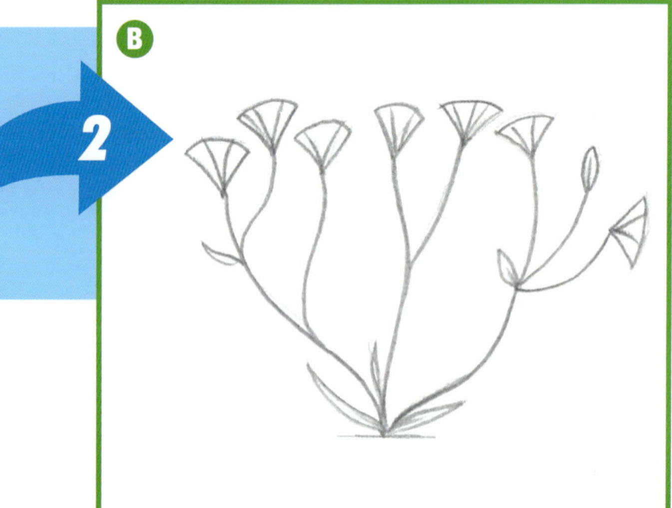

3

C

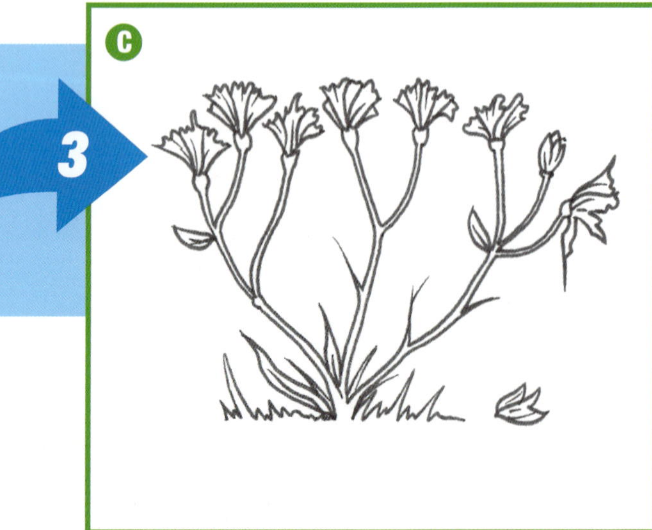

4

D

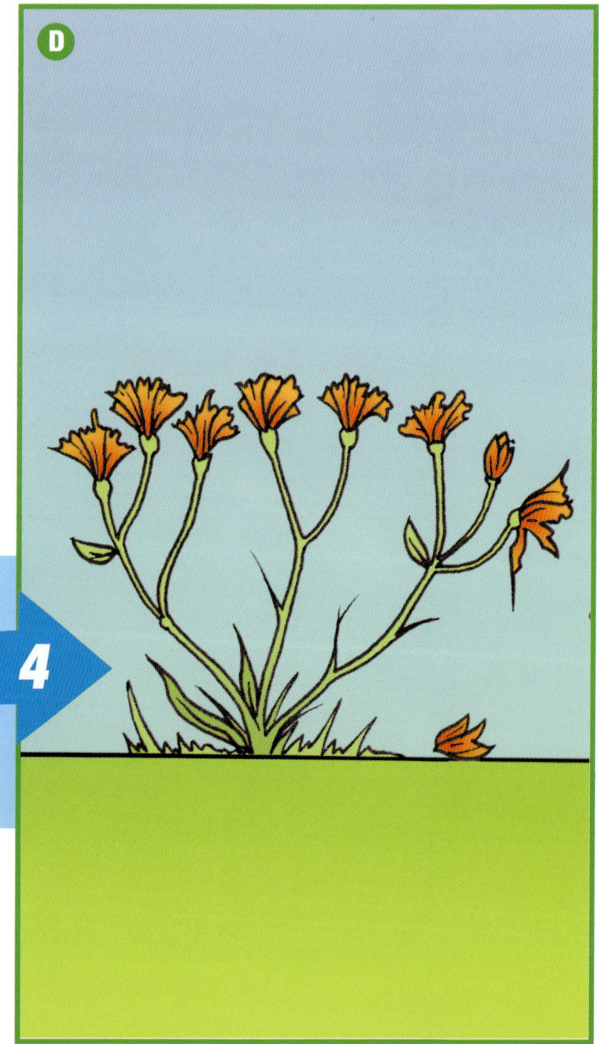

SPORTS

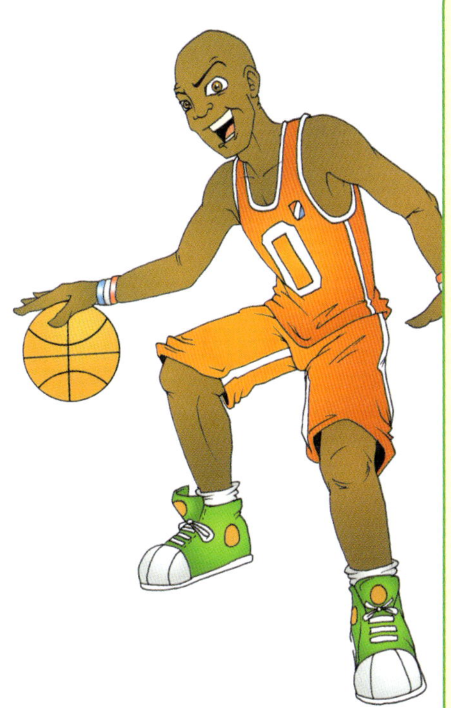

"Work hard, play hard." It is a great mantra to live by and hopefully, when you're not hard at work, you've got some sort of hobby—but if you're reading this, one of your hobbies must be drawing! Chances are though that you also have an interest in a sport, whether it be football, baseball, or skateboarding.

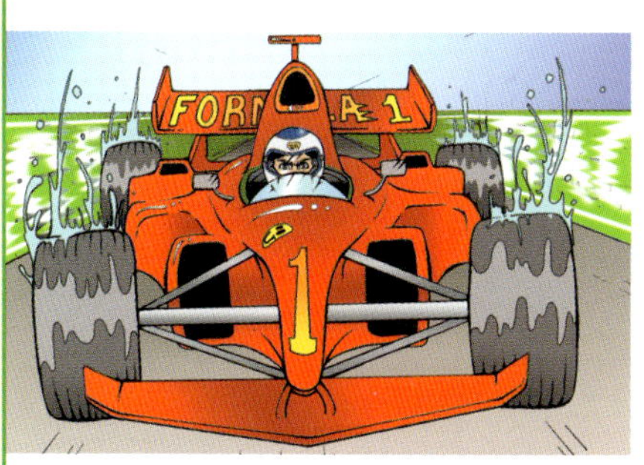

While sports are great to play or simply watch, it can also be a lot of fun drawing sporting characters. This section of the book is dedicated to helping you draw various sportsmen and women. It covers mainstream sports like football, basketball, and Formula 1 racing, but also deals with extreme sports such as surfing, snowboarding and skateboarding.

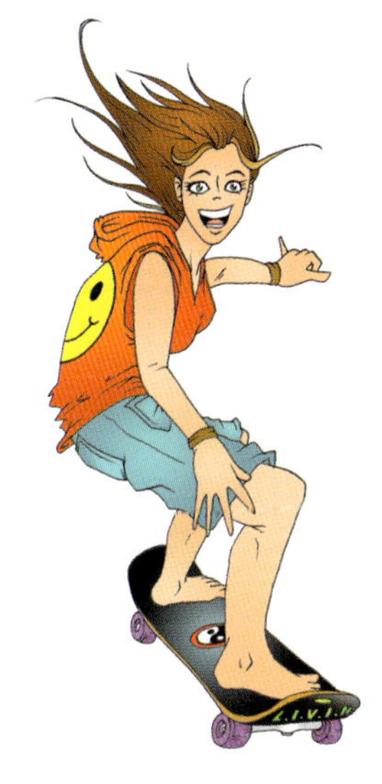

Maybe you want to draw your favorite sports hero or perhaps just a regular girl or guy enjoying their pastime. Either way, it'll be worth calling time on your busy day to check this out. So be on the ball, ride your creative wave, and bring these characters to life!

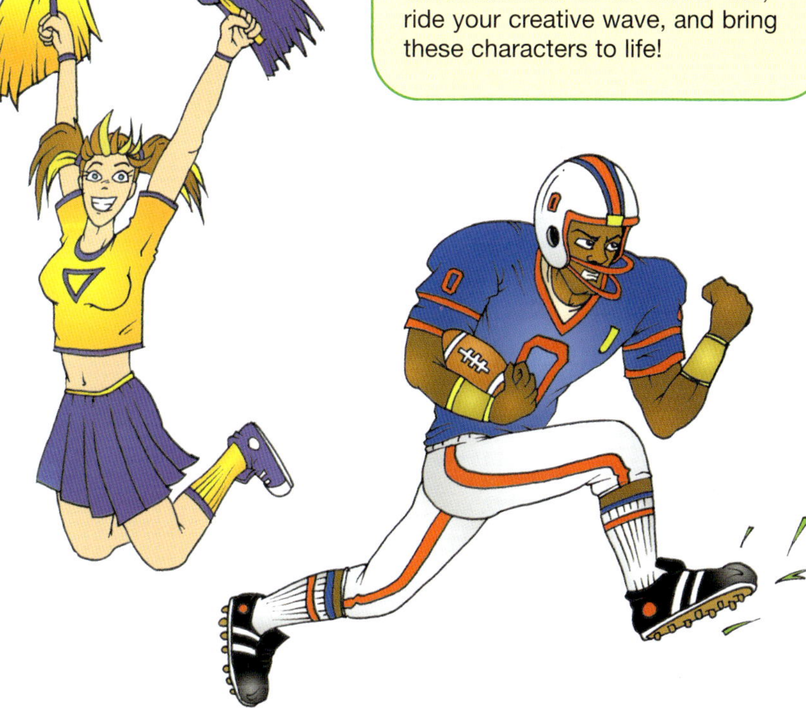

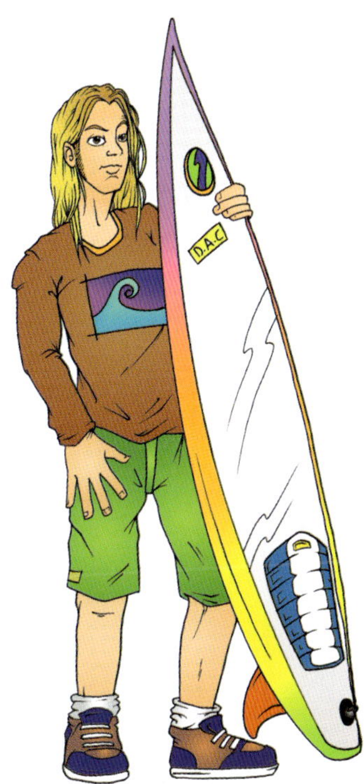

STEP 1

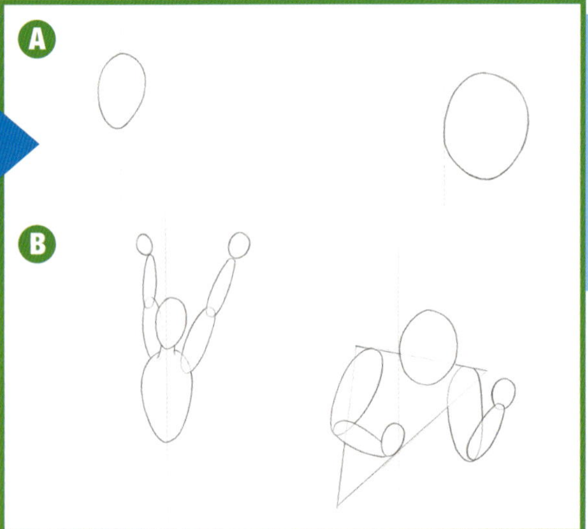

A Place your sheet of paper horizontally, and sketch two vertical lines roughly a third of the way in at each side. Use these as a guide, and draw two eggs. The left egg needs to be small, with the line running through the center, while the right egg needs to be bigger and fatter, with the line running down the left side.

B The left egg is your cheerleader. Her body is an egg shape about twice the length of the first shape you drew, and her arms are made using ovals and circles; each oval is slightly longer than her head. The right egg, your footballer, has a triangular body that overlaps his head slightly. His arms are drawn in the same way as the cheerleader's, but are bent at the elbow.

2

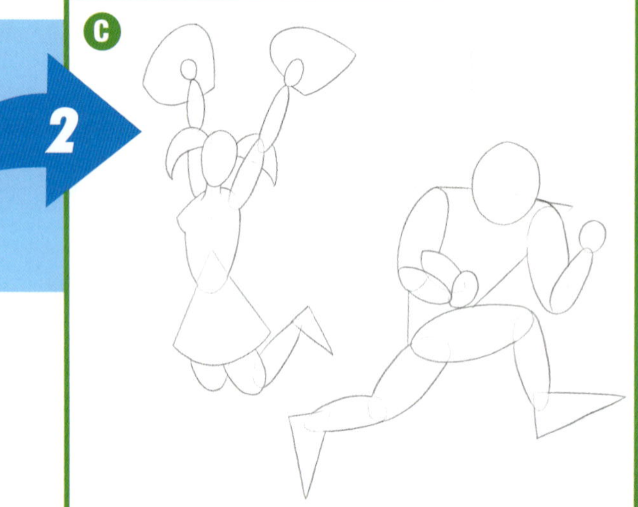

C Both characters' legs are drawn using two overlapping ovals and a triangle for each foot. The cheerleader has her legs bent back, as she's jumping in the air. Connecting her legs to her upper body is a large fan-shaped skirt; line this up using the center line. She has two pom-poms and wears her hair in bunches. The footballer's legs are in a running position, his front leg bent close to his elbow. Finally, he has an almond-shaped football.

D Start to put some details on both characters, such as their clothing and faces. The cheerleader's face is central, as she's looking forward. The footballer's face, however, is turned slightly away, so you need to shift his features to the

3

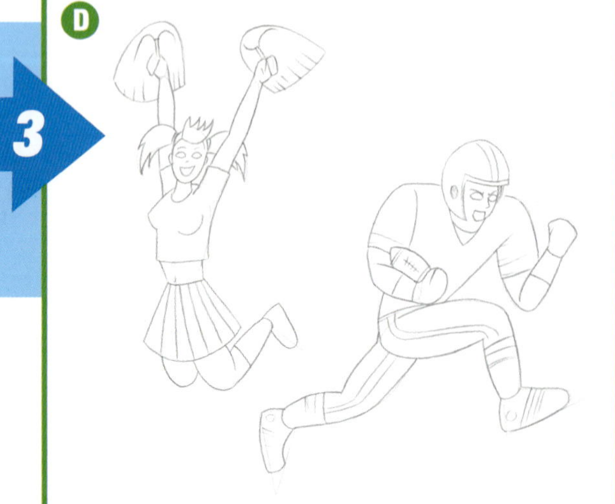

4

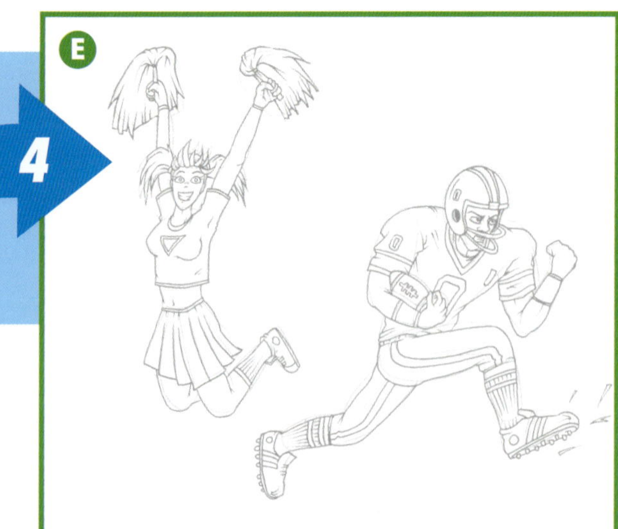

5

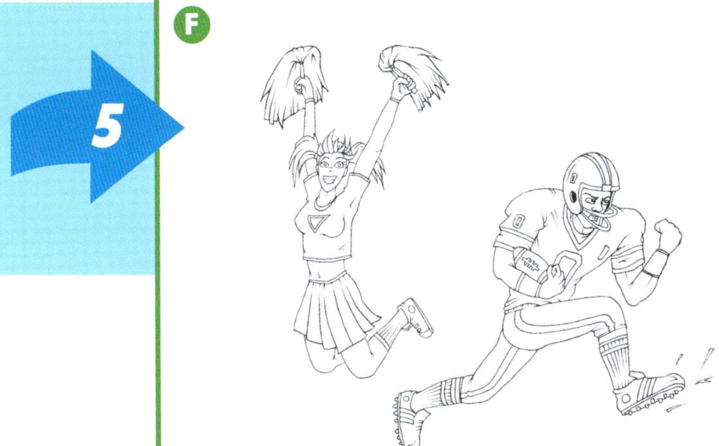

right a little. His face is sketched lower down in your egg shape—the rest is his helmet. Round off both characters' feet to form their shoes and sketch the shape of their outfits. It's time to start drawing the final detail.

E Your footballer's duds need to look authentic, so give his shirt a number on the front and sleeve, and you can also draw one on his helmet. Draw the stitching on the football, and give his boots a row of studs to help him grip the field. Give your cheerleader's pom-poms a fluffy look by drawing a spiky edge to them; her hair has a similar look. On both characters, draw pupils in the eyes and don't forget their teeth. These can be drawn with a single line through the center of the mouth.

F Before adding any color to your footballer and cheerleader, trace over your pencil version in black pen and erase the pencil lines. This prevents any smudging of the outline when you color them in.

G Color your characters in your favorite team colors. The two characters here are wearing different colors, because the cheerleader is cheering for the rival team. That is making the footballer pretty mad!

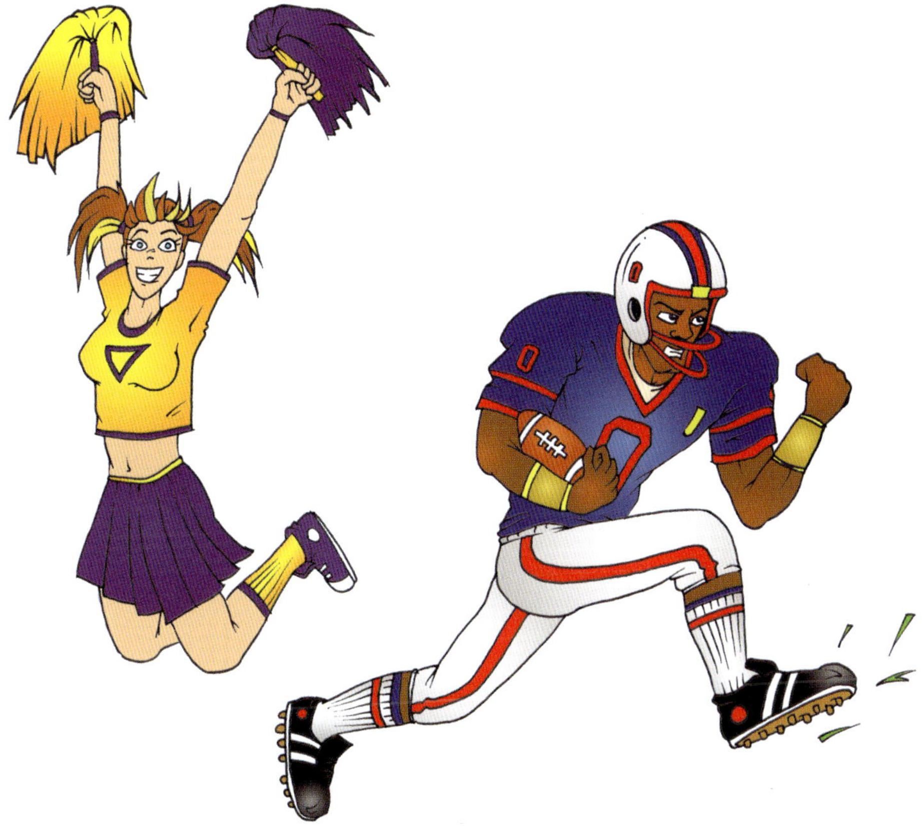

STEP 1

A B C

A Start your basketball player by sketching a feint vertical line down the center of your paper. Using this as a guide, draw an oval shape to the left of it and quite high up on the page.

B The body of your basketball star is exactly the same shape as his head, only twice the size. This shape overlaps your center line, but is positioned mainly on the right-hand side. Join the two shapes with a simple neck shape.

C Basketball players have long arms—handy for that hook-shot from the three-point line—so you should draw them using quite long, thin oval shapes. Both hands are triangular, although the one palming the ball is thinner.

D Complete the basketball player's frame by giving him two muscular legs to help him run up the court. His back foot is triangular, and the foot closest to you is fan-shaped to begin with.

E At this stage, you will need to add detail to your drawing. Using the shapes as a guide, connect them together using simple, bold lines. The basketball star is wearing knee-length shorts and a singlet. Start sketching his face, ball, and boots. The boots are drawn by rounding off the foot shapes, and the lines on the ball are created by drawing a cross and two semi-circles.

2

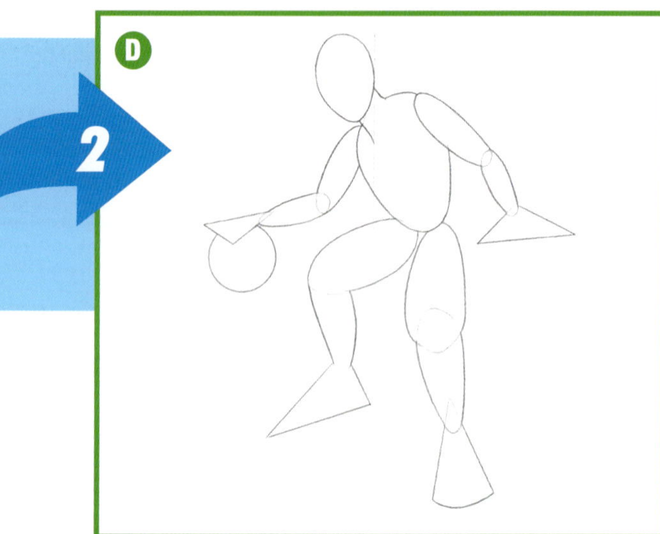

3

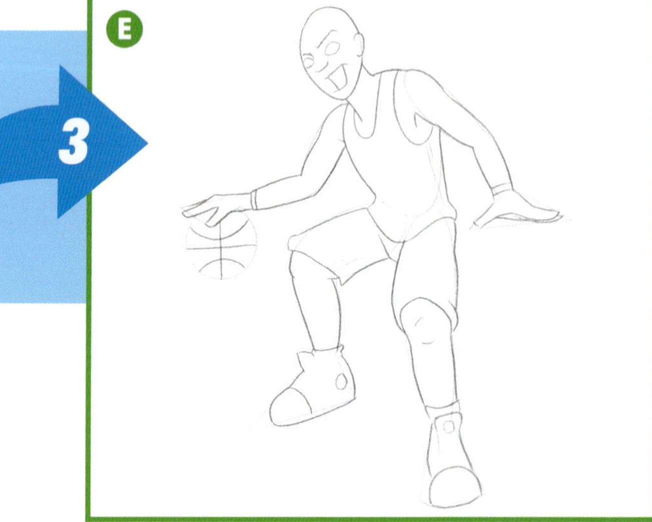

4

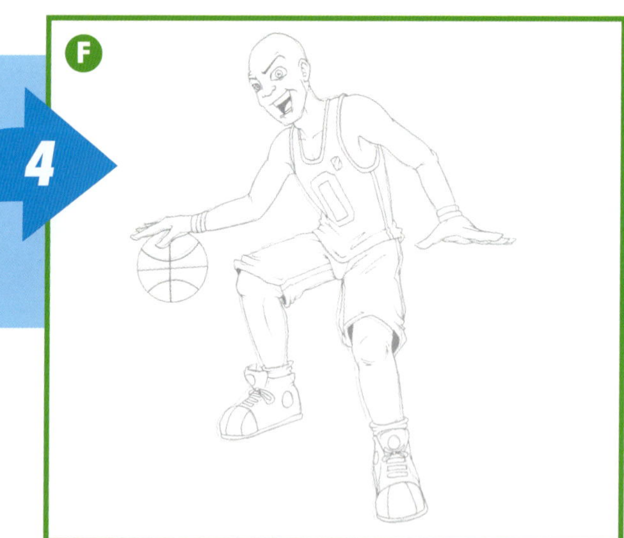

5

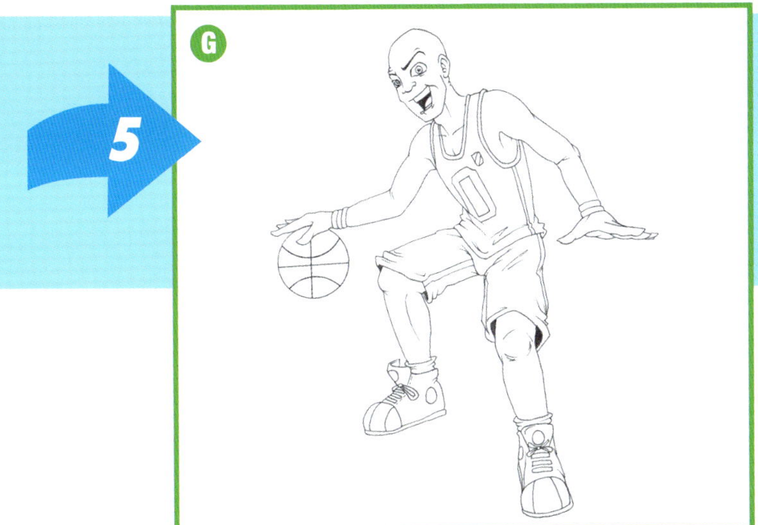

F Now it's time to finalize the detailing, specifically the designs on the basketball star's clothing and his facial features. Firstly, the face. He has a bald head, raised eyebrows, and almond-shaped eyes. The singlet has a large number on it and piping around the edges. The shorts have a stripe running down the length of the fabric. Finally, the laces on his sneakers are tied in a bow, and the sneakers have a separate rubber toecap.

G Now trace over all the lines you have drawn so far using a black pen. Then erase any pencil markings that are left. Your basketball star is now prepped and ready for coloring.

6

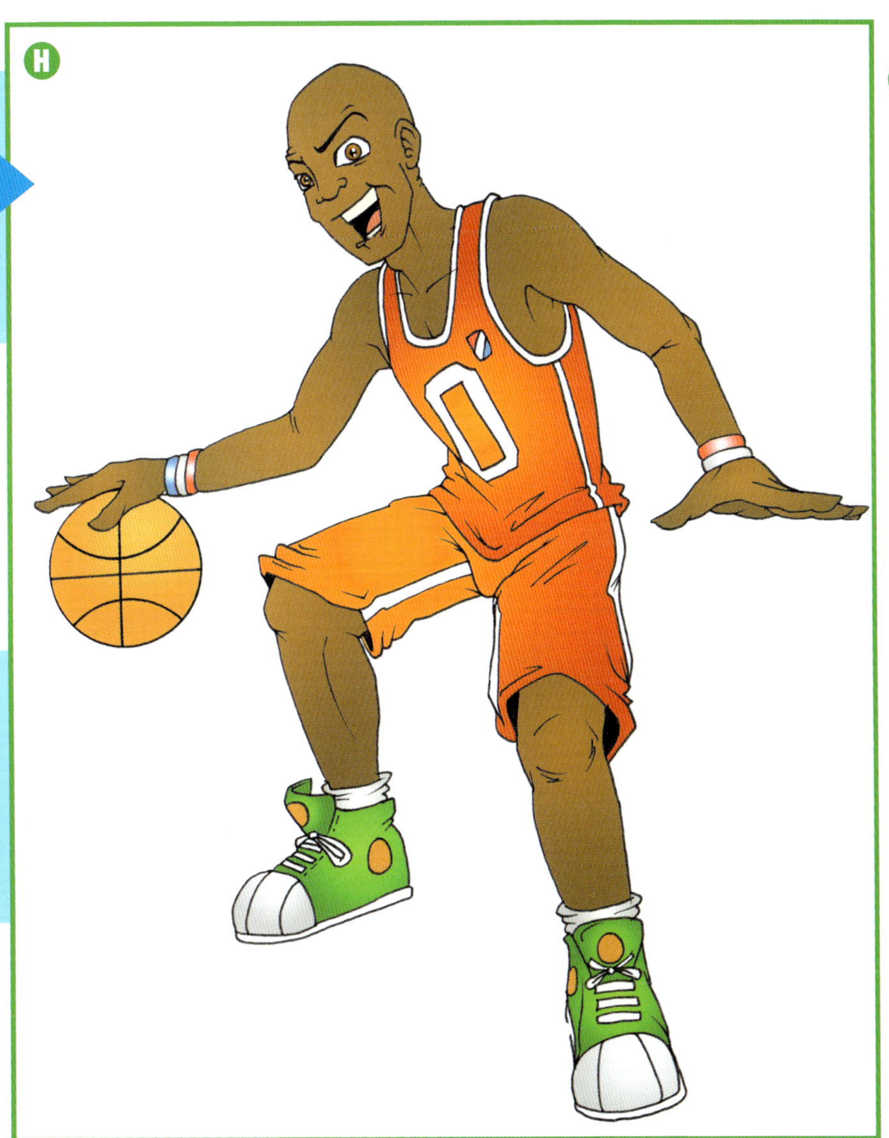

H Coloring this guy is easy. Just sit back and think of your favorite team and your favorite player. What are the team colors? If you don't have a favorite team, look around and see what colors are used often, or you could always just use the same colors as featured here.

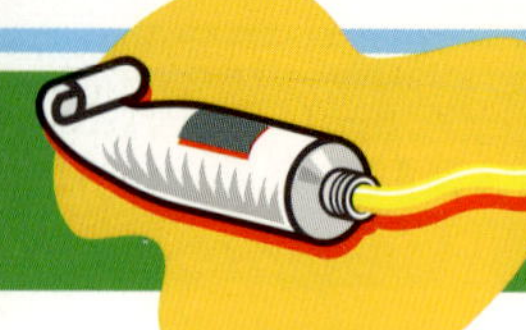

STEP 1

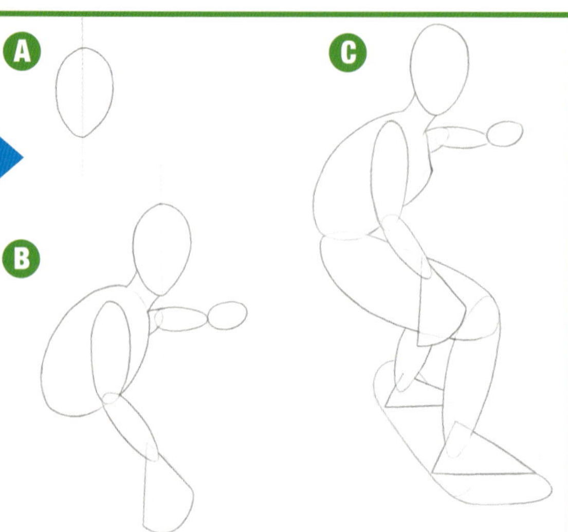

A Your skateboarder begins life as an egg shape with a vertical line running through the center. This egg is going to be her head, so it needs to be quite small and high up on the paper.

B The body of your skateboarding girl is also an oval shape, only it's about twice the size of her head—don't worry, you don't have to be exact! Her body is drawn to the left of your center line, diagonal to her head. Next, the left arm is drawn in front of the body, and consists of two long, thin ovals and a fan shape that is going to be her hand. Her other arm is partially hidden behind her body, so just draw the lower part of this limb.

C Now your skateboarder needs some legs to help her get around. The legs are created in a similar way to the arms, but with an added triangle at the base for the feet. As with the arms, one leg is prominent and the other is half-hidden. Finally, the board she's cruising on follows the line of her feet, and is slightly wider at the front to give a sense of depth.

2

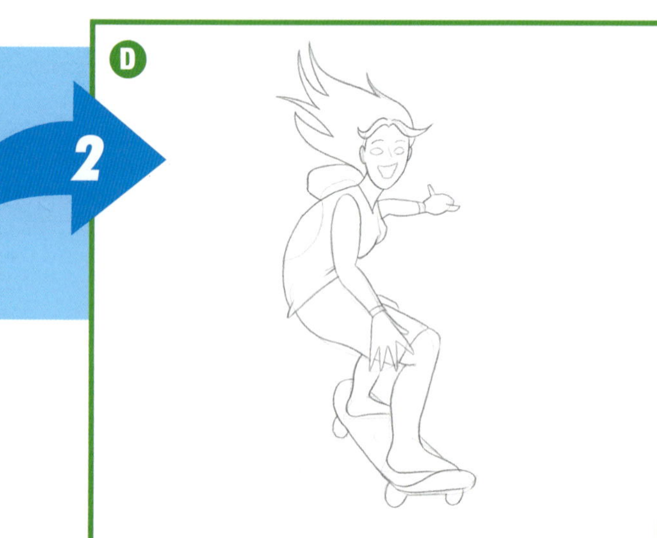

D Draw your skater's outline using the shapes as a guide. Connect the shapes, remembering which ones are supposed to overlap and which ones aren't. Start sketching a face for your skateboarder—give her a huge smile and have her hair flowing behind her in the wind, which adds to the feeling of motion. Draw the individual fingers on the left hand using the

3

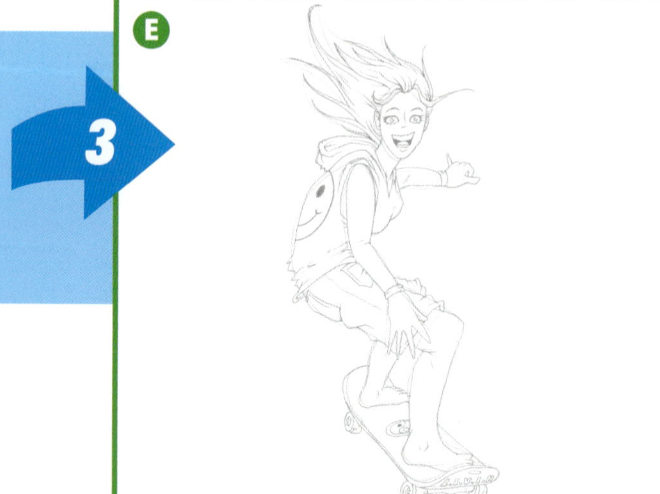

4

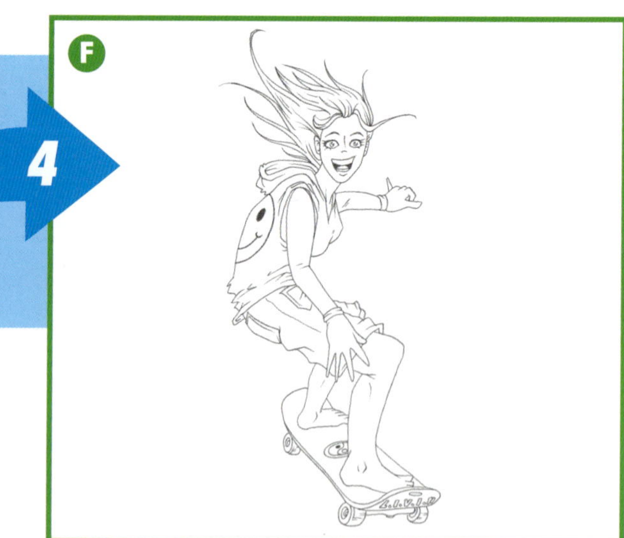

5

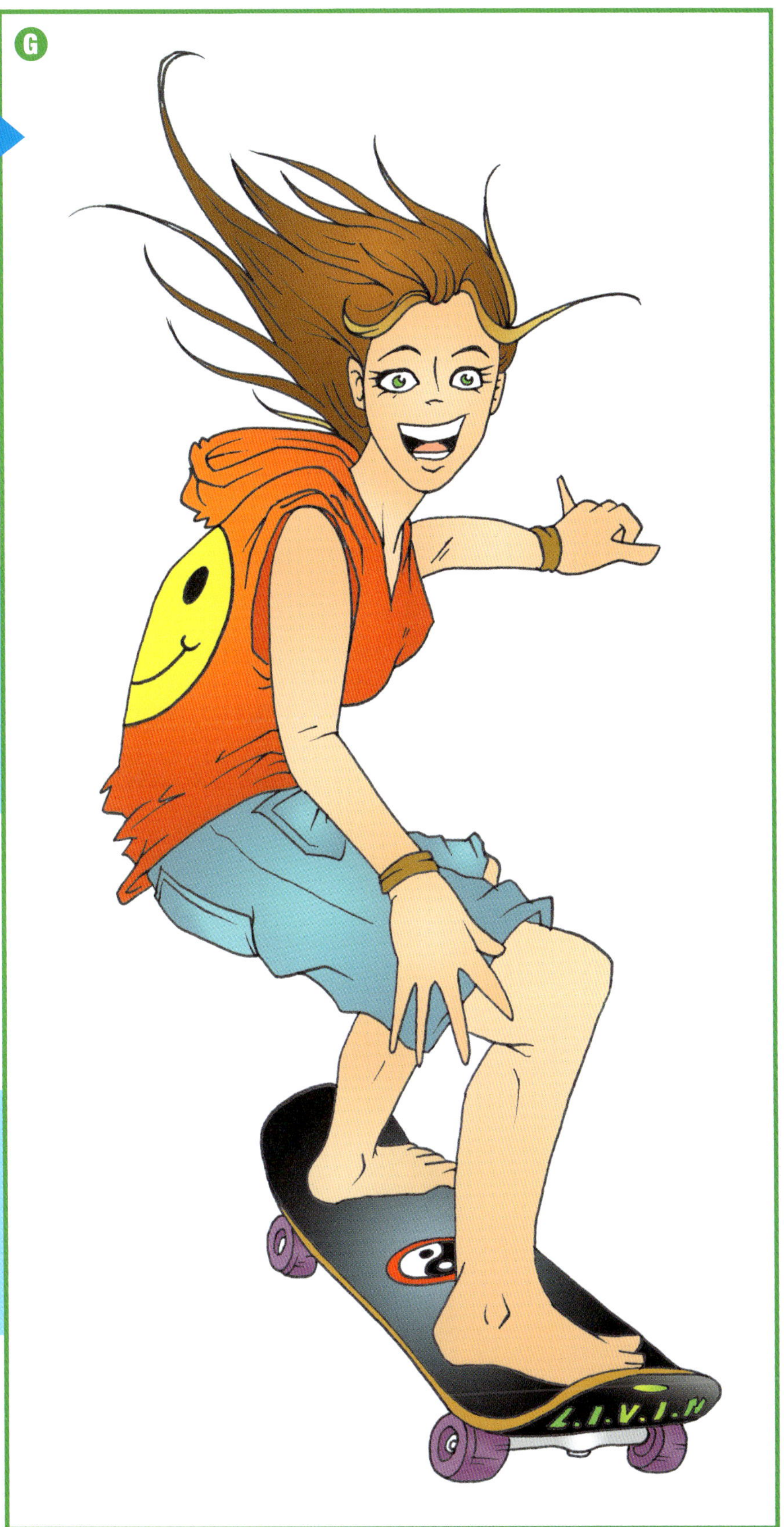

fan shape as a guide. She's wearing a hooded top and cut-offs. The skateboard's wheels are oval-shaped.

E Your skateboarder should be looking almost finished by now. To make her clothes look more realistic, draw creases where the wind is blowing the fabric, and where her body is hunched over. Her skateboard and top need some graphics. Remember, you can do whatever you want with the graphic—maybe put on the names of bands you're into or draw on some of your favorite cartoon characters.

F Once you're happy with the finished pencil sketch, you can draw over the pencil lines with a black pen, and erase any lines that you don't need.

G Color in your skateboarding girl using paints, colored pencils, felt-tip pens, or a computer. Using bright, strong tones really lifts your design up off of the page and adds to the positive atmosphere.

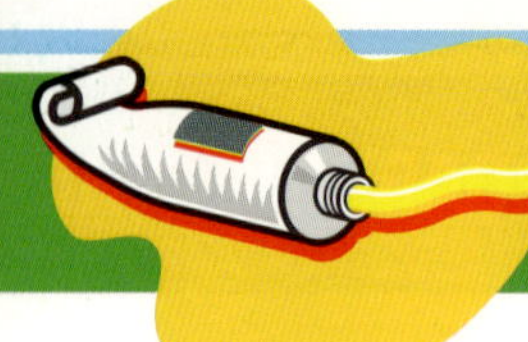

STEP 1

A

B

C

A The main element of your Formula 1 race car is a large rectangle drawn in the center of your page. This is roughly twice as long as it is high, but don't worry about being exact. Draw a center line running vertically through your rectangle as this will help you in the next few stages.

B Using your center line as a guide, draw a long, thin diamond shape through the center of your rectangle. Start this by drawing a horizontal line just under half an inch below the top of your rectangle. Then draw a triangle above this, and another below. The lower triangle should drop below the base of your rectangle. Draw a circle on the center line of your diamond—this is going to be your driver's helmet.

C Draw a large oval in the center of the diamond shape you drew in Step B. This will become the car's cockpit. Next, draw a thin rectangular "wing" behind the diamond, at roughly the same height as the helmet.

D Because you're drawing the wheels head-on, they are rectangular. The rear wheels are half the size of the front wheels, and are partly covered by both the car body and front wheels. Join the rear fender to the main body by two triangles, and start to sketch the detail onto the driver's visor and windshield.

2

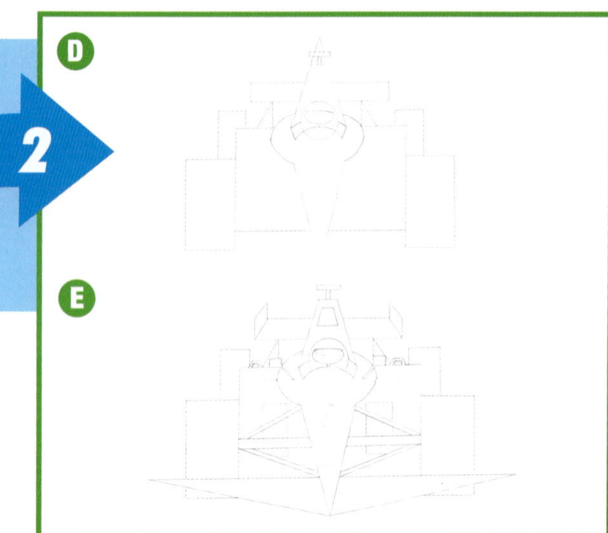

3

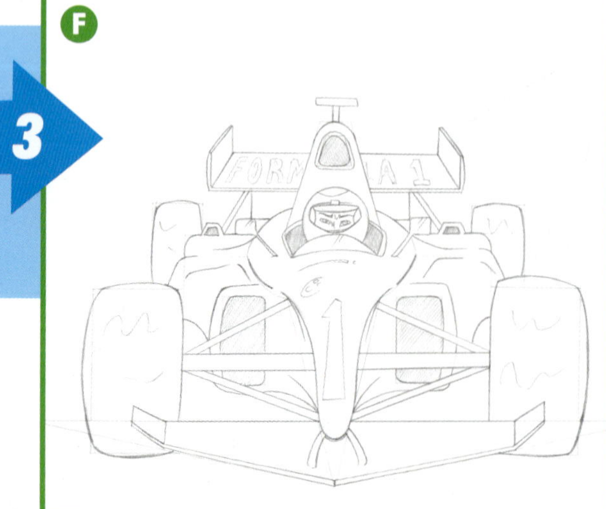

4

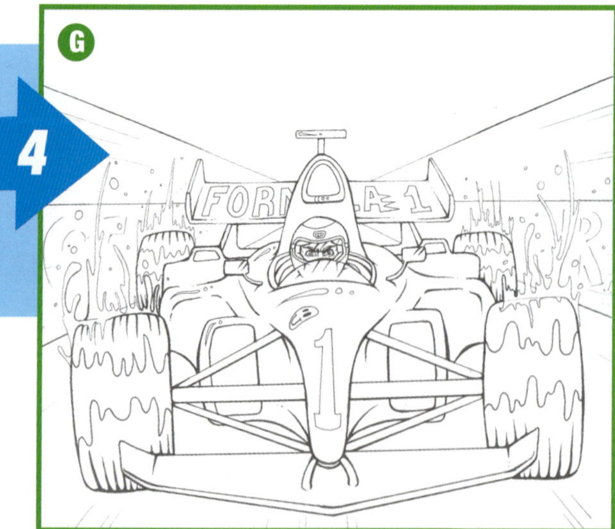

E Chop the top off of your diamond shape and draw a tee-bar on top. Draw a vent below this, and turn up the edges of the rear fender. Next, draw side-mirrors on either side of the cockpit and sketch in your driver's face behind the visor. Finally, we move on to the front section of your car. The axles that connect each wheel to the chassis form a diamond shape. The front spoiler is a large, flat triangle, and the front vents are dark rectangles, hidden behind thc axles.

F Round off those sharp edges—a F1 race car needs to be aerodynamic. The wheels are given a shine to make it look as if the track is wet, and the car is covered in decals—a huge "No. 1" on the hood, with a smiley face and the words "Formula 1" across the rear fender.

5

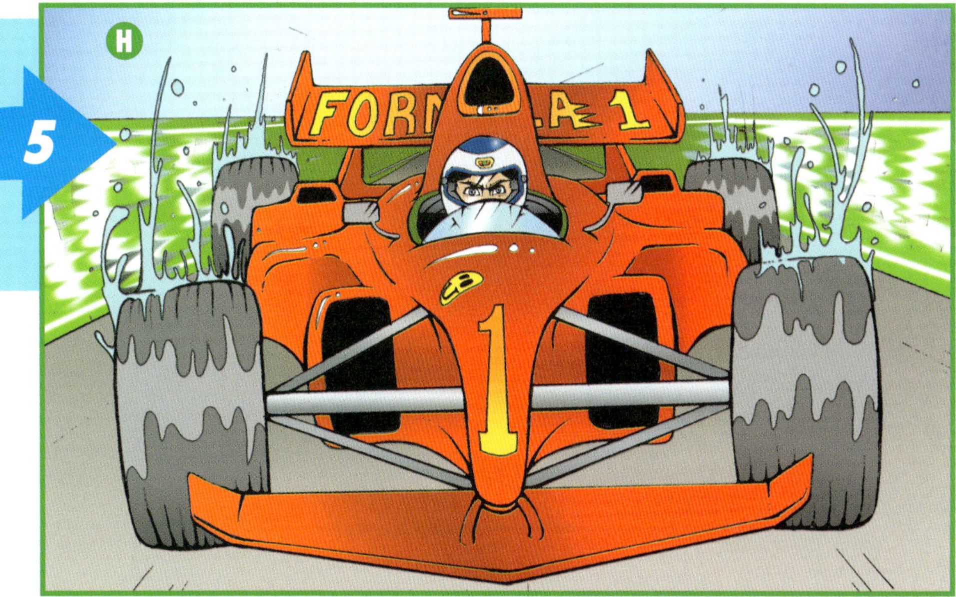

G Draw ovcr your F1 race car with a drawing pen, wait a few minutes for the ink to dry, and then erase any remaining pencil lines.

H The final stage of the picture involves adding the color. Use bright colors, as these will make your race car leap off the page—primary colors are great!

I J Adding speed lines or drawing a close-up section of the cockpit will add dramatic impact to your race car. When only the driver and cockpit are showing, this shifts attention to the racer's expression of determination. In this kind of picture, only a suggestion of the car is needed.

6

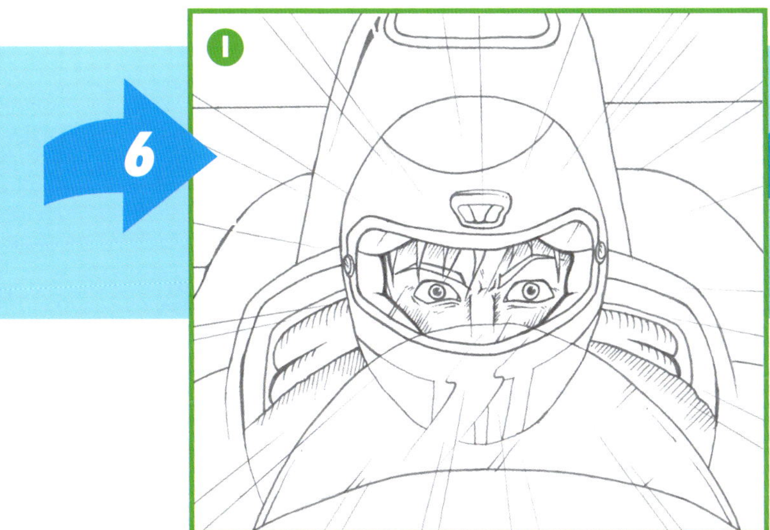

7

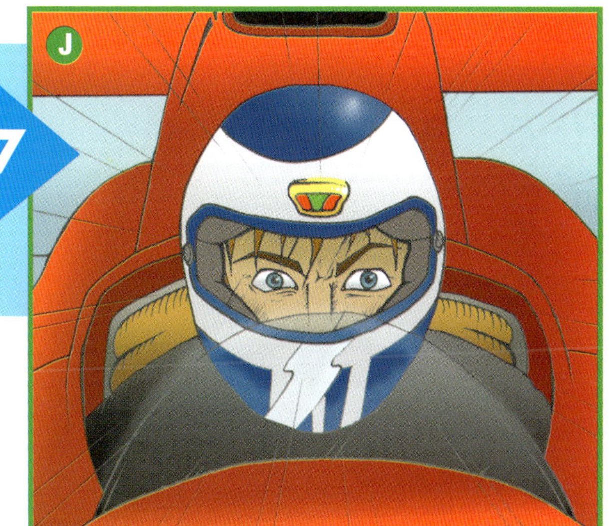

STEP 1

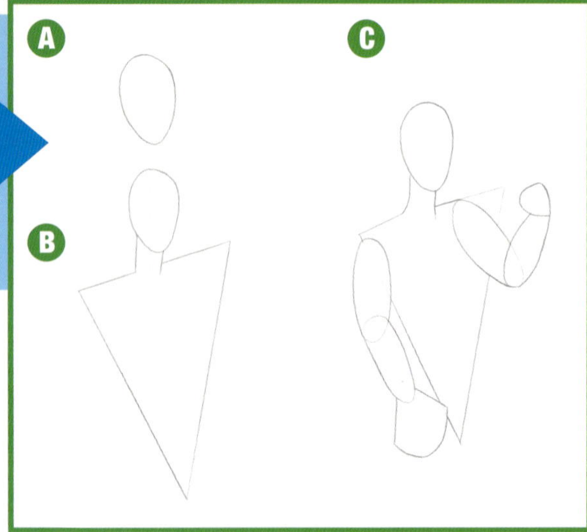

A Draw a feint vertical line down the center of your page. This is going to be helpful when placing the shapes that make up your surfer. Next draw an oval shape on the line, quite high up on the page.

B Your surfer's body is a large triangle shape, slanting over to the right so that the "shoulder" line lifts on the right-hand side. This is joined to the head by a simple two-line neck shape.

C It's time to give your surfer some arms. Draw two long ovals for each arm. The left arm is slightly bent, with a fan-shaped hand. His other arm is going to hold his surfboard, so it is bent at a sharper angle, with a semicircular hand ready to grab the rail.

2

D

D The legs of your surfer are constructed in the same way as the arms—in three connecting shapes. These ovals should be about 1.5 times the length of those used for his arms, and a little wider too. His feet are triangular and the right leg should be slightly bent. The other leg is straight and lines up with the center line. This is his "weight-bearing" leg.

E Begin sketching in some simple detail, such as his wavy hair, his sweater, and his shorts. Use the arm and leg shapes as a template for drawing the outline of his clothes. Round off his triangular feet to form his shoes and draw where they meet his legs. Next, draw his

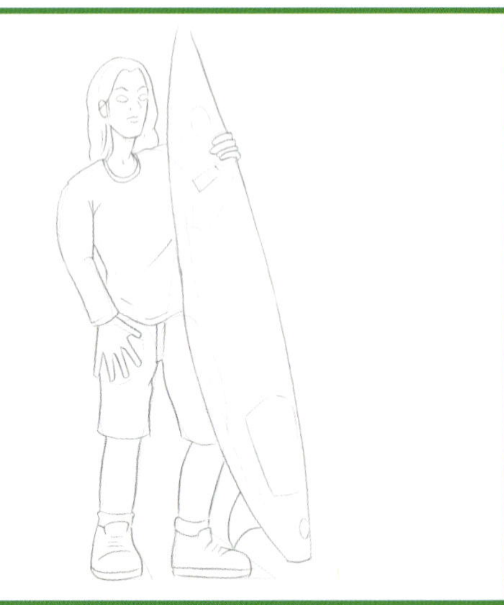

4

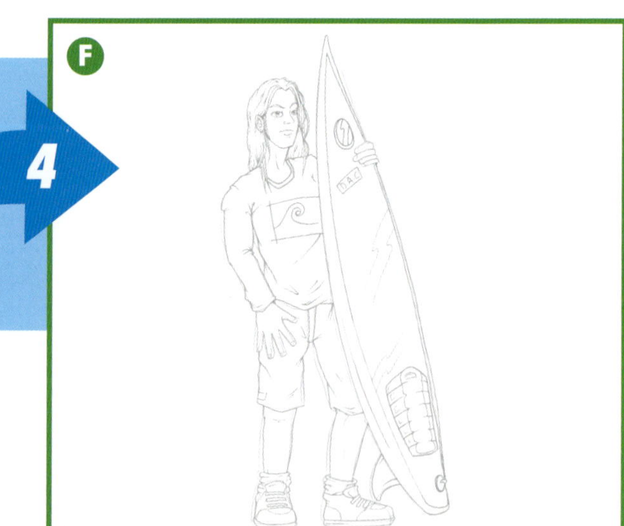

5

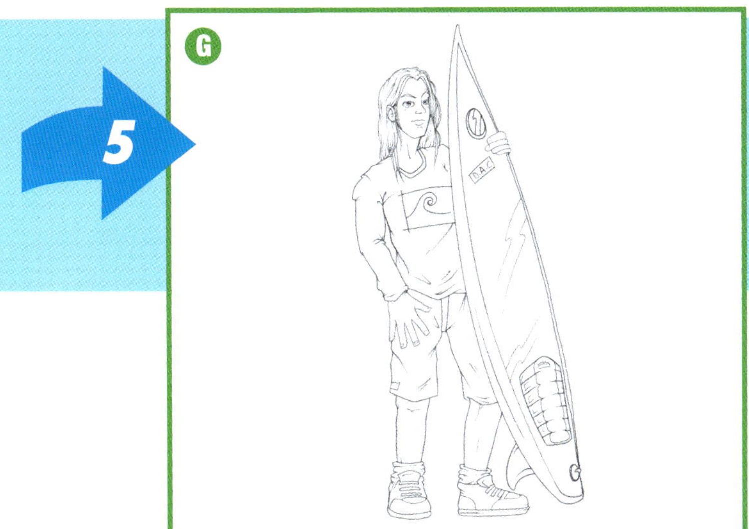

6

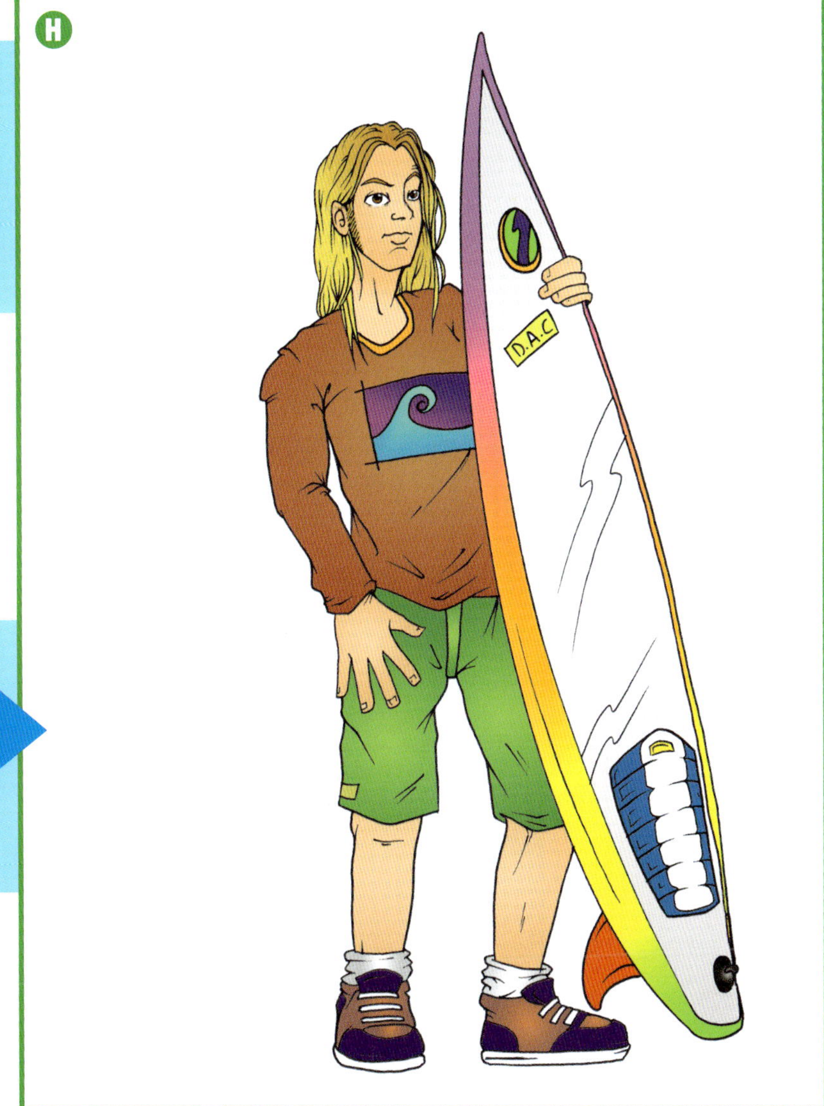

board—this is a large, thin almond shape with a curved fin on the bottom. Finally, sketch his eyes, nose, and lips.

F Now try to give your surfer's clothes a more lived-in, baggy appearance by using jagged lines—try to get rid of any rounded lines. Add final detail to his face, such as the pupils in his eyes and his sideburns. Make sure he looks amped-up and ready for the next morning's session in the surf!

G When you're happy with the overall look of your surfer, you can draw over him using a fine black pen. Only draw over the lines you want to keep, and then erase the pencil lines—he's ready to color!

H Time to choose some colors for your surfer's clothes. Check out the colors of your clothes, or the ones your friends are wearing, for ideas. The surfer here is wearing earthy shades, but his surfboard is brightly colored. This was the look in the '80s and '90s! You may want to use colors that are easier on the eye, though.

By using the same frame as your surfer, you can actually turn him into a daredevil snowboarder, simply by altering the clothes and the board. Follow the steps for the surfer up until Step D, and then follow the instructions over the page to create your very own snowboarder who'll be ready to risk life and limb to take on those death-defying slopes.

→

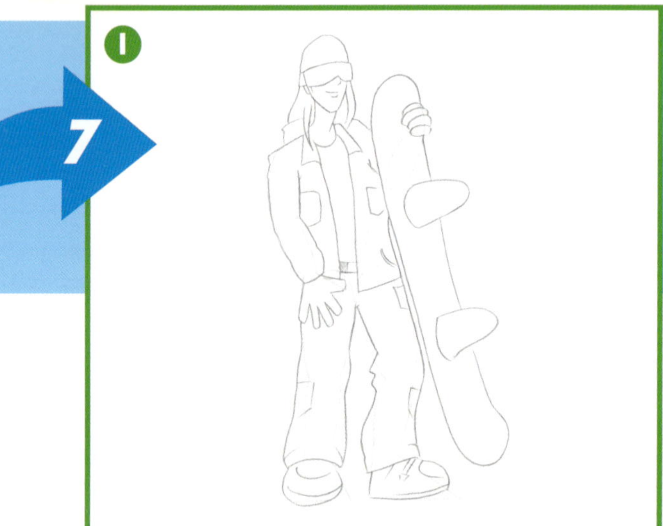

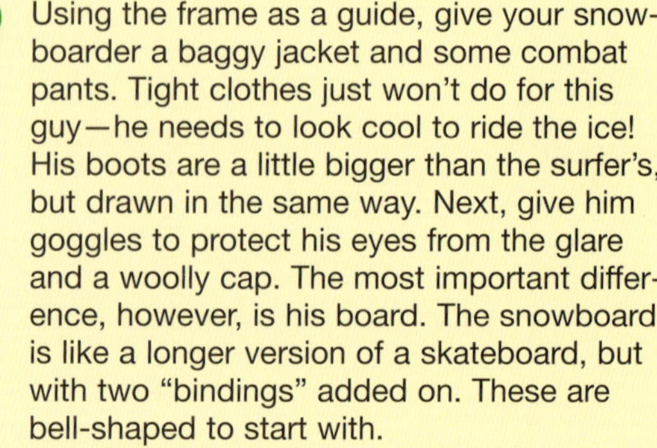

I Using the frame as a guide, give your snowboarder a baggy jacket and some combat pants. Tight clothes just won't do for this guy—he needs to look cool to ride the ice! His boots are a little bigger than the surfer's, but drawn in the same way. Next, give him goggles to protect his eyes from the glare and a woolly cap. The most important difference, however, is his board. The snowboard is like a longer version of a skateboard, but with two "bindings" added on. These are bell-shaped to start with.

J Add lots of crease lines to his pants and jacket. Draw reflection lines on his board and goggles, and the pockets on his clothing. His woolly hat has a flame emblem on it. The snowboard's bindings have a scooped back section, with four screw holes in the base of each one and two curved straps to hold keep his boots in place when he's riding the snowboard.

K When you're happy with your picture, and you've traced over it with your black pen, erase the pencil lines ready for coloring.

L The snowboarder's jacket is gray-and-green, his pants are blue, and his board is an icy cool shade of blue.

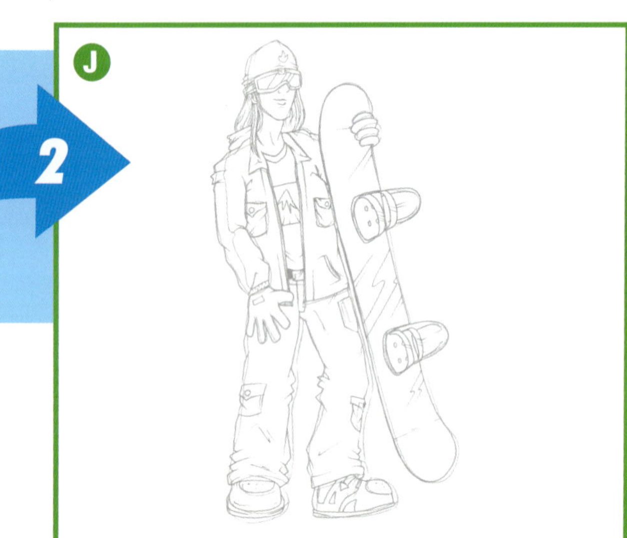

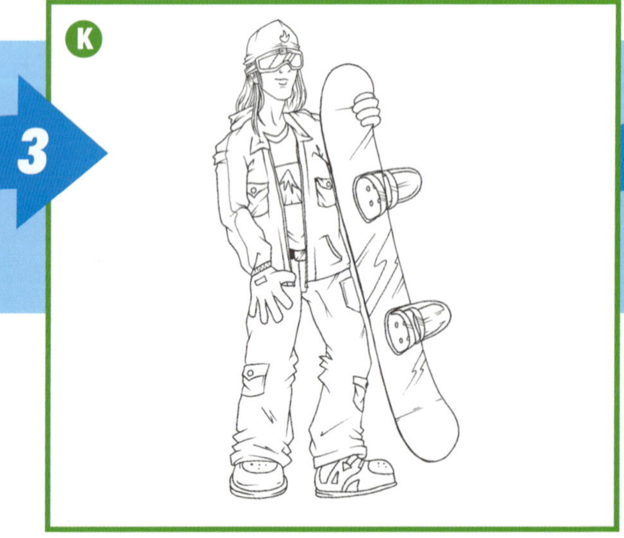

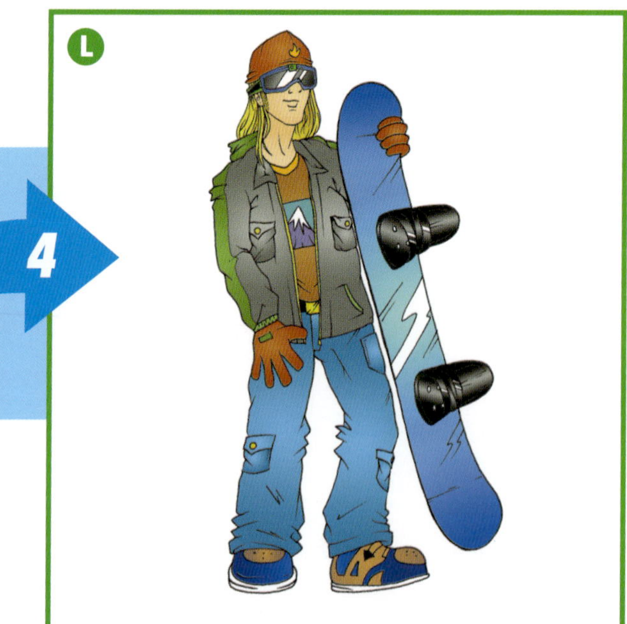

DINOSAURS

The word "dinosaur" means Terrible Lizard. Well, they're not so "terrible" now because they all died out around 65 million years ago, and to this day nobody is quite sure why. Scientists believe that a huge asteroid may have collided with Earth, causing a phenomenal impact that threw up a massive blanket of suffocating dust.

When dinosaurs did roam the Earth, however, they were the kings of their world. The reign of the dinosaur was divided into three main periods, the Triassic, Jurassic, and Cretaceous. The earliest of these, the Triassic period, dates as far back as 225 million years ago.

Dinosaurs flourished during the Jurassic and Cretaceous periods. They included the terrifying Tyrannosaurus Rex. who was one of the Cretaceous period's largest carnivores. The Tyrannosaurus is also one of our favorite dinosaurs.

In this chapter, along with T-Rex, you'll be learning how to draw the herbivores, Stegosaurus and Brachiosaurus. You will also find out how to create an airborne Pterodactyl.

Due to the three separate time periods, some of these creatures would never have had the chance to come into contact with each other, but there are no time boundaries in drawing, so you'll be able to draw them all on the same piece of paper if you want. So hop into your time machine and get ready to go Jurassic!

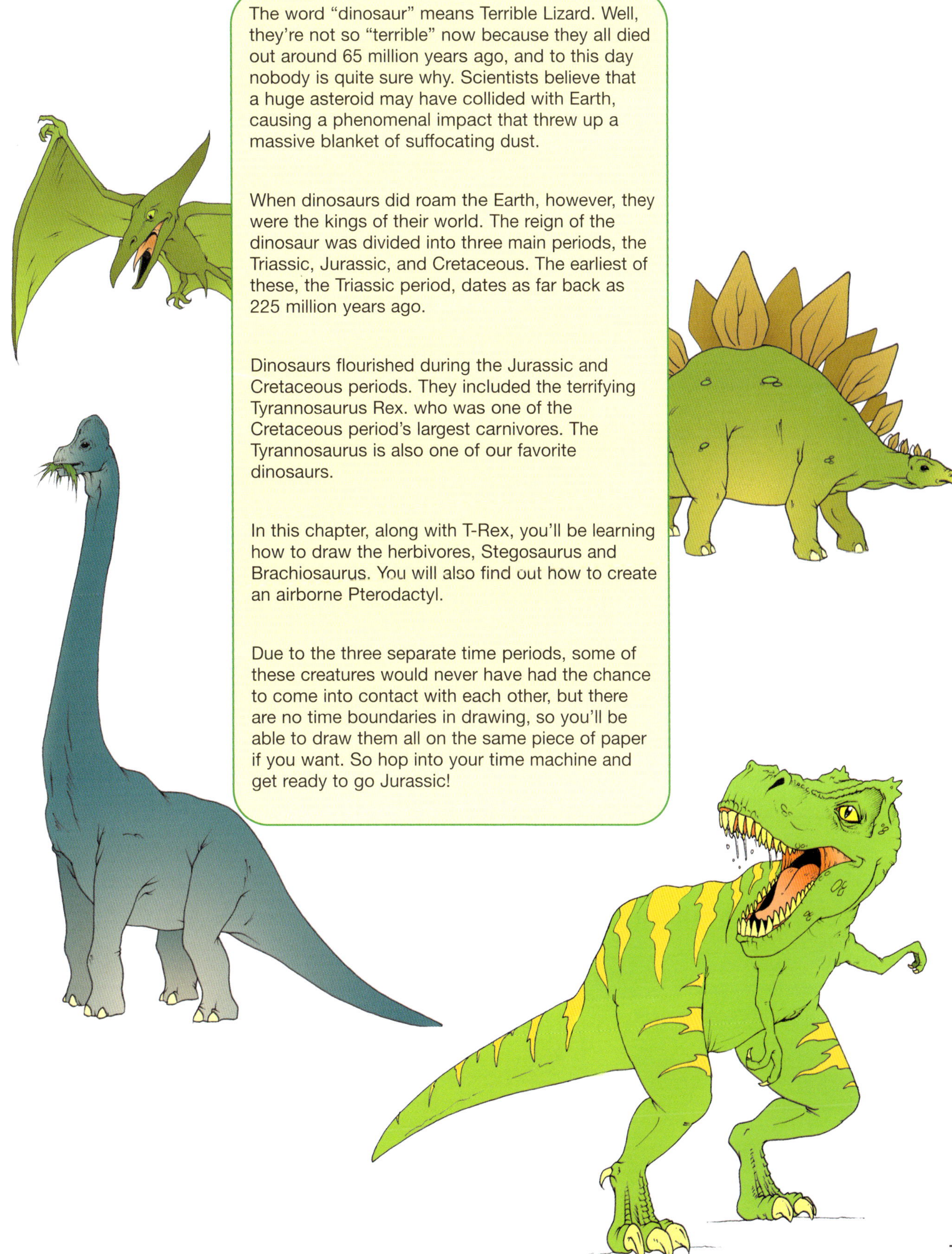

STEP 1

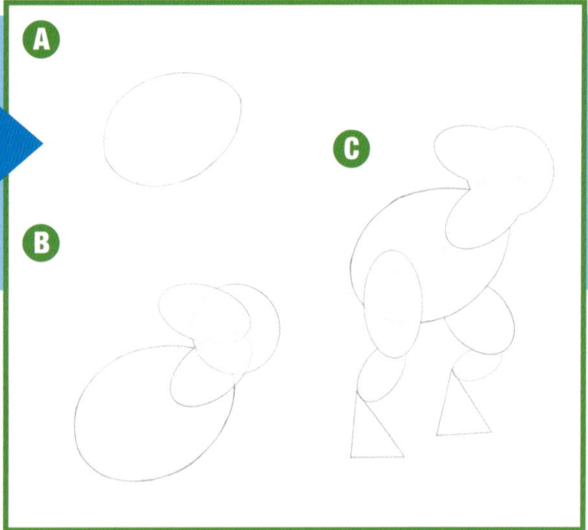

A The king of all dinosaurs began life as an egg. Draw an egg-shape at an angle on your page, with a feint line running through the center, which will help you to place his tail and head.

B Your T-Rex has a head consisting of a circle joined to the “egg” body, and two large oval shapes for his mouth, which is going to be wide open as he roars.

C T-Rex’s legs are drawn using two overlapping ovals and a triangle for each foot. The leg on the right side is partially hidden behind the body, and it should be slightly smaller as it is further away.

2

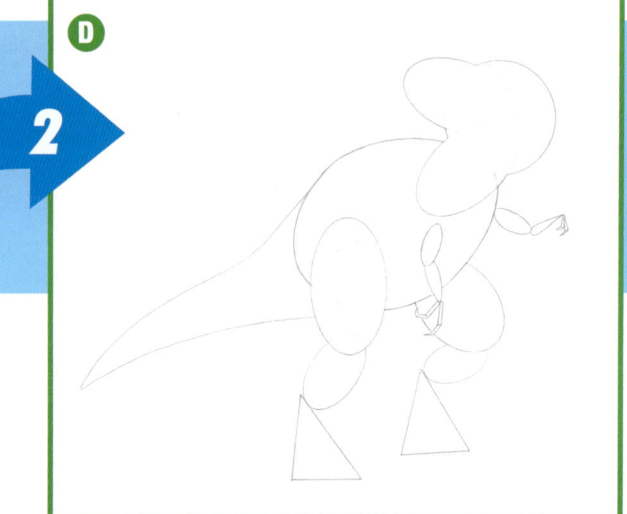

D Tyrannosaurus, although a carnivore, only had very small arms. Draw them just below the head, using two thin ovals which end in two-clawed hands. Next, his tail is a long triangle shape. This would have helped him balance, so don’t draw it dragging along in the dirt!

E After your framework is finished, you can start adding the features that make T-Rex so ferocious. Sharp, triangular teeth fill his mouth, and he has claws on his hands and feet. Give him small, beady eyes and flared nostrils. Join the body shapes together to produce a smooth outline of your dinosaur.

3

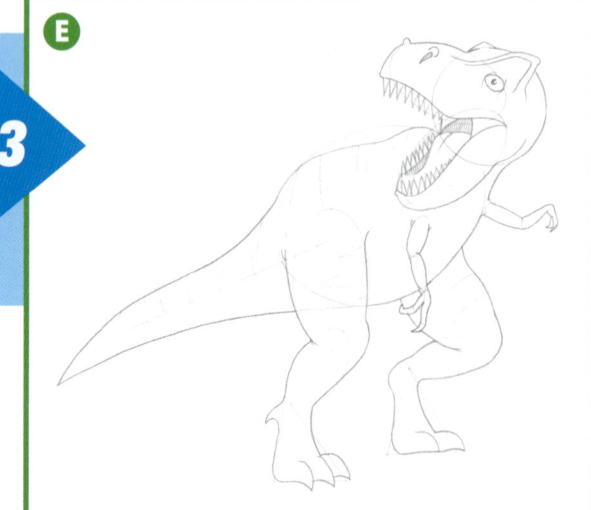

4

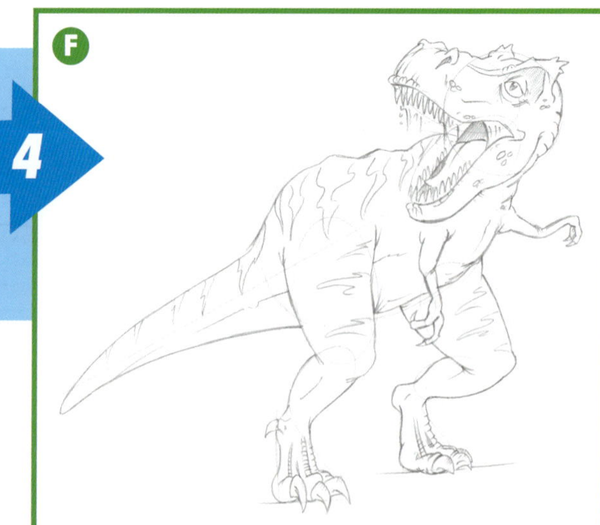

5

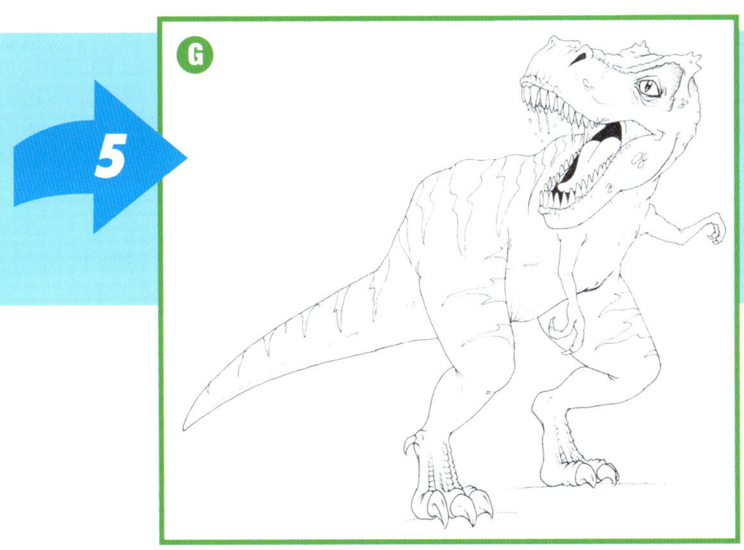

F Sketch detail onto his skin, such as wrinkles where the legs meet the body, and scales. Emphasize the look of his feet with lines of thick ridges running down to his toenails. You could also put a pattern on his skin. The one used here features stripes for camouflage.

G Before adding any color to your Tyrannosaurus, draw over your pencil version in black pen and erase the pencil lines.

H Color your "King of Lizards" in earthy tones, such as green or brown. This would have helped T-Rex to hide in the undergrowth while stalking his prey.

6

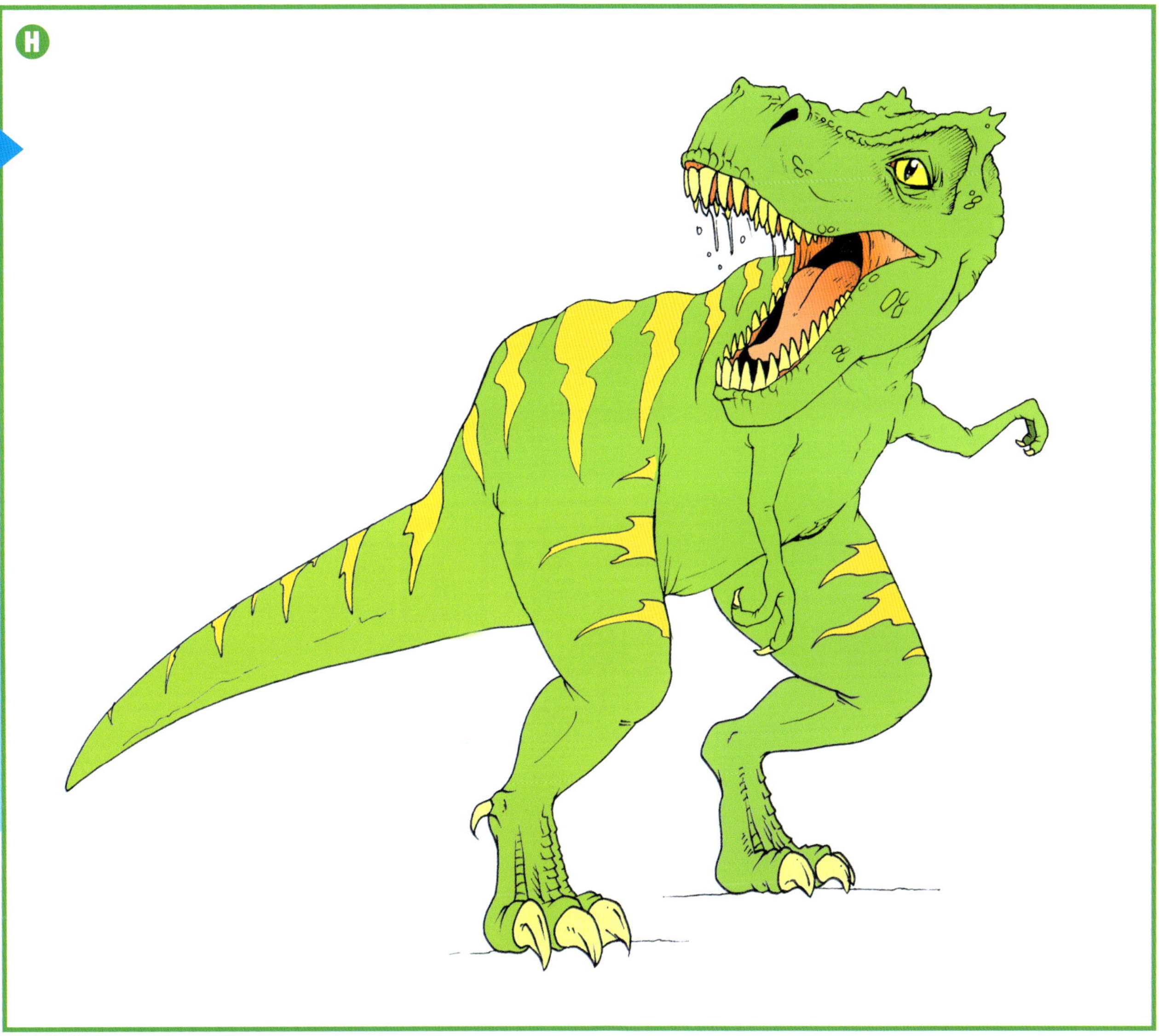

H

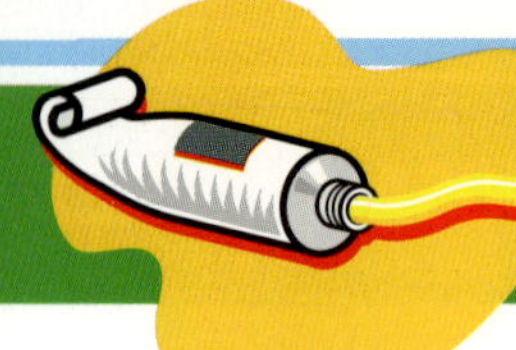

STEP 1

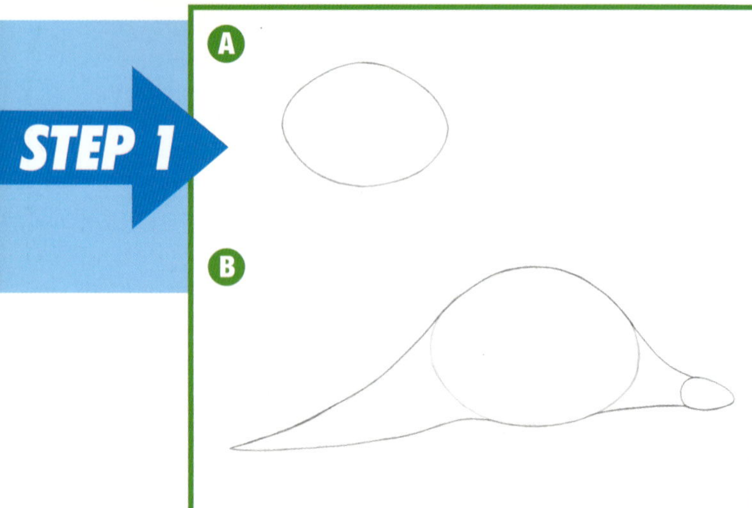

A The Stegosaurus's body is shaped like a large egg. Start by drawing this shape in the center of your paper.

B Now draw his head and tail on either side of the egg-shaped body. The tail is shaped like a large, curved triangle, and the head is a very small egg shape, joined to the body by a short neck.

C Your dinosaur will need some legs. These are constructed using an oval shape for the upper part of the leg and a bent "tree stump" shape for the lower part. Remember that two of his legs are hidden behind his body, so don't be too firm with the pencil as you will have to erase these lines later.

D Now you can start adding some simple details to the dinosaur's frame. Stegosaurus is best known for the huge plates of bone that line his back. These are diamond-shaped. He also has curved spikes on the end of his tail, a beaked mouth, and rounded toenails.

E Finally, your pencil sketch should include some texture on the dinosaur's skin. Stegosaurus would probably have had tough, scaly skin like many of today's reptiles. You can get the effect of this by drawing small clusters of two or three ovals. Next, put some folds on his legs and add detail to his eye and back plates.

2

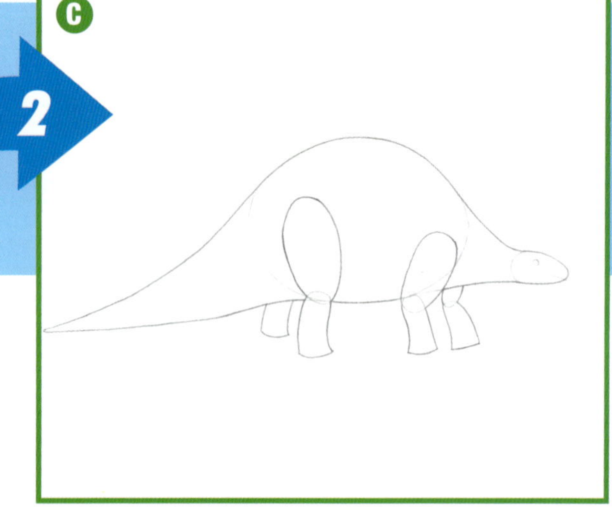

3

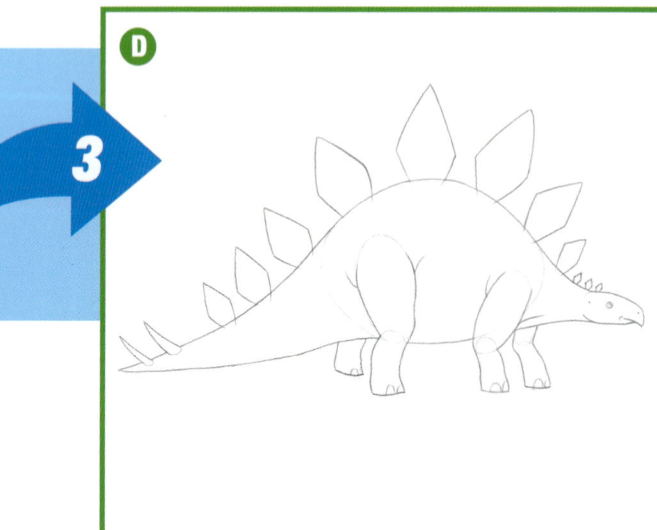

4

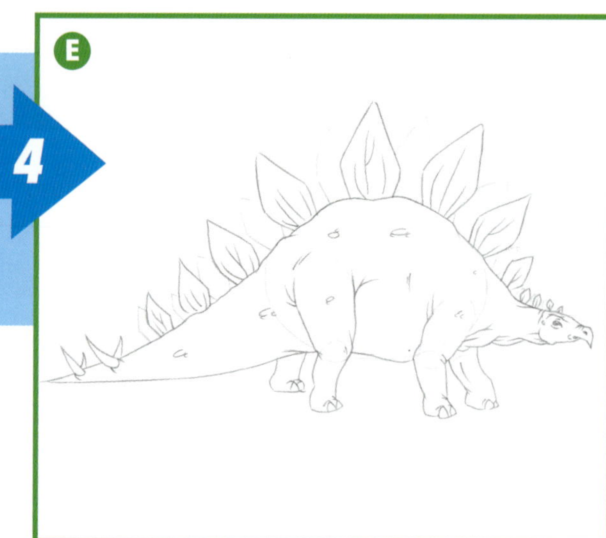

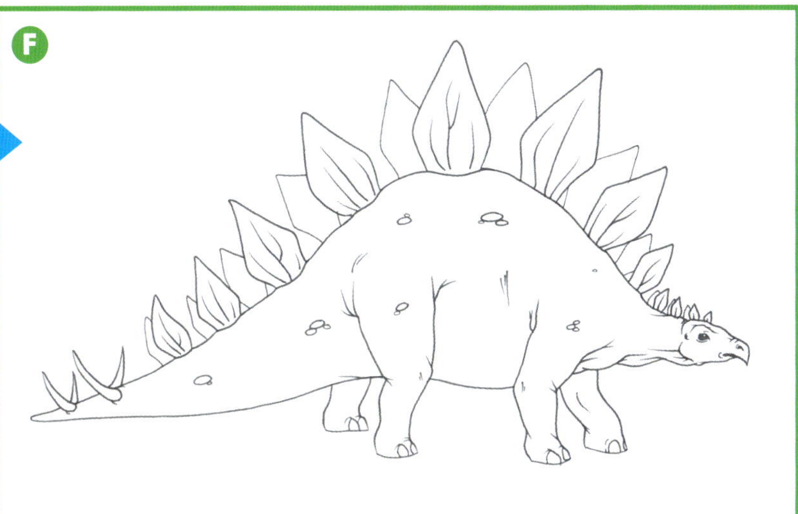

F Once you have all the details that you want, you can draw over the lines in black pen, before erasing the original pencil framework.

G Nobody is exactly sure what color dinosaurs would have been, so it's up to your imagination. The Stegosaurus here is green, to give him a reptilian look, but your picture could be completed using brighter colors.

G

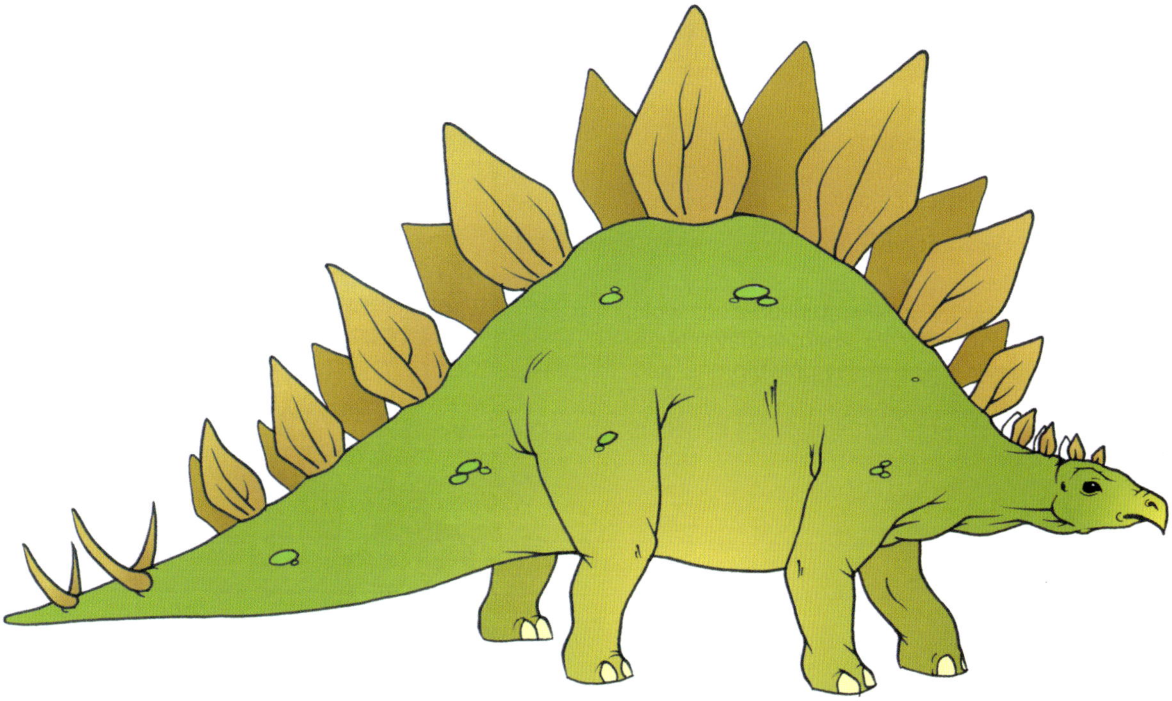

STEP 1

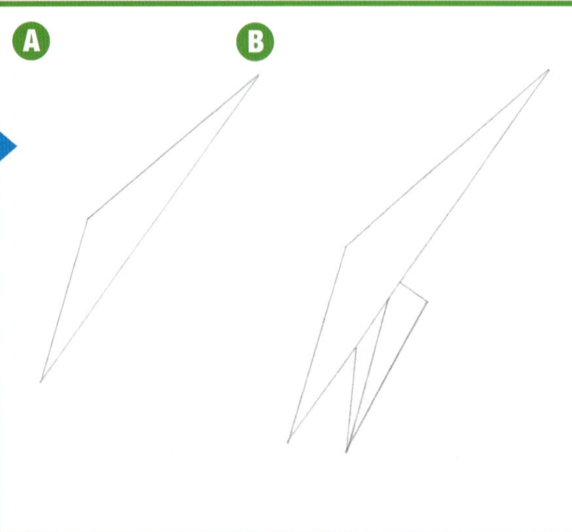

2

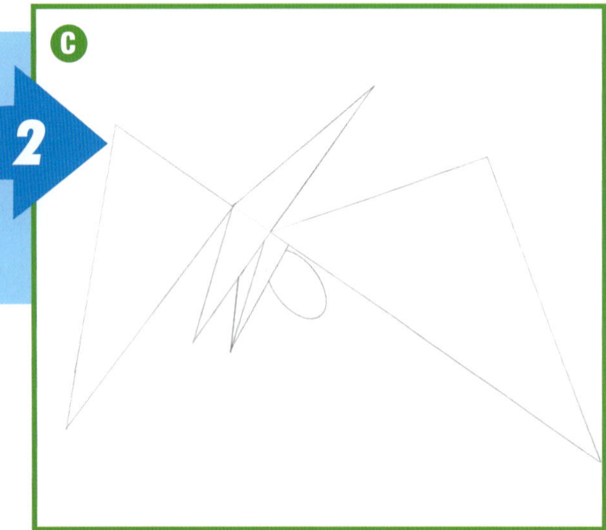

3

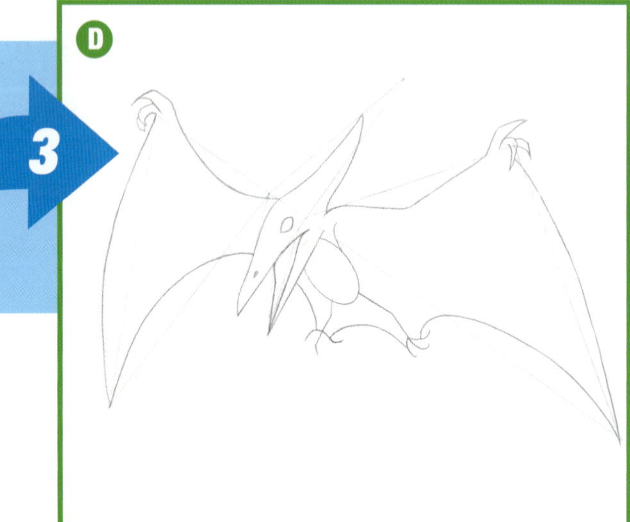

4

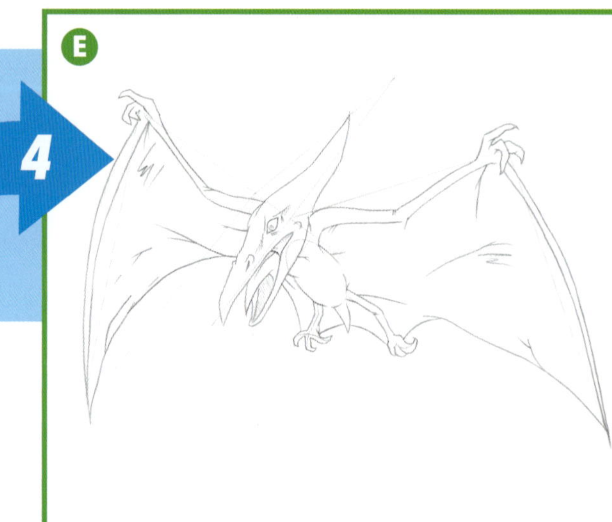

A Start your Pterodactyl by drawing a long, thin triangle in the center of your paper. Make sure that it is at a 45-degree angle, and that the top half is slightly longer than the bottom half. This is going to be the head.

B Now draw his mouth, which is also triangular. Make this shape slightly overlap the first, and run a line from the larger triangle through to the tip of this triangle.

C Your Pterodactyl needs wings if he is to fly; these are also triangular. Draw a large triangle on the right side of the head, with the base at 90 degrees to the main head shape and with a slightly smaller triangle to the left side; this triangle is smaller because it is further away in the picture. Finally, your Pterodactyl's body is an oval shape tucked under the head.

D Time to work on the dinosaur's simple details. Using your frame as a guide, start to round off the sharp edges. Draw some stick legs on the body and join these to the wings. Begin adding the facial features and some claws on the tips of his wings.

E Draw some final details on your Pterodactyl, such as the tongue and the thin "arms" that connect the body to the claws on the tips of the wings. Thicken the stick legs and draw a pointed tail. Next, you can sketch some creases and wrinkles on his skin to give the picture depth.

5

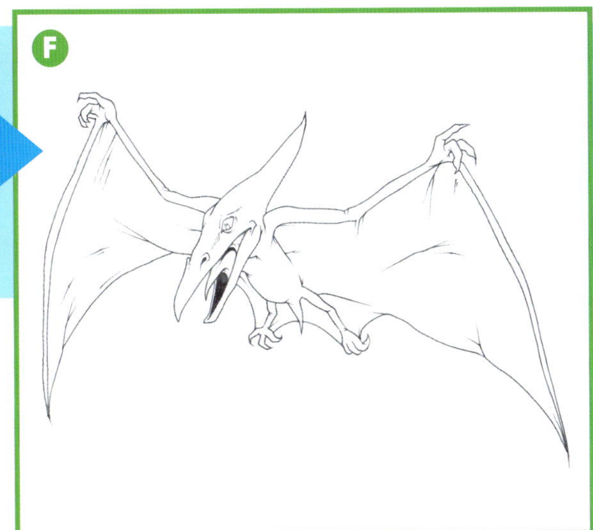

F Draw over your pencil sketch with a black pen in order to create your final outline. Then erase the pencil, and he's ready to color.

G Lastly, it's time to color your Pterodactyl. Greens and browns always look effective on dinosaurs, but you can use any color you like. Color the tongue a fleshy pink and the eye a reptilian lime green.

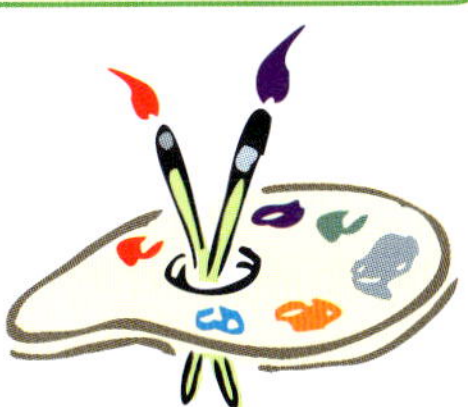

G

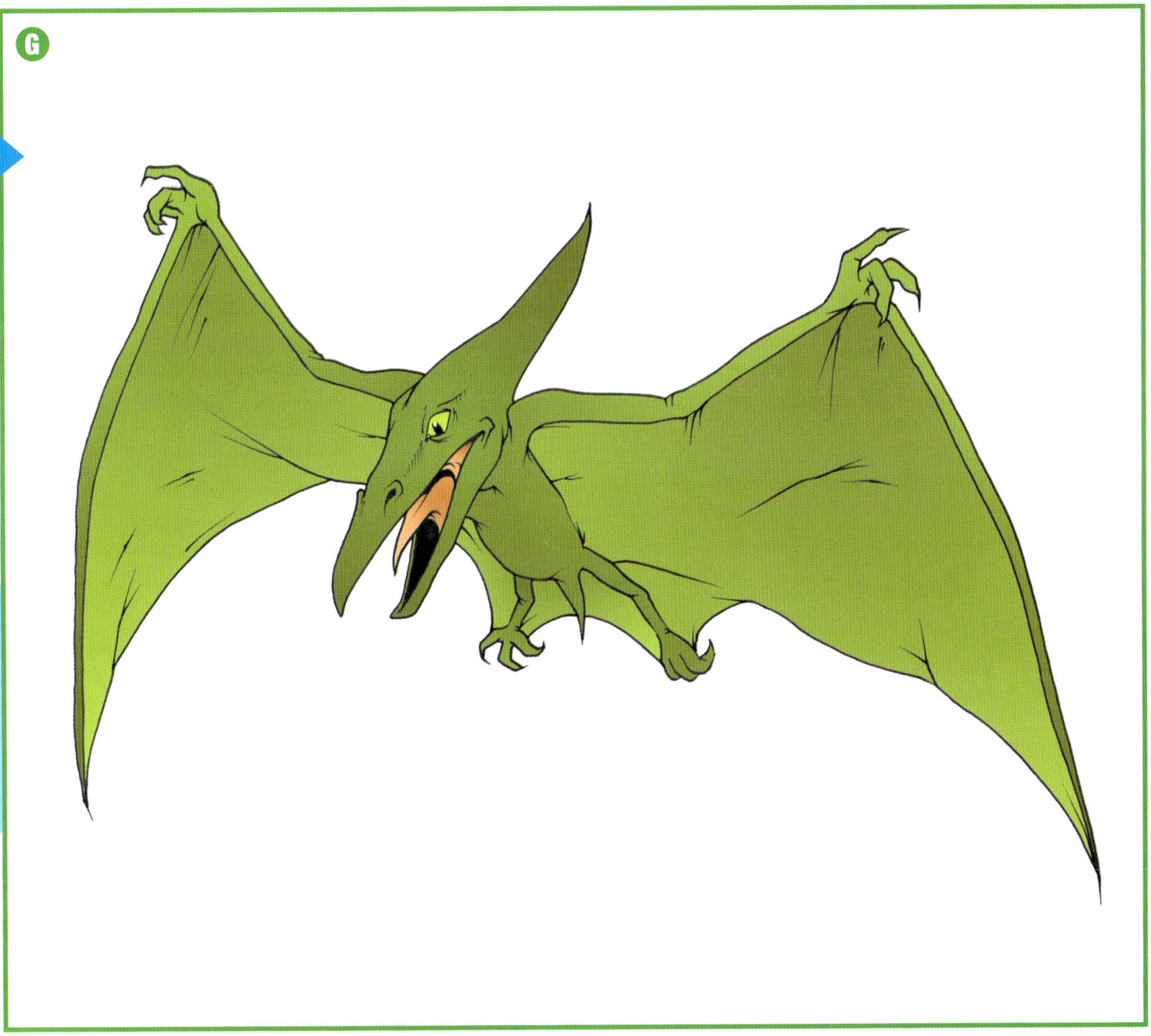

HOW TO DRAW BRACHIOSAURUS

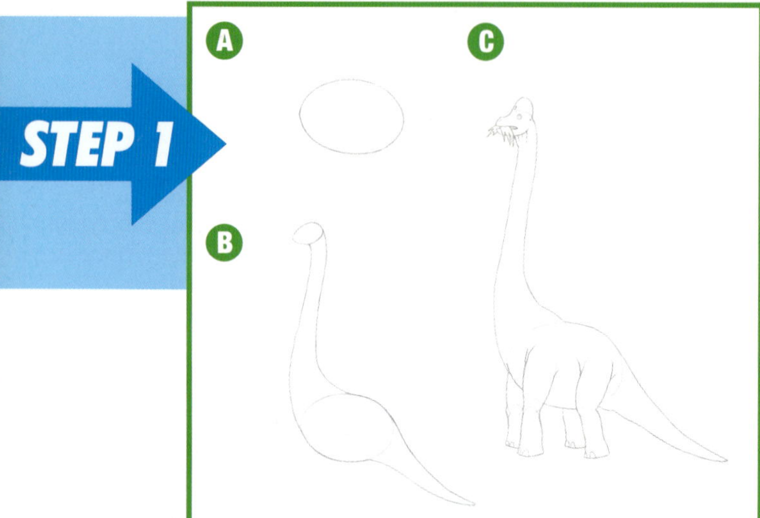

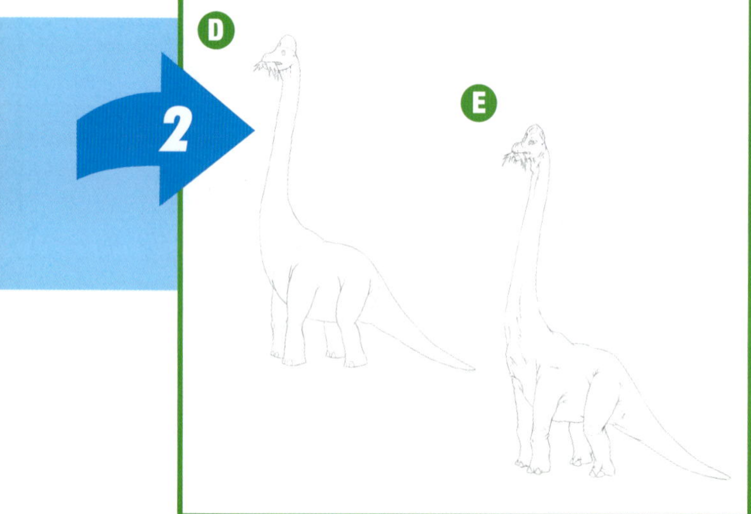

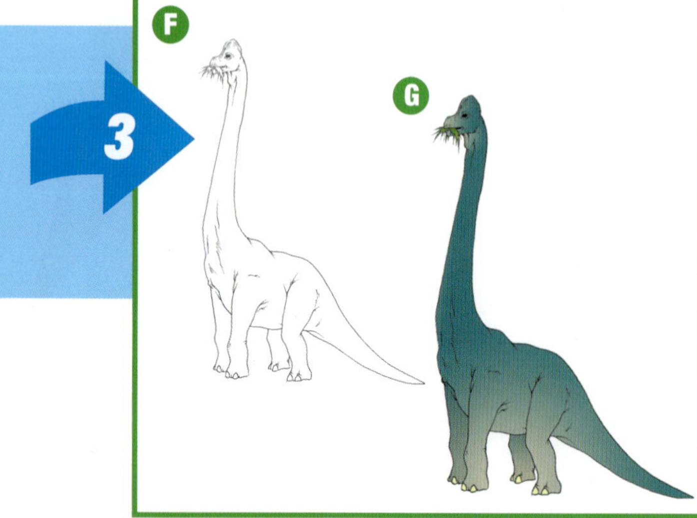

A The Brachiosaurus begins the same way as the Stegosaurus, as a large egg shape on your paper. Make sure you draw it closer to the bottom of your paper—you'll find out why in step B.

B Draw the Brachiosaurus's tail in the same style as that of the Stegosaurus—a large, curved triangular shape attached to the "egg" body. Now, the reason for drawing this dino at the bottom of your page is to make room for the dinosaur's neck. It is similar in shape to the tail, only twice as long and joined to his tiny egg-shaped head.

C The Brachiosaurus's legs are pretty much the same as the Stegosaurus's, but longer. The upper leg is a large oval, and the lower leg is slightly bell-shaped.

D Add some simple detail to your dinosaur's frame, such as wrinkles in his skin and toenails on his feet. The Brachiosaurus had a bony, oval ridge on the top of its skull. These dinosaurs were herbivores, so you could give yours some grass to chew on.

E In the final pencil stage, enhance the thick, aged appearance of the skin. The Brachiosaurus pictured here has fairly smooth skin, except for a few wrinkles, but you may want yours to have some scales.

F Trace over your drawing using a black felt tip or drawing pen. Then erase the pencil lines, and your dinosaur is ready to color.

G You can fill in your Brachiosaurus with any choice of color you want. It's a good idea to shade from one color to another, as this will make him look three-dimensional.

MONSTERS

Have you ever been told a really good monster story? The kind that keeps you awake at night, wondering if the creatures you heard about are lurking inside your closet waiting to burst out?

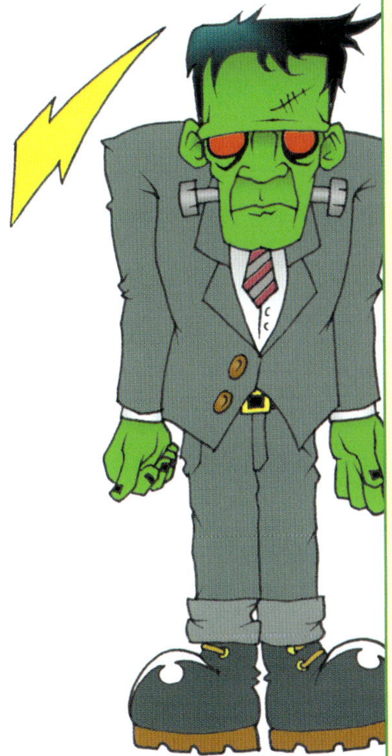

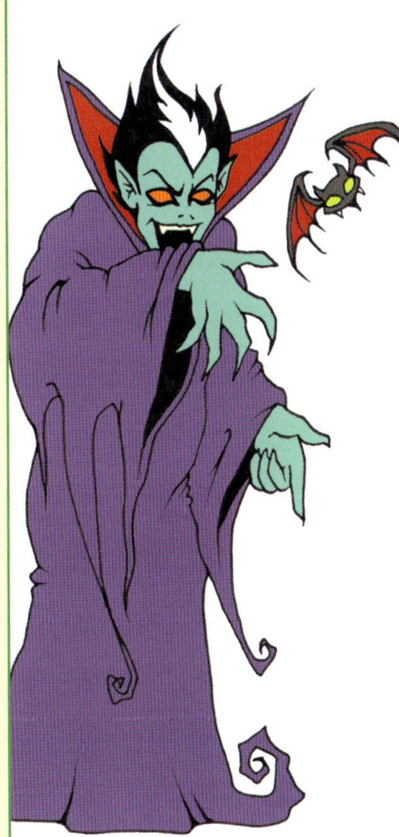

There are many "favorite" monsters, and you'll find three of the most popular creatures featured over the next few pages. First, there's the dreaded vampire. It is said that anyone bitten by this fanged creature in human form is doomed to become one of the "undead." These "undead" then survive by drinking the blood of their victims. Vampires are only able to walk the earth after the sun has set. Direct sunlight or a sharpened stake through the heart are said to be sure-fire ways of disposing of this evil fiend.

Then, we come to "Frank." He was created by his master, a mad scientist, out of various human body parts. He was brought to life when the bolts on his neck were connected to a lightning conductor during an electrical storm. He has no emotions, and feels no pain.

Finally, we have the werewolf. It is said that if a person is bitten by one of these half-man-half-beast creatures, then they will change into a werewolf themselves when there is a full moon. Once the sun comes up, werewolves return to human form until the next full moon. It is also believed that only a silver bullet can kill this beast.

Scared yet? Well, whether you are a fan of horror movies or not, this is definitely a chillingly good chapter to sink your creative teeth into!

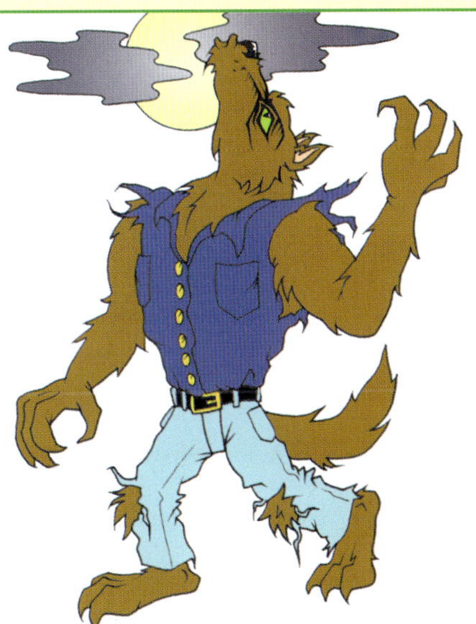

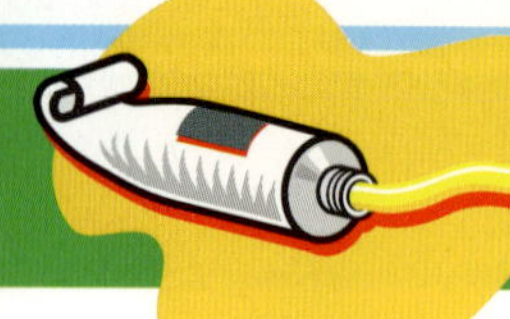

STEP 1

A

B

C

A The first stage of your vampire drawing will look a little like a giant thumb. Draw a feint line down the center of this as it will help in later stages of the picture.

B Draw a triangular collar on top of the thumb shape, slightly overlapping it. Next, your vampire's head should be an oval shape, drawn inside the lower half of the collar.

C Give your vampire tall, spiky hair and a large triangular sleeve on his robe. His hand also starts off as a triangular shape, and the right arm consists of simple blocks.

D Start adding detail to your vampire, such as ripped edges to his sleeves, long pointed fingers, and spiral corners to his cape. You can also begin sketching in the face and hair. Give him narrow, sinister eyes and spiky, raised hair.

E Draw a white stripe down the center of your vampire's hair and give him pointed eyebrows and teeth to match his narrow eyes. Add further detail to his cape and collar. Above one of his shoulders, the vampire has a bat helper, whose frame is a simple circular body with triangular wings.

F Give the vampire's cape a crinkled look by making the spirals of material on his robe more irregular and sharp. Next, add the final touches

2

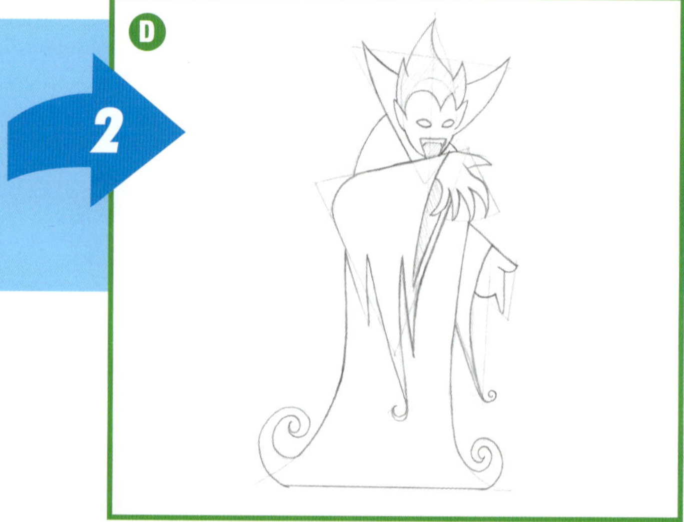

3

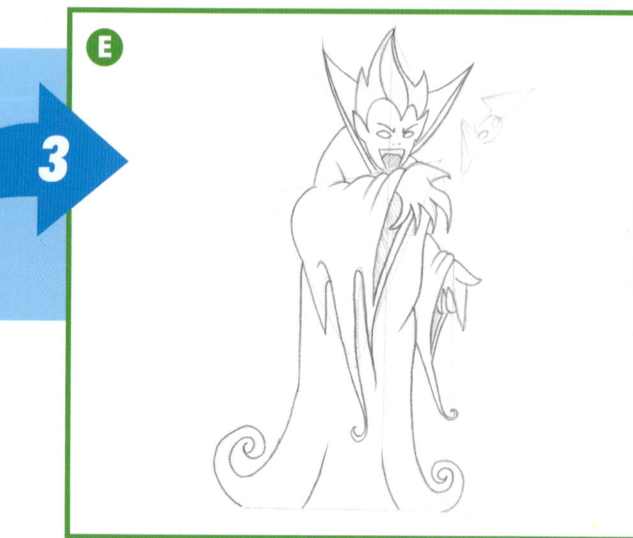

4

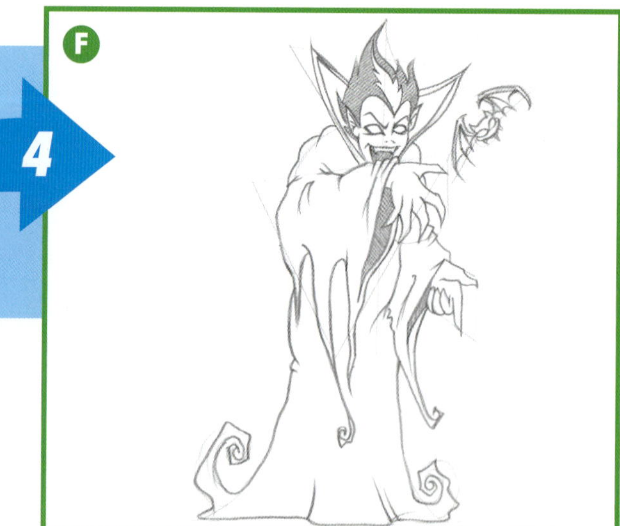

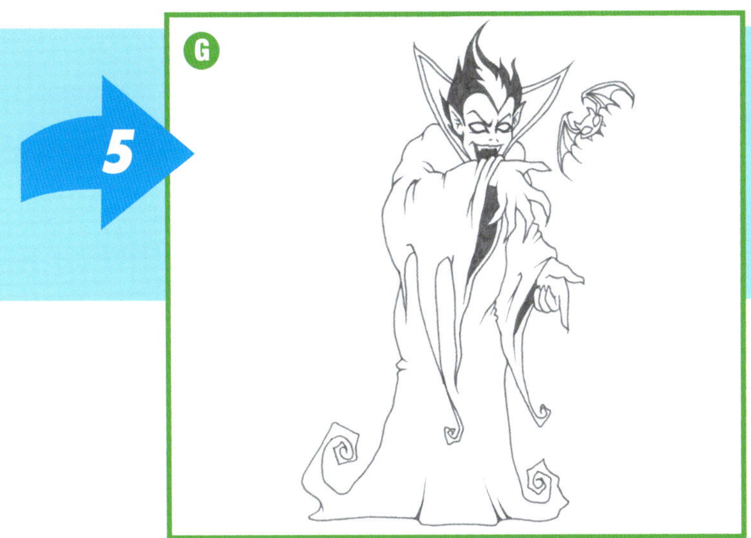

to his face by putting dark rings around his eyes. Finally, his bat helper has evil, almond-shaped eyes, pointed ears, and spiky wings.

G Use a black pen to draw over your design before erasing the remaining pencil lines. This will leave you with a crisp line drawing that's ready to color.

H Use blue-gray tones for the vampire's undead skin. Darker colors are best for his robe, and use red for his brightly glowing eyes. The bat helper should also have evil, glowing eyes, so go with a light green color. As you can see, together the vampire and the bat make a scary pair!

6

H

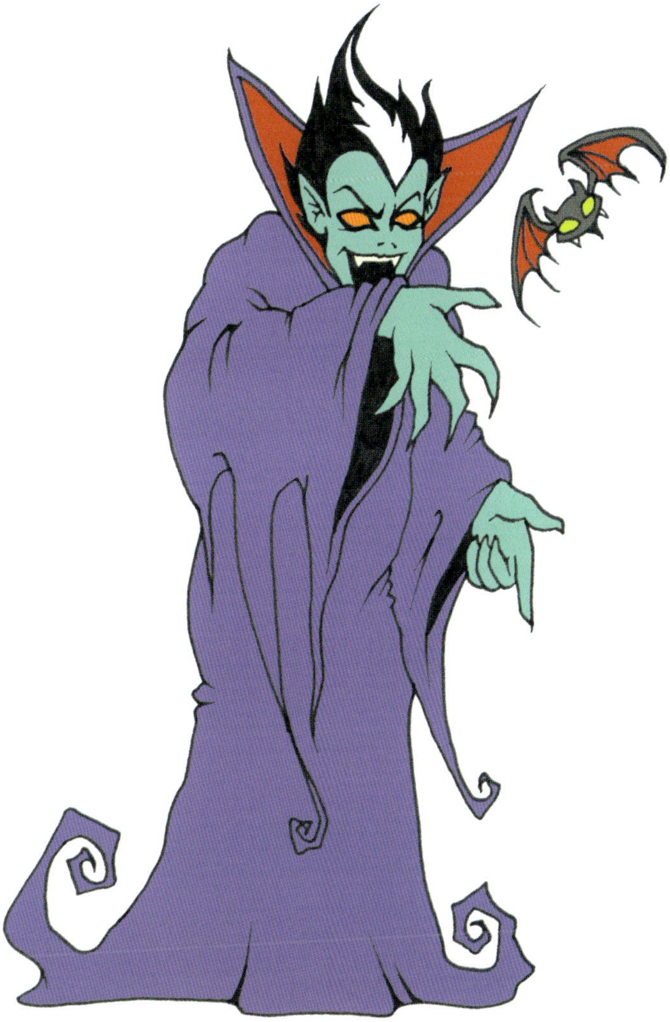

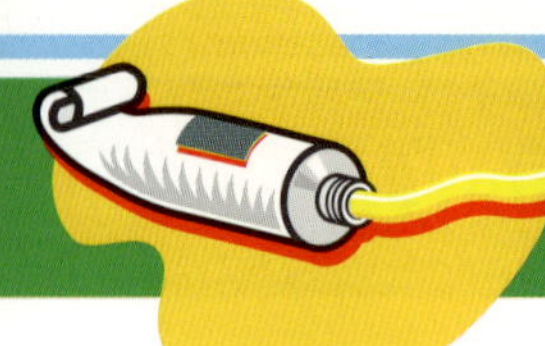

STEP 1

A

B

C

A Frank is quite a boxy character, so the first shape you should draw on your page is a large square. Draw a feint line down the center of this, which will help keep him symmetrical.

B Draw an upturned triangle and chop off the point to form Frank's head. This should overlap his body roughly in the center. His legs start off as a simple rectangle drawn below the body.

C Frank has huge, boxy feet and oval-shaped hands. Remember that he's mainly symmetrical, so whatever you do to one side of his body has to be mirrored on the other.

D Although Frank is boxy, his shoulders and feet need to be slightly rounded. He is wearing a suit, so you can add details to the jacket, such as buttons, and turn-ups to his suit pants. Sketch a frowning face featuring wide eyes and a flat head of hair.

E Continue adding details to Frank's suit jacket, such as cuffs and lapels. Give him a triangular, striped necktie, and bolts on either side of his neck. Draw pockets on his trousers and fat, stubby fingers on his hands. Next, sketch some bolts of lightning at either side of his head—these were essential in bringing big creepy Frank to life so he can live to scare us out of our wits!

2

D

3

E

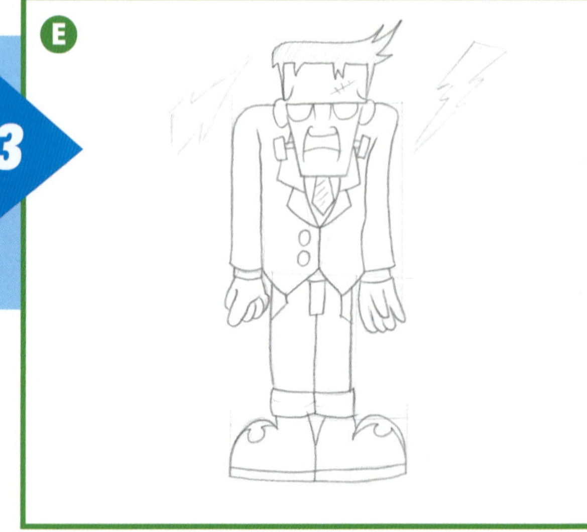

4

F

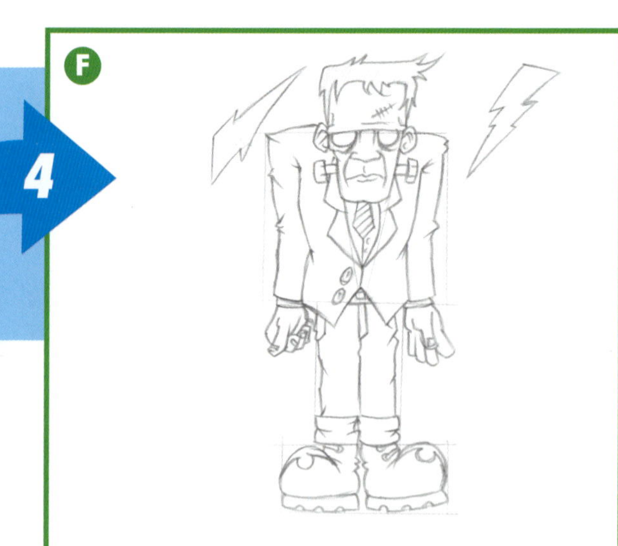

5

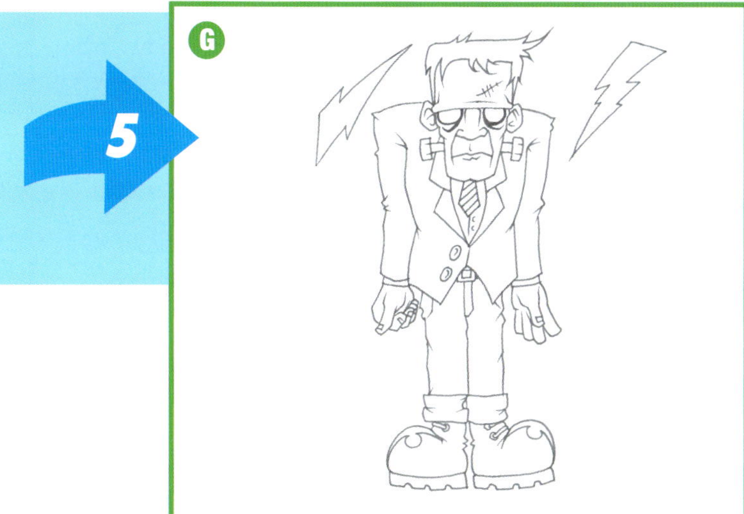

G

F To give that look of realism to your character, draw some creases in the fabric of his suit. Also, draw dark rings around his zombie eyes, and add a shine and some laces to his boots.

G Draw over the character with a thin black pen, before you erase the remaining pencil lines.

H Frank has green skin and a dark, gray-colored suit. You can use pencils, paints, or even a computer to complete your Frank. Finally, color the lightning bolts in yellow, and he's alive! It's probably best if you start hiding around about now!

6

H

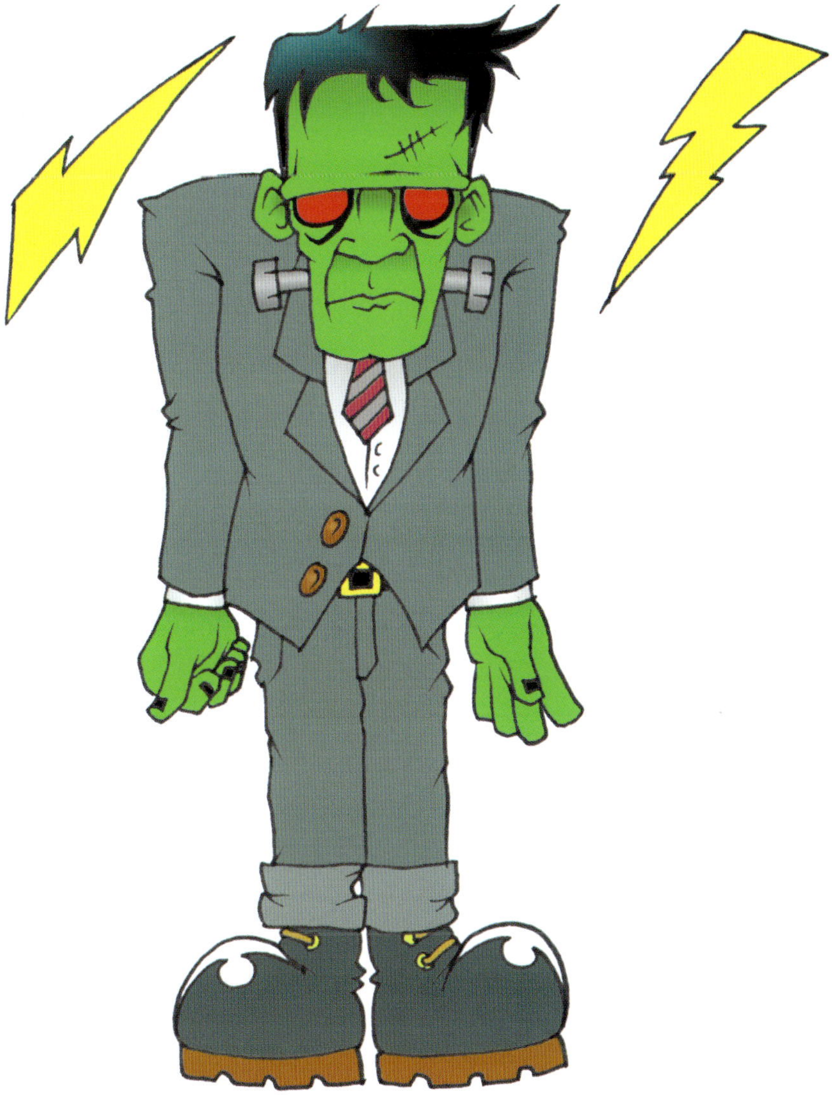

STEP 1

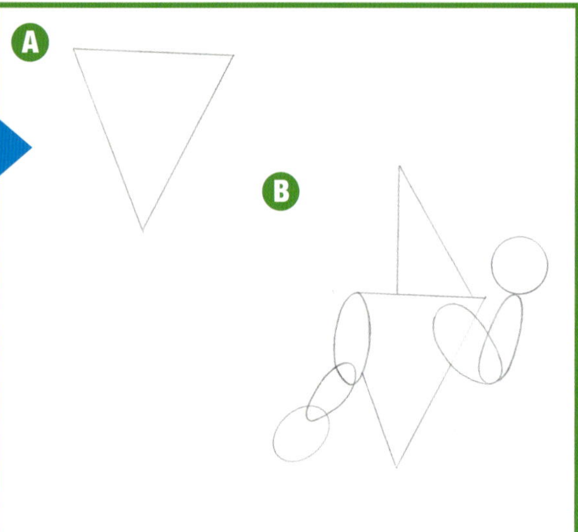

A Start your werewolf by drawing his body. This is a large triangle, pointing downward. Draw a feint line down the center of this as a guide.

B The head of your werewolf is also a triangle; its left edge should line up with the center line. His arms consist of two ovals and a circle.

C The werewolf's legs are constructed using two oval shapes and a triangular foot. Finally, a wolf needs a crescent-shaped tail, reminiscent of the new moon.

D Using the frame as a guide, start to put a few details on your werewolf. Round off the head and draw some pointed ears, an oval eye, and a dog-like wet nose. Begin sketching the clothing, which includes a shirt and jeans. Next, give him sharp, curved claws on his hands and feet.

E Give your werewolf a furry appearance by drawing a jagged outline on his arms, legs, and face. Draw pockets on his shirt and jeans, and some tufts of fur pushing through his clothing. Start to sketch in a full moon behind him. After all, this is the very reason for his transformation! Without that full moon re-appearing once a month, he really wouldn't be scary at all—he'd just be an ordinary man.

2

C

3

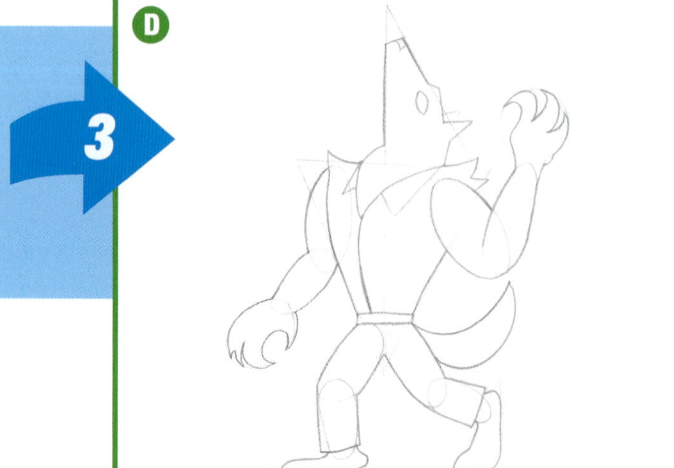

4

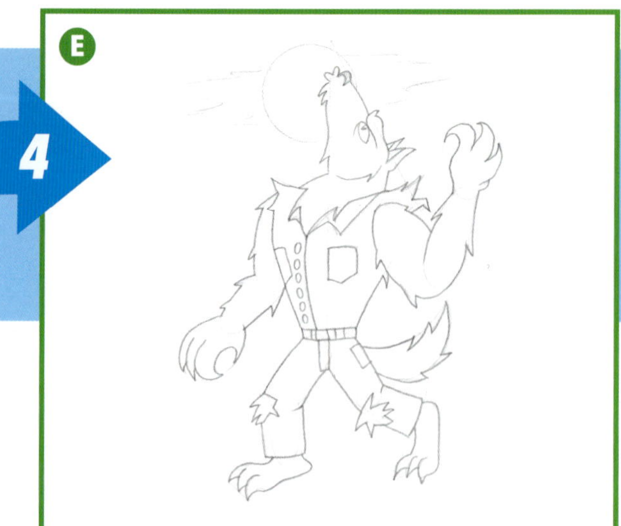

5

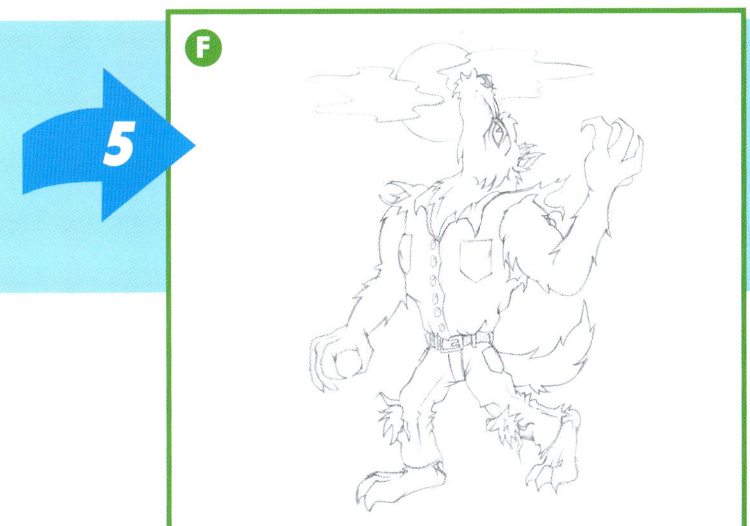

F Your werewolf will need a mouth to howl at the moon with! You can also darken his eyes by adding thick lines around them. Draw creases in his clothing to give a more realistic appearance, and use sharp lines to add texture to his ripped sleeves and knees. Lastly, sketch some clouds in around the moon.

G Draw on top of your picture with a black pen or felt-tip. Once you have traced over all of the lines, erase the leftover pencil marks.

→

G

6

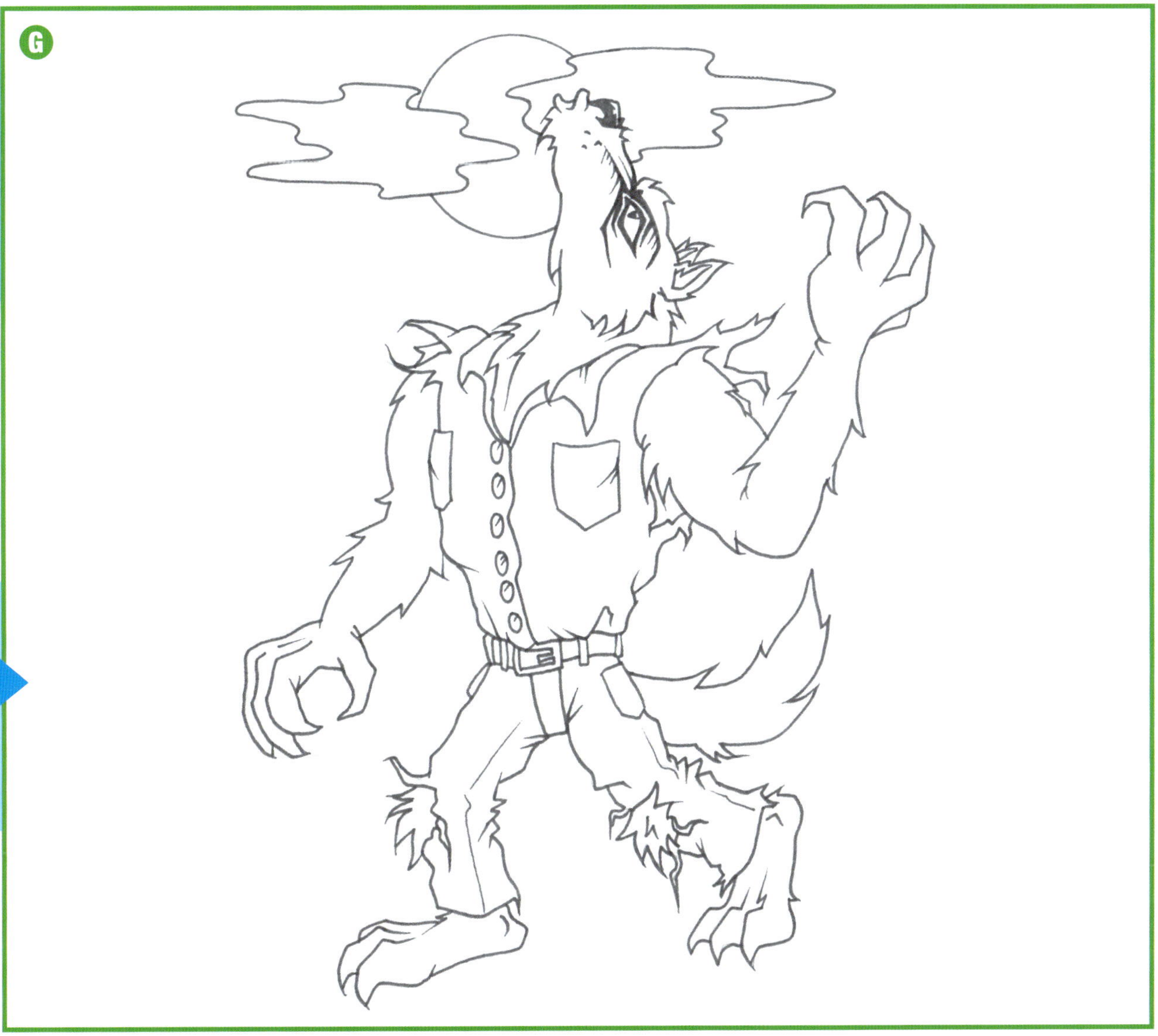

7

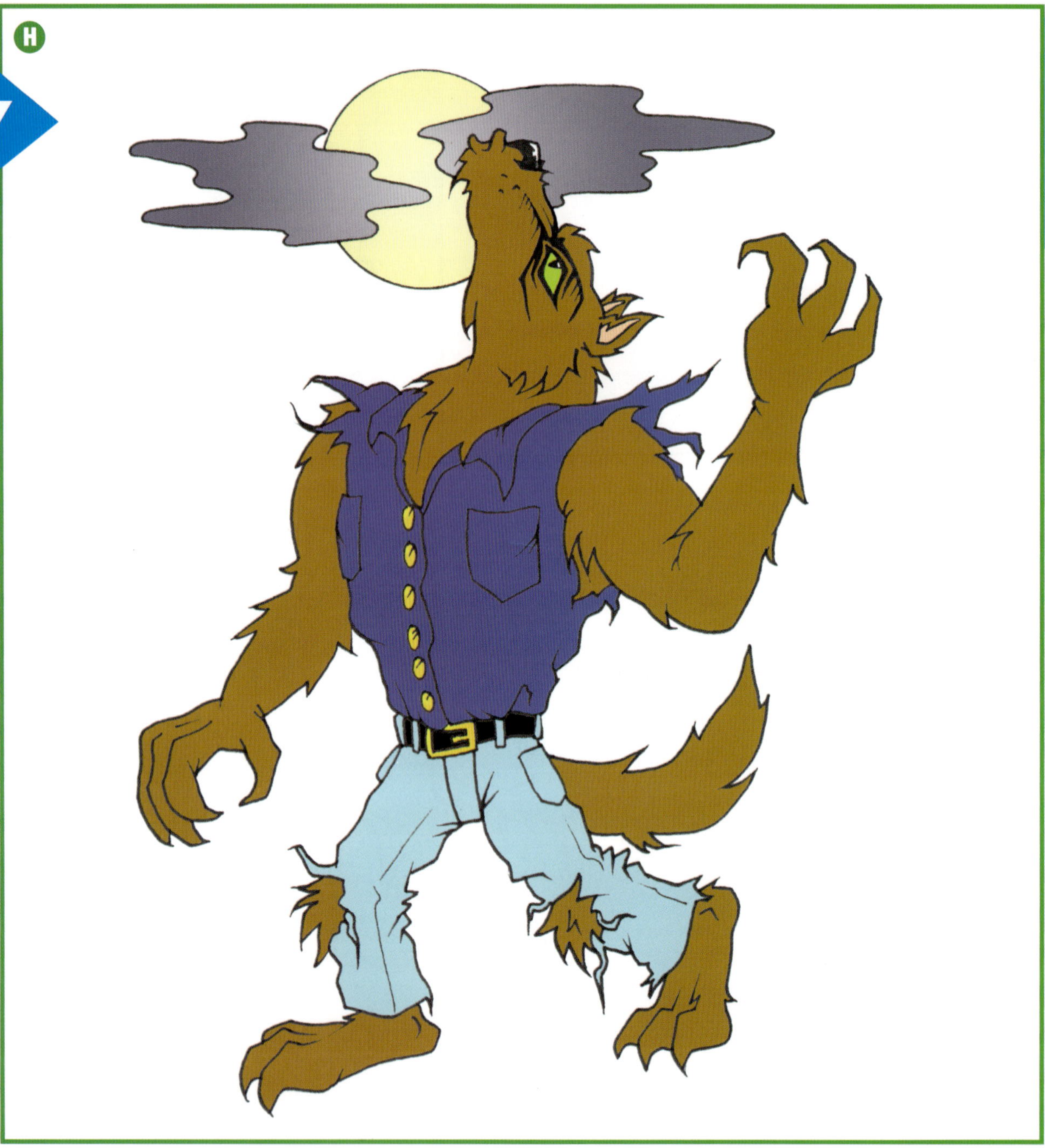

H

H Now it's time to choose which colors to use to really bring that terrifying werewolf to life on your page. Wolves are naturally either brown or gray, so it's best to stick with these colors if you want the werewolf to look realistic. The color of his clothing, however, is really up to you. Whatever colors you choose, just make sure you have a howling good time doing it!

FAIRYTALE

Once upon a time in a land far away...

Yes, in this chapter, you're going to be drawing a set of characters from a fairytale. In the story, we are introduced to a beautiful, yet lonely Fairy Princess. She falls in love with a strong, courageous knight who has fought many a battle for his kingdom.

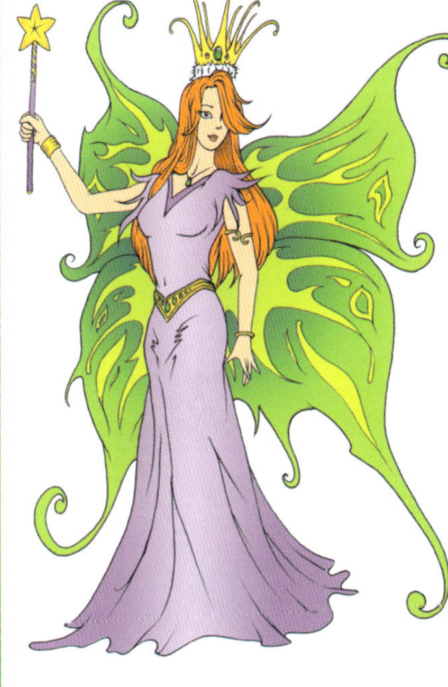

One day, the Princess is taken prisoner by a wicked witch, who locks her up in a castle dungeon, deep in the darkest forest. The knight sets out to save the Princess, hoping to win her love in return for his bravery.

Alas, he has not realized the true power of the wicked witch, and the old hag senses that the knight is drawing close. So, as soon as our hero enters the forest, the witch conjures up a dragon to destroy him.

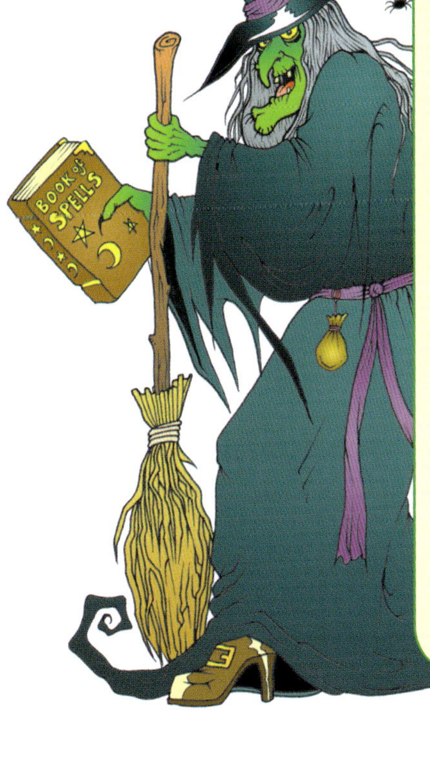

The hero and dragon fight ferociously, and eventually the dragon is defeated by our hero's steely blade. The victorious knight gallops off to save the beautiful Princess.

The cowardly witch flees as our brave hero enters the castle. He strides into the dungeon in which the Princess is being held captive, and frees her. In return, he receives a kiss and the Princess falls in love with him.

Now imagine that story told with your own pictures! It is a great way to bring your very own fairytales to life, and this chapter will inspire you...

THE END

STEP 1

A

B

C

A The body of your princess is triangular, so begin by drawing a fairly long and thin downward-facing triangle. Draw a center line through it to help place the rest of her outline.

B At the top right-hand side of your triangle, draw a funnel shape for your princess's neck. On top of this, add a shape that resembles an upside-down egg—this will be her head. Then, on top of the egg, draw a tall, spiky crown, consisting of a series of thin triangles.

C The rest of your fairy princess's body is constructed using simple shapes. First, there is her dress, a long bell shape flared at the base. Use your center line as a guide when placing this. Next are her arms, two thin ovals with a smaller oval on the end for each hand. The left arm is bent upward at the elbow, ready to hold a wand.

D This is where you start to give your princess a more feminine appearance. Draw her long hair that falls over her shoulders and down her back, using curved, flowing lines. Next, sketch in the shape of her belt and chest, including the v-shaped neckline of her dress. When drawing these, remember to curve them slightly so that they follow the contours of her body. Finally, draw her wand using a long straight line with a five-pointed star on the top.

2

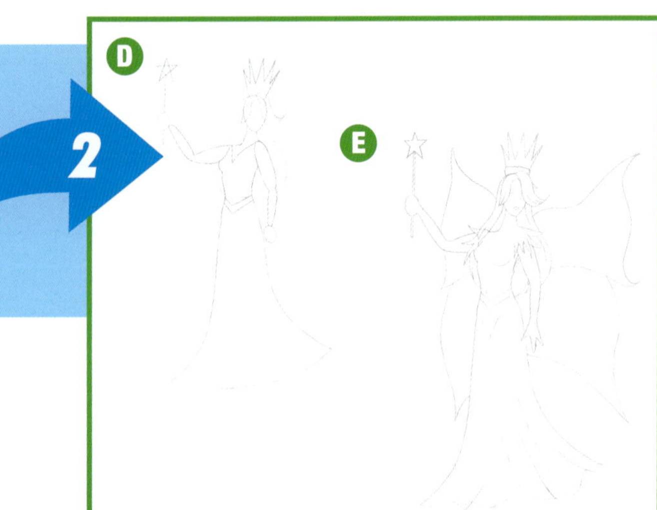

3

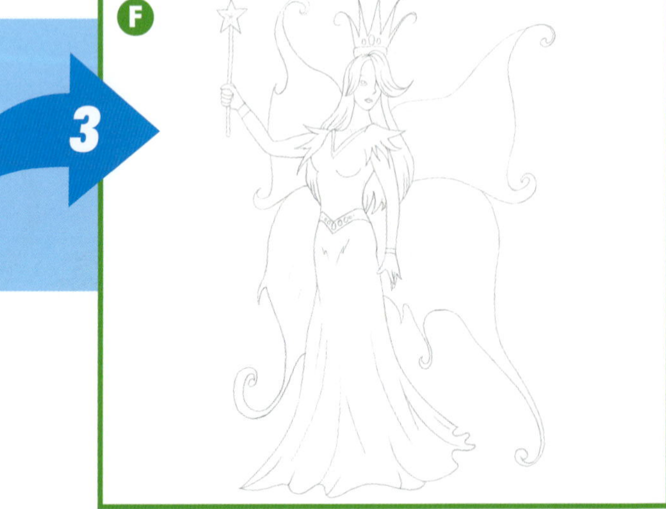

4

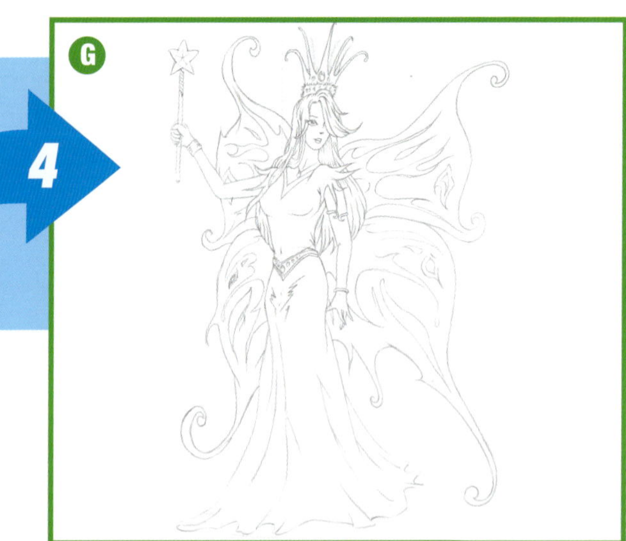

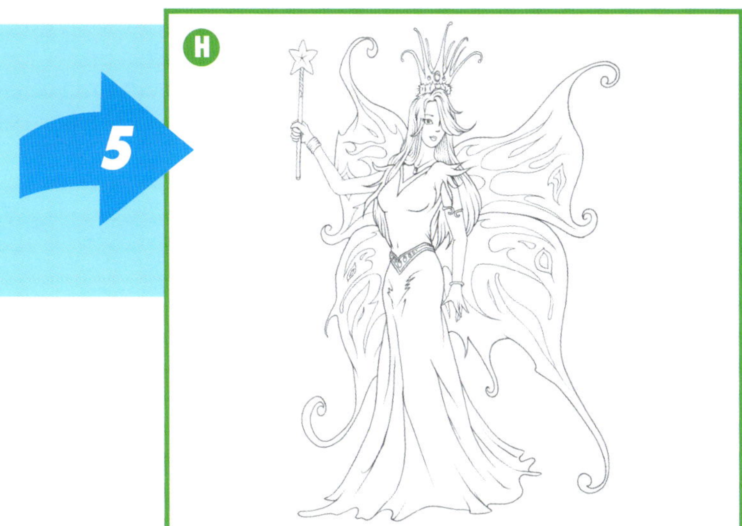

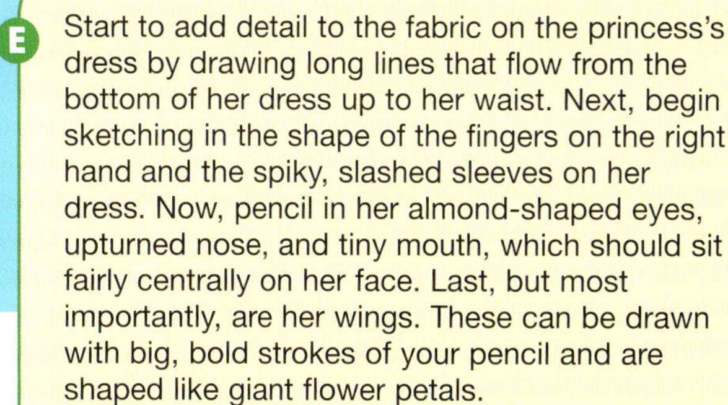

E Start to add detail to the fabric on the princess's dress by drawing long lines that flow from the bottom of her dress up to her waist. Next, begin sketching in the shape of the fingers on the right hand and the spiky, slashed sleeves on her dress. Now, pencil in her almond-shaped eyes, upturned nose, and tiny mouth, which should sit fairly centrally on her face. Last, but most importantly, are her wings. These can be drawn with big, bold strokes of your pencil and are shaped like giant flower petals.

F Your princess's wings should look like those of a butterfly. You can draw some beautiful flowing curls and spirals on the tips of her wings; this will give a really organic look, as if they were floating in the wind. Curl over the tips of the crown and add detail to her hair, belt, and dress. Draw elegant, pointed fingers on each hand.

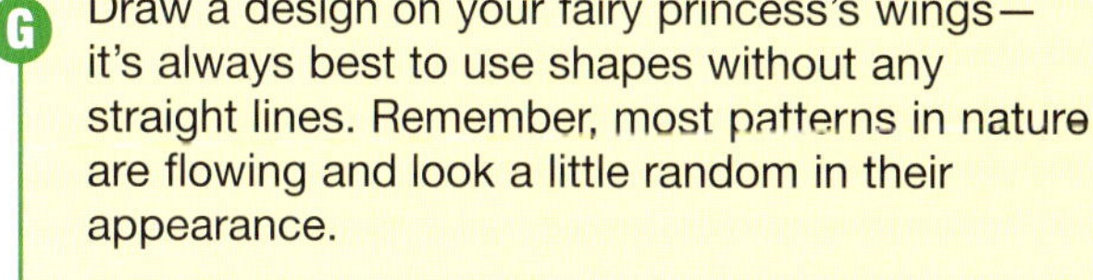

G Draw a design on your fairy princess's wings—it's always best to use shapes without any straight lines. Remember, most patterns in nature are flowing and look a little random in their appearance.

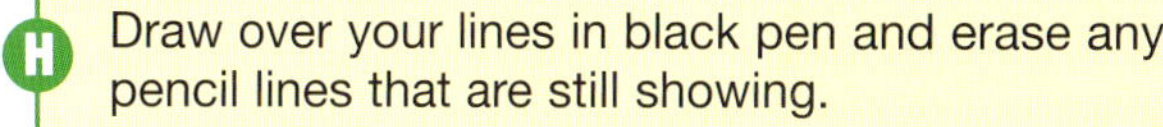

H Draw over your lines in black pen and erase any pencil lines that are still showing.

I Your princess should be colorful and magical in appearance. She's dressed in lavender and lime green here, as they give her a floral look.

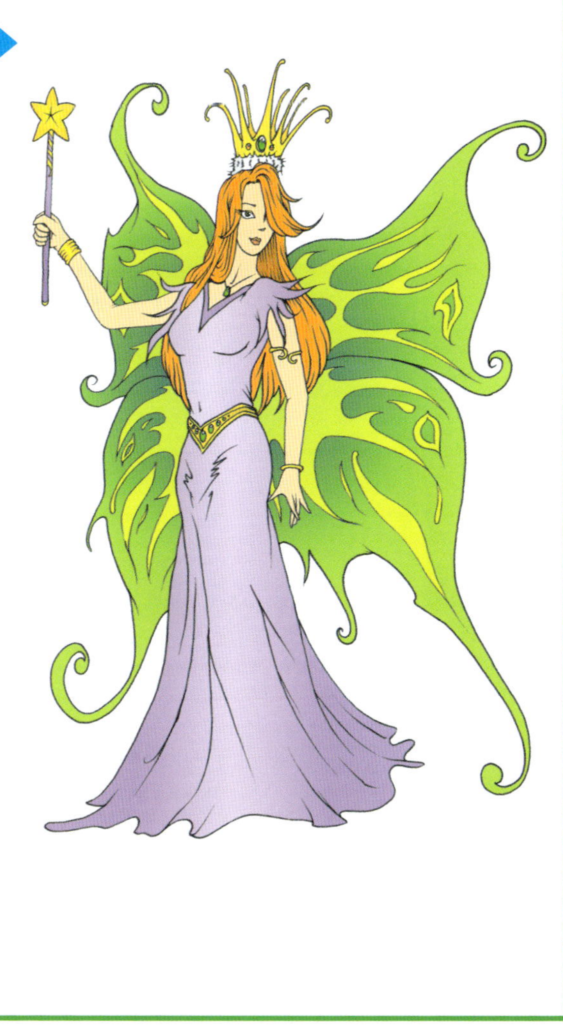

STEP 1

A

B

C

A Start your crooked, old witch by sketching a feint vertical line down the center of your paper. Using this as a guide, draw a large oval shape (a bit like a stretched circle) for your witch's body.

B The witch's tall, pointed hat is triangular. To draw this, sketch two straight lines from the top to the bottom of the oval, meeting at a point on the top left-hand side of the picture. Then, using a ruler, draw a line that cuts across these before sketching a curved brim. To make the sleeve shape, draw a large oval that overlaps the body, then cut a curved section out of the top of it.

C Your witch's legs are covered by a robe, so pencil in a large bell shape that leans to the right (as if her knees were bent). A witch needs her broom, and this is constructed from three shapes, consisting of a long rectangular handle with triangular and almond shapes attached to the bottom. The hand holding the broom is oval-shaped.

D Give the witch's hat a silk trim, and sketch in her long hair and the outline of her face, which is crescent moon-shaped, with a crooked, hook nose. Her robe needs a long fabric belt and slashed sleeves. Add some simple detail to her broom and put a book of spells in her other hand—this is important because it is the secret of her power.

2

D

E

3

F

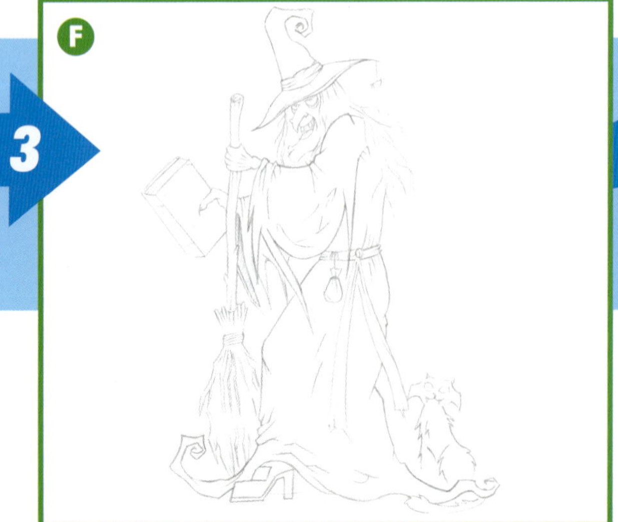

4

G

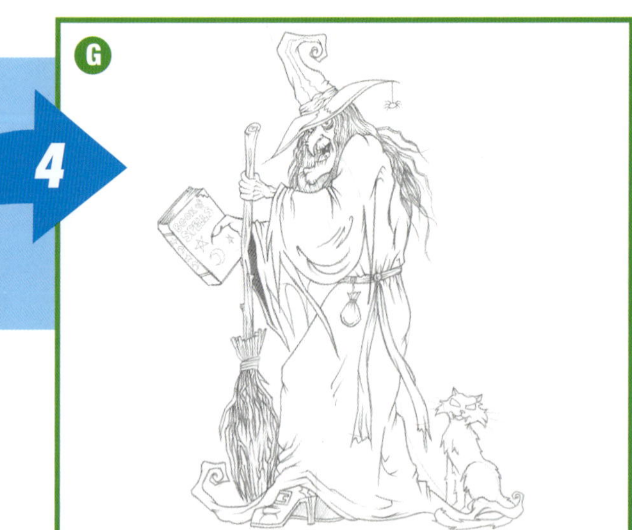

5

H

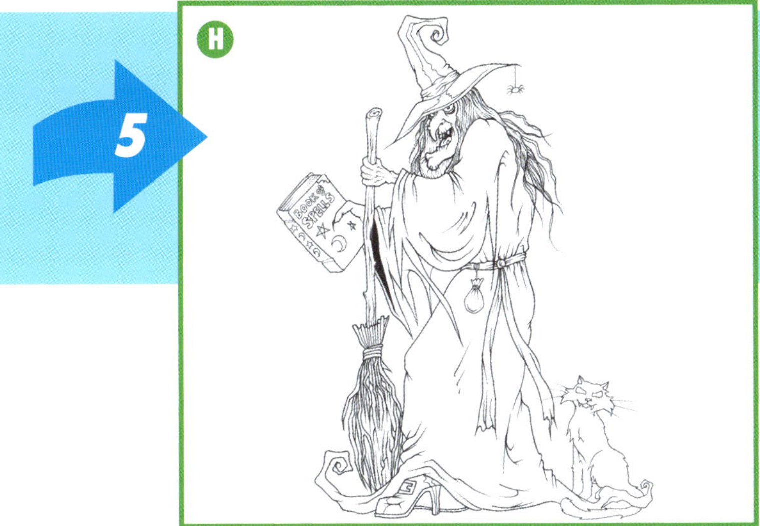

6

I

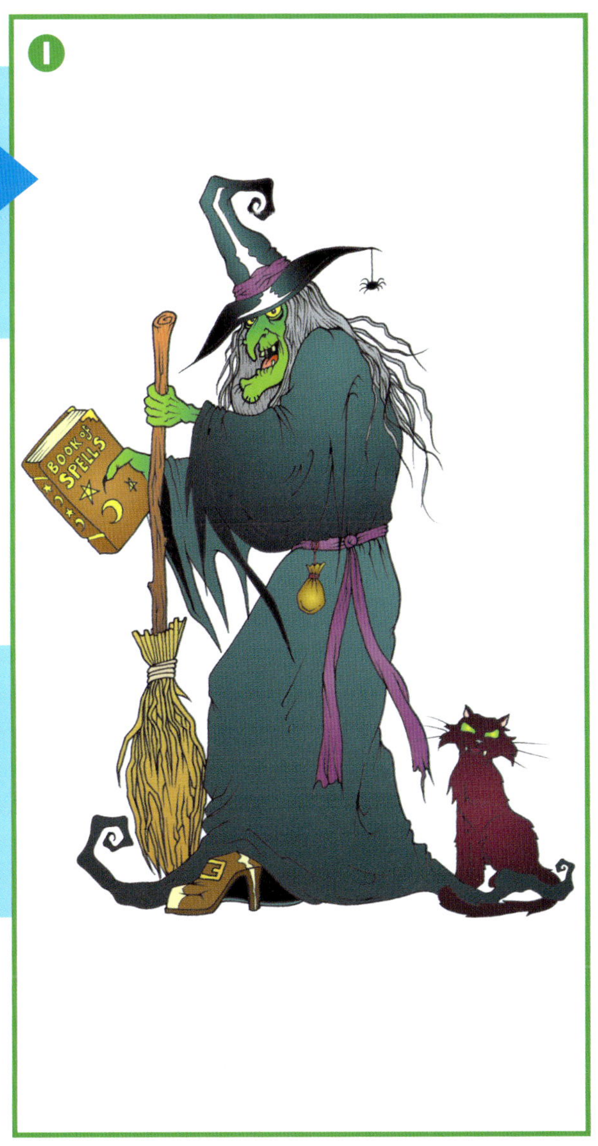

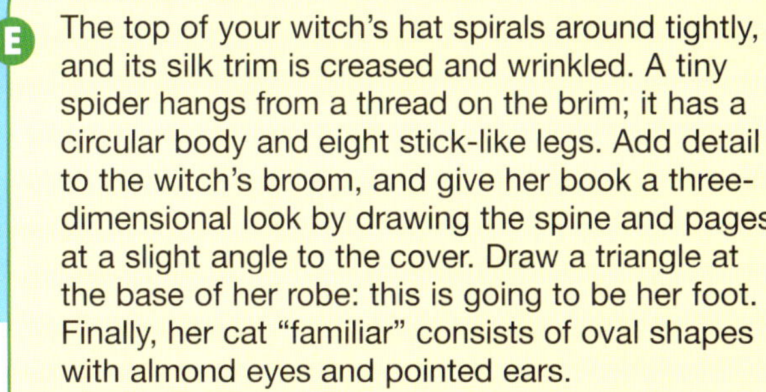

E The top of your witch's hat spirals around tightly, and its silk trim is creased and wrinkled. A tiny spider hangs from a thread on the brim; it has a circular body and eight stick-like legs. Add detail to the witch's broom, and give her book a three-dimensional look by drawing the spine and pages at a slight angle to the cover. Draw a triangle at the base of her robe: this is going to be her foot. Finally, her cat "familiar" consists of oval shapes with almond eyes and pointed ears.

F Draw the witch's square-toed boot inside the triangle you sketched in step D. It has a large square buckle on the front. Add creases to the fabric on her robe and spiral the bottom corners to give a twisted appearance. Next, work on her face. Draw a wart on her nose and dark rings around her eyes. Finally, give your witch only a couple of teeth, because the rest have fallen out! Give her cat a jagged outline to represent its fur.

G Final detail can be drawn on your witch's thin, wispy hair and wrinkled face. Draw lots of angular lines on her broom to make it look like it's made out of twigs.

H The final stage of drawing your witch involves tracing over all of the lines drawn so far with a black pen. It gives a cleaner, stronger appearance to your witch. Erase any pencil lines.

I Now she's been drawn, color the old crone in dark, mystical tones. Give her green skin, gray hair, and glowing yellow eyes. Her cat also has glowing eyes, so it can see little children in the dark and hiss at them!

STEP 1

A Your Hero and Dragon picture begins with two simple shapes. For your hero, draw a compressed circular shape with a feint center line. Draw a much larger egg shape at a 45-degree angle on the other side of your paper; this is going to be your dragon's body.

B The head of your hero starts off as an oval shape. His arms also consist of ovals; give the right arm a circular hand, and the left arm a shield that overlaps his lower arm slightly. The next stage of the dragon is to draw his head and tail. Draw his neck and tail in one curved, snaking shape before joining the oval-shaped head to the top of the neck, which should be tilted down toward the hero.

2

C Your hero's legs are two simple ovals with a triangular foot attached. Put a large sword in his right hand, and now he's ready to fight! Your dragon will need some legs and arms to fight back, and these are constructed in much the same way you drew the hero's arms and legs only much bigger!

D Now add detail to your hero's and dragon's outlines. Your dragon is going to need some wings and a pair of sharp horns. Next, work some facial details into the oval head shape; give him menacing eyes and a beaked mouth. Your hero's face will need a huge square jaw and a determined expression in his eyes. He also needs a full head of heroic hair, which will

3

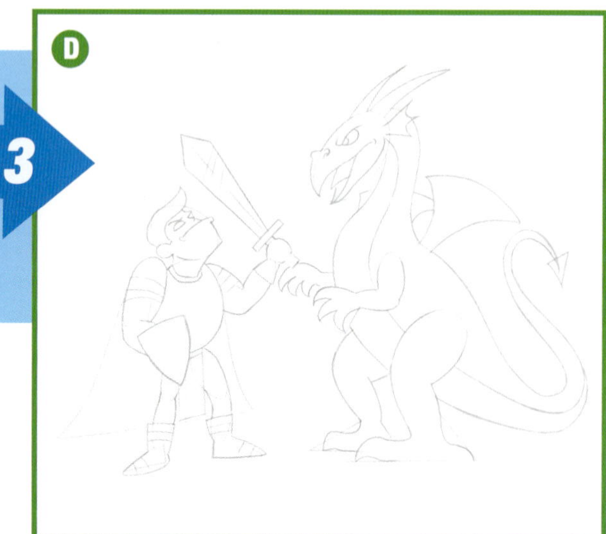

4

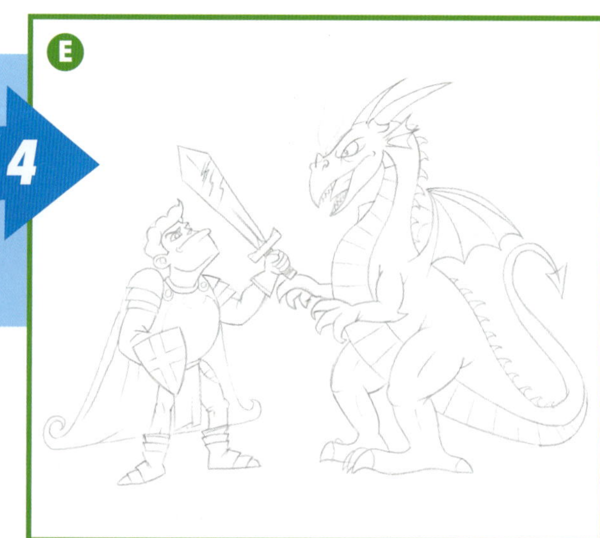

5

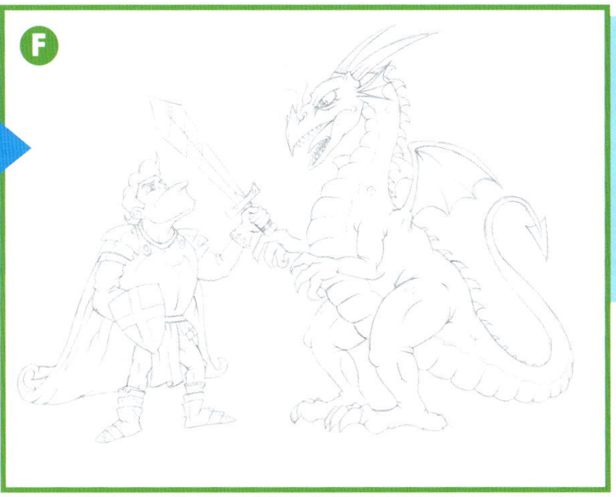

F

his king's emblem on his shield. Add detail to your hero's face, such as the pupils in his eyes. Your dragon's wings are like a bat's: split into sections and wavy along the bottom. He's going to need some sharp talons and long, curved toenails if he is going to fight the hero. Armor would come in rather handy too, so give your dragon a spiny back and tough, leathery sections of skin all the way down his neck and stomach.

start off at this stage as one giant curl. Add some layered armor to his boots, add shoulder pads, and a large triangular cape.

E Give your hero's hair a curly appearance by sketching it in the same way you would draw a cloud. Curl up the ends of his cape, and draw

F Now it's time to add the all-important finishing touches to your hero's armor, such as reflections, and add elements to the dragon's skin like his muscle tone and scales. Draw some smoke pouring out of the dragon's nostrils and a reflection of light flashing across your hero's sword.

G Draw over your image with a pen so that the lines stand out. Erase any leftover pencil lines. →

G

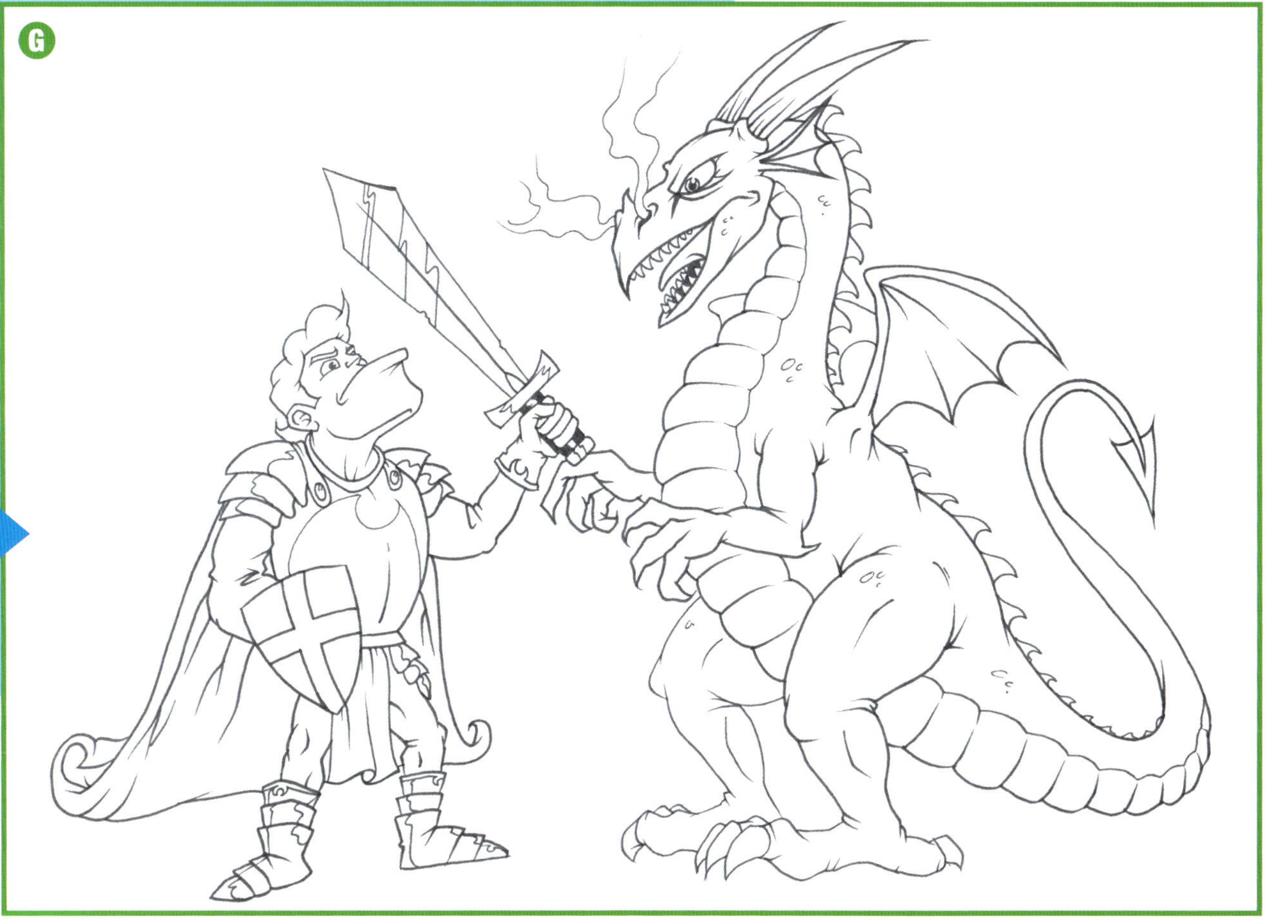

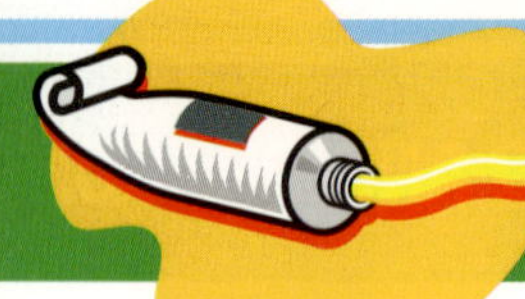

7

H

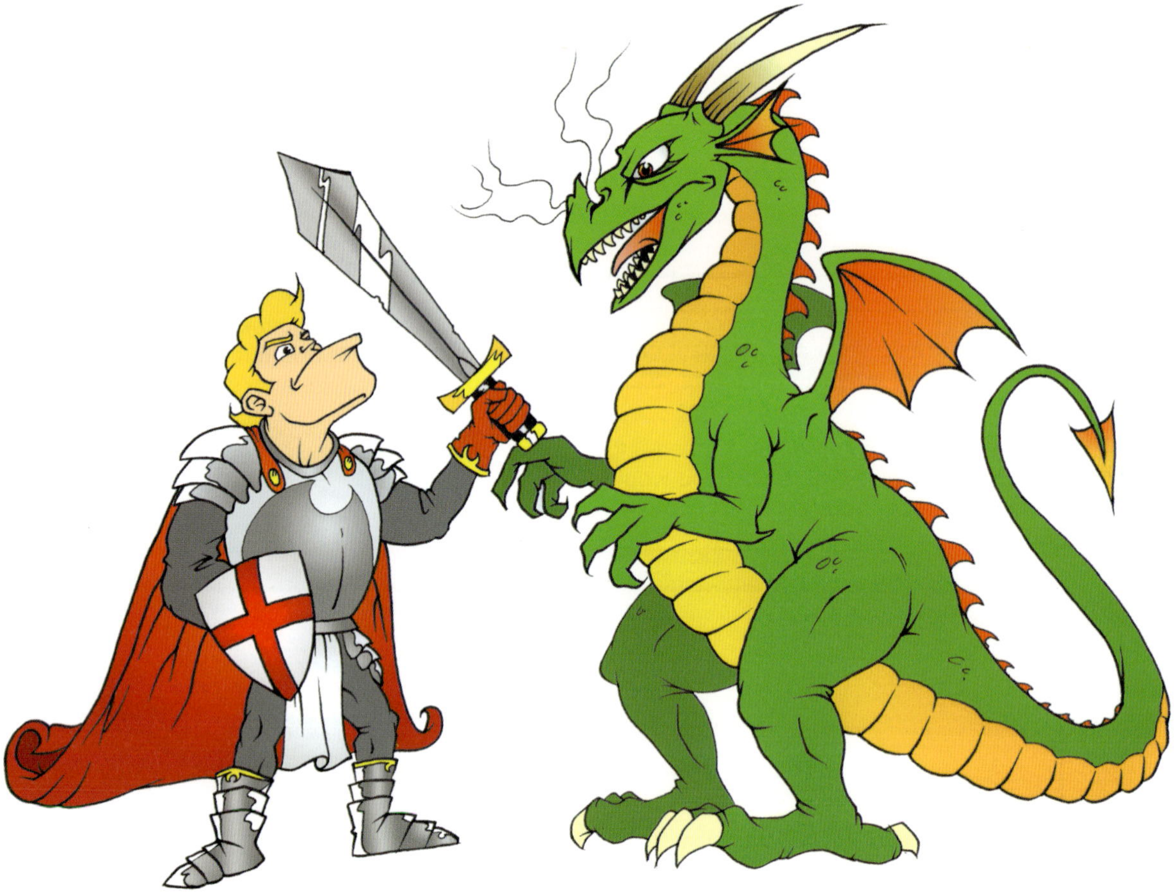

H Color your dragon in bright, cartoon colors such as reds or greens. This will make him practically leap off of the page! Your hero's armor should look silvery and metallic. You can achieve this by shading with a pencil, or by using gray and silver pens.

MANGA

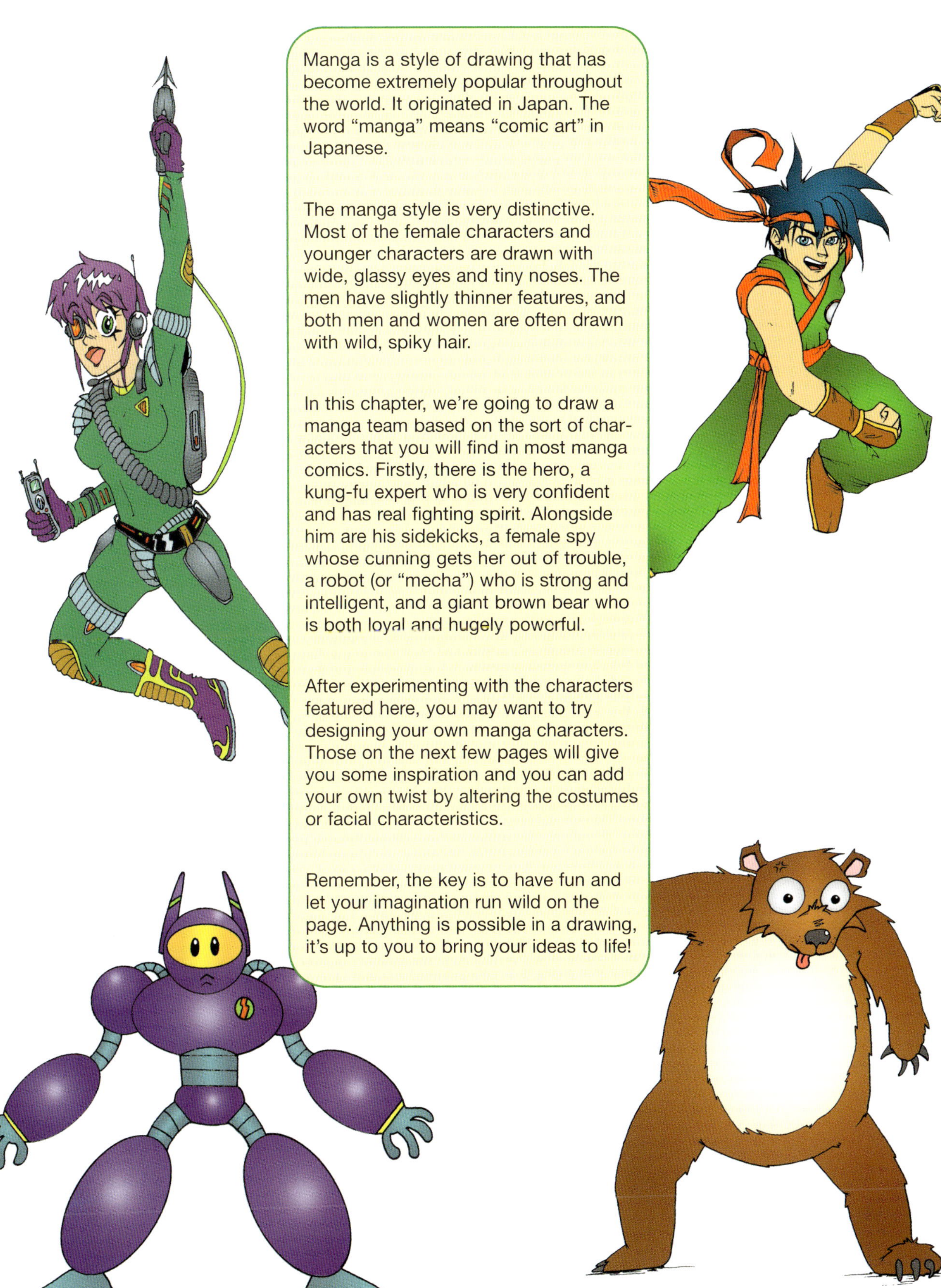

Manga is a style of drawing that has become extremely popular throughout the world. It originated in Japan. The word "manga" means "comic art" in Japanese.

The manga style is very distinctive. Most of the female characters and younger characters are drawn with wide, glassy eyes and tiny noses. The men have slightly thinner features, and both men and women are often drawn with wild, spiky hair.

In this chapter, we're going to draw a manga team based on the sort of characters that you will find in most manga comics. Firstly, there is the hero, a kung-fu expert who is very confident and has real fighting spirit. Alongside him are his sidekicks, a female spy whose cunning gets her out of trouble, a robot (or "mecha") who is strong and intelligent, and a giant brown bear who is both loyal and hugely powerful.

After experimenting with the characters featured here, you may want to try designing your own manga characters. Those on the next few pages will give you some inspiration and you can add your own twist by altering the costumes or facial characteristics.

Remember, the key is to have fun and let your imagination run wild on the page. Anything is possible in a drawing, it's up to you to bring your ideas to life!

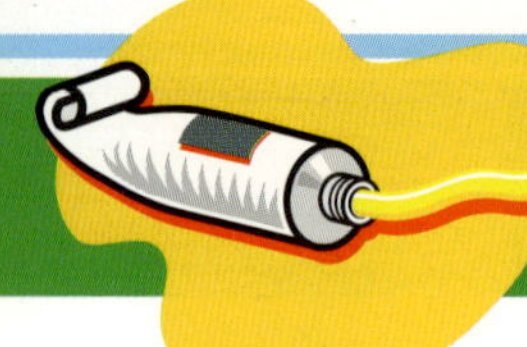

STEP 1

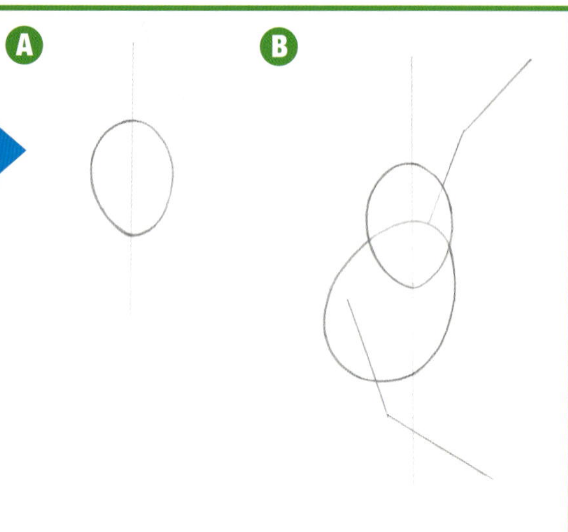

A Draw a feint vertical line down the center of your page. This is going to be helpful when placing the shapes that make up your manga hero. Next, draw an egg shape on the line, slightly above the center of your page.

B Your hero's body is based on another egg shape, that is rather larger than the last. Make this overlap the head, and only lightly pencil it in where it crosses the face because you'll need to erase this later. Next, draw bent lines where his arms are going to be.

C It's time to bulk out your hero's arms. Using the lines you drew in Stage B as guidelines, draw two long ovals and a circle for each arm, making sure that the upper arm is slightly fatter than the forearm.

D The legs of your hero are constructed in the same way as the arms, in three connecting shapes. These ovals should be about 1.5 times the length of the those used to make his arms, and wider too. Your hero's feet are triangular and the right leg should sit behind the arm. Start to sketch his face. It is tilted slightly away from the front, so his features should be offset instead of centered.

E Begin sketching in the detail, such as the hero's huge, spiky hair, his headband, and his wristbands. Use the arm and leg shapes as a

2

C

3

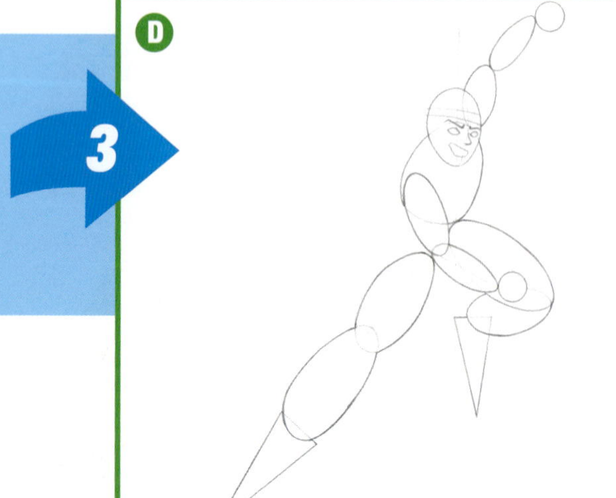

4

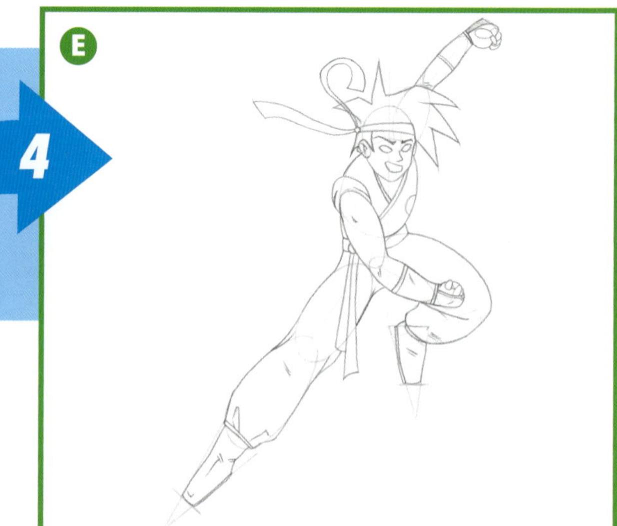

5

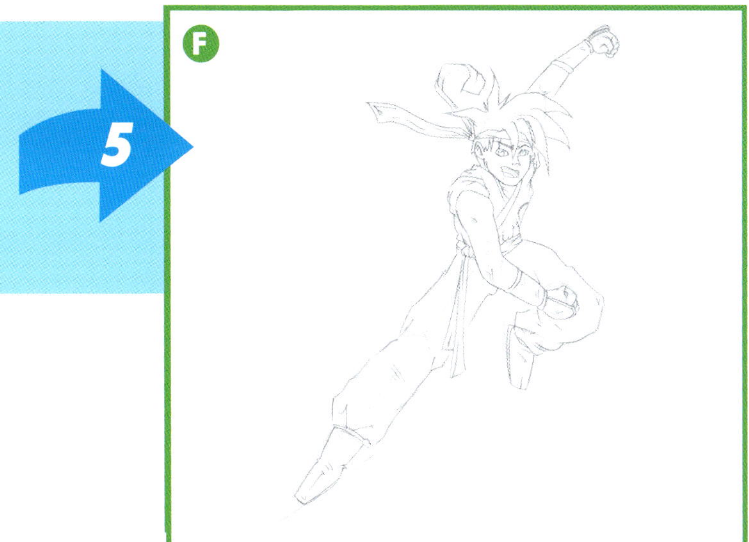

template for drawing the outline of his costume. Round off his triangular feet to form his boots and draw the lines where they meet his pants.

F Now, give your hero's costume a crisp but baggy appearance by using jagged lines. Try to get rid of any rounded lines on his suit. Add final detail to his face, such as the pupils in his eyes and his teeth. Then draw over him using a fine black pen. Erase the pencil lines, and he's ready for coloring.

G You can use any colors you like for his clothing, the ones shown here are just a suggestion. You can photocopy your drawing and experiment with different colors on the copies until you're satisfied.

6

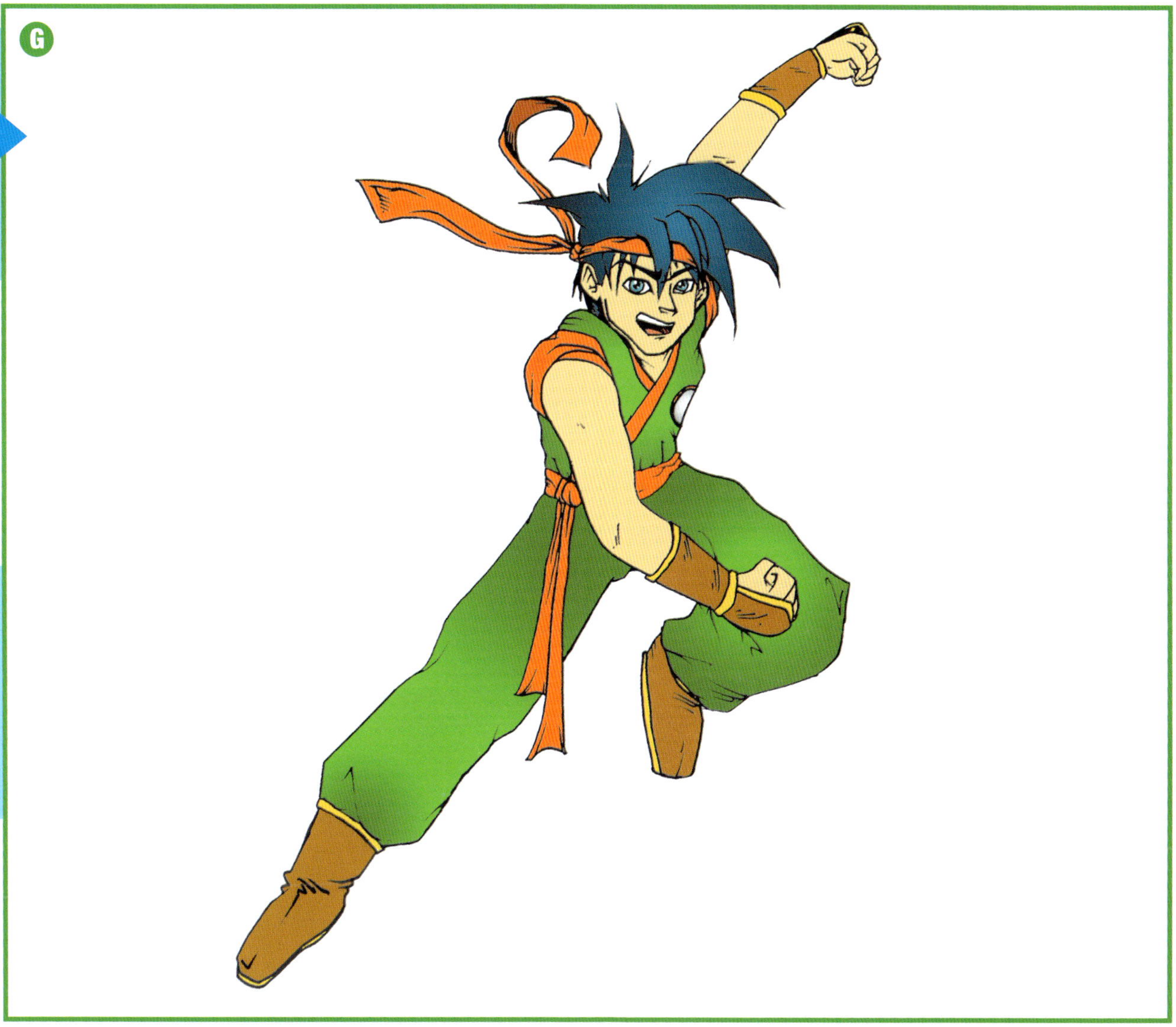

G

STEP 1

A

B

C

A Start by drawing an oval shape on the page. This is going to be your manga spy's head. Next, draw a feint vertical line down the right hand side of the oval. This will act as a helpful guide when drawing the rest of her frame.

B Draw a larger oval, roughly 1.5 times the length of her head, below the first shape and slightly to the right, so that the feint line runs through the center. Join the two ovals together with a neck shape. Next, sketch in lines where her arms are going to be.

C Your spy's arms are made by using two long, thin oval shapes and a circle on the end for her hands. Make sure that the forearm oval is thinner than her upper arm. The left arm is bent behind her body.

D The legs of your spy are built up in the same way as her arms, using two ovals. These need to be approximately twice as wide and 1.5 times as long, but you don't have to be exact. Her feet are simple triangular shapes at this stage. Begin adding simple detail to her face and chest. Her face is turned slightly away, so don't draw her features too centrally.

E Now you have a basic shape for your spy, you can start to draw her costume. This starts as a tight, figure-hugging bodysuit. Using your frame as a guide, draw the spy's outline by joining the shapes together. Start to pencil in

2

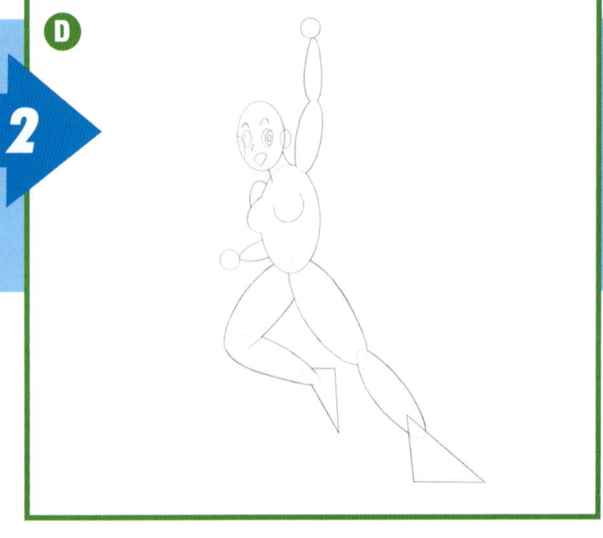

3

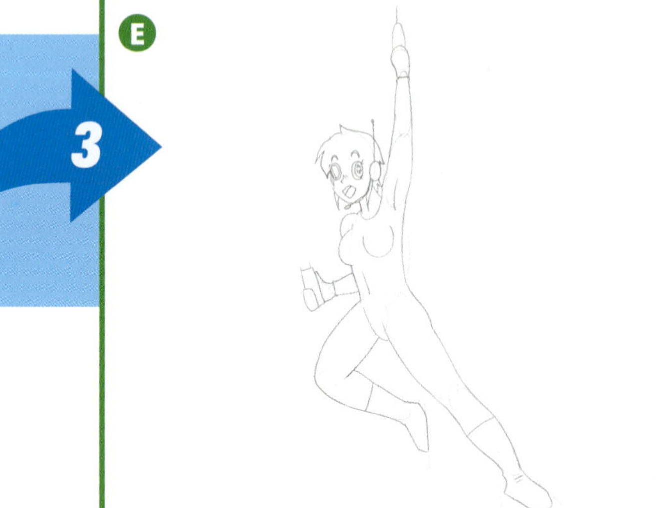

4

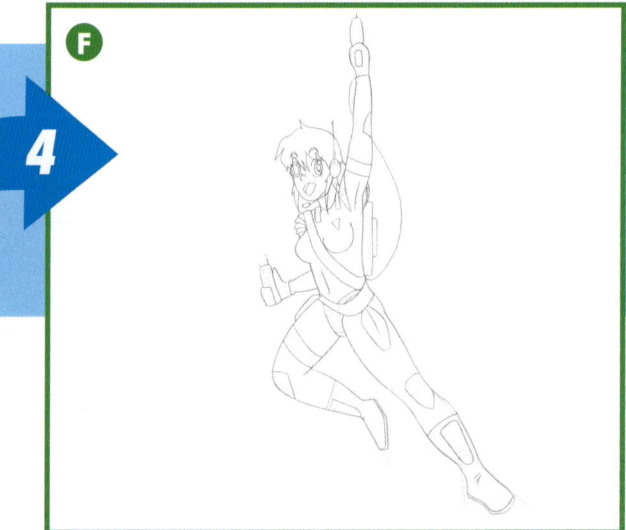

5

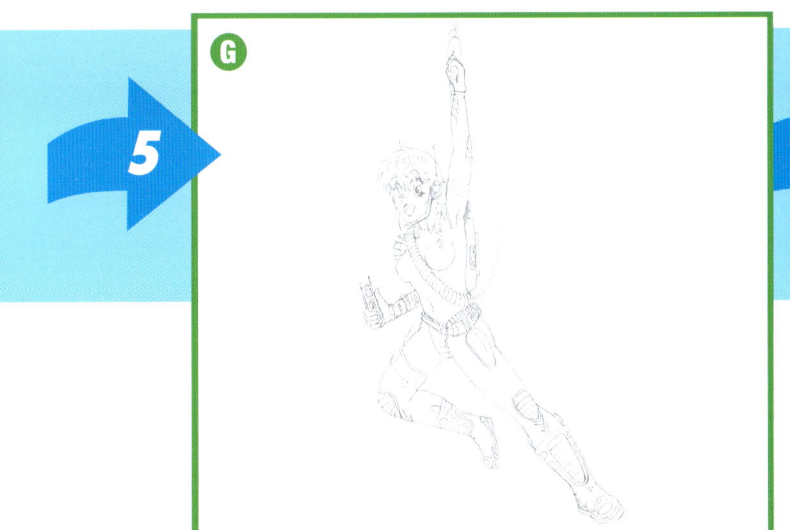

6

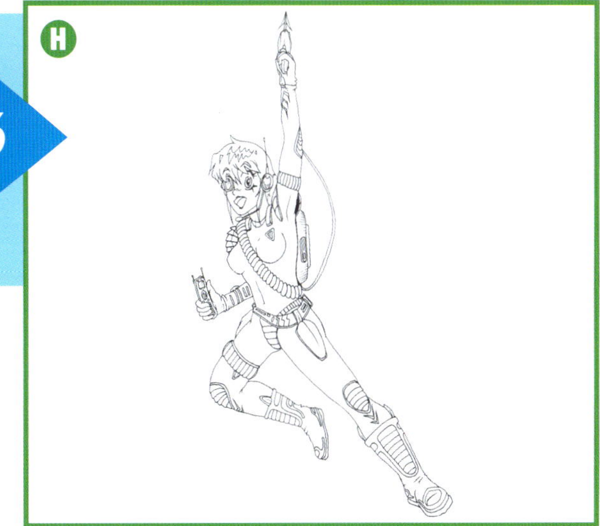

7

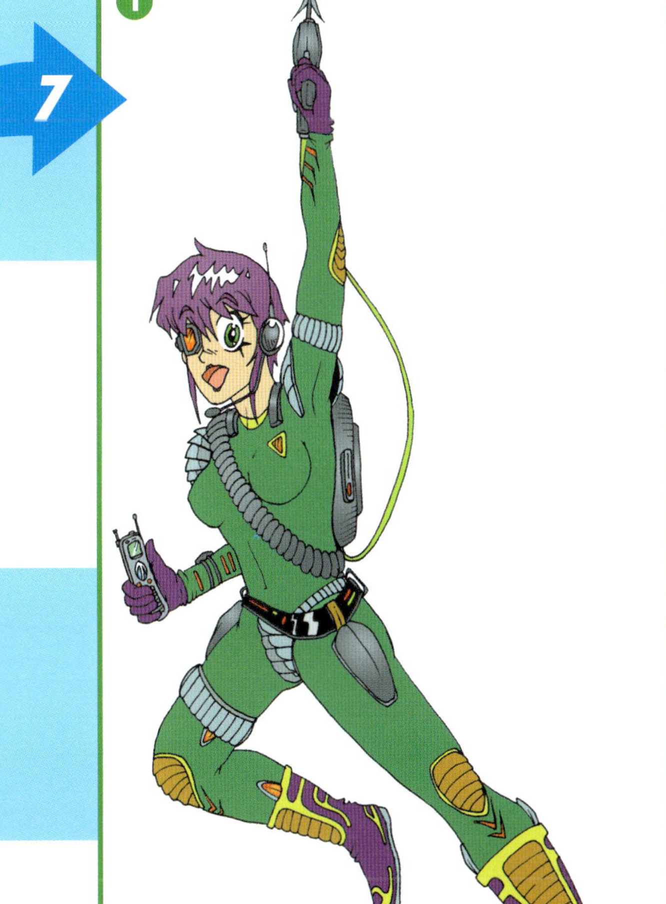

her hair; manga hair is usually spiky and quite simple. Round off her feet and sketch in where her boots and gloves overlap her bodysuit.

F You can now begin adding her hi-tech gadgets and body armor. She has leather pads on her elbows and knees, metal shoulder pads, and a harpoon gun in her hand to help her escape from danger. When drawing her arm, leg armor, and her belt, curve them to follow the contours of her body. Continue adding detail to her face, such as her infrared eyepiece and communications headset.

G Add finishing touches to your spy's boots, armor, face, and hair. Fine detail, like the buttons and lights on her belt and intercom handset, give an extra look of realism. Finally, add a glossy shine to her hair. This is typical of manga women.

H Trace the picture with a black pen, then erase the original pencil lines. You may want to add some extra gadgets or detail to her suit.

I Color your spy using bright tones. Go wild! It's a good idea to use different shades of gray to give a metallic effect to her shoulder pads and backpack.

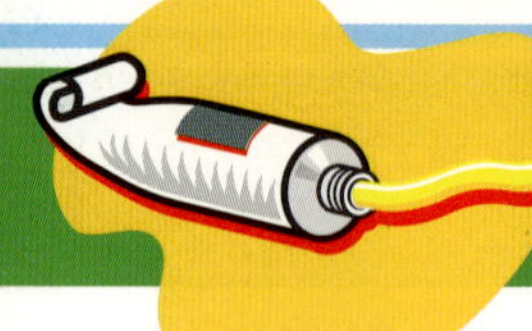

STEP 1

A First draw an oval shape for the robot's chest-plate. Start with a vertical line to represent the center of your picture, and then draw the oval horizontally across it. The line will help you to form the rest of the picture, as your manga robot is going to be symmetrical.

B Draw a circle on either side of your oval, slightly overlapping it. These are going to be your robot's shoulders. Then, using the center line as a guide, draw a slightly larger circle for the robot's head. Once again, this should overlap the chest a little. You can draw these circles in freehand, but drawing around different-sized coins may make it easier, and will look much tidier.

C Your robot's arms are created by drawing an oval slightly smaller than the one used to create the chest. Connect this oval to the chest by a simple tube shape. Do the same on both sides. Remember, your robot is symmetrical, so whatever you do to one side must be mirrored on the other. Next, your robot's waist and pelvis are built up using a block and triangle. This should end up looking like a downward-pointing arrow.

2

D To complete your robot's basic frame, it will need some legs. As with the arms, these are made up of an oval and a tube. This time, the oval is the same size as its chestplate. Finally, the feet begin as a simple triangular shape.

3

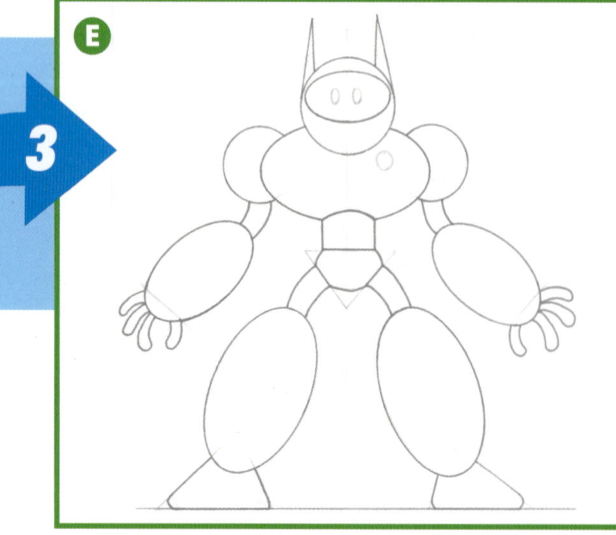

4

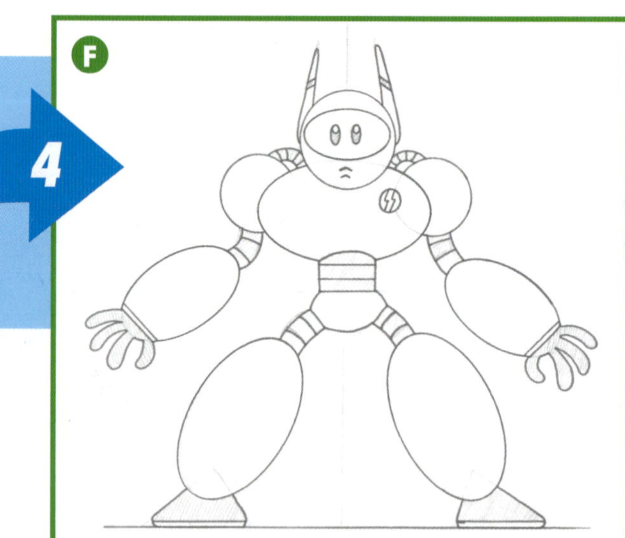

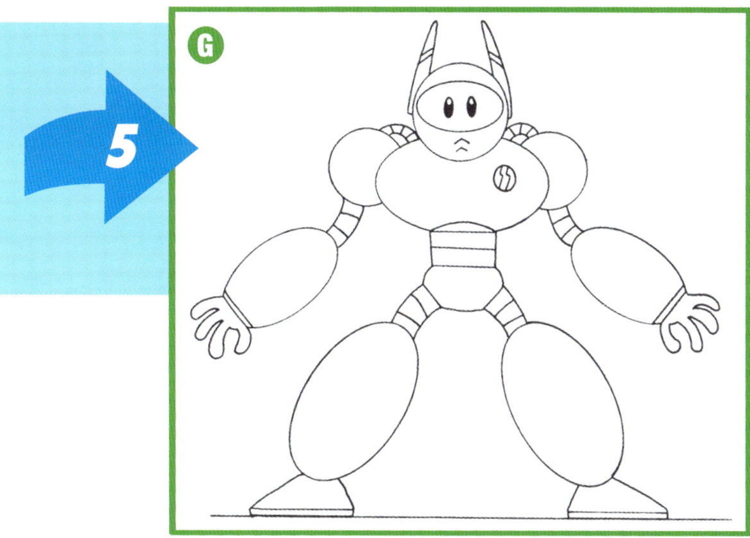

E Start adding simple detail to your robot, such as its ears and fingers. The ears are thin triangles on either side of the head, while the fingers are created using cylindrical shapes. Next, round off any sharp corners on the feet and pelvis, and draw an oval visor on its head, just above the halfway point.

F Add some final detail to the robot. It now has eyes that peep out from behind the visor, an intergalactic badge on its chest, and tubes that connect the shoulders to the body. You can also draw lines across the arm and leg tubes.

G H Before coloring your robot in, draw over your pencil lines with a black pen. You can now color your robot in various ways—use paints or colored pencils.

6

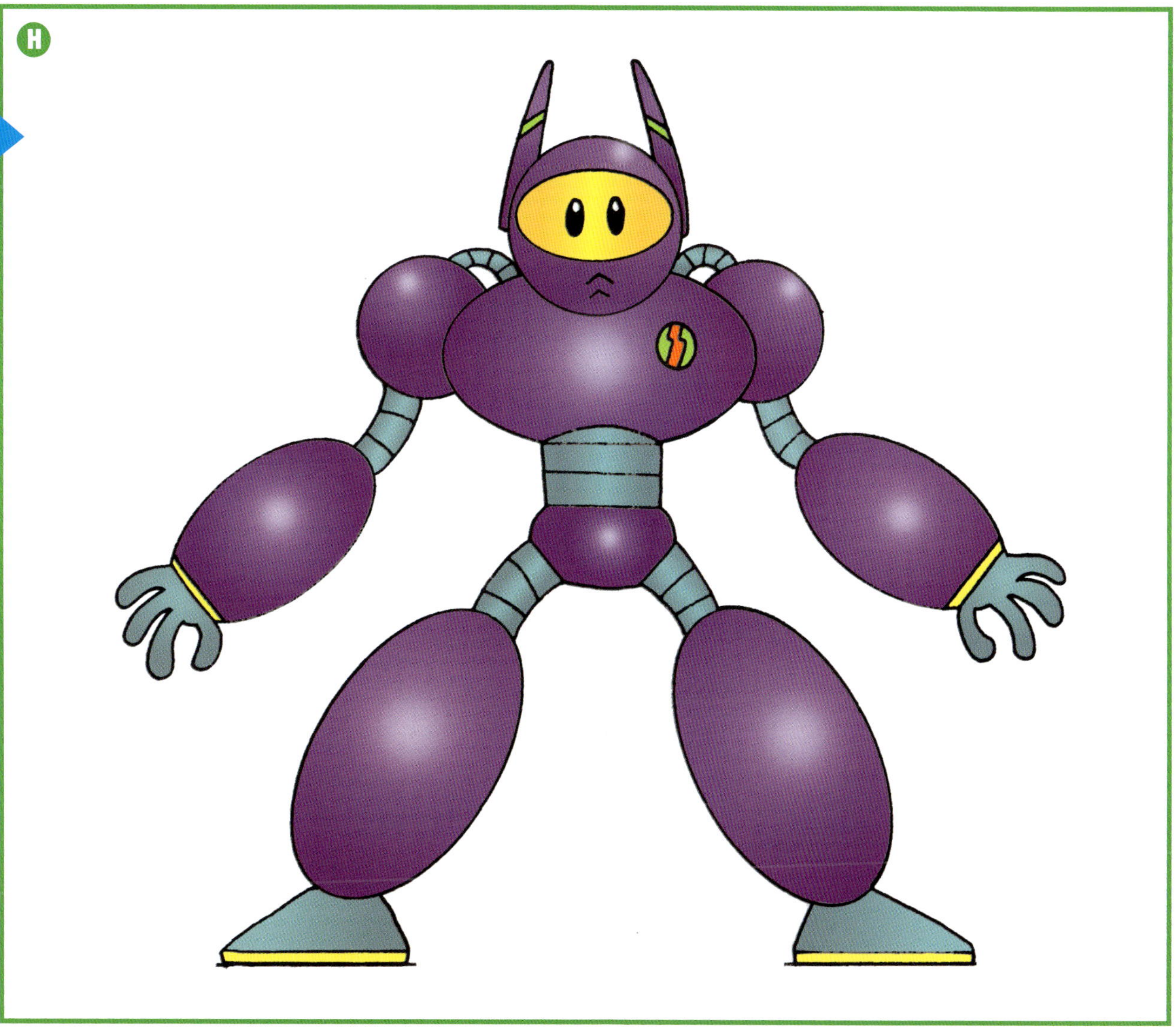

H

HOW TO DRAW A MANGA BEAR

STEP 1

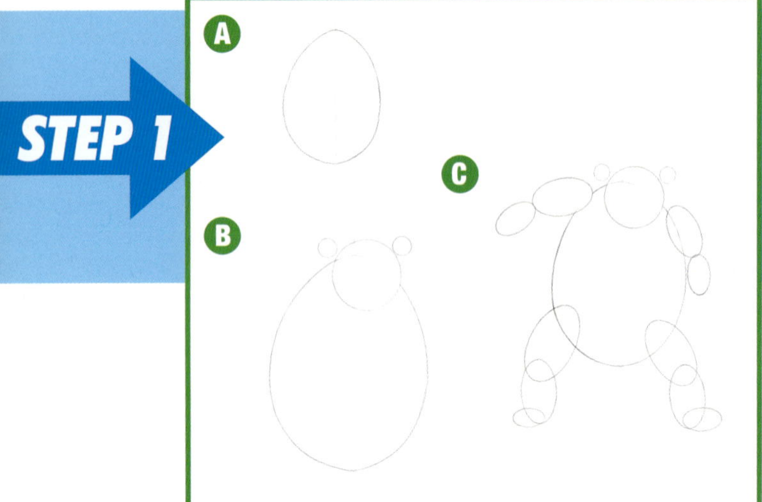

2

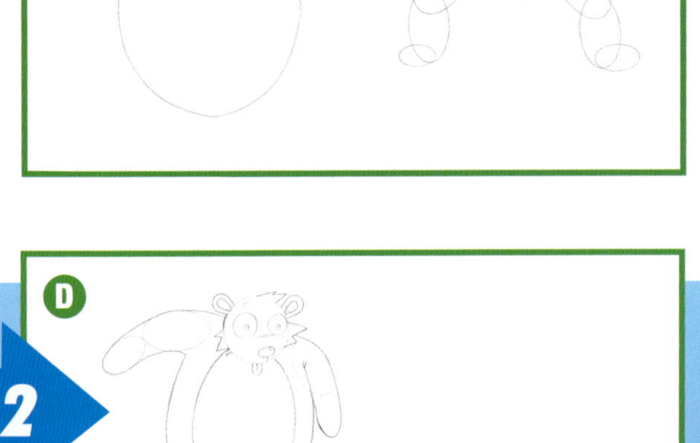

A Your manga bear begins life as a large egg shape, with a vertical line running through the center. This is going to be his body, so it needs to be quite large on the paper.

B The head of your bear consists of circles. There is a fairly large circle for the main bulk of the head, with two smaller circles at either side for the ears. Make sure that the large circle overlaps his body.

C The bear's arms consist of a larger oval as the upper arm, and a smaller oval as the forearm. These are connected to the body just below the head. Next, the bear's legs are created in a similar way, but with an added oval shape at the base for the feet.

D Draw your bear's outline using the shapes as a guide. Connect the shapes, remembering which ones are supposed to overlap and which are not. Start sketching a face for your bear. He looks kinda stupid here, but you might want your bear to look happy or even angry.

E Your bear's claws are sharp, curved shapes at the end of its arms and legs. To give the fur a shaggy appearance, trace around your outline, and draw little spiky bits here and there.

F Once your bear is looking fuzzy enough, you can draw over the pencil lines with a black pen, and erase any lines you don't need.

G Color your bear using short colored pencil strokes. This is a great way to give his fur that all-over shaggy look, or you may want his fur to look glossy and simple.

3

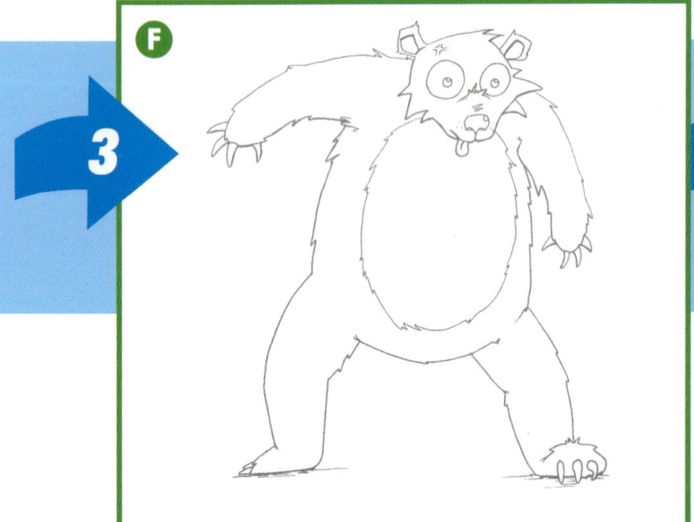

4

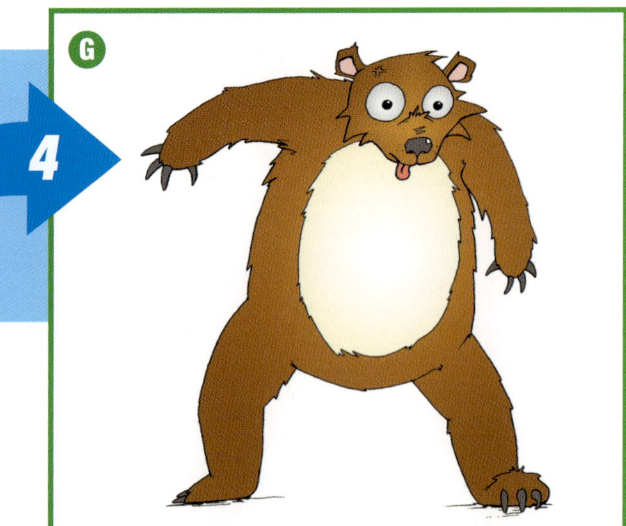

SPACE

"Are we alone?" Scientists and the public have been asking this question for hundreds of years. Is it possible that there is intelligent life on other planets, far away in another solar system? Many scientists would reply with a definite "yes."

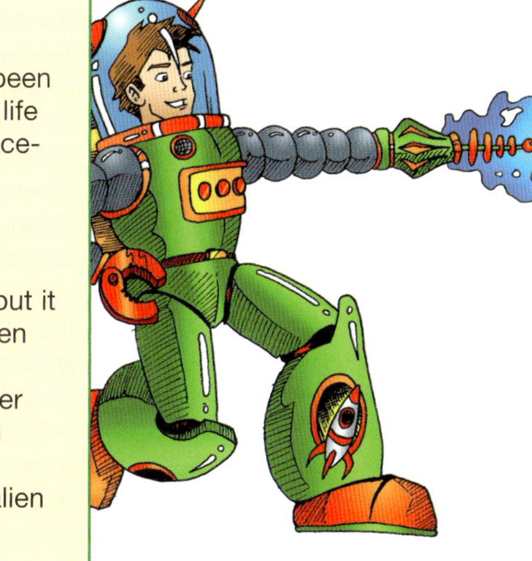

In this chapter, an astronaut from Earth has been sent to a distant planet to check for signs of life there. The astronaut is wearing a special spacesuit that enables him to breathe and he has weapons, in case of intergalactic conflict.

When he arrives, though, there is a conflict, but it is between two resident aliens, who don't even notice our astronaut. Zog, the smaller purple alien, has pulled his ray gun on Bob, the larger blue alien. Both seem equally scared of each other—it is an extraterrestrial disagreement! Meanwhile, a UFO piloted by a small green alien zooms by overhead.

As most of us have never met an alien life form (even though some people claim to have done so), this chapter is all about using your imagination. You may want to design your own aliens with ten legs, six eyes, and huge, sharp teeth! Hopefully, Zog, Bob, and friends will give you some fuel for thought.

So strap in, blast off, and search the corners of your mind. These guys will take you to another world!

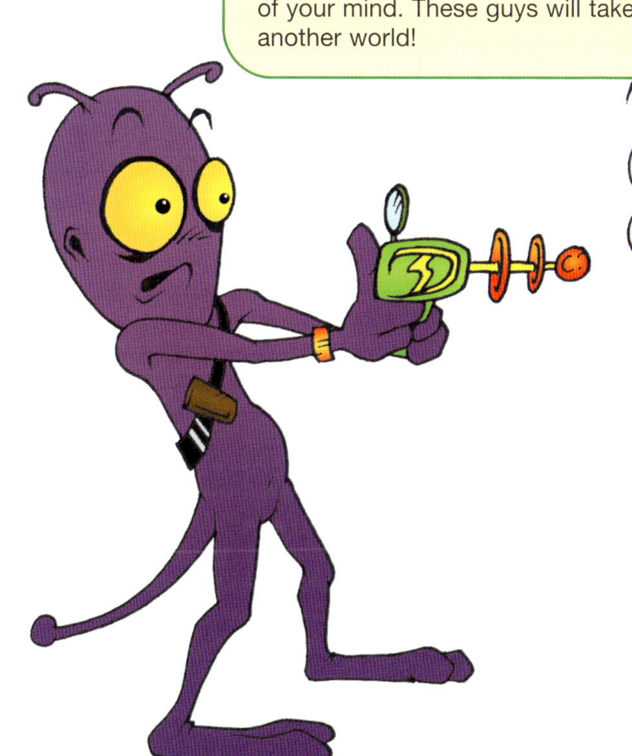

STEP 1

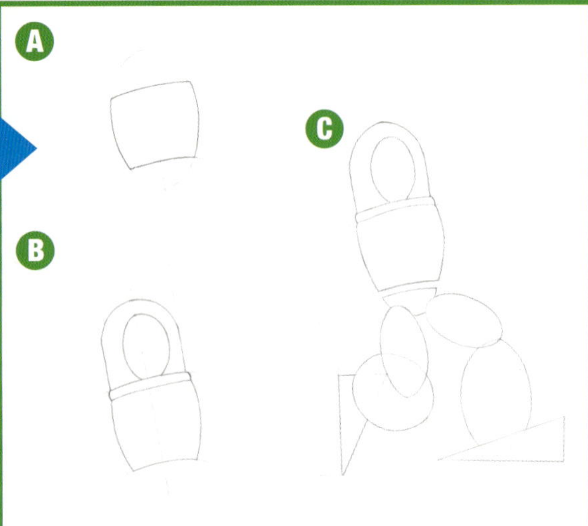

2

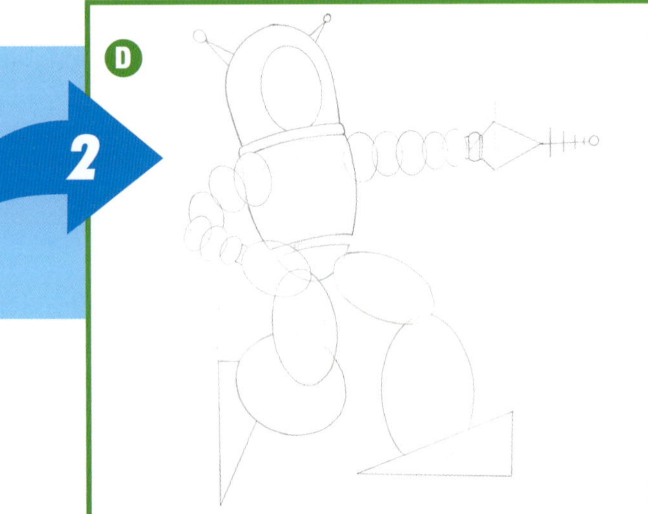

A Begin by sketching a large oval shape in the center of your page, placed at a slight angle. Draw a straight line through the center of this and trim the oval down to a barrel shape. This is going to be the main body of his spacesuit.

B Draw a dome shape on top of the body, with a rim along the base of it joining it to the spacesuit body. A compass or circular template may help when drawing the dome. Next, draw an oval shape inside the dome; this will be your astronaut's head.

C Your astronaut's legs are constructed using simple shapes. His feet are triangular, and the upper and lower parts of the leg are both oval-shaped. As the left leg is tucked back whilst running, make sure the shapes overlap each other. This will give depth to the picture and make it appear that he is striding forward.

D The arms of the spacesuit are drawn using lots of overlapping ovals. Add a diamond-shaped laser on the right arm and a claw on the left arm. You can also put two antennae on his helmet, so he can pick up any transmissions from ground control.

E Round off your astronaut's triangular feet and begin putting detail onto the different sections of his legs, remembering which parts overlap each other. Start to sketch his facial features and spiky hair. Remember, his head is turned,

3

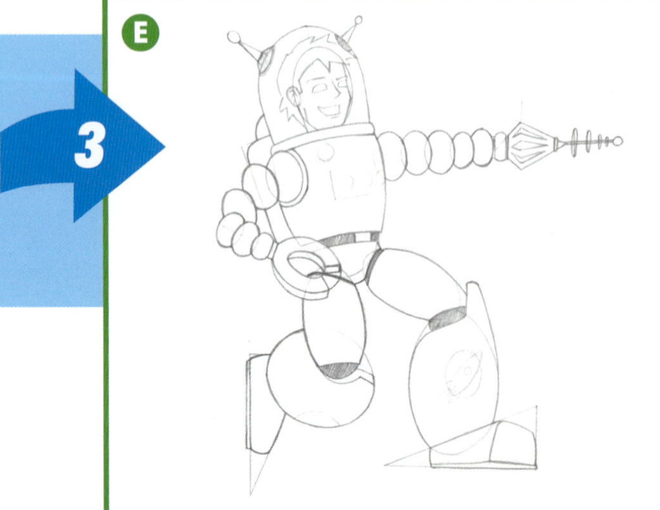

4

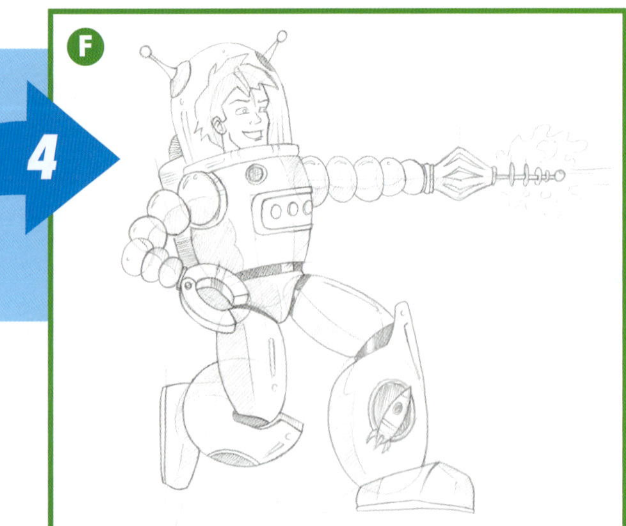

5

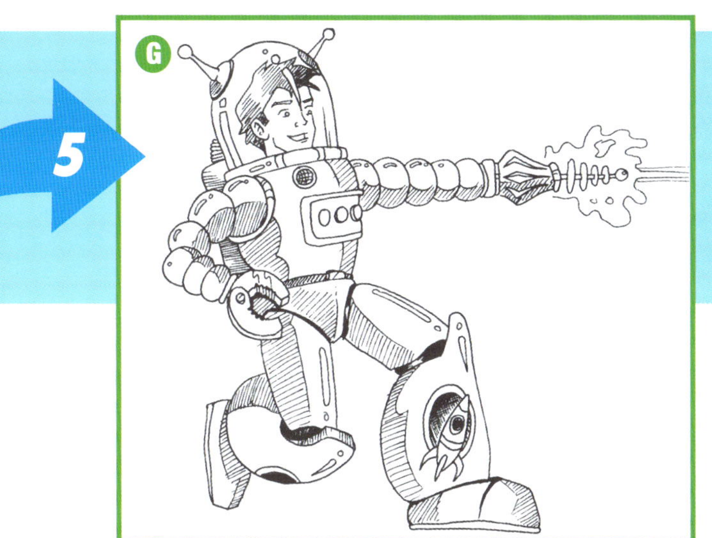

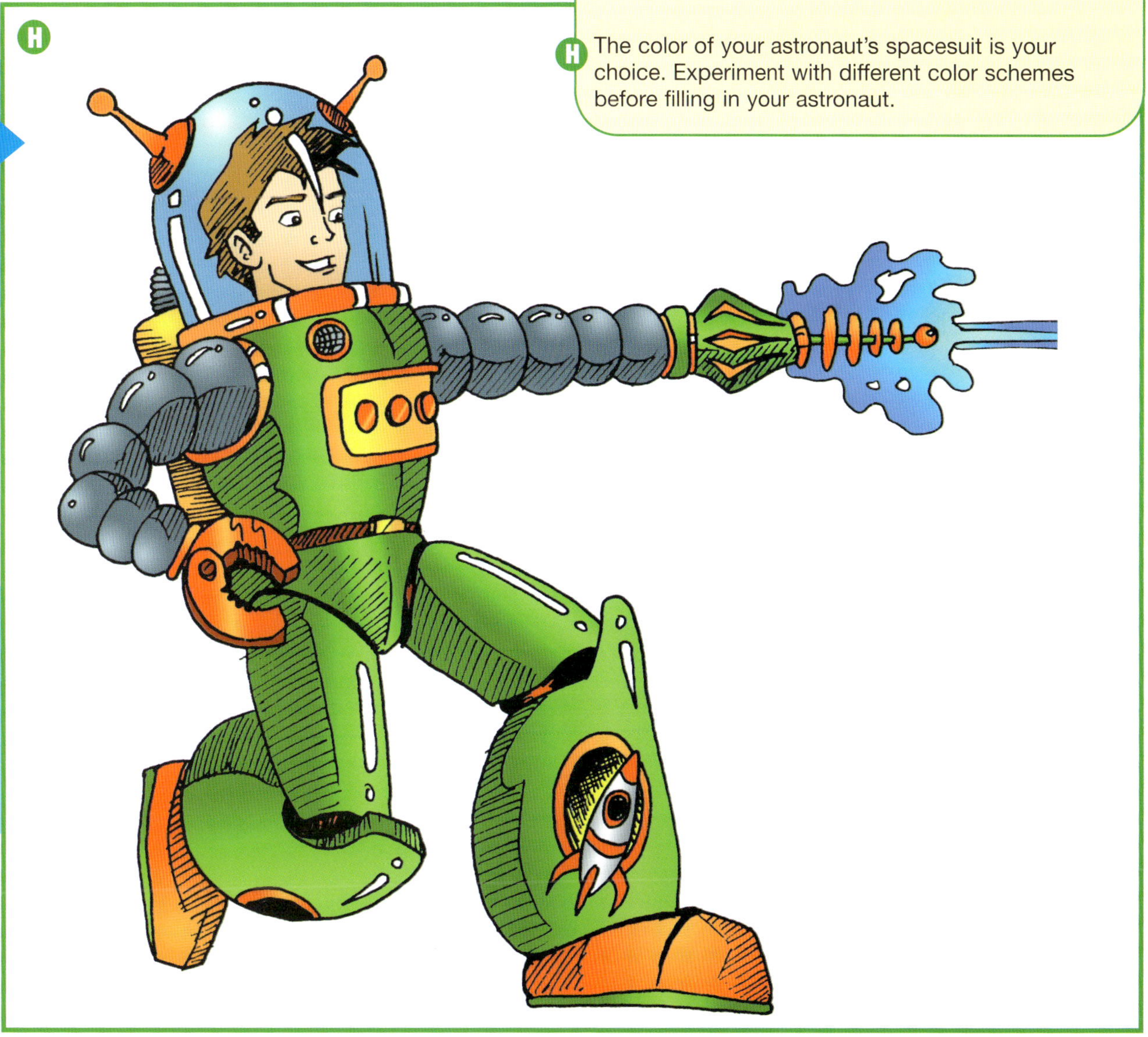

so his eyes and nose are drawn slightly to the right. Next, start sketching in the claw, using its oval outline as a guide. Draw more detail on the laser and place a control panel on his chestplate. Finally, give your astronaut a rocket motif on his leg.

F In the final stage of pencil sketching, alter anything you aren't happy with before developing the face of your astronaut. Give his eyes pupils and add some extra detail to his hair and mouth. Finally, work on his badge design. You may want a different logo to that featured on the rocket ship.

G Trace over all of the pencil lines that you're happy with using a black drawing pen and then erase any you don't want. Your astronaut is ready to color.

H The color of your astronaut's spacesuit is your choice. Experiment with different color schemes before filling in your astronaut.

6

H

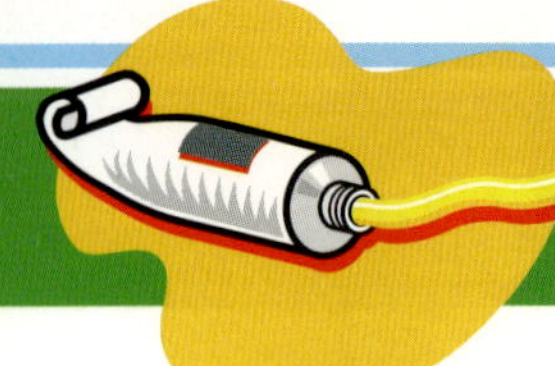

STEP 1

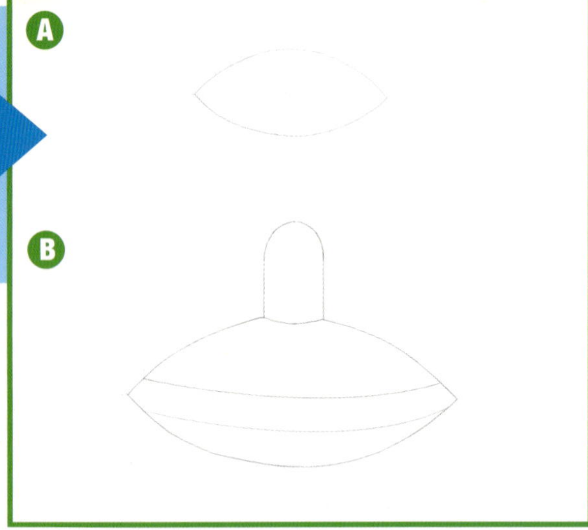

A Draw a large feint cross in the center of your page. This is a guide to help you work out the dimensions of your UFO. Measure 4in either side of your center point, and make a mark there. Next, measure 2in above and 1.6in below your center point, marking both of these as well. Join the four points using curved lines to form a large almond-shaped alien craft.

B On the top of your UFO shape, draw a dome in the center. It may help you to use a compass or circle template when drawing this. Once the dome is complete, draw two curved horizontal lines through the center of your UFO—these are the basis for the strip of rotating lights.

2

C Start to draw your alien pilot inside the dome. He can be drawn like a stick man, but with a much larger, egg-shaped head. Give him two gear sticks to hold onto, to help him drive the spaceship. Draw a row of circles inside the curved lines you drew in stage B; these are going to be the rotating lights. On the under-side of the UFO, in line with the top dome, draw a booster flame. This is a similar almond shape to the spaceship, but only half of it is actually showing.

D Give your enthusiastic alien traveler some big round eyes and a huge, grinning mouth. You should also add detail to the glass dome, such as the gleam from the stars. Next, start to draw some large panels on the body of the

3

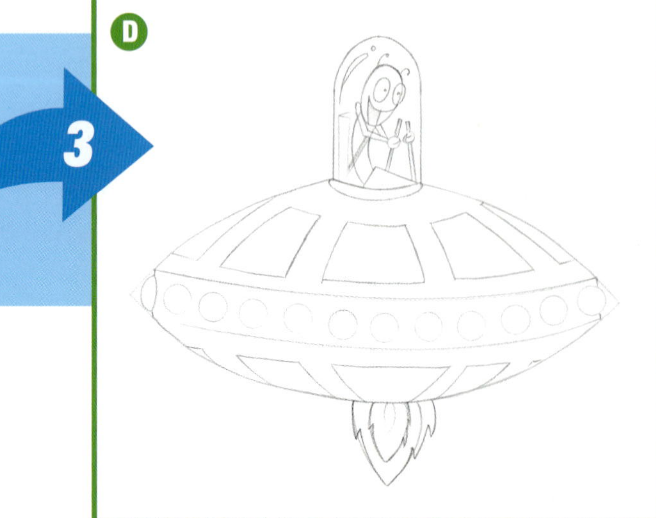

4

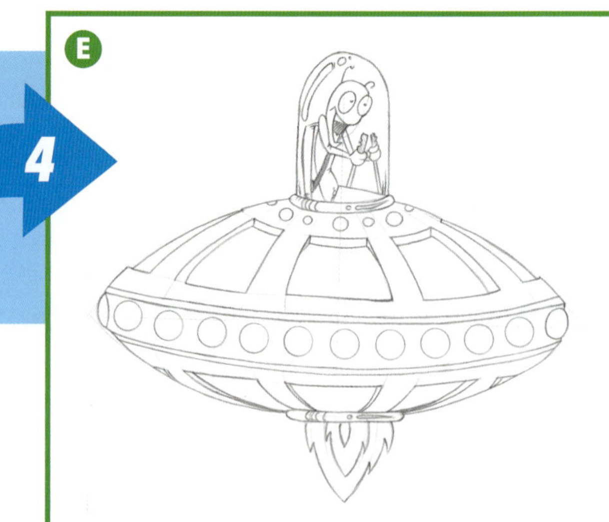

5

F

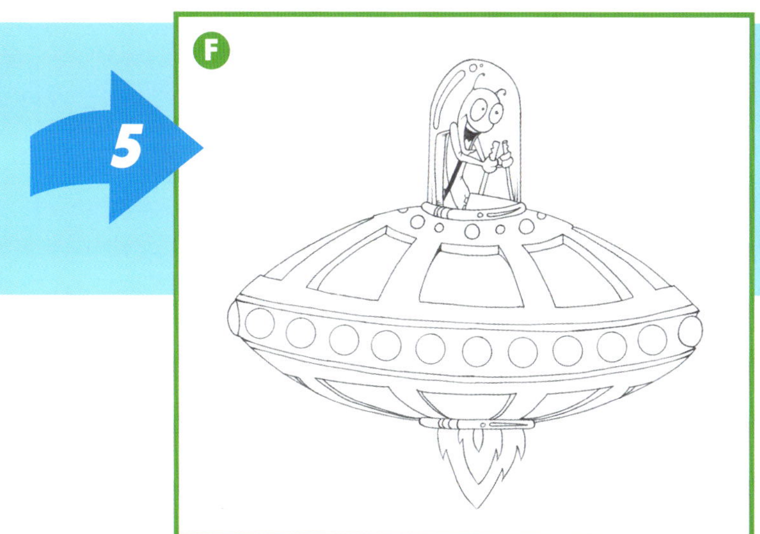

UFO. These panel lines are drawn by curving each of them toward the central point at the top and bottom of your UFO.

E Draw some extra lights on the UFO just underneath the dome. Finally, you can make the booster flame look more powerful by adding a couple of layers of fire inside the original almond shape you sketched in step A, and by giving the flame a jagged outline.

F When your UFO is looking the way you want it to, trace in the outline with a black pen and erase any pencil marks.

G It's best to use metallic colors for the ship itself, such as gray, blue, and silver. The alien here looks like a typical "little green man," but you can paint him purple or red, or maybe even blue!

6

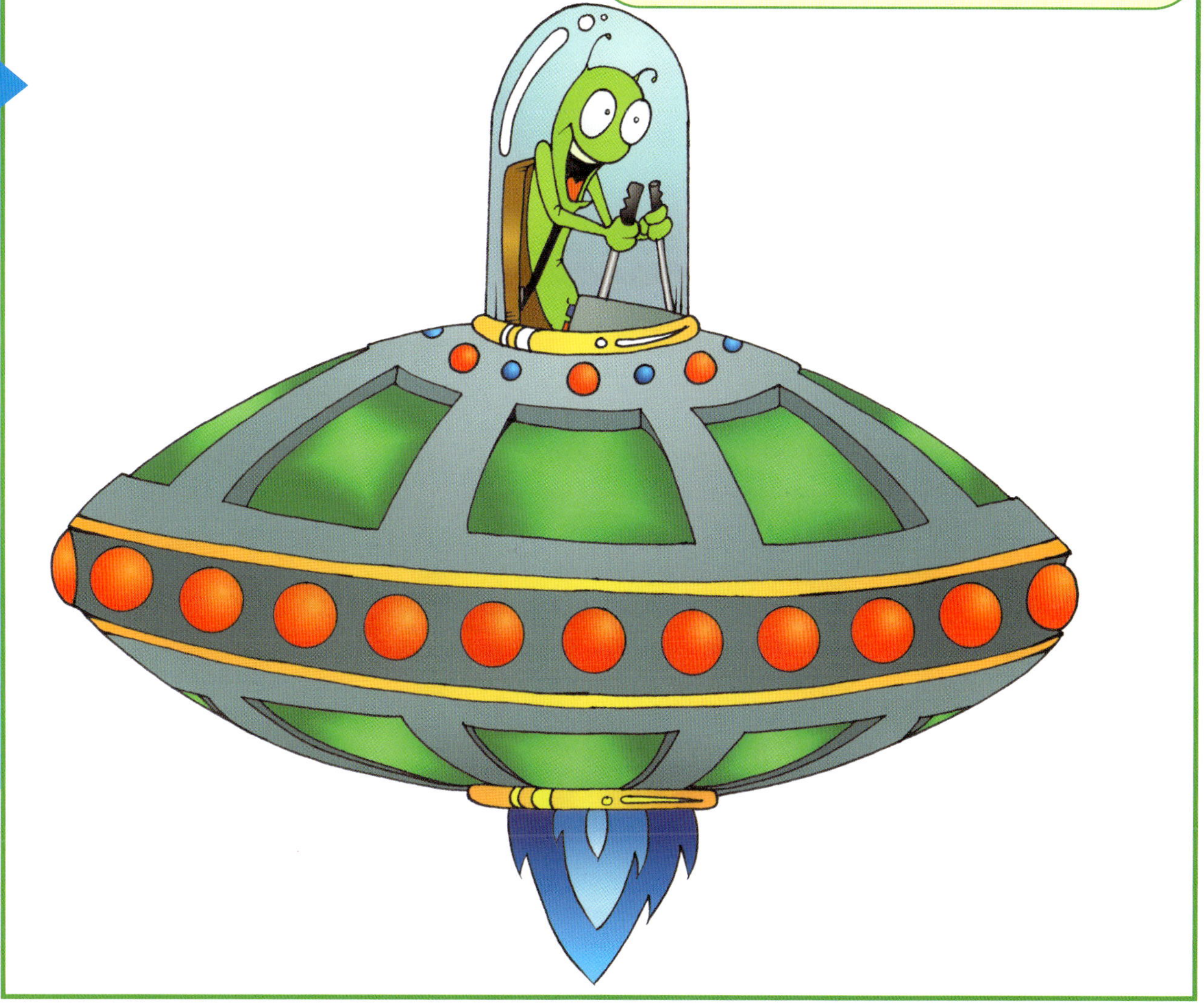

G

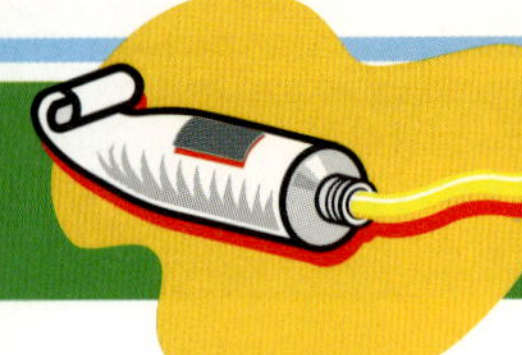

STEP 1

A

2

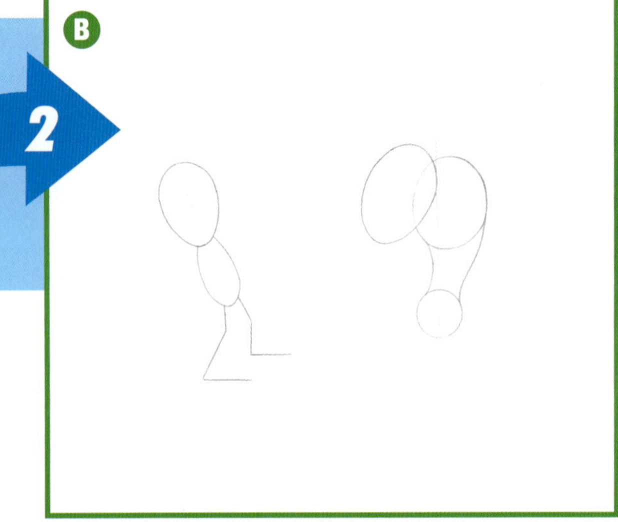

A Both Zog and Bob's heads are egg-shaped. Draw Zog's head to the left of the page at a slight angle. Next, draw Bob's head a little larger than Zog's on the right-hand side of the page, slanting in the opposite direction.

B Zog's body is an oval shape that's smaller than his head, but tilted at the same angle. Draw some simple stick legs, bent at the knee; one of these will be slightly bigger as it's closer to you. Bob's body is more complicated: it consists of another egg shape, the same size as his head, joined to a small circle by two wavy lines.

C Draw Zog's arms in the same way you drew his legs. Give him a ray-gun to hold, which is a simple square shape. Next, add two antennas, huge round eyes, and a downturned mouth. Draw a long, thin tail with a bobble on the end. Bob's going to need some eyes too—four of them in fact! The lower two are slightly smaller, and he has a wide-open mouth. His legs are constructed using simple shapes, and his tail is long and curved.

D Zog's legs and arms need padding out a little at this stage. Round off the square gun's corners and give Zog's hand a large thumb. Draw a strap across his chest with a gun-holster on it. Finally, give him pupils, eyebrows, and ears. Draw Bob's second set of legs the way you drew his first set, but make sure that they are

3

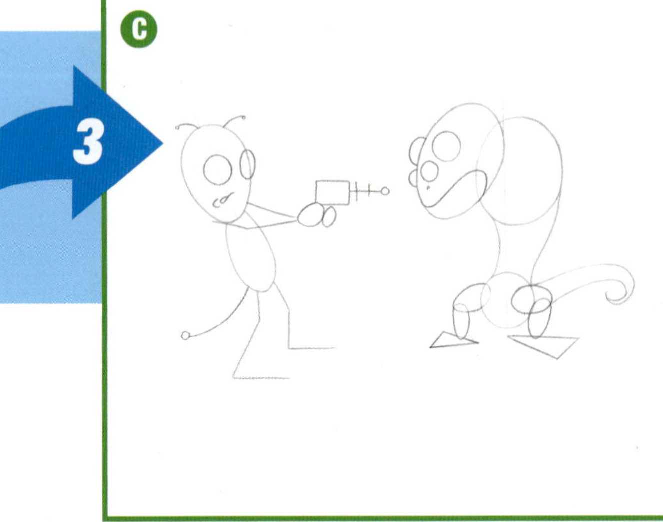

4

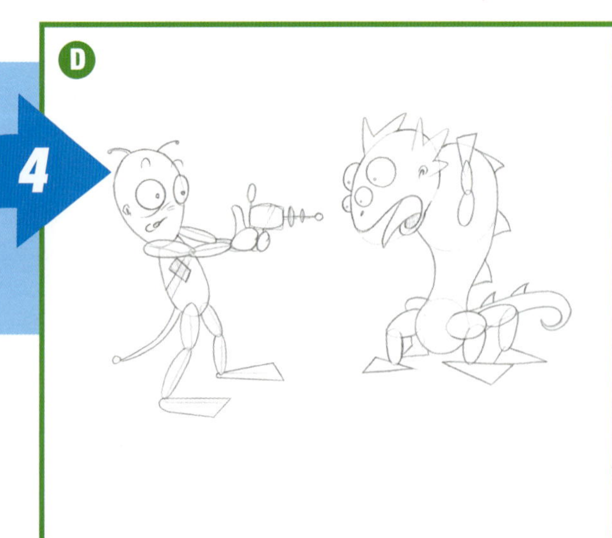

5

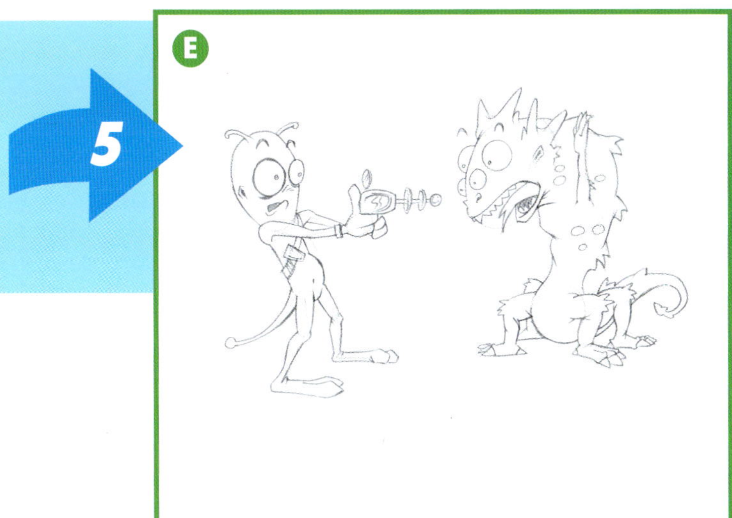

tucked behind him. Add detail to his face, like his tongue and spiked crest. Then give him a spiny back, and an arm held up in horror!

E Give Zog's ray gun some final details, such as a wavy shine and the aiming sight. Next, his fingers, toes, and wrinkles can be added, along with dark rings under his eyes. Bob has polka-dot skin in places, and you can make his spines more jagged. Finally, give him some goofy teeth and big, sharp toenails.

F Draw in both aliens with a pen. Then erase the pencil lines. This will leave you with a clean line drawing of the aliens arguing!

→

6

F

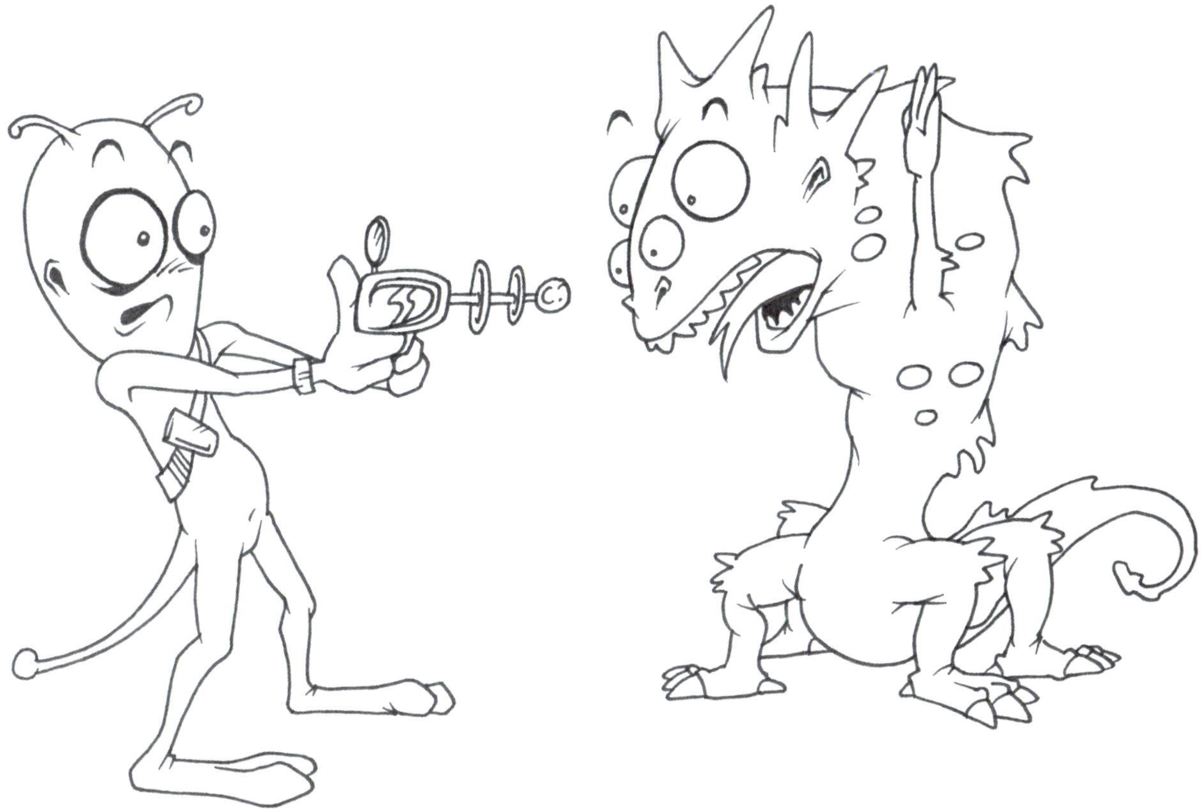

7

G

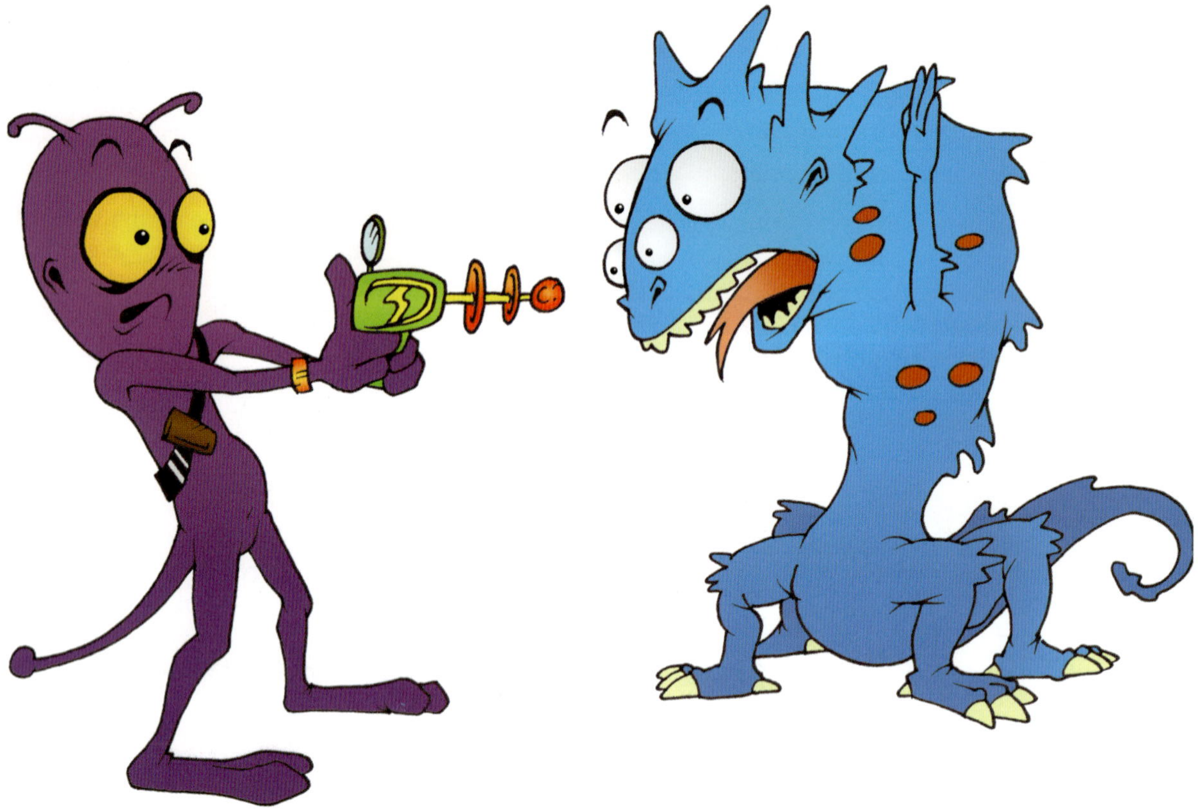

G Aliens can really be any color. After all, have you ever actually seen one? Maybe you have, but most people don't know what aliens look like, let alone what colors they are. This is one for your imagination, so go crazy—and see what happens!

SUPERHEROES AND ARCH-VILLAINS

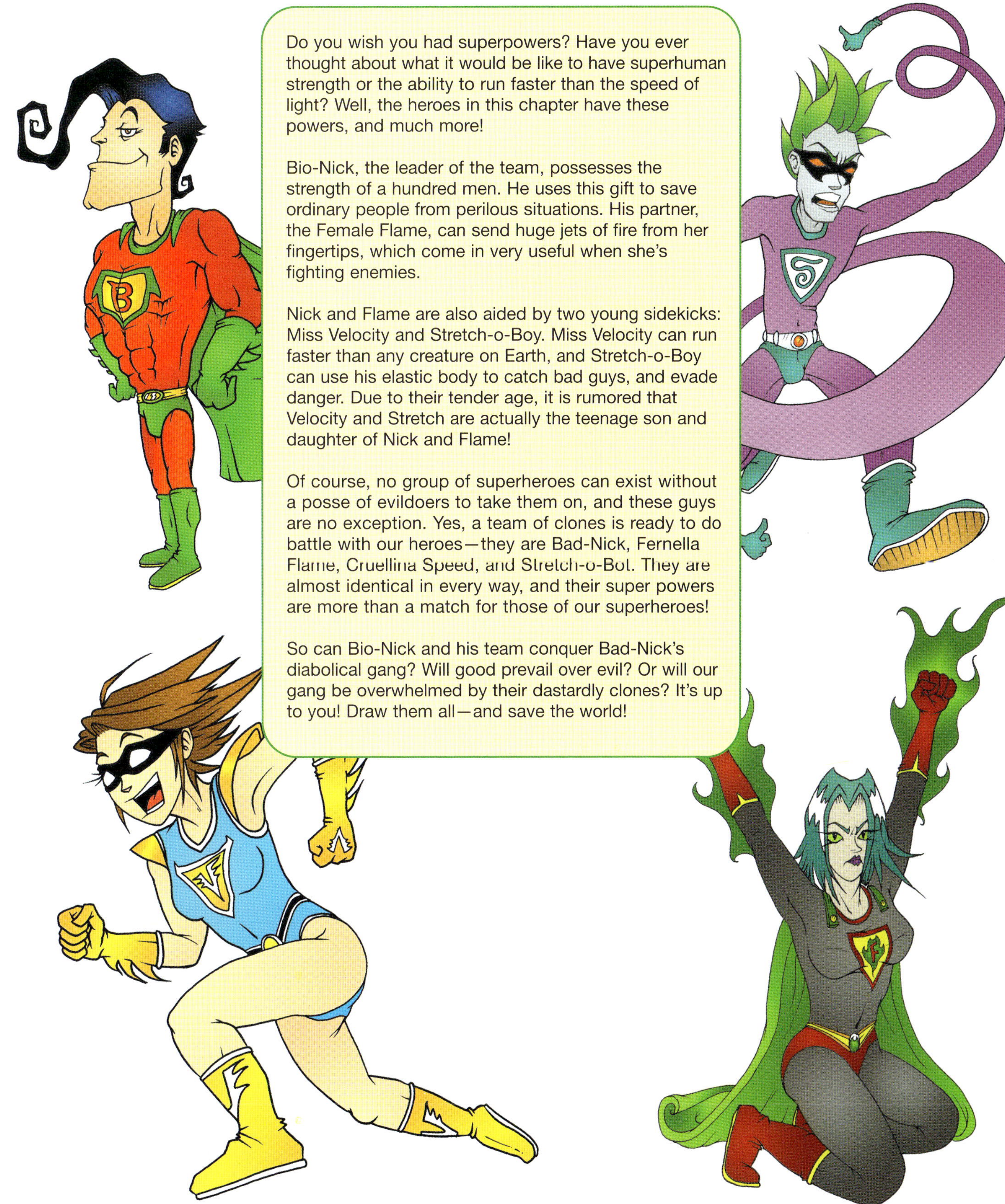

Do you wish you had superpowers? Have you ever thought about what it would be like to have superhuman strength or the ability to run faster than the speed of light? Well, the heroes in this chapter have these powers, and much more!

Bio-Nick, the leader of the team, possesses the strength of a hundred men. He uses this gift to save ordinary people from perilous situations. His partner, the Female Flame, can send huge jets of fire from her fingertips, which come in very useful when she's fighting enemies.

Nick and Flame are also aided by two young sidekicks: Miss Velocity and Stretch-o-Boy. Miss Velocity can run faster than any creature on Earth, and Stretch-o-Boy can use his elastic body to catch bad guys, and evade danger. Due to their tender age, it is rumored that Velocity and Stretch are actually the teenage son and daughter of Nick and Flame!

Of course, no group of superheroes can exist without a posse of evildoers to take them on, and these guys are no exception. Yes, a team of clones is ready to do battle with our heroes—they are Bad-Nick, Fernella Flame, Cruellina Speed, and Stretch-o-Bot. They are almost identical in every way, and their super powers are more than a match for those of our superheroes!

So can Bio-Nick and his team conquer Bad-Nick's diabolical gang? Will good prevail over evil? Or will our gang be overwhelmed by their dastardly clones? It's up to you! Draw them all—and save the world!

STEP 1

A

B

C

A Begin your picture of Bio-Nick by drawing an upside down egg shape in the center of your page. Draw this at a slight angle. This egg shape will eventually be Nick's head.

B Now draw a triangle directly below the head, and join it to the head with two curved lines to represent the neck. The top edge of your triangle should slant down to the left—this will give the illusion that one shoulder is further away than the other. Nick's arms are created using two oval shapes with a fan shape on the end for each hand.

C To complete the frame for Nick's body, he's going to need some bionic legs. Like his arms, these are made up of three shapes. This time, though, it's two ovals and a triangular foot. Due to Nick's strength, his arms are actually bigger than his legs, so make sure you draw the leg ovals smaller and thinner.

D At this point in the drawing, you can start adding detail to your character. Bio-Nick's hair is styled in one long, heroic curl with a smaller curl at the nape of his neck. Sketch in his eyes and mouth. Draw lines on his suit to represent the seam of his gloves and boots before adding triangular spikes to his gloves. Finally, give him a flowing cape and some underpants on the outside of his tights—as all superheroes should have!

2

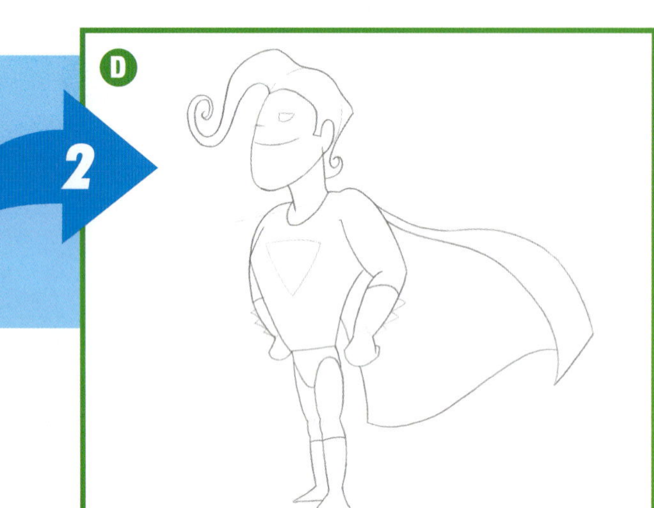

3

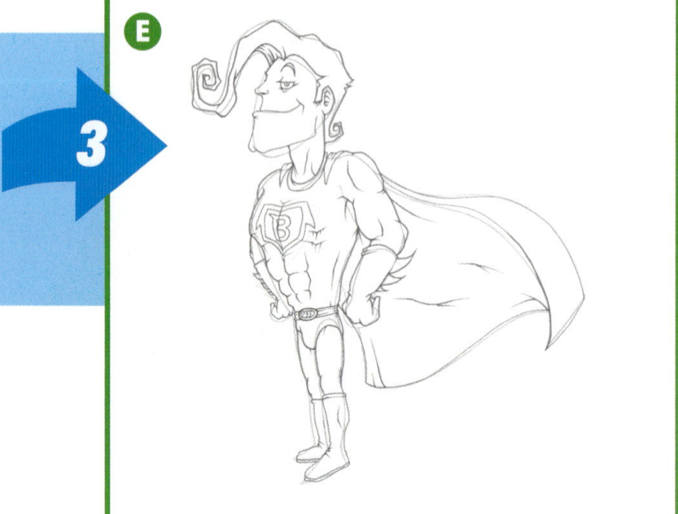

4

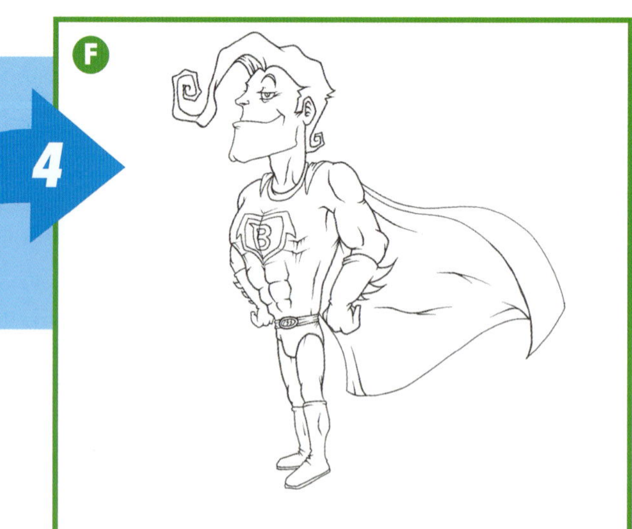

5

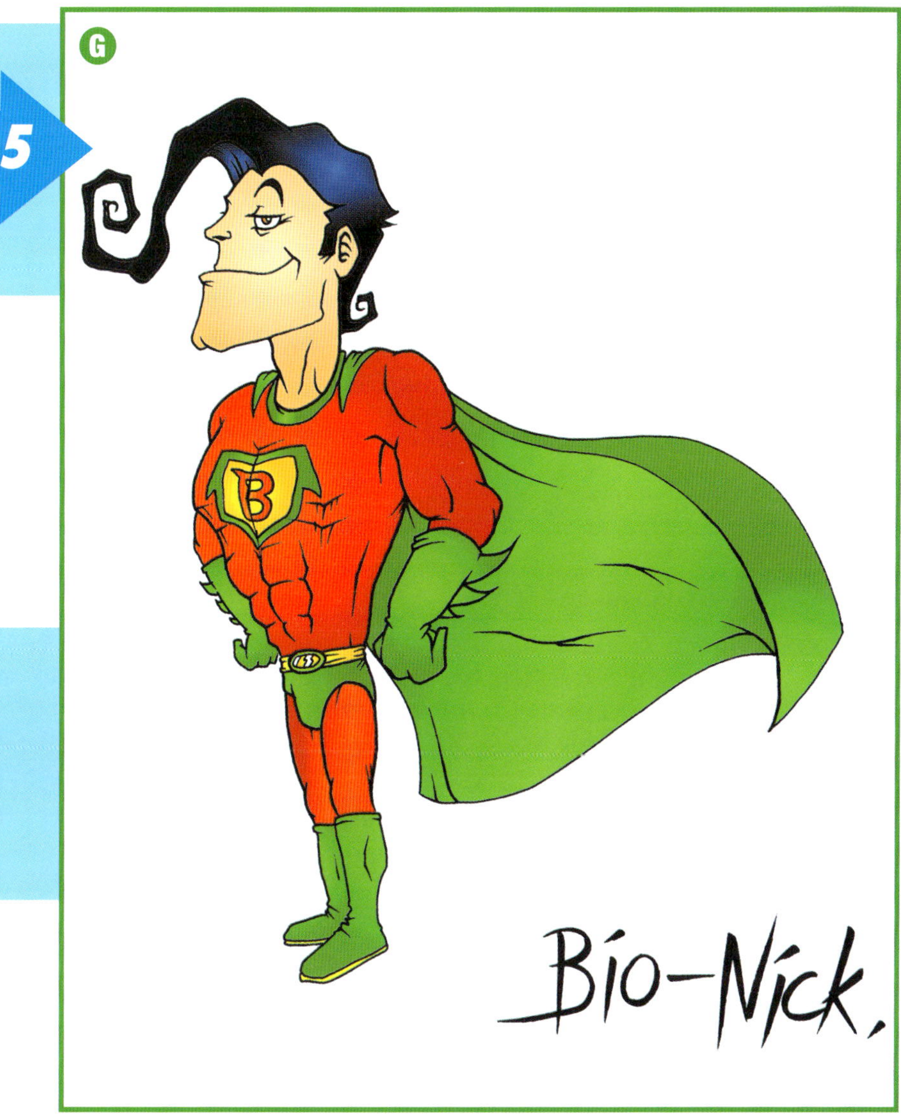

E Start to put the finishing touches to your superhero by adding some detailing to his suit and face. Superheroes are very muscular, so draw lines to show where his muscles are, including a "six-pack" on his stomach. Final touches such as the superhero logo (a large letter "B") on his chest add to his image, and make Bio-Nick instantly recognizable.

F Once your hero is looking the way you want him, draw in the outline using a black pen, and erase the pencil marks.

G Heroes are normally painted in strong primary colors, so Bio-Nick's suit is predominantly red, with green gloves and accessories. Blue and yellow also make a great combination.

H I To draw Bio-Nick's utterly evil nemesis, Bad-Nick, all you need do is change his facial features slightly, and recolor his all-important special suit. Now you should take a close look and see if you can spot what else has been changed to make Bad-Nick into a true bad guy!

6

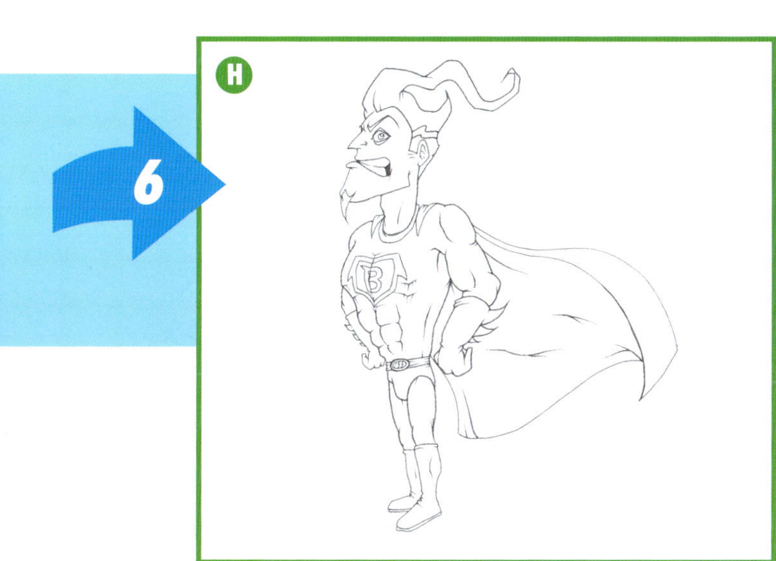

7

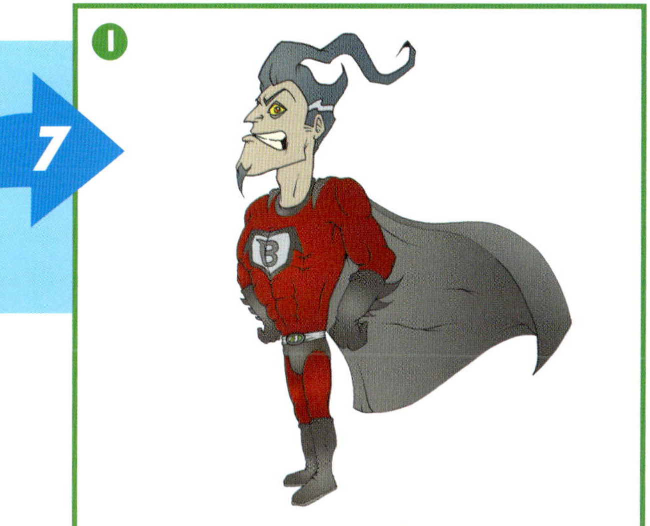

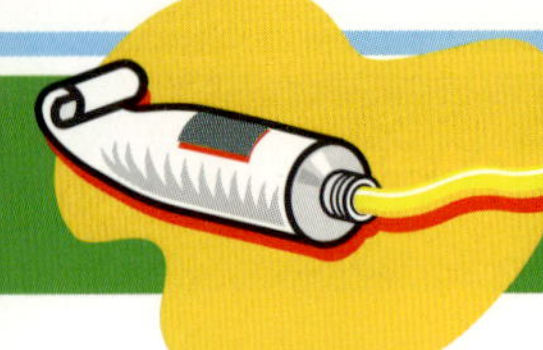

STEP 1

A

C

B

A The Female Flame's head is shaped like an egg, so start by drawing this shape in the center of your paper. Next, draw a very pale vertical line through the center, from the top of your page to the base.

B The second stage is drawing Female Flame's main body shape below her head. This is shaped like a large triangle. The head is joined to the body by a short neck.

C The Female Flame's arms are drawn in a similar way to the other characters' arms. Draw them using three simple shapes, stretched up above her body. Make sure that the right arm is closer to the neck, and slightly obscured by her head.

D Your heroine is going to be kneeling down, so the shapes that make up her legs overlap each other slightly. The leg closest to you is larger than the other leg, and her foot starts off as an upward-pointing triangle. Her other leg tucks in behind the first. Once you've drawn this, curve a line from her arm to the base of her back. Then chop the top right-hand corner off the large triangular body to give the shape of her chest.

E Give your heroine a cape, and add some simple detail to her costume, such as the gloves and boots. Pencil her eyes, nose, and mouth onto the egg shape before giving her a simple, spiky shoulder-length haircut. Female Flame, like her superhero friends, has a triangular logo on her chest.

2

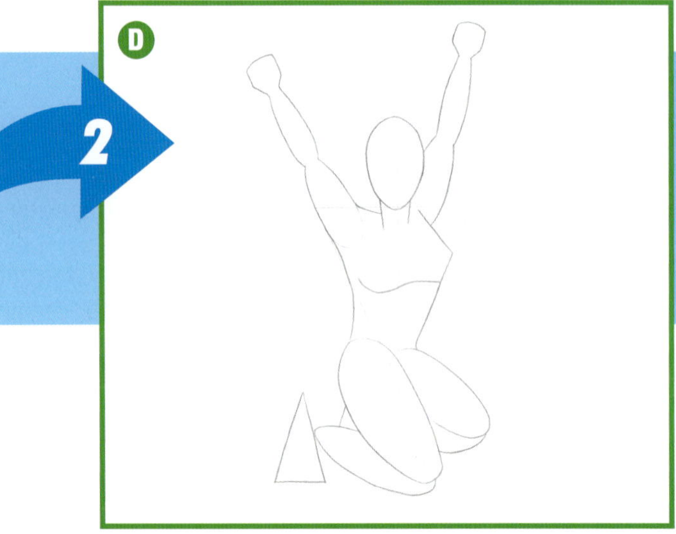

3

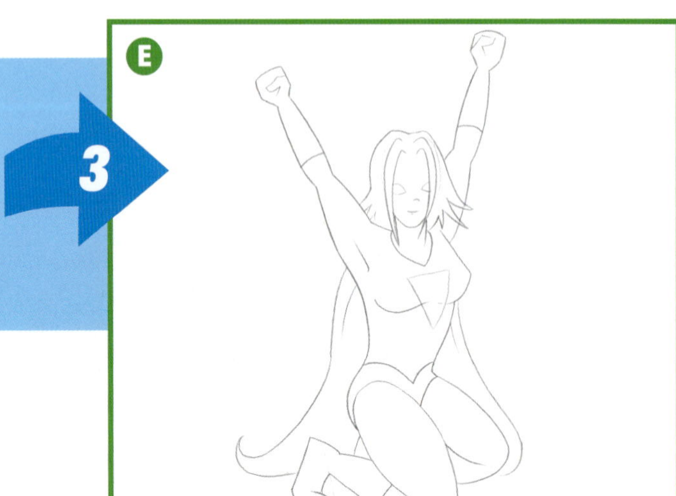

4

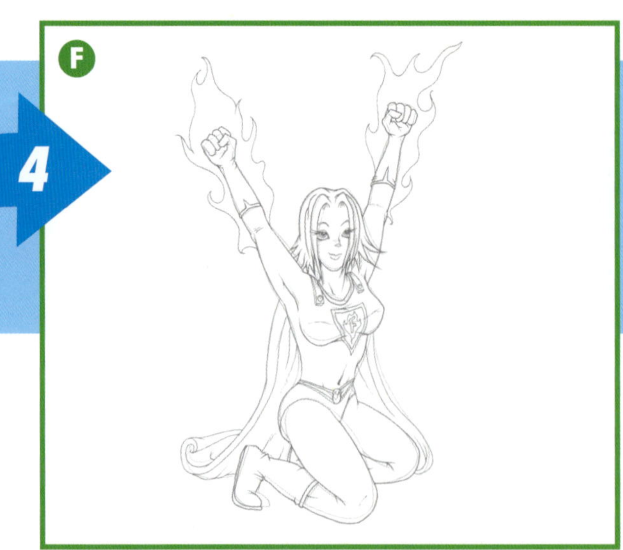

5

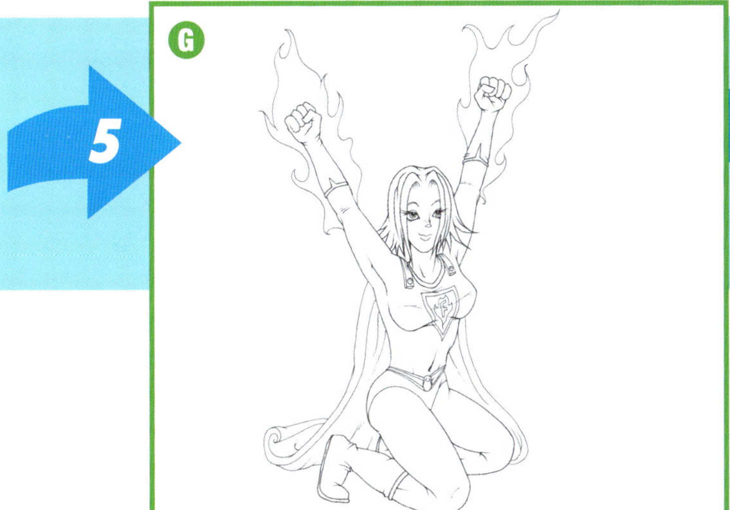

6

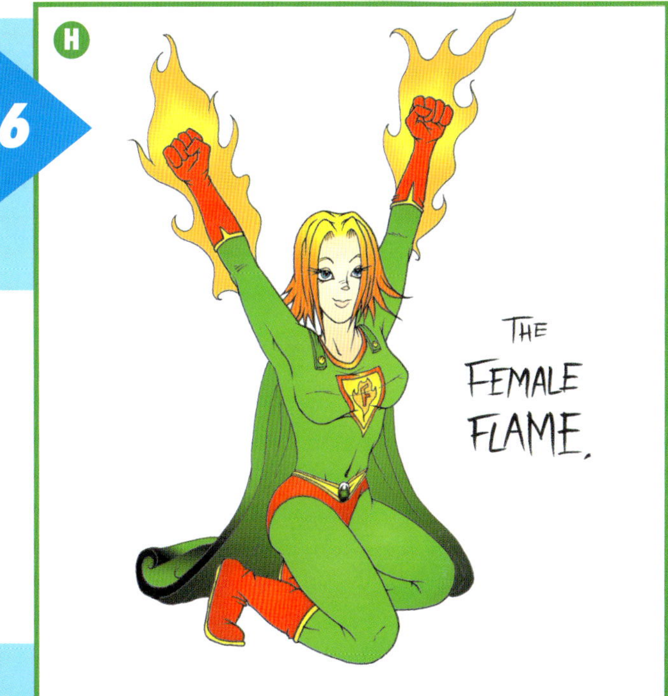

F Using heavier pencil lines, you can start to add detail to your picture. Female Flame's eyes should have dark outlines and long, pointed eyelashes. The fingers on each hand are cylindrical, with the thumb bent over the other digits. Final touches to the suit, like the flaming "F" logo, will help add an authentic look to your superhero. The most important detail, however, is the scorching flames pouring from her hands—remember, this is her special power. Every hero has to have one!

G Once you have all the detail you want, you can then draw over the lines with a black pen before erasing the original pencil drawing. You're now ready to begin coloring!

H The Female Flame has a similar color scheme to Bio-Nick, as they are a team—using the same colors gives a visual unity to their heroic partnership. The colors are reversed though, the green is used as the main suit color, and the red for her accessories.

I J The evil Fernella Flame is drawn using the exact same frame as her heroic doppelganger, but her face is sharper, as are her features—her eyes are snake-like and she is scowling.

7

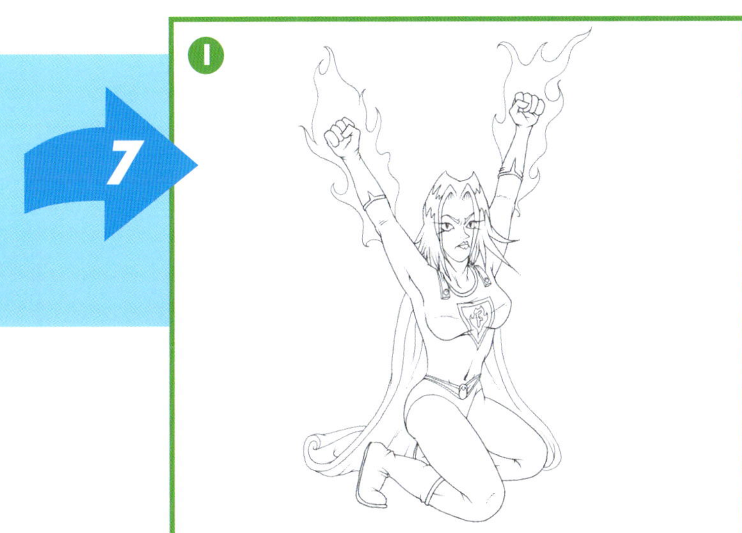

8

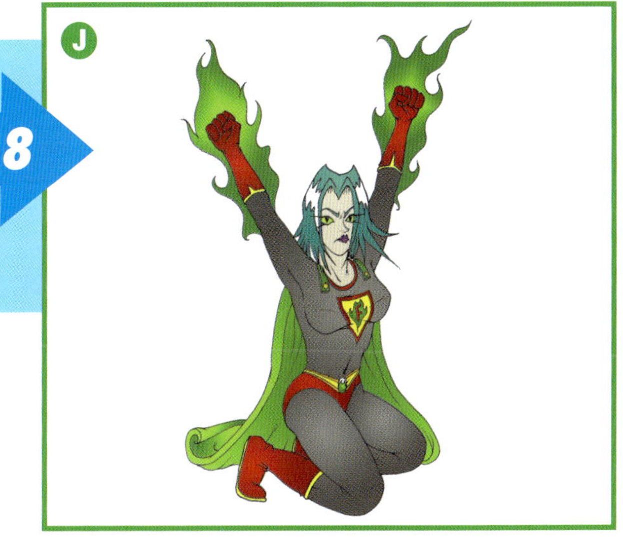

STEP 1

A

C

B

2

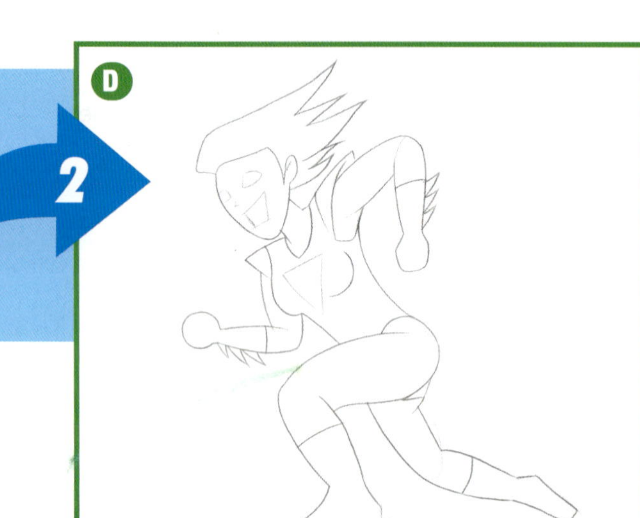

3

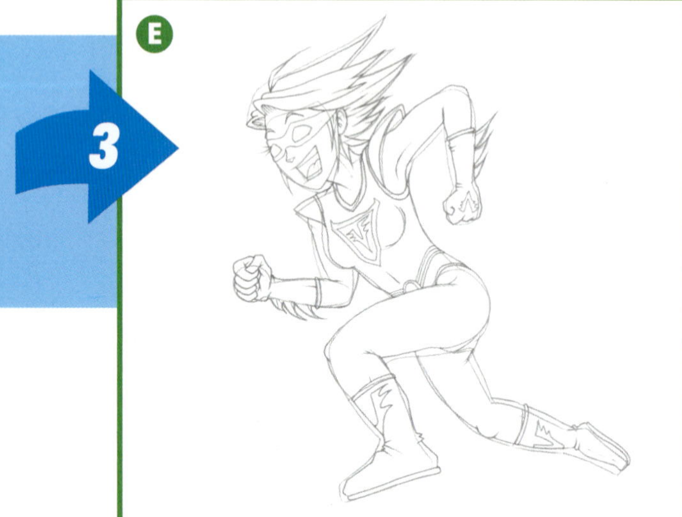

4

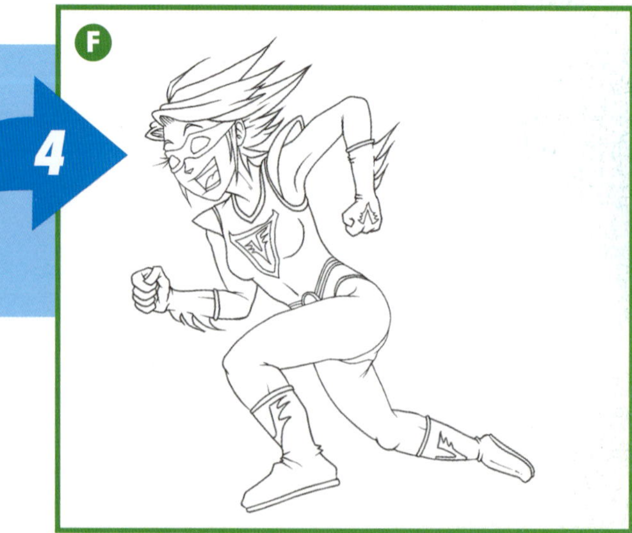

A Start your drawing with a simple egg shape, with the pointed end facing downward. Remember that most human heads can be started in this way.

B Now, draw a large triangle beneath the head, joined by a "neck" consisting of two curved lines. Attach two arms to the triangular body. One arm is bent backward, while the other is thrusting forward. The arms are created using two ovals with a circle on the end of each, that are going to be her hands.

C Miss Velocity's body is completed by giving her two striding legs. One leg is out in front, bent at the knee. Remember to draw her upper leg wider than her lower leg, just like yours. Her other leg is stretched out behind her, so it must be drawn smaller and thinner to give the appearance of perspective. Finally, she needs triangular feet and curved lines to represent her chest and the curve of her back.

D This is where you begin working on Miss Velocity's details. Using your frame as a guide, start to round off the sharp edges on her feet and shoulders. Begin adding her facial features and her long, flowing hair. Draw a triangle on her chest where her logo is going to be, and give her gloves a row of spines.

E Start cleaning up the lines of Miss Velocity's body, and give her face, hair, and costume more detail. Separate her hair into sections, and give her a mask to hide her identity. Final touches, such as the letter "V" on her gloves,

5

G

chest, and boots give Miss Velocity a look that is all her own!

F Draw over your pencil sketch with a black pen in order to create your final outline. Then erase the pencil marks, and she's ready to be filled in with your own choice of colors.

G "Velocity" means speed, so the colors that have been used are ones that will remind people of the wind—her suit is mainly a pale blue color, with a gold tone added to the boots and gloves.

H I Cruellina Speed is as fast as Miss Velocity, but much, much more scary. Just look at her! Her skin is swamp green, and her eyes are a bright, creepy yellow. Worse still, she has sharp, fanged teeth that can pierce through anything—so watch out when she's about! Her suit is the same as Miss Velocity's, only it is a dark purple-black to reflect Cruellina's dark nature.

6

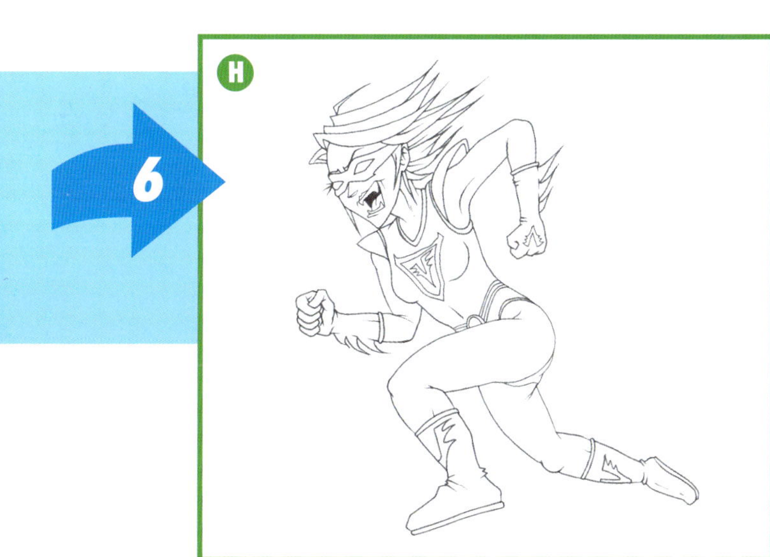

7

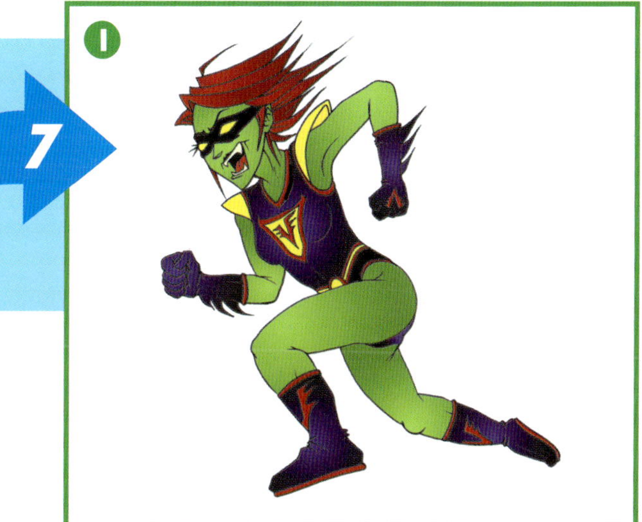

STEP 1

A

B

2

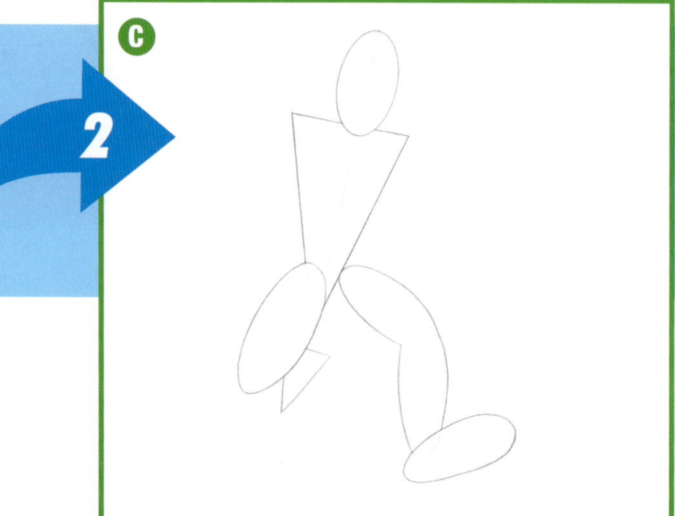

A Stretch-o-Boy's head is oval shaped, and set at a very slight angle to the right. Draw a center line through this shape—it will help you when drawing the rest of his body.

B As with Bio-Nick, Stretch-o-Boy's body is a triangle. Set this at the same angle as his head, and make sure it is slightly overlapping.

C Draw your superhero's legs using simple shapes. The right leg is bent at the knee, and jumping toward us. His foot is an oval shape, but narrower at the heel. The left leg is tucked back, so only draw a single oval for his upper leg, and a triangular shape for the visible part of his foot.

D Stretch-o-Boy's elastic arms are drawn in one long, snaking line. The right arm wraps around his body, so be careful not to pencil it in too heavily. Finally, draw in his facial features using the center line as a guide, and start to give his suit detail.

E Stretch-o-Boy isn't as muscular as Bio-Nick, so his suit is fairly smooth. The all-important details are on his face and utility belt. He has a mask over his eyes, sharp eyebrows, and floppy spiked hair. His belt has a large circular buckle and some small capsules lining it. Don't forget to put an "S" on his chest, and to make it snake-like to represent his super powers—after all, every superhero must have an instantly recognizable logo to make sure that the people he's saving know exactly who he is!

3

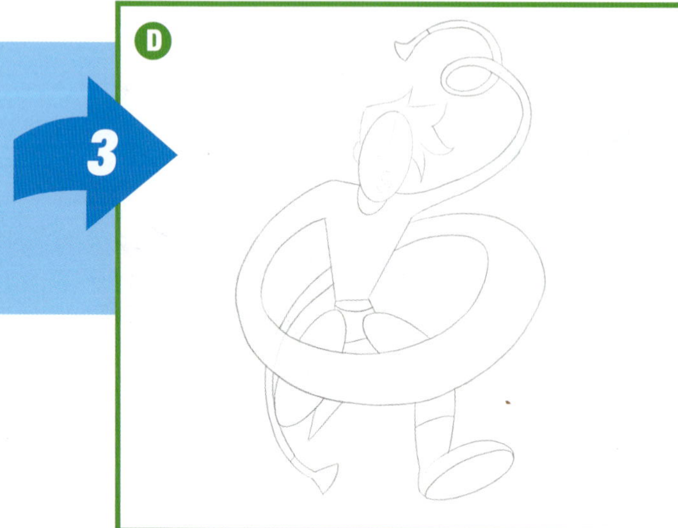

4

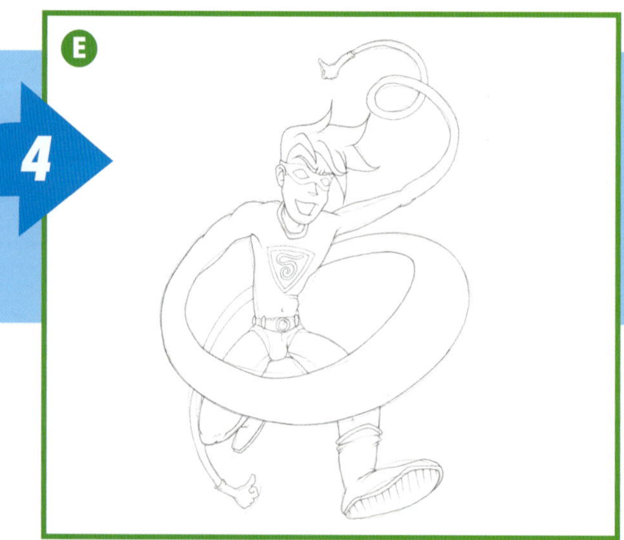

5

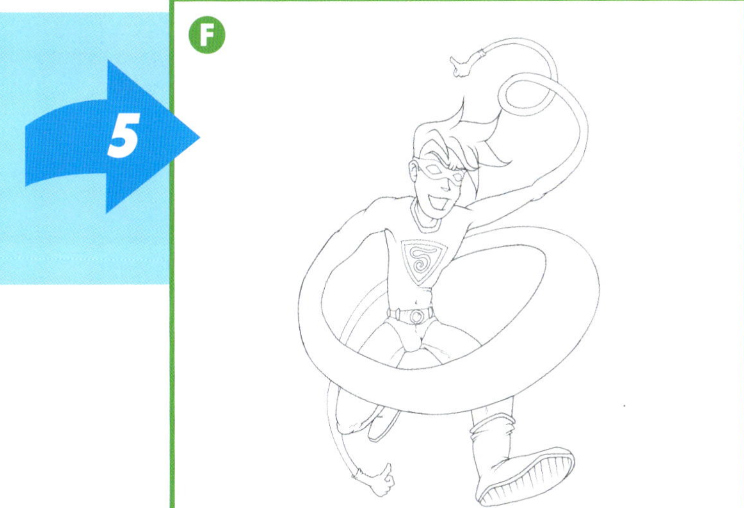

6

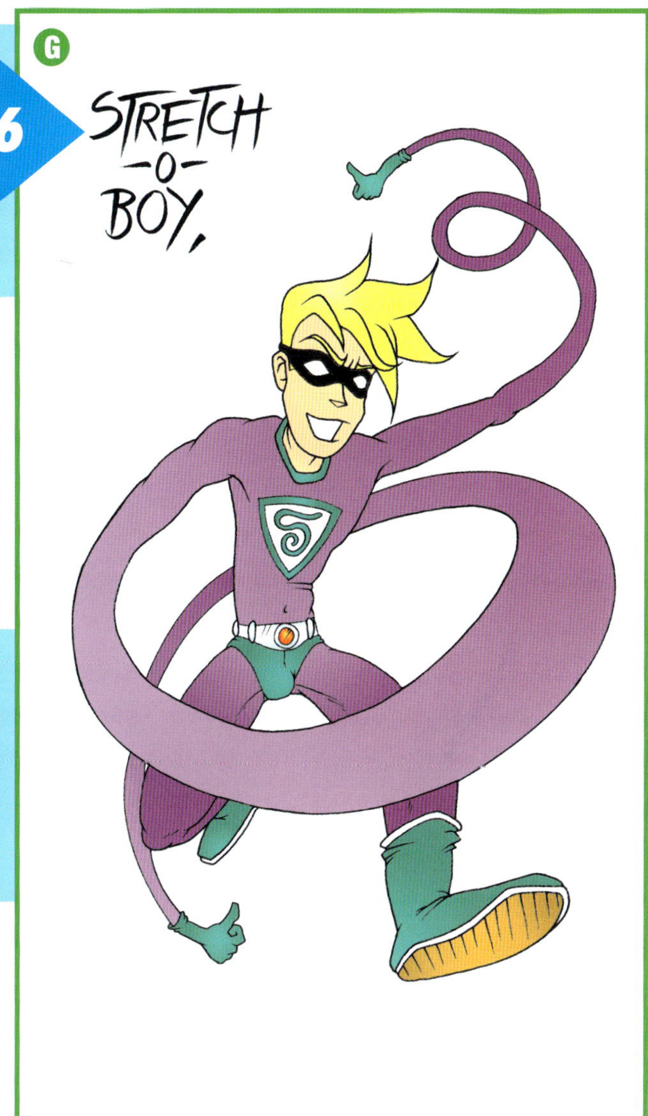

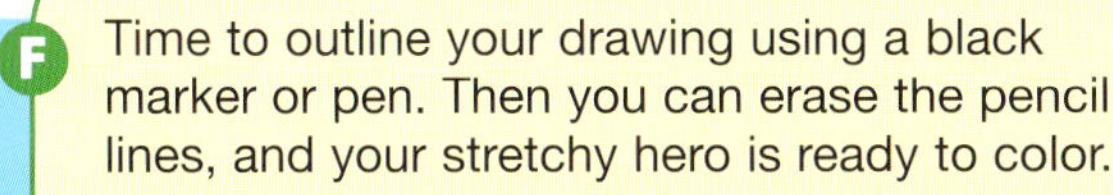

F Time to outline your drawing using a black marker or pen. Then you can erase the pencil lines, and your stretchy hero is ready to color.

G You can color your hero in any way you want. It's a good idea to shade from one color to another to give him form. In the finished picture here, his suit is purple and his accessories green.

H **I** Stretch-o-Bot is Stretch-o-Boy's evil robot double. His hair is wild and spiked, and his eyes are an unforgiving, soulless red. His "skin" has a metallic appearance which is created by using shades of gray, instead of pink flesh tones.

7

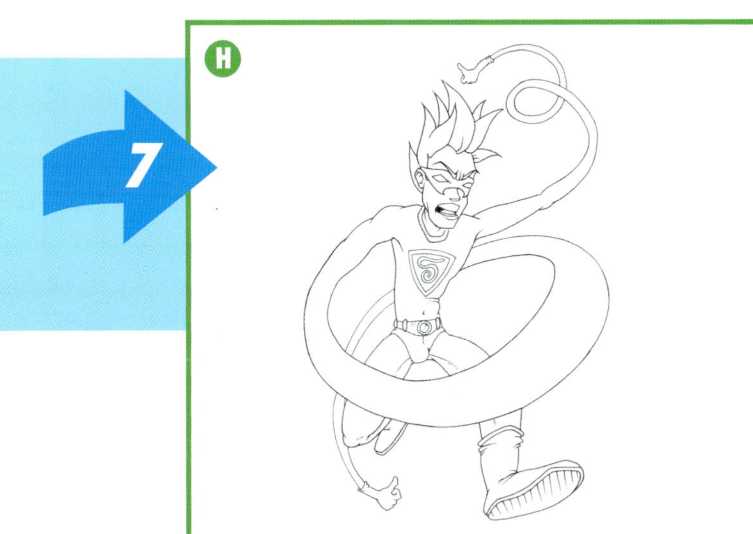

8

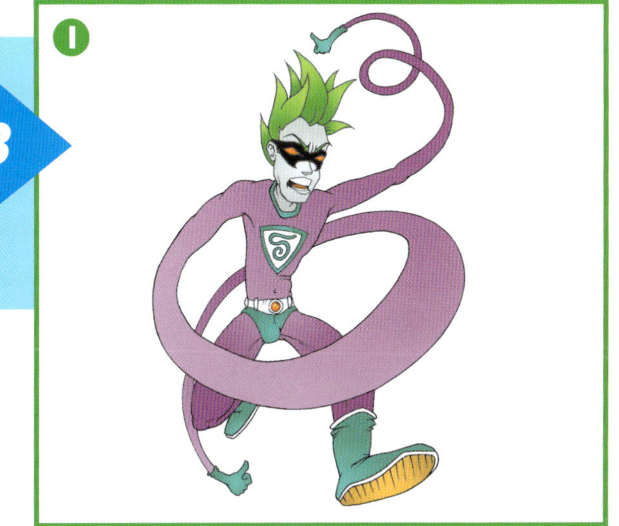